THE HEATH
Handbook of
Composition

THE HEATH
Handbook of Composition

TENTH EDITION

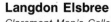

Langdon Elsbree
Claremont Men's College

Nell G. Altizer
University of Hawaii

Paul V. Kelly
Boston University

D. C. HEATH AND COMPANY
Lexington, Massachusetts Toronto

TEXT CREDITS

Robert L. Heilbroner, from pp. 33–34 in *The Great Ascent* by Robert L. Heilbroner. Copyright 1963 by Robert L. Heilbroner. Reprinted by permission of William Morris Agency, Inc., on behalf of Author. Copyright © 1961 by Robert Heilbroner.

Langston Hughes, from "The Negro Artist and the Racial Mountain." Copyright 1954 by Langston Hughes.

Ogden Nash, from *Verses From 1929 On* by Ogden Nash. Copyright 1939 by Ogden Nash. First appeared in *The New Yorker*, 1930. By permission of Little, Brown and Company.

International Standard Book Number: 0-669-03353-7

Library of Congress Catalog Card Number: 80-81881

There is not so poor a book in the world that would not be a prodigious effort were it wrought out entirely by a single mind, without the aid of prior investigators.

—*Samuel Johnson*

PREFACE

When this *Handbook* was first published in 1907, its author, Edwin C. Woolley, announced that its aim was to be "practical." Since then, much has changed in the study and teaching of composition, but we strongly endorse that aim. Conscious of the different editors, critics, and writers whose efforts shaped the first nine editions, we see ourselves working within their tradition, a tradition that views writing as a craft based on knowable principles and conventions. Now, in 1980, we would like to celebrate an anniversary and share with students and teachers who use the *Handbook* our understanding of what this tradition means to us, the current authors. The anniversary is the tenth edition of the *Heath Handbook*, the seventy-third year of its use by readers. We understand our tradition to include the privilege of working together in making major revisions.

Like most of the previous editions, this one is the product of collaborative authorship, for we consider composition itself to be a corporate activity involving fellow readers, writers, and teachers. The process of trying out one's ideas in rough draft and sharing them with others for comment, discussion, and modification is the process of effective communication. Although one person, one unique sensibility usually lies behind the final copy, that person's authority has been increased, not diminished, by the contribution of others. Often, in the choice of a particular example or detail for the *Handbook*, each of us speaks individually. So far as basic principles are involved, we intend a common point of view. We are skeptical about the star system—the notion that any single performer can or should pretend to do it all alone—as a model for writing. In this edition as in others, the authors have mutually aided one another.

The current edition of the *Handbook* includes the following major revisions:

First, we have substantially reorganized and expanded our materials. We start with two wholly new chapters, "Beginning" and "Discovering and Focusing." The first provides an overview of what follows and our strategy for organizing the book as we have; the second suggests ways of examining experiences or ideas to locate the details and to gain the focus necessary to get a paper under way. Building on these first two chapters and their topics, we have also rearranged the subsequent chapters—from planning the entire paper, through building paragraphs, to writing and polishing sentences, to choosing and sharpening words. The remaining chapters are concerned with sound reasoning, the long research paper, and the history of the language. Obviously, not all teachers will assign the chapters in this order; but we believe that by moving from the general to the particular and from the early stages of exploration and planning to the later ones of polishing and revising, we have a usable, coherent structure.

Second, we have substantially revised the chapters themselves, sometimes condensing, sometimes expanding, and always with an eye to refining them. We have partly rewritten three chapters on paragraphing and made them into one. We have added a new section on writing under pressure, which should be especially helpful to you when writing tests, for example. In reworking the chapters on sentences and diction, we have made special efforts to increase your sensitivity to words and your pleasure in using them effectively. We have also added the chapter "Sharpening Your Wording" and altered the chapter on the history of the language with these aims in mind.

Third, we have adhered to one of the strongest traditions of this *Handbook*: the inclusion of frequent student sentences, paragraphs, and papers. We have added several more examples throughout, the most important of which is the student research paper on autism.

We call particular attention to this paper because it concerns a kind of social problem you may choose (or be called on) to write about, and because we think you will find well-handled student papers to be the most convincing and helpful models.

In addition to these major changes, we have made many minor revisions in phrasing, detail, and choice of exercise throughout the book. Whether major or minor, all revision depends on the help and criticism of others. We continue to be grateful to colleagues, students, and reviewers who assisted with the seventh, eighth, and ninth editions, upon which this edition builds. We are again indebted to our editor, Holt Johnson, for his contributions during all stages of writing. We wish to thank James P. Doyle of Fordham University, Nora B. Leitch of Lamar University, and Peter T. Zoller of Wichita State University for their thoughtful reading of the manuscript and their comments, both general and specific. We wish to acknowledge especially the help of Gertrude P. Brainerd of Area College, Belleville, Illinois. Her rigorous and detailed critique has improved many pages of this edition.

Our last debt is by far our greatest. It is to Frederick Bracher, one of the *Handbook*'s authors for more than thirty years. He has brought in some of us as collaborators, held us to his own firm standards of clarity and usefulness, and provided much of the book's continuity. Though his name no longer appears on the cover, he is still present in the text, not only in his own words but in the spirit suggested by Dr. Johnson's words. To Fred, a wonderfully precise and vigorous teacher and co-author, we affectionately dedicate this tenth and anniversary edition.

L. E.
N. A.
P. K.

CONTENTS

13 SENTENCE FRAGMENTS AND COMMA SPLICES 381

THE HEATH
Handbook of
Composition

1

BEGINNING

We all know the excitement of learning. A new idea gives us power, insight into ourselves or the world, a sense of the majestic—as when we see a skyscraper, a prairie, or a seascape for the first time. Others may have seen such things before us, but that does not make the sights any less impressive. Often, our first desire is to express our surprise and awe.

This is so even in college. After the first week, most students discover that they have entered a world that is quite different from high school. They have heard lectures, taken part in discussions, asked and answered questions. New terms—acculturation, *Bildungsroman*, ethnocentrism, Reformation, mitosis—enter into their thoughts. The prospect is both exciting and challenging.

With learning come responsibility and qualms. Each student must master the ideas taught and show that mastery in class discussions, papers, and examinations. The knowledge that our statements will be judged makes some of us hesitant about speaking up in class, and most of us wonder about the outcome of our writing. Will we be able to say exactly what we think? How will our writing be graded? Often, these questions worry us so much that we find it difficult even to begin writing. The aim of this handbook is to give you confidence and pleasure in your writing by showing you how to communicate your knowledge in accordance with the standards of most college instructors.

We start with the problem of beginning. Professional writers begin in a thousand different ways. Some mull over their ideas until they have a first sentence, and then begin writing. Some write disjointed paragraphs, cutting and pasting and rearranging until they are satisfied. Some write and rewrite each sentence until it seems perfect. Some write a whole composition at once, marking problems that they intend to return to later. Others begin with a word that fascinates them. Some writers begin with outlines. Each has his or her own approach to the craft of writing.

What can we learn from this variety of beginnings? First, we see that writers find out what approach suits them and then make that approach habitual. Second, we see that none of them are satisfied with the first try. The essence of composition is revision (re-seeing): rewriting until you are satisfied with your essay, or until you have to turn it in. Third, we see that each writer starts by emphasizing one set of writing problems at a time, whether diction or sentence structure, paragraph coherence or organization. A writer can begin anywhere.

Similarly, a handbook can begin with any of several sets of problems and proceed according to a plan. You do not have to follow the plan of this handbook, especially if you have already formed a successful habit of writing. Most students, however, need a clear, practical plan to help them acquire the craft of writing. This handbook provides one such plan.

Thinking of ideas and focusing them is often the first and most difficult problem students encounter. Chapter 2 suggests two techniques for finding a subject. One is to jot down your impressions in fragments of sentences and words. The other is to write your thoughts down as quickly as you can, without regard for spelling, punctuation, grammar, or sentence structure, using the pen and paper as a sort of tape recorder for your inner voice. Both techniques help you to think of ideas for composition by putting off judgments about how well you have expressed those ideas. In addition, Chapter 2 will show you how to focus your ideas so that your writing has an original point.

Another set of problems that college students have trouble solving concerns the organization of their writing. Many students cannot decide what shape to give their ideas or how to make that shape clear. Chapter 3 focuses on the thesis sentence and the topic sentence as aids to clarify the shape of an essay. Because the major divisions of an essay are marked by paragraphs, the paragraphs, too, help to show its structure. To help you to master this aspect of the writer's craft, Chapter 4 discusses the organization of paragraphs.

The next three chapters explain sentence structure. Because sentences are the basic units of communication, it is important for you to construct your sentences well. To make the right choices among structures, you need to know how sentence structure affects the meaning and emphasis of your statements and how to make sentences more compact and more effective.

To neglect words in a consideration of writing would be like a carpenter's omitting wood from a discussion of his craft. Words transmit the color of your personality if you choose them well; poorly chosen, they can make you seem dull and ordinary. Chapter 8 shows how words serve as social indicators in your writing, identifying you in relation to your audience. Chapter 9 describes some aspects of word choice that give your writing flair, as well as some pitfalls to avoid. We have added Chapter 10 so that you may enjoy the history of words themselves and acquire an understanding of the origins and variety of your language.

In Chapter 11, we explain some principles for examining the logic of your writing. Our placement of this discussion is somewhat arbitrary, since logic may falter at any point in the process of writing, even in word choice. It is simply for your convenience and for clarity that we discuss logic after language. Ideally, you should examine and correct faulty or unclear thinking after each revision, whether you have revised paragraphs or words. When you have mastered the craft of revision, you will be able to correct errors in logic while you are revising.

The most common assignment any college student receives is the long research paper—the term paper. Three sets of problems arise in connection with writing research papers: finding material, finding a focus for your paper, and learning the system for footnotes and bibliography. In Chapter 12, we recommend some procedures and guides for research, some ways of focusing research material, and one of the three most common methods of documentation.

After every other problem has been solved, you have to eliminate grammatical and spelling errors. Up to this point, you often have freedom in deciding the aim of your essay, the structure of your paragraphs, the flow of your sentences, the flavor of your words. Grammar, punctuation, and spelling, however, are not matters for you to decide. In a way, this lack of freedom is an advantage: you have no difficult decisions to make, merely conventions to follow. Hence it is possible for you to commit the rules to memory and never worry about them again. These rules are set forth in Chapters 13 through 16.

Finally, you are ready to recopy your essay to hand in to your teacher. Chapter 17 lists some conventions of presentation that teachers expect assignments to follow. We also discuss proofreading. It would be foolish to have worked several hours on an essay, only to allow half a dozen errors in copying slip by to reduce your grade or your reputation as a writer. Proofreading, the final check, must be done.

It may appear from the length and organization of this handbook that writing is a dismaying, complicated task. However, if you work intelligently to solve each writing problem as it arises, you should have a good chance of success. And your achievement can mean more to you than a mere passing grade. Mastering new skills, learning about yourself through writing, you can keep alive the invigorating sense of beginning that came with you to college.

2

DISCOVERING AND FOCUSING

Your first challenge as a writer is having something you want to say. Through this concern you may avoid an essay that merely repeats common knowledge to support a stale idea. Even if you only give a fresh turn to an old idea or apply common sense to solve a problem, you will be extending knowledge and understanding. In general, if you can bring your own experience and insight or new information to bear upon your subject, you will be more likely to write a persuasive essay.

To develop a sense of what is interesting, consider the first assignment of a college writing class. Tens of thousands of students will be asked to write about any subject that interests them, and thousands will choose to write about their career choice. Let's say you decide to write about becoming a business executive. After you have said that there are many opportunities in management and that jobs in business pay well, what remains to be said? A dozen students in your class may have written the same thing.

Does the vast number of essays making the same arguments about the value of a business career mean that an original essay about that subject is impossible to write? Almost all such vapid essays are written without much reflection or research. Research will often help to distinguish a good essay from a bad one, for several reasons. In the first place, an essay that argues its point with details and statistics and examples is more convincing than one that has no supporting material. Second, many writers find that their research requires them to change their opinions, to qualify them, or to include arguments that do not support their first beliefs. In other words, they try to tell the truth that research and rethinking suggest. Third, research often forces writers to narrow their subject because of the great amount of information that they have found. It is certainly true that you can find in a library a great deal of information about business, if you know where to look. In Chapter

12, you will find an extensive list of resources that will make your library research quicker and easier. Almost every large library has a reference librarian who can help you should your own efforts fail.

What about other kinds of research, in which you explore the files of your memory, interview your classmates, or search through your lecture notes? How can you discover something worthwhile? The solution lies with you.

Almost as soon as you see the information, you will probably respond to it in some way, even if only to groan, "I don't know what that means." If you groan in incomprehension, you will need to determine the meaning of the material you have found; if your response is more articulate than a groan, it will become the basis of your essay. This response can be intellectual, focusing on a pattern you have detected in your research. It can be moral, focusing on your sense of right and wrong as you consider the facts. It can be emotional, focusing on the feelings the details arouse in you. Your response will probably be a combination of the three, with one focus predominant.

Suppose that you have been paging through *Business Week*, looking for information about chemical engineering. You find an article that states that many American chemical engineers who work in the Middle East are paid twice as much as those working in the United States. The engineers who work in the Middle East receive three months of vacation a year, and they often get housing, food, and clothing allowances, the article claims. "It must be hard to get people to go there, but I'll bet it's interesting work," you think. Your response is principally intellectual: you are wondering about the conditions that lead people to demand high salaries. However, your response is also moral and emotional. You don't think there is anything wrong with the salary scale, and you think you might like working in the Middle East. The important thing is not to forget your discovery—but, in fact, to keep it in mind as long as possible.

At this stage, writing can be an invaluable aid to memory if you do not pay special attention to correctness in spelling or grammar. Keep in mind that the first writing that you do when you have an essay to complete has the aim of recording your thoughts as you think them. Therefore, you will need to find a shorthand method of recording your own thoughts.

What sort of thinking should you do? That depends on the assignment that you are trying to fulfill. We can classify assignments into two categories: open assignments, which allow you to choose the subject of your essay; and restricted assignments, which limit the subject and sometimes the structure of your essay. These two types of assignments require different types of thinking because they have different aims.

In an open assignment, you often have to choose your writing objectives in accordance with those of the course. If your political science teacher asks you to write a term paper about a subject of your own choice, it is quite unlikely that a paper about rock music will fulfill the assignment. Your political science teacher wants you to choose a subject that shows your understanding of the concepts and methods of political science. You might still be able to write a paper about rock music that satisfies this expectation: a paper about the politics of rock musicians, perhaps focusing on the participation of Linda Ronstadt in the 1980 Presidential campaign of Jerry Brown, might raise some interesting issues.

The more explicit your assignment is, the more limitations there are upon your choice of subject, of structure, and of the point you will be able to make. In almost every assignment, however, there is an opportunity for independent thought. The first question you should ask yourself when you begin to think seriously about your assignment is: "What sort of insight or understanding am I expected to show? In other words, why is my instructor asking me to do this assignment?" The first idea you might jot down, because it will guide the rest of your writing, is the answer to that question.

2a

Jotting

Since our thoughts rarely wait for our hands to catch up with them, most of us need a technique for capturing those thoughts as they race by. One such technique is jotting, taking notes of our thoughts much as we would take notes in a history or biology lecture. These notes are often merely a collection of sentence fragments. You should include among your jottings any facts or details that come to mind as well as your opinions about the subject you are exploring.

1. Open Assignments

When you are writing in response to any open assignment, your first task in jotting is to find a focus, to discover a subject that is narrow enough to enable you to say informed things about it. Here are a student's jottings about the 1979 baseball umpires' strike:

> *in favor of umpires striking*
> *cause is just*
> *owners don't like to give in*
> *reaction to players' strike, free agency*
> *unfair to fans*
> *substitute umpires not very good*
> *Jim Rice knocking sub umpire over*
> *don't even wear same uniforms*

At this point, the student stopped jotting, looked over the list to see what was most original, and discovered that the last two jottings were more concrete than the others, so he wrote them at the top of another page and began again. He found his focus.

> *Jim Rice knocking sub umpire over*
> *subs don't even wear same uniforms*
> *some wear blue jacket some gray some black*
> *why uniform bugs me*
> *expect them to look the same, call same kind of game*
> *uniform like rules*
> *break rules = violence*
> *why Jim Rice knocked ump over—couldn't trust ump's*
> *   knowledge of rules*
> *arguments about calls—different now*
> *baseball without trustworthy consistent umpires = baseball*
> *   without rules = violence*

After ten minutes of jotting the ideas down, the student had found an informed insight into the subject. He began his second set of jottings by recalling a vivid scene in a game he had witnessed, and by contrasting the substitute umpires' uniforms with those of the umpires on strike. His first insight was that the uniforms are a symbol of the game: identical dress reflects a set of unchanging rules. Without those rules, violence can erupt; and violence, the student believed, was the result of the substitute umpires' ignorance of the rules and their violation of the uniformity of dress. The student concluded that Jim Rice's act was violent because neither he nor the other players could trust the umpire to control the conduct of the game. This insight into baseball was only sketchily outlined in the jottings, but at least they had provided the student with the means to organize and write his paper.

Jotting will work for you only if you examine your brief notes and try to identify the most concrete and suggestive ideas among them. Usually, your first ideas are vague; two or three sets of jottings, however, will often help you find a focus for your essay.

Exercise 1

Examine the following sets of jottings. Decide which jottings in each set are the most original and likely to serve as a basis for an interesting paper. Do not correct any errors of spelling or grammar.

1. many people think gymnastics is boring
   they're right
   practice boring, esp. exercise, setting up and breaking down equipment
   leg lifts are very boring
   very painful
   how you do them
   flat on your back
   if you do them wrong you get extras
   leg-lifts for punishment as well as exercise
   gymnastics is good for you though
   getting a high score gives a good feeling
   one of the top sports
   more people should enjoy it
2. heroes of today
   not military
   no John Waynes

rock stars
people who have ideal
strange ideal—negative not positive
maybe Mork is hero
not from earth—kind of negative even though positive
M*A*S*H is military but antiwar
3. energy crisis
fuel shortage
learn to live with less
go to war for fuel + energy
nuclear power
woodburning stoves
relaxing controls on pollution
oil spills
these are too abstract, I don't know enough
general energy—why we can't solve problem—too abstract
how does energy touch us what do we know
maybe if I try
other sources of power—windmills
changes in our lifestyle
4. my father's death
what it meant to all of us
cancer is an awful thing
getting the news
great tension and sadness
no one wanted to believe
trying to live normally
going to Japan to try a new drug
how we argued against it
accused of not loving him
discovered drug in New York
another relapse
into the hospital
phone ringing—pneumonia and death

Exercise 2

Choose one of the sets of jottings in Exercise 1 and add items that you think will serve as starting points for an original essay. Feel free to draw on your own experience and add details if you have chosen set 1 or 4.

Exercise 3

Write your own set of jottings. When you are finished, copy the most informed ones and begin again. Is your second set of jottings more detailed than your first? Does it suggest a focus? Write an essay based on the focus you have found.

2. Restricted Assignments

When a teacher gives you a restricted assignment, the problems of discovering and focusing become slightly different, because you will usually have to find material in printed sources and because your teacher usually limits the subject. It is important for you to ask yourself what your teacher believes the assignment will teach you. Try to fulfill that aim; if you cannot see the aim of the assignment, discuss it with your teacher.

Your jottings for a restricted assignment should include three types: your idea of the aim of the assignment, jottings from your textbook or lectures or library research, and jottings of your own responses to this material. Do not incorporate into the writing your jottings about the aim of the assignment; keep them as a guide for what you will write. The jottings will help you to decide how to take notes from books, articles, and course material, as well as what to say about that material.

Here is an assignment from a freshman sociology course:

Compare the structure and the functions of the family and the values surrounding children and community in modern China and the Israeli kibbutz. Refer to Melford E. Spiro, "Is the Family Universal?" and Bruce Dollar, "Child Care in China." Length: 2-4 pages, typed.

One student used her preliminary jottings to guide her note-taking from the two articles (adding the page number of the article so that she could check her accuracy and refer to the articles for details). Here are selections from her notes:

> *"Is The Family Universal?"*
>   *Murdock: four functions of nuclear family*
>   *1st sexual*

2nd economic
3rd reproductive
4th educational   839
Kibbutz one such subgroup   839
    an agricultural collective in Israel: communal living,
        collective ownership of all property, communal
        rearing of children   840
Education + socialization function of "nurses" and
    teachers, not parents   843
Parents are important to psychological development of
    child

"Child Care in China"
Several major ideas about childrearing   1
    themes: subordination of personal to social needs,
        respect for productive labor, altruism, cooperation,
        integration of physical w/intellectual labor—tend to
        develop kind of citizen China wants—values
Importance placed on group activities   2
Toys too heavy for one child
"Multiple mothering" of Chinese children   4

These notes seemed to apply best to the assignment. She then jotted down the following thoughts:

likenesses
    both value children
    both emphasize group rather than individual
    both separate economic function from others
    also educational function
    cooperation preferred to individual
    both provide psychological security for the child
    family life strong
    both altruistic

> *why important?*
>   *family is institution that guarantees future of society*
>   *I see this now better than before—all values are focused*
>   *on children*
>   *society's way of life and values are impressed in the way*
>   *children are treated—socialization isn't just education,*
>   *it's the whole atmosphere of the society in its attitude*
>   *toward children*

Her jottings focus on "likenesses" because the assignment asks her to compare the values and childrearing methods of the two societies. (If the teacher had asked her to contrast them, she would have focused on the differences between the two societies.) She then turns to the question "why important?" because she wants to have her own insight into the comparisons she has drawn. Such questions will help you to understand your own perspective on your material. After you have finished taking notes for your assignment, ask yourself focusing questions such as these:

Why is this set of ideas and details important?
How do these things go together?
Do these details have a cause in common?
Do these details lead to one result?
Can I compare this set of ideas and details with any others I know?

Once you have jotted down the answers to one or several of these questions, you may find, as this writer did, that you have a focus for your essay.

Exercise 4

Write a set of jottings for an assignment from one of your classes. Include notes about the aims of the assignment. Use these jottings to help you to take notes from your reading and focus an essay. Write an essay based on your jottings.

2b
Free-Writing

Another way of capturing your thoughts in flight is free-writing. Free-writing differs from jotting in that you attempt to catch the flow of your thoughts by writing them not as a list of ideas, but as a thread of sentences.

To begin free-writing you need an opening question, whether it is supplied by your jottings or whether you invent one. The opening question merely helps you get started. You do not need to limit yourself to answering it in your free-writing. Your opening question may be as vague as "What can I say that's worth reading?" or as specific as "What does Ruth Benedict mean by 'cultural integration'?"

Once you have written down your opening question, write quickly whatever follows as you think about your reply to it. (Do not stop to correct yourself as you write, unless leaving obvious errors uncorrected worries you so much that you cannot continue. Especially, do not interrupt your writing to puzzle over an error; you can take time to find the answer later.)

Here is an example of one student's free-writing:

> *How are TV hospitals different from real ones? TV hospitals are very unreal. When a patient arrives at a emergency room everyone stops what they're doing and their attention goes to patient—That's on TV. In real life its different. When I had a bad accident, not only was no one concerned, but it took an hour for Dr. to arrive. This one lady was yelling and crying desperately that her baby needed help and treatment but no one came to help as they do on TV.—A clerk told her to wait because there were others waiting and she had to fill out forms before the Dr. could examine the baby.*

There are errors of spelling, punctuation, and grammar in the free-writing above. It would be too soon to correct them if the writer has more to say. Instead, because the writing focuses to a greater extent on the real hospital than on the television view of hospitals, the writer begins the next paragraph of free-writing by focusing on some details for expansion:

What is emergency room like? On TV it is antiseptic, well-lit focus on one patient, a very dramatic place with music to underline the drama. People are all very good looking, only the "star" patient is sick because of the drama. The one I was in was darker. Two-tone walls green and white— not dirty but not sparkling white either. It hadn't been painted in a while, a noisy place and not with music either, <u>full</u> of sick people, no drama, basically it was boring. Sickness is basically boring in real life.

In this free-writing sample there is often no clear sentence structure, but there is quite a bit of informed detail and an insight into one difference between television hospitals and real ones.

Sometimes you will run out of things to say, or you will not be able to think of the words for what you do want to say. On these occasions, try rewriting your last five words again and again until something new comes to mind. Your object is to fill the pages with writing, not to compose a perfect essay in ten minutes. Not even Samuel Johnson, who was a champion procrastinator, could compose that speedily when he finally started to work. There are other questions you can ask yourself that will help you write more about your subject. You will recognize some of these questions from the discussion of jotting.

What's the best detail here?
How does it look?
How does it sound?
What is it like?
Why is this important?
What do I mean by this?
What happens after this?

Why is this true?

How many kinds are there?

Another way of expanding your writing is to use transitional devices:

Moreover, . . .

The next step is . . .

Therefore, . . .

However, . . .

When you are editing your writing, you will eliminate many of the clumsy and wordy transitional devices. Now, however, they can help you clear the clogged pipes of your thinking.

Exercise 5

Choose one of the following opening questions and write for ten minutes.

1. Do we pay too much attention to children?
2. What do I think of my roommate (husband, wife, children, parents)?
3. Do we really need cars?
4. Should college students be allowed to drink?
5. What should we do about whale hunters?
6. Why is water skiing so much fun?
7. What do I need to succeed in college?
8. What is my fondest memory?
9. What are my parents (children, neighbors) really like?

Exercise 6

Examine your free-writing, identify the best details, and write another paragraph based on one of these details, using one of the questions or one of the transitional devices for expansion.

2c

Free-Writing as a Supplement to Jotting

When you have jotted notes about your assignment and already found a focus, your free-writing usually comes more easily. You can use your jottings for the assignment as a guide for the free-writing.

The method of jotting first and free-writing afterward is especially useful for restricted assignments, when you should jot down the aim of the assignment and notes from relevant reading. When you fill out jottings with free-writing about your reading, you are trying to find more to say about your subject, and the result should be several disorganized pages of writing, some of it fairly specific. In Chapter 3, we will discuss how to give your material structure; first, though, you need to find material. You will always start with notes, readings, reflections, or memories, but then you must write. A useful guideline is to write at least twice as much as you need for the assignment. When you have more material than you need, you can choose and condense the best of it into an effective essay.

Here is some of the free-writing of the student who compared Chinese childrearing with that of the kibbutz. The jotting that opens her free-writing is underlined.

<u>both emphasize group rather than individual</u>
What does this mean? The community values of the societies are focused on communal success not on the individual. First the Chinese—best illustrated by the way children are brought up—most activities occur in groups not in individuals—examples of the building blocks that are too heavy for children to pick up. This forces (Chinese teachers said) group cooperation. More than one child was needed to pick up blocks—whole Chinese society is focused on group effort. Thus we see that children are taught values they will live by for the rest of their lives, thus maintaining the society's values (maybe this should be part of the introduction). Well, it's not really teaching—the blocks are designed to force students to learn to cooperate. It's the whole atmosphere that is intended to reinforce the values.

How is this related to the family? <u>Family is institution that guarantees the future of a society.</u> In China the family has three of the four functions which what's his name mentions (look it up): economic, sexual, reproductive, not educational, also one that Spiro mentions, affection. This

---

> *means that the family is not fully part of educational
> system because the family would tend to individualize—in a
> society that emphasizes group identity you would have to
> take children away from the family, but even the substitute
> family is very loving. Do not punish, only correct.*

Neither of the two "paragraphs" above is coherent. Both have material that can be developed into other paragraphs. In the second paragraph, the writer has not allowed her forgetting Murdock's name to interfere with her writing down everything she can think of.

After she has written two or three more pages of free-writing, she can begin to reorganize them. She may underline sentences or fragments about the same part of the subject with a colored pencil, using a different color for each part; she may rewrite the sentences one by one, putting those that go together on the same page; she may number the sentences according to the part of the subject to which they belong. At this point, she can begin to consider structuring her essay.

Exercise 7

Using your own jottings as a guide, identify their focus and free-write for five minutes. Choose a detail from your free-writing and write for five minutes with an opening question about that detail.

2d

Beginning with Free-Writing: Finding a Focus

It is not a good idea to begin a restricted assignment with free-writing: usually, you need to jot down notes about the aim of the assignment and about your readings for it. In addition, you can find a focus for a restricted assignment more easily from jottings than from free-writing. For an open assignment, however, beginning with free-writing can help you discover your subject and theme quickly.

Since free-writing is basically thinking aloud on paper, you can review your thoughts and find the ones that arouse the most interest. Many of us have a tendency to elaborate upon the ideas we believe or those that engage our curiosity. When these ideas appear in free-writing, you can expect that they will be followed by explanations or details that reflect your interest in the idea.

Sometimes, of course, the opposite can be true: you may have an original insight and not know what to say about it. As a result, you may turn to a more familiar idea that you can explain at length, as this student did:

> *I was sitting in the commuter's lounge the other day when someone left the room, I don't remember who. The minute she left, someone else, I don't remember her name either, said something about her. That made me think about what goes on behind closed doors, behind closed doors, behind closed doors. People talk about other people because they don't care, and society has become so involved with the ultimate that it has lost the ability to love. No longer are people concerned with others—all anyone cares about is himself—the old song, What the world needs now is love sweet love is so true. People are so mixed up and lost because of the realization that no one cares. If only society would slow down and take advantage not of prestige but of love, half of the problems would be resolved. If only people would reach out to each other.*

This student began his free-writing with some remarkable details. Even the phrase, "what goes on behind closed doors," which is a little worn, suggests that the closed doors have locked up his memory. In reviewing the rest of his free-writing, the student should recognize that his original thought is more concrete than the succession of clichés that follows the phrase "behind closed doors." That thought may be the focus of an essay.

To decide whether to pursue a line of thinking in your free-writing, ask yourself if you would want to read what you are writing. What bores you will bore others. If your writing does lack interest, you may be able to improve it by searching out engaging detail. Here is some free-writing that begins with a cliché, yet develops vivid detail.

I long for true tranquility in my life once again, as I had in the worst blizzard in Montana's history. I had no means of communication with anyone. There was no television no telephone, and no radio—I was the only human being within seven square miles, stranded for three full days in literally the middle of nowhere with no human voice, no ring of the telephone, no honk of the car horn, and no media propaganda. The three most relaxing days of my life, I wrote poetry and read by kerosene lamps. I loved it. Outside the snow was already two feet high blowing and drifting steadily up to heights of twenty feet. It was forty below 0. With the wind's howl a spit-freezing eighty-five below 0. All the machinery had been immobilized, the wind compacted the snow so tight you could walk on top of a drift without leaving a footprint. To look out over the landscape was like looking into a hazy dream, not earthlike at all. the wind filled the air with tiny pieces of ice which had once been snow that burned your skin to the point that you could not stay out for ten minutes. It was pitch dark at high noon.

Once the free-writing turns to a description of the blizzard, the student's imagination transforms a fairly standard praise of solitude into a paradoxical vision. The earth becomes unearthly, the snow-drifts harden, the snow burns, the day turns dark. In his next free-writing, he might try to explain what these reversals of nature meant to him, or to ask if he had similar paradoxical feelings about himself, or to specify what thoughts he had during the blizzard to find if his thoughts were as paradoxical as his perceptions.

Exercise 8

Examine the following pieces of free-writing. Identify the sentences, phrases, words, and details that are likely to focus a good essay. What additional questions might the writer ask to expand the writing into enough material for a 500-word theme?

1. My own view of the strike was often a confusing sea of half-truths contradictions and rumors. Being ignorant of certain issues at hand as were many people, definitely did not aid me in making a responsible decision to support the union or management. However since the strike I have gained the knowledge necessary for taking a stand and as a result of this gained information. My previously uncommitted sympathy and support now lies with the members of the AFL-CIO local.

2. For me, the first year of college has been a great change, I have had to learn to live in a different environment than that of my protective home. to try to take it slowly and easily because during my first few weeks of college I noticed a drastic change in my eating habits. I began to eat more and eat when I was not hungry. If I had kept this up, I could have been a model for the Goodyear blimp advertisement. I also did not care about my appearance. Now that I look back at this, I can see that I was deeply depressed.

3

CONSTRUCTING THE PAPER

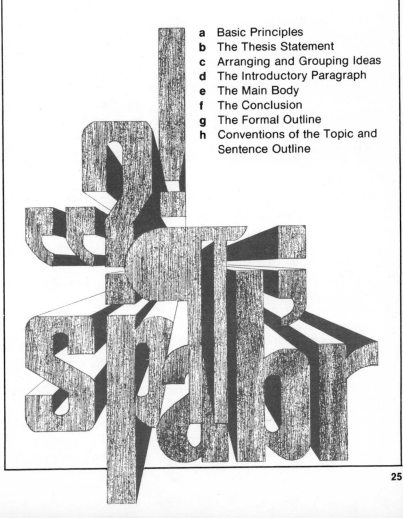

Before considering some of the techniques for constructing a paper, we need to review a few basic principles. These have already been touched upon in the opening chapters, but since they are essential to all orderly writing, they need to be spelled out here. They are strategies for coherence—tactics of effective planning.

3a

Basic Principles

The first two principles concern the type of paper required and its length. If a topic for a paper is assigned, you must be sure you understand what you are being asked to do. This is especially important if you are asked to write an "essay" question on an examination. If you have any doubt about what the question calls for, ask for clarification. If a theme assignment requires that you comprehend certain reading materials, do the reading early enough so that you can discuss obscure points with the instructor or members of the class. Talking about a subject generates critical thinking and makes for fluent writing.

Word limits are usually assigned as an indication of approximate scale, not as absolute restrictions. Your instructor is not going to count the number of words in your paper; don't waste time doing it yourself. Ordinarily, you will find that the real problem is not filling up space but keeping within the rough limits set by a teacher or editor. If your first draft seems too short, look for more material, not more padding. It is a courtesy to your audience to present your argument as incisively as possible, but if your first draft goes far beyond the set limit, cut down the topic instead of trying to compress everything into a few pages.

The third principle is that of *depth* of information and understanding. Perhaps the major cause of vague paragraphs, errors in logic, and incoherent papers is your failure to know enough about the topic. The more you know about a topic, the more likely it is that you understand certain basic interconnections and can make them plain to a reader; and the more connections you are conscious of, the more likely you are to realize that only a few, not all, can be discussed with adequate fullness.

Suppose, for example, that you have been concerned about the importance of conserving the world's natural resources. When you begin to explore this large subject, you may be tempted to throw up your hands in despair. Such topics as natural scenery, agricultural lands to grow food for increasing millions of people, limited supplies of oil and natural gas, other possible sources of energy (solar, geothermal, nuclear) and their potential hazards and advantages, pollution of the air by exhaust gases from factories and cars, pollution of rivers and lakes by industrial wastes or sewage, inadequate water supply in urban areas, the necessity of controlling population growth—even a book would be too short to cover it all. How do you start?

The answer is "Don't start, yet." That is, don't begin to write until you have limited the topic to a size you can handle comfortably. Instead of trying to say something about all the topics included under "Conservation of Natural Resources," choose one of them, and start to explore it in detail.

Suppose that you choose other sources of energy than the now prevailing oil, coal, and natural gas. Alternative sources are, mainly, solar, nuclear, and geothermal. In its direct form, solar energy is relatively simple—heating space or water by concentrating the sun's rays. But the possibilities of utilizing indirect solar energy—harnessing the wind, developing natural water power, taking advantage of temperature differences in the sea, recycling organic wastes such as garbage or sewage, converting vegetable fuel to alcohol or artificial "natural" gas—are still too broad for a single paper. You might choose one of these subtopics and explore it, or you might move on to consider nuclear power. Here you would find two main subdivisions—energy from nuclear fission (splitting the atom) and energy from nuclear fusion. The latter, still in an experimental stage, would involve some highly technical special knowledge.

Unless you know a good deal about nuclear physics, you'd better try the simpler process—nuclear fission, now used widely to generate electricity. This process, you will soon discover, is highly controversial. Its advantages and disadvantages are hotly debated by physicists, whose expert knowledge does not keep them from violent disagreement. Is the process economically justifiable, considering the enormous cost of building nuclear reactors? Is the process safe enough to justify tripling the number of our nuclear plants?

If you decide to limit yourself to exploring the latter question, you may have cut down your topic to a manageable size. When you begin reading on the relative safety of present nuclear power plants, you will find that critics of nuclear power point to three chief hazards: the danger of the accidental escape of radioactive material at a reactor, the danger of plutonium falling into the hands of terrorists bent on nuclear blackmail, and the problem of safely disposing of the violently poisonous nuclear "ash." These three points may still be too much to cover in a short paper. How about taking only one of them?

Suppose that you choose only the first of these—the possible danger of accident at a nuclear power plant. You will still find differences of opinion, and you may gather more material than you will actually use. That is normal; don't worry about it. You will now be in a position to select items to suit your topic. You may, for example, come across an account of a near-accident at the Browns Ferry plant in Alabama or the emergency at Three Mile Island in Pennsylvania and decide to use either or both as examples of the risks involved.

It should be clear by now that you cannot limit a subject to an appropriate size by just sitting at your desk and thinking. You need to get to the library and inform yourself a little. The more you read, the more possible lines of development will suggest themselves; and by a process of narrowing and eliminating, you can arrive at a unified topic of about the right size for the space at your disposal. As you organize and write up this material, you may want to cut a bit here, or add there, depending on your purpose, but at least you will have something to work with.

3b

The Thesis Statement

Before you do much actual writing, you should *clarify* your purpose in writing. Ask yourself, "What am I trying to do with this material? Do I want to present objectively both sides of some controversial question? Am I trying to convince my audience that nuclear reactors are safe or dangerous?" Unless you have clarified your purpose, you may wander from the main point of the paper.

How do you identify your main point? By the end of the first draft, your stand on the issue, your attitude toward a personal experience, or your judgment of a book's value should be clear. You should be able to express your main point in a single, unambiguous sentence. This sentence sums up the central thesis to be developed in the paper: it is the *thesis statement*. If the draft explores several possible alternatives or policies, the thesis statement is a kind of map or proposed route of places to be visited. If the draft argues a point of view or particular interpretation, the thesis statement is a commitment you make to yourself and the reader, an agreement that one route is better than another or that one way of looking at the scene is more complete than another. If the draft is a muddle, the thesis statement should be a new contract that makes a definite claim and omits irrelevant considerations.

The thesis statement is usually expressed in the opening paragraph. Sometimes, though, it is not finally stated until the concluding paragraph. Such holding back of the thesis statement can provide a dramatic turn to the essay and give the reader a sense of discovery. No matter where the thesis statement is placed, it should be specific, not general, sharply phrased, not vague. Such sentences as "Football is an *exciting* game," "During my summer vacation I had *some very interesting* and *educational experiences*," and "High school plays offer *many excellent opportunities* and *beneficial aspects* to the aspiring actor" are useless as theses. Note that the offending italicized phrases do not commit the writer to anything specific, do not give him any real control over his subject. He still has to decide by analysis what is "exciting" about football (Is it the variety of plays? The body contact? The dramatic run? The crowds and cheerleaders?) and to whom (To spectators? Players? Both? Always?). Unless he faces the task of thinking analytically toward a thesis, his writing will probably wander from impression to impression as he tries to make up his mind about what he does mean.

To take another example, a thesis such as "Adolescence is a difficult period in the life of an American" gives no clear focus, makes no sharp commitment. Be relentless in cross-examining yourself about your views. Your preliminary notes might read like this:

adolescence is hard because my body and my thinking seem out of gear with the rest of the world. I want everything and never have any money. I have to make decisions that will affect my whole life, and yet I don't know what I want. No one ever gave me any guidelines about sex, and I'm still muddled about it. I never had enough allowance to treat my friends, so when I'd find money I'd pocket it and feel guilty about it later. I had to take College Boards when I was seriously considering dropping out of school, and that's why I'm not in the advanced English class.

Depending on your purpose, the topic, "Adolescence—What About It?" can be turned in a number of directions and lead to a number of thesis statements:

Some American adolescents lie, steal, and commit vandalism because they are frustrated at a critical period of their development.

Adolescent misbehavior can be cut down by a strict curfew enforced by jail sentences for those who violate it.

The creation in American families, schools, and churches of puberty rituals like those of primitive societies would help the young to bridge the gap between an immature individual and adult society.

Whatever the topic, a clear thesis often contains within it an implied pattern of development. For example, the thesis "For the average football spectator the long run makes up for all the dull line play" suggests the pattern of comparison and contrast: first the description of the spectator's boredom during a quarter filled with two-yard plunges and shoving linemen, and then the description of his excitement during the few seconds he is on his feet to watch the long run. A vague or disunified thesis, however, contains no implied pattern of development. Your thesis, once it is formulated from your analytic thinking or writing, becomes the foundation of your paper. When it is formulated accurately, the rest of the paper becomes easier to organize.

3c
Arranging and Grouping Ideas

Sometimes, especially with "how to do it" papers, the material will determine the best order and the main headings for your working outline. For example, after reviewing his list on resurfacing a floor, a writer might note that the items fall naturally under three main headings:

I. Materials

II. Preparations

III. Laying the tile

Often, though, the topic will be more complicated. Consider the example of the writer whose subject was "What I Expect from College" and whose first thesis is "What I want from college is the freedom to make choices independently." After thinking about it, the writer might realize that the essential thesis is the need for enough freedom from the past to make clear choices. An informal working outline—one that spells out the thesis with the intended emphasis—might be set up as follows:

I. Hope for enough personal freedom from the past to make clear choices

II. Distance from relatives

    To make up mind between engineering and teaching

      Family encourages engineering

      But have worked with people, and liked them, in camp and Scout jobs

    To choose courses without outside pressure

      Have done well in physics and chemistry

      But might like more work in history and psychology

III. Distance from high school groups

    To choose new friends and views

    To keep up old friendships on more relaxed basis

    Escape high school habit of having to go steady

    Look back on group I was in

Remember that the preliminary organizing is temporary and can be changed at any time. Remember, too, that in a short paper you can develop only the most significant aspects of the points listed; probably none of them can be fully developed in a short assignment. Don't take your categories so seriously that they become a straitjacket instead of a support. The actual writing of a composition may suggest new material, or reveal a lack of material, and thus lead you to modify your original plan.

When the material doesn't clearly determine the order of presentation, try what is the standard, safe form: *begin with your conclusion and experiment with several kinds of arrangement, each based on a different method of categorizing.* If you are arguing that grades are an obstacle to education, you might begin by classifying your arguments according to the psychological effects grades can have on students:

Grades become an end in themselves
Direct students into easy courses
Cause cheating in hard exams
Mean concentration only on what is required for tests
Cause anxiety, which interferes and disrupts

Then you could try classifying according to the effects on teachers:

Makes teacher a cop, set against class
Makes teacher a showman to hold attention
Makes teacher into a judge passing on the accused and defending verdict

Finally, you might reclassify both these lists according to the effects grades have on the students' attitude toward the teacher and toward the course:

I. Attitude toward teacher
    A. Is expected to be an entertainer and spoon-feed dull, required material
    B. Is thought of as cop and judge defending verdict on tests
II. Attitude toward course
    A. Makes easy courses attractive and popular, hard and challenging courses unpopular

    B.   Means concentration only on what is required for tests
    C.   Provokes fear of subjects that have caused anxiety before

Section 3h concerns itself with outlining as an aid to grouping ideas, and Chapter 4 discusses some basic patterns for arranging materials by paragraphs. The point here is that you should *look* for a pattern, and, if necessary, play around with possibilities until you develop an arrangement that makes sense. You may want to revise and tinker after the entire design is constructed, but at this stage of writing pay attention to your mind's inclination for making divisions, shaping, and concluding. As an example of a writer's trust in the natural divisions of his topic, consider the outline, thesis, and opening paragraphs from the following student essay:

"Harpo and the Marx Brothers"

Thesis: Whereas Groucho and Chico relied on verbal means, Harpo played with the language visually: since he was mute, almost all of his jokes had to be related to sight.

  I. Thesis
 II. Harpo's visual style of punning
III. Harpo's visual use of overcoat
IV. Harpo's visual play with clichés

    When I read Peter Farb's *Word Play,* I was delighted with his four pages devoted to the Marx Brothers and their attitude toward language. Although I believe that Farb accurately summarized the Marx Brothers' style of comedy (they attacked the rules and conventions of the English language), I don't think he caught Harpo's style as well as he did those of the other brothers. Farb was correct when he described Groucho's puns as those of a shrewd and "fast-talking sharpie" and Chico's speech as a "phony-Italian dialect" that "misconstrues both the meaning and manners of the 'foreign American speech community.' " However, his analysis of Harpo's manner of comedy, as one that throws language "back to the level of the beasts," is incomplete. Whereas Groucho and Chico relied on verbal means, Harpo played with the language visually: since he was mute, almost all of his jokes had to be related to sight.

    An excellent example of Harpo's style can be found in *Monkey Business* (1931). Harpo is leaning against a sign on one side of a door appearing to be marked in bold letters, "MEN." Along ambles a well-dressed fellow who opens the door, enters the room, and seconds later is seen by the audience flying out the door and landing on his rear. At this point, Harpo strolls away from the wall, revealing that the sign actually reads "WOMEN." Harpo also leads his brothers in the taking of English homonyms and other words literally. A movie packed full of many of these gems is *Horsefeathers* (1932)—the *Animal House* of the 1930s. For example, when Groucho demands a "seal" to make the contract process valid and binding, his mute brother extracts a live, black, slippery, flipper-clapping sea mammal from his baggy overcoat and dumps it on the desk. In another scene, when Chico and Harpo pose as icemen and enter carrying a large chunk of ice in each other's arms, Groucho questions the practicality of their methods. He demands, "Where's your tongs?" whereupon the other two open their mouths wide and stick out their tongues.

Harpo's magical overcoat is essential to this visual style of comic punning. He always comes up with anything a person demands, as in the episode with the seal and in the gag where a ragged hobo approaches him with the request, "Say, buddy, I'd like to get a cup of coffee." The man is obviously looking for a handout of money, but Harpo's response is to reach into the inside pocket of his tattered overcoat, pull out a white saucer and a cup of steaming coffee, and hand it to the dumbfounded bum. A witty variation of this style—a put-on—occurs in *Monkey Business* when the brothers are trying to get off a steamship and they cut through a line to the customs table. When they are stopped by officials, a bald, uniformed man demands a "passport" from Harpo. Harpo proceeds to pull everything out of his overcoat that has a somewhat similar sounding name, from a washboard to a cupboard, infuriating the inspector a little more each time.

Harpo even takes clichés and trite phrases literally and vivifies them. In *A Night in Casablanca* (1949), a policeman spots Harpo loitering and leaning against a wall and asks him, "What are you doing? Holding up the building?" Harpo vigorously nods his head affirmatively. As the policeman drags him away, the bricks, glass, and wood of the building rumble to the ground, leaving a rising cloud of dust, a stunned cop, and a grinning Harpo. . . .

Although this is only part of the essay and its outline, this example illustrates *how* a writer can achieve concreteness and momentum through a clear thesis and a clear sense of his topic's stages or divisions. Having devised a unified, specific thesis, the student was able to factor out the distinct aspects of Harpo's style that most interested him.

3d

The Introductory Paragraph

Few rules of writing are binding, but it is usually desirable that the introductory paragraph (1) seize and hold the reader's attention, (2) indicate efficiently and gracefully the subject matter of the paper, and (3) reveal, implicitly or explicitly, the writer's attitude toward the subject matter. Most writers write the introductory paragraph a number of times. Since the success of your introductory paragraph depends on your understanding of the complete essay, especially of the conclusion, you may well write its final version last.

Don't be timid about taking a first plunge into writing. Just begin, remembering that any beginning can be changed, or even discarded, in the final draft. Try to create in a reader the illusion that you are beginning at the beginning, even though you have written and discarded three or four versions before you were satisfied. Polishing for tone—the selection of this word rather than that—may be the last thing you do before handing in the essay.

One way of getting started, especially for short papers, is to begin with your thesis. Another way is to open with a sharp contrast, as in the paragraph that compares Harpo's comic technique with those of his brothers. Sometimes, the contrast depends on controversy:

> There is no longer just a generation gap. Today, the feelings are often open, deep indifference. In the 1960s youth was attacked for its involvement in political and peace movements and its rebellion against sterile education and the war-as-usual. In the 1970s it was criticized for its preoccupation with careers, its apathy about social issues, and its interest in "doing one's own thing." Knowing that earlier generations were denounced for contradictory reasons, many students can see no reason at all why they should listen to adult America.

Another method is to open with a key quotation from the work under discussion, as the student writer of the following example did:

> It is the "quick, compact imagery of a single statement that forms the basis of Navajo poetry," says Oliver LaFarge. This remark can well be illustrated in LaFarge's own story of Navajo life, *Laughing Boy,* a novel

in which things are perceived and identified through "quick, compact imagery." The first image ties the protagonist, Laughing Boy, to his environment: "His new red headband was a bright color among the embers of the sun-struck desert, undulating like a moving graph of the pony's lope"—a simple statement, surely, but nonetheless a "compact image" of the movement of a man on his horse over flat ground.

Still another way is to begin with a short, clear summary or characterization and lead up to a focusing statement:

The Hawaiian Islands are anchored in a position where they receive sea swells the year round. The contour of the ocean floor and the structure of the reefs turn these swells into beautiful breaking waves, which make Hawaii a surfer's paradise. I have been surfing in this paradise every day for the last seven years, and I can tell you that there probably is no more purely natural act than surfing. You are at one with nature's most basic element—the living sea. But as changing times bring "progress" to the islands, so is there a change in surfing.

Avoid beginning essays with generalities and platitudes: "Pollution nowadays is a very important issue" or "It is obvious to everyone that children watch too much television." Such openings discourage even the most determined reader. Neither is the proclamation "This essay will discuss" likely to spark reader interest. Avoid scrupulously the complaining tone, "While no one can write on a topic as difficult and complex as this one, I will nevertheless attempt . . ." or the apology, "I am but one small sail in the sea of human opinion. . . ." Confidence, assertiveness, authority characterize the most successful opening paragraphs.

3e

The Main Body

The sections in this chapter on outlining and the discussion in Chapter 4 about paragraphing offer the fullest treatment of the main body of the paper—the material that comes between the introduction and the conclusion and constitutes the body of the argument. Nevertheless, a few general principles are relevant.

First, remember that the more space you give an idea, the more important it may appear to the reader. While the middle of the paper should take into account all the points listed in an outline, each heading need not require full paragraph development. Whether to devote more than a sentence or two to a specific heading depends on your judgment of the importance of a point. Commonly accepted judgments or matters of fact and history can be stated briefly or summarized, but stands on controversial issues may need the support of concrete evidence and the reasonable proof a logically developed paragraph provides.

Second, in papers that argue a thesis through the analysis of particular examples, arrange the evidence in ascending order of importance. Otherwise, you miss the opportunity to convince a skeptical reader through the accumulation of solid proof and run the risk of jarring your audience with anticlimax. Keep your reader alert by varying the length and structure of your sentences and paragraphs, and fasten paragraphs together with strong transitional sentences.

Third, check your transitions, especially the last sentence of the opening paragraph and the first sentence of the last paragraph. Transitions hold an argument together, helping to ensure the persuasiveness of your paper. Be sure that the first and last paragraphs are joined to the rest of the essay.

3f

The Conclusion

While the conclusion of the paper is a vital part of the composition, if only because of its final effect on the reader, it is the one most often neglected by student writers: either they end too abruptly or meander through a tedious summary of the major points of the agreement. Unfortunately, there are too many formulas to end a paper—the grandiose "therefore"; the limp but modest "so"; the circular and soporific "in conclusion I have shown . . . ." Resist these pat transitions since they avoid the task of demonstrating the significance of the argument, which is the obligation of a well-written conclusion.

A conclusion is not a one-sentence tag; it should not apologize for itself or the essay, and it should never introduce a new idea. Rather than summarize what has gone before, the best conclusions mark the arrival of the essay at the destination announced in the introductory paragraph. An essay should end with the ease and authority of a musical composition that brings its themes to a unified, harmonious resolution, giving the reader a sense of finality. One student ended a 700-word theme on Chekhov's play *The Seagull* this way:

> When the curtain falls on *The Seagull,* one has the feeling that the story is not at all ended, that the action continues behind the curtain. Reflecting on this, one may find that the secret of Chekhov's effect lies in avoiding the overly dramatic, the play in which everything builds to one climax centered in one character. Chekhov has allowed the themes of love and death, of dreams and reality, to unfold in the random, senseless way that they occur in our lives.

Often the feeling of completeness that a well-written conclusion conveys can be created by picking up a word or phrase from the introduction or recalling an earlier example. Such returns, of course, should make it clear that since we have read the body of the essay, we understand these references in a new way. An essay is not a circle. If we only arrive where we began, we have not gotten anywhere.

The student who argued that the increasing number of surfers in Hawaii would either have to discipline themselves to share the waves or expect state regulation of the sport picked up from the opening paragraph the key word, *sea*, and echoed *living* in the noun *life*, to tie together the beginning and the end of his paper:

> Unless we treat the sea with the consideration that it deserves as a source of wonder, pleasure, and life, sacrificing our own selfish desire to catch the big wave regardless of who or what is in the way, we can look forward to the regulation of surfing. Police patrolling the beaches, floodlights stuck into the sand for day and night surfing, licenses, permits, tickets—these are not pleasant prospects. But neither are the fights, the racial name-calling, the indifference to another surfer's safety which one encounters all too often in Hawaiian waters. To live in a world of change we must learn to change ourselves.

A writer may conclude strongly not only by returning to key words but also by emphasizing continuity. Beginnings and endings are connected: the basic pattern is shown—and seen in relation to our lives. In the following student example, an analysis of the protagonists in Pirsig's *Zen and the Art of Motorcycle Maintenance* and

Ellison's *Invisible Man,* note how the writer makes these connections.

> Participation in life and the celebration of its possibilities are what both Phaedrus and the Invisible Man finally affirm. They are able to do so as a result of their personal quests. Yet they both set out in ignorance, not knowing the direction they are actually headed in. At the end, when the Invisible Man says, ''Who knows but that, on the lower frequencies, I speak for you?,'' it is a warning that most of us are still back at the very beginning simply because we think we're not or, worse yet, because we don't even think about it.

No competent writer dashes off a conclusion at the last moment. When we finish reading an essay we should feel that it could not have ended any other way. Writing that creates this sense of completion is the result of thought and revision, but the result—a satisfied and agreeable reader—will justify the effort.

3g
The Formal Outline

In this section, we stress outlining because it is one of the most effective means writers have for planning and revising papers. Outlining is an active analysis to discover a paper's full meaning: it is a *systematic listing* of an essay's most important points—a visual model of its plan and structure. Even the most experienced writers usually begin with some kind of informal outline, however much they may modify it or deviate from it as they expand upon their subject. For less experienced writers, formal outlines are often essential. The usefulness of either the topic or sentence outline depends, however, on how well the writer understands and observes its conventions.

The most obvious use of the formal outline is to help the writer to anticipate the main divisions of the topic and the connections between ideas and evidence, and to show these to the reader. Writing about almost any complex topic in economics, history, psychology, or biology—really, in any field worth writing about—*should* entail an outline.

A second use of the formal outline is in the revision of a rough draft or of an unsatisfactory final version. If your writing is criticized for lack of coherence or unity or the logical relationship of ideas, try to outline the defective composition. Use a formal outline to diagnose the paper. Translate the generalized impression that "something's wrong with it" into specific knowledge of how and where the subject needs restriction or development, where paragraphs need transitions or internal coherence.

Finally, you can use a formal outline to discover and test another writer's plan and structure. If, for example, you have read three essays on Lincoln's use of power during the Civil War and are to write on the authors' differing assumptions about the presidency, you can avoid hectic rereading by constructing three accurate outlines. By isolating crucial differences in visual form, you save yourself from skimming over and over the same paragraphs and snatching at random phrases or details. Formal outlining is also helpful when you are asked to refute someone else's position or case. By outlining his argument, you discover what it is, what the key issues are, and what may be the fallacies in his logic or the limitations of his evidence. By outlining your reading, you not only discover someone else's views but also clarify your own.

1. Types of Outlines

There are three types of formal outlines: the paragraph outline, the topic outline, and the sentence outline. Each has its particular uses and limitations; instructors usually indicate which form they want submitted with papers.

The first of these, the PARAGRAPH OUTLINE, is a list of topic or summary sentences numbered so that sentence one is the gist of paragraph one; sentence two, the gist of paragraph two; and so on.

For example:

1. Outlining is a systematic listing of an essay's most important points—a visual model of its plan and structure.

2. The first use of the formal outline is to help writer and reader anticipate the main divisions of the topic and the connections between ideas and evidence.

3. The second use of the formal outline is in the revision. . . .

By enumerating, the paragraph outline helps you recall a loose sequence of ideas. What it *doesn't* show so clearly are the logical relationships within and between paragraphs and the kinds of evidence and argument the writer employs. For your own writing and revising, you need a form that shows the main ideas, their logical relationships, and the evidence—the topic and sentence outlines.

The TOPIC OUTLINE consists of brief phrases or single words, numbered and lettered to show the order and importance of the ideas. Topic outlines use no complete sentences, except occasionally in the main head, which stands at the beginning:

Anne Bradstreet's Homespun Cloth:
The First American Poems

I. Biographical introduction
    A.   Anne Bradstreet's voyage to Massachusetts Bay
    B.   Her reaction to the New World
II. The Puritan Dilemma
    A.   Conflict between impulse and dogma
        1.   Love of this world
        2.   Love of God and submission to His will
    B.   Bradstreet's dilemma
        1.   Rebellion against the New World
        2.   Submission to God's will
III. First volume of poems
    A.   Publication without author's permission
    B.   Bradstreet's reaction
    C.   Public reaction
        1.   Favorable reception in her day
        2.   Modern preference for her later poems
IV. Handicaps of a woman poet in colonial America
    A.   Physical handicaps
        1.   Harsh living conditions
        2.   Endless labor raising eight children
    B.   Psychological handicaps
        1.   Woman's duty to do housework
        2.   General distrust of poetry as "Devil's Library"
        3.   Writing believed dangerous for tender female minds
            a.   Governor's wife
            b.   Sister Sarah
            c.   Anne Hutchinson

    V. Bradstreet's best poetry produced by tension
        A.   Conflict between love of this world and of Heavenly Kingdom
        B.   Increased interest in personal experiences
           1.   Fear of death and love of husband
           2.   Autumnal splendor declaring the glory of the Lord
           3.   Adjusting to early death of grandchildren
           4.   Loss of home and possessions in a fire
        C.   Bradstreet's solution of this dilemma
           1.   God's providence to be accepted
           2.   Inevitable human rebellion against such dogma.
   VI. Conclusion: Final success of Bradstreet's homespun muse

For brief papers in class, tests, and short analyses or reports, the topic outline is useful and usually sufficient. Carelessly used or misunderstood, it merely deceives the writer and very often causes vagueness and disorder if he writes from it. Headings like "Introduction," "Main Body," and "Conclusion" and subheadings like "Example," "Reasons," and "Results" delay concrete thinking and reveal nothing. Consider the following typical examples:

VAGUE TOPIC OUTLINE

The Change from School to College

   I. Introduction
      A.   High school ideas
      B.   Reasons for these ideas
  II. What my first impressions were
      A.   Two examples
      B.   Results
 III. Conclusions
      A.   Why I have changed my mind
      B.   Advice to high school seniors

In this first example, quite aside from irregularities in form, neither the reader nor, apparently, the writer knows what his "high school ideas" were (Were they misconceptions? Partial truths?), why he had whatever "first impressions" he did about college, or the reasons for whatever "advice" he would give to seniors.

OUTLINE DEVOID OF CONTENT

The Mob in the French Revolution

I. Types during the early days
    A.   Leadership
    B.   Effects on the course of the Revolution
II. Types during the Reign of Terror
    A.   Leadership
    B.   Effects on the course of the Revolution
III. Types immediately before Napoleon
    A.   Leadership
    B.   Effects on the course of the Revolution

The second example has an ornamental patina of meaning and may look like a usable outline, but it has no real content and is of doubtful value to the writer. An interesting topic, it is also a complex one, as the writer discovers when he investigates the differences between the mobs in Paris and rioters elsewhere in France. Not all of the possible differences and distinctions would necessarily be relevant to the paper (e.g., are twenty or thirty pillaging peasants a mob?), but the outline does not analyze any distinctive features.

For longer papers, the SENTENCE OUTLINE is often the best form. The sentence outline has a complete statement, a sentence, for every item in the outline and has a thesis at the beginning. In the following example, note how a topic outline can be expanded into a sentence outline.

TOPIC OUTLINE

The Complexity of Experience of Laughter

I. Single explanation theories of laughter
    A.   Social punishment
        1.   Mocks differences
        2.   Shows feeling of superiority
    B.   Defense against social taboos
        1.   Relies on dirty jokes
        2.   Is relief of tension
    C.   Sudden surprise
        1.   Stimulated by the unexpected act
        2.   Is delight in being startled

II. Complex experience of laughter
    A.   Descriptions of feelings
        1. "To have the last laugh"
        2. "To laugh at"
        3. "To laugh off"
    B.   Descriptions of vocal expressions
        1. "To chuckle"
        2. "To giggle and titter"
        3. "To snicker"
        4. "To guffaw"
III. Inadequacies of theories of laughter to experience of laughter
    A.   Failure to account for description of feelings
        1. No sudden pleasurable surprise in social punishment theory
        2. No sense of superiority in social taboo theory
        3. No self-embarrassment in pleasurable surprise theory
    B.   Failure to account for sheer joy
        1. No explanation of lovers' spontaneity by any theory
        2. No explanation of delight in success by any theory

EXPANSION TO SENTENCE OUTLINE

The Complexity of Experience of Laughter

Thesis: Although there are several theories of laughter, no single one accounts for the quite distinct emotions that cause it.

I. The theories tend to explain laughter by a single emotion or cause.
    A.   Laugher is social punishment inflicted by the majority.
        1. It mocks differences in dress, behavior, and belief.
        2. It is a feeling of superiority and satiric awareness.
    B.   Laughter is a defense against social taboos.
        1. It is stimulated by the dirty joke and obscene remark.
        2. It is a safety-valve response relieving tension.
    C.   Laughter is the expression of pleasure in the sudden surprise.
        1. It is stimulated by the unexpected physical or verbal act.
            a. The physical is often the sudden fall or thump.
            b. The verbal is usually a witty remark.
        2. It is delight in being startled.
II. The experience of laughter is not a simple one.
    A.   Our feelings while laughing vary.
        1. Vindictively we "have the last laugh."
        2. In amusement we "laugh at" something.
        3. In embarrassment we "laugh it away."

   B.   The vocal expressions of laughter vary.
      1. We "chuckle" in a low tone when inwardly satisfied.
      2. We "giggle and titter" in rapid, high-pitched sounds when silly.
      3. We "snicker" in sly, half-suppressed tones at another's plight.
      4. We "guffaw" in loud tones when heartily enjoying ourselves.

III. The theories are inadequate to the experience of laughter.
   A.   No theory accounts for the ways we describe our feelings.
      1. The theory of laughter as social punishment neglects the laugh of sudden pleasurable surprise.
      2. The theory of laughter as a defense against social taboos minimizes the laugh of punishment and mockery.
      3. The theory of laughter as pleasurable surprise slights the laugh of self-embarrassment.
   B.   All theories omit the laughter of sheer joy of being and doing.
      1. They do not account for the spontaneous laughter of children, lovers, and parents.
      2. They do not account for the triumphant, delighted laugh of the successful artist or athlete.

In comparing the two outlines, notice that the sentence outline contains far more information and reveals a more detailed analysis than the topic outline. The sentence outline has the advantage of compelling you to *formulate more explicitly* the material you intend to use. For longer papers on complex topics—say, 1,500 words on the effects of automation on the unions or 2,000 words on the methods of crime prevention—a sentence outline may be the best means of organizing the paper or revising an unsatisfactory one.

3h

Conventions of the Topic and Sentence Outline

The following system of numbering and lettering is nearly universal:

I. _____

  A.   _____

  B.   _____

    1.   _____

    2.   _____

      a.   _____

      b.   _____

II. _____

Coordinate points—those of equal importance—should be indented the same distance from the left margin. The main heads (I, II, III) are farthest to the left; the subheads (A, B, C) are indented several more spaces to the right. Rarely will you need to go farther than the third subhead (a, b, c).

For topic outlines, capitalize the first letter of the word beginning the heading, but do not punctuate the end of the entry since it is not a sentence. For sentence outlines, begin with a capital letter and end with a period or other terminal punctuation.

The headings and subordinate items in the topic and the sentence outline should correspond to the logical divisions and subdivisions of the material. The indentation and numbering of items should indicate parallelism or subordination of ideas. The pattern

I. _____

  A.   _____

  B.   _____

II. _____

indicates that A and B are parallel ideas under I, and that the larger division II is parallel in content with I.

These conventions matter. When one sees the pattern

I.
    A.
    B.
II. etc.

he expects to find the two parallel ideas A and B under I, and he expects to find the larger division II parallel in content with I. The writer *misleads himself and his reader* if he divides his material this way:

ILLOGICAL AND CONFUSING

  I. Advantages of outboard motors
    A.   Relatively inexpensive
    B.   Attachable to any small boat
  II. Easily transportable

"Easily transportable" is logically a subtopic under I, "Advantages of outboard motors." It should be made parallel with A and B:

CLEAR COORDINATION AND SUBORDINATION

  I. Advantages of outboard motors
    A.   Relatively inexpensive
    B.   Attachable to any small boat
    C.   Easily transportable
  II. Disadvantages of outboard motors
    A.   Troublesome to repair on the water
    B.   Limited fuel capacity

When one subheading includes material covered in other parallel headings, the subdivisions are said to overlap. Overlapping subdivisions show that you have not analyzed your material fully.

POORLY ANALYZED—OVERLAPPING

  I. Organized welfare groups
    A.   Early relief organizations
    B.   Red Cross
    C.   Community Chest
    D.   Relief organizations today

Logically, "Relief organizations today" *includes* the Red Cross and Community Chest. If you are subdividing on a chronological basis, stick to it consistently, and make a subdivision for Red Cross and Community Chest:

CLEARLY SUBDIVIDED

   I. Organized welfare groups
      A.   History of early relief organizations
      B.   Relief organizations today
         1.   Red Cross
         2.   Community Chest

One last word about subdivisions: convention demands that each topic which is subdivided must have at least two headings. The argument runs that dividing something must produce at least two parts. Occasionally, however, a lone subhead is a useful means of *reminding yourself* of an example, illustration, or reference you don't want to forget:

REMINDER FOR FULL ILLUSTRATION

    1. Extension of Mohammedan power under the early caliphs
       A.   Eastward and northward
          1.   For example, Persian and Greek lands
       B.   Westward
          1.   For example, Syria, Egypt, and northern Africa

Lone subheads should be eliminated from outlines that are to be turned in, and usually should be revised in your own working outline; free your mind by recording the needed reminder and reclassifying it later.

Exercise 1

Analyze an essay in the text used in your writing course or a chapter in a text for another course you are taking or an article in a magazine such as Scientific American, Atlantic Monthly, *or* Natural History *to discover what the thesis of the essay is. Does the essay have a thesis statement, and if so, where does it appear?*

Exercise 2

Decide what your position or commitment is regarding the following topics. On the basis of that decision, formulate in one sentence the thesis statement that would be the foundation for a 500- to 700-word essay about the subject. Then analyze your statement to see whether or not it leads to a pattern of organization or development. If not, reexamine the thesis statement for vagueness and generalities.

The media's treatment of violence
The appeal of science fiction on television and in film
Laws discriminating against homosexuals
The use of the SAT to determine college admissions
The right to abortion
Defense spending in the current fiscal year
The meaning of "sexual freedom"
The eating habits of American children

Exercise 3

Select some controversial subject about which you have strong convictions—pollution, drugs, child-care centers, education. Prepare a thesis and sentence outline of the position you oppose. Then construct a thesis and sentence outline for a 1,000-word composition that answers the most telling arguments of the opposition.

Exercise 4

Take an in-class theme, an essay test, or a short composition you had trouble organizing and make paragraph, topic, and sentence outlines of it as it was written. Then construct revised paragraph, topic, and sentence outlines for it. Be prepared to write a revised version from one of the new outlines if your instructor should ask you to.

Exercise 5

Make a tentative topic or sentence outline for a long research project or term paper assigned in another course. Submit it to your English instructor or your course instructor, if either is willing. Go over the outline with your instructor in as much detail as you can, noting particularly gaps in the evidence and needed reorganization. (The sentence outline will be more helpful to both of you, but it will be hard to construct if you are still in the very preliminary stages of planning and research.)

4

CONSTRUCTING PARAGRAPHS

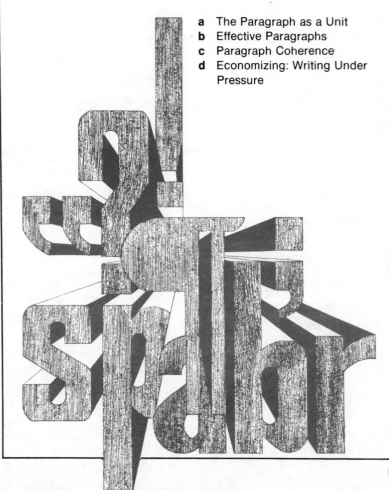

Paragraphing is one of the skills most important to the craft of writing. The following chapter focuses on three essential aspects of this skill:

1. The paragraph as a unit, which stresses some of its basic traits.
2. Effective paragraphs, which stresses development and coherence.
3. Economizing, which stresses ways to control paragraphs when you have little time for revision (as during exams, or when you are trying to save space).

For continuity, try to keep two basic considerations in mind: *What* is it that I am trying to *do* in this paragraph or these paragraphs? and *How* can I rework it or them to be more effective?

4a

The Paragraph as a Unit

Let's begin with a few simple questions about paragraphs and agree that because these are simple questions, they may be hard ones. Exact definitions and pat examples would be neat, but they are unlikely to reflect the varied possibilities and uses that writers have discovered in paragraphs. So let's try to answer the following questions: What are paragraphs? What can they do? How can they be made more effective?

First, what are paragraphs? The standard answer is that a paragraph is both a unit in itself and part of a larger whole; that paragraphs help to indicate the structure of a composition; and that paragraph division is a conventional sign that one point is completed, the next point about to begin. As far as it goes, the answer is true enough. What a word is to a sentence, or a sentence to a paragraph, the paragraph may be to an essay, a story, or a chapter— a part that is integral to the whole and gains its full meaning from the whole. Or, like certain words ("Ouch!") and sentences ("Trespassers will be prosecuted"), a paragraph can stand alone, more or less contented and self-contained—a gem of an answer, a smug point of view, another way of looking at things. What, then, is insufficient about the standard answer? Nothing, except that it suggests paragraphing is like drawing static squares:

We still want to know about the different ways in which the boxes can be made to hold a variety of things:

We will take up these considerations later when we answer the second and third questions.

What can paragraphs do? Well, we know they break up a page of type and make it more readable: they provide both focus and rest stops for the reader. They isolate individual features of a landscape the writer wishes to look at, and thus they allow both writer and reader to linger over—or hurry by—this feature. Too many paragraphs, like too many commands to "See this!" "Note that!" and "Look here!," fragment our attention and make us glance at a page superficially. Too few paragraphs in a work, like the guide who wants us to take in the whole landscape at once, lead us to see nothing clearly. Most beginners probably want to look at too many things too quickly, or skip from one sight to another because they don't know how to focus. In either case, the consequences are brief, fuzzy paragraphs. We need not only to look more steadily and fully at the individual parts but also to study the way each part contributes to the total impression.

Paragraphs single out, connect, and control tempo. But they obviously do other things. They help tell stories, describe processes, distinguish differences, report findings, and push conclusions. They help clarify feelings, understand motives, and excite emotions. Paragraphs *make something happen.* When we are writing well, we find that we are getting into our subject and discovering new connections and examples as we go along. On such lucky occasions, we usually paragraph by the dynamic feeling that one section is complete and that we're eager to get on with the next one, which is already teasing our consciousness. Later, during the rewriting and revision ("re-seeing"), we combine, break up, thin out, or rework our paragraphs more systematically. We now have an overall view, a clear structure, to work with and to improve.

Finally, how can paragraphs be made more effective? You can employ a number of techniques for improving paragraphs, or you can imitate models used (often unconsciously) by experienced writers to accomplish particular ends. One trait of any effective paragraph is that it is *unified,* and we can ask certain questions (after the writing) that help ensure unity: Does the paragraph read smoothly? Does it hang together? Unified paragraphs are not magically created by indented openings or by other graphic devices, but they do have certain elements we can look for.

1. Paragraph Division

As a unit in itself, each paragraph should deal with a single topic or aspect of a topic. It should have a central idea or purpose, and each sentence in the paragraph should aid in developing this central idea and making it clear. But before you test for unity in any single paragraph, you should consider the relationship of that paragraph to the work as a whole. *The essential principle in dividing material into paragraphs is making sure that each paragraph will show a significant turn in your thought.* (If you have been working from an outline, check back and be sure that your paragraphs come at important points in it.)

One way to achieve unity in paragraphs is by careful analysis of your material and the coverage of the thesis statement when it comes near the beginning. This technique works well when you can sort out distinct stages or steps in a process, requirements for a particular job or position, distinct aspects of a person's character, and so on. Notice in the opening paragraph of the following student theme *how* the writer names three different requirements for the task of beet gathering—stamina, a sharp eye, and mastery of special techniques. Each of these requirements can (and does) become the basis for a well-organized paragraph. The composition is unified as a whole by its thesis.

A Beet Gatherer

A mechanical sugar-beet gatherer, like many other agricultural machines, is far from perfect. Its main imperfection is that it leaves beets behind, either by breaking them off or missing them altogether. Thus, someone is needed to walk behind the machine, pick up all the beets missed, and toss them into the truck. This is not a complex task, admittedly, but **it is one that requires a good deal of stamina for walking, a sharp eye, and the mastery of some special techniques.** [THESIS]

As an example of the complete essay, consider the following student paper (edited and condensed for publication here). It began as a satire of undergraduate *machismo* and as a parody of "How to do it" papers, which often concern themselves with trivial matters. Like all good parody, it makes fun of the object by mimicking its basic form: it makes us conscious of what the original really looks like by laughing at its features.

How to Fling a Keg

If you travel to a rowdy college beer party, particularly if it's mostly male, you may be asked to participate in the last rites for the beer dispenser, commonly known as the keg. Such a ritual commences with the hauling of the keg up onto someone's shoulders and climaxes with its being tossed down a stairwell or out a window, punctuated by cries of "t-t-timber" or "fore." In such an ethos, nothing will produce obscene ridicule more quickly than a keg that is weakly slung from the hip and bounces off each step until it settles on the linoleum landing. Most often the keg is half full when heaved, so unless you are a six foot two, 220-pound tackle, you may not find your task easily or gracefully accomplished. **But you can save yourself from embarrassment and** hernias by making the right preparations, employing the right technique, and being well versed in the etiquette for retrieving it and explaining to the dorm president how the beer keg got there in the first place [THESIS], along with the broken black pump.

Preparations are important. You should know what kind of party you are venturing into and what traditions are tied to the social gathering. There is more possibility of a keg heaving if the festivity is held at a fraternity or on the night following the final football game than if it's an alumni get-together. When checking out the parties, avoid ones where aggressive and enthusiastic fathers insist on teaching their sons how to toss a pony keg in order to awe lodge members at the next picnic. Care should also be taken to select the appropriate clothing. Wear shoes with good traction, such as sneakers or Topsiders, since by the time the ritual occurs refuse beer has accumulated on the floor. (A pair of wingtipped French Shriners will put you on your back if you attempt throwing a keg under the typical prevailing conditions.) And since kegs are not handled with the care or cleanliness of a six pack of Heineken, do not plan to wear your "I'll-impress-the-hell-out-of-them with my Lacoste shirt and khaki slacks outfit." Even if you doubt that you will be lobbing Schlitz depth charges, forget about your best clothes. Your best bet is a pair of Levis and an old shirt.

Technique is essential. When it is you whom the brewmasters volunteer to complete the task, the first thing to do is to throw back your shoulders and suck in your gut. This ritual heave is by no means to be performed as a routine on "Beat the Clock," but the appearance of brute strength is appreciated more than ingenuity. (You do need ingenuity, but it should be disguised as strength.) Next, assume a good stance and take a good grip—the keg should be thrown in the same way a track and fielder would heave a shotput. With feet spread shoulder distance apart, bend over the keg and grasp the silver edges on the top and bottom. As you lift the container slightly off the ground, swing it back, swaying your body with it to gain momentum, so you can move it easily up to your shoulder. When you are ready to toss the keg, place most of your weight on your back foot so that you can drive off of it as you throw: this is where proper shoes can make the difference among a Charles Atlas heave, a Chevy Chase dribble, or a back operation. Finally, be sure to follow through and snap your wrist after you have released the dispenser. As in basketball when you were taught to concentrate your aim on the front of the rim, you should direct the keg to the front base of the wall near the landing. The best method to improve your technique is practice—a household hallway and an old wooden chair are excellent aids in refining your throw.

Finally, there is the necessary mastery of the post-throw etiquette. When replying to questions asked by the proper authorities (for example, the dorm president or Campus Security), attempt to discourage any efforts to finger any specific person by using phrases like "To the best of my ability I cannot recall" or "At this moment in time." The practice and experience of these touchy post-ritual situations can be gained by reading a lot of Watergate books, viewing *All the President's Men,* and watching reruns of the David Frost–Richard Nixon interviews.

Let's summarize what the essay does. It specifies, in its thesis, the minimum precautions a keg thrower should take; it establishes an *orderly sequence* of significant ideas and, therefore, makes paragraphing much easier. Each paragraph discusses *only one set* of precautions, complete with relevant detail. Each paragraph, in short, is unified in itself and a logical subdivision of the whole composition.

2. The Topic Sentence

You may have noticed that a writer often begins a paragraph with a sentence that summarizes the paragraph's content, as in the preceding piece, "How to Fling a Keg": "Preparations are important," or "Finally, there is the necessary mastery of the post-throw etiquette." These are topic sentences. Topic sentences perform the same function for the individual paragraph that the thesis does for the whole paper. *A topic sentence summarizes the central idea of a paragraph.* It is a valuable aid in securing paragraph unity: the writer can use it in the rough draft as a guide to the paragraph's content, and in revision as a means of ensuring that everything in a paragraph is connected. It helps a writer to control the paragraph's focus and to cut out irrelevant details.

Topic sentences are usually found at or near the beginning of a paragraph. Here, they are a kind of promise writers make themselves of what is going to be talked about. Topic sentences also prepare the reader for what is to come. They are the declaration of the paragraph's independence. A topic sentence, however, may be placed anywhere in the paragraph—in the middle, after some transitional sentences, or at the end, as a conclusion. There is nothing sacred about starting with a topic sentence; the beginning of the paragraph just happens to be the place most writers naturally pause, reflect, and center their thoughts. Notice in the following student paragraph how the topic sentences at the beginning help unify the material that comes after.

OPENING WITH A TOPIC SENTENCE

Rachel Carson has used simple illustrations to get important information over to the reader without using complex technical terms. Rather than tell her readers that scarps mark the upper part of a great fault, along which the crustal block under Valley X moved in relation to the range, she simply mentions that the crust of the earth fell into folds and wrinkles and that valleys were formed. Miss Carson's statement is clearer to the average reader than the technical one, and yet it gets the same point across. Similarly, because most people already know what sponges, jellyfish, worms, and starfish look like, Miss Carson has chosen these to represent her specific examples of early animal life. They give the reader a general idea of all primitive animal life, since each one is representative of a specific phylum.

In this example, the writer uses the topic sentence at the beginning as a broad generalization which she then illustrates. The key phrases "simple illustrations" and "without using complex technical terms" give the writer a framework into which to fit her observations.

When a topic sentence comes in the *middle* of a paragraph, it usually ties the sentences that precede it to the material that follows it. When it *concludes* the paragraph, the topic sentence usually pulls together a long series of details that have been designed to lead up to it, often serving as a climax. Notice how the topic sentence functions in each of the following examples. (You might try reading each paragraph aloud to get a feeling for how the topic sentence works.)

TOPIC SENTENCE IN THE MIDDLE

Then something unforeseen happened. The waters of the River, shut out from much land, rose higher upon the lands that were left, and so broke over many dikes and again flooded the farms. The white men cursed, thinking that the rains must have been heavier than before; they decided to build levees a little higher and be safe for ever. **In those years** that followed, a confusion as of a nightmare fell upon the Valley. More and more levees were built, and each one made the water rise so that men had to build up the old ones higher still. The white men would not withdraw from the lands, and neither in their peculiar madness would they all work together against the River. Instead, in the dark rainy nights a man might break his neighbor's levee to lower the water-level against his own; so, not with shovels, but with loaded guns, men patrolled the levees, like savages brandishing spears against the river-god.

TOPIC SENTENCE AT THE END

At last, although the white men hated the very sound of the words, they began to talk more and more of "the government" and "regulation." Then finally came engineers who looked shrewdly not at one part of the River, but at the whole. They measured snow and rain, and the depth of streams. They surveyed; they calculated with many figures how high the levees must be and how wide the channels between. Gradually even the fiercest fighters among the white men came to see that the River (which was always the whole River) was too great for any man or company of men. Only the Whole People could hope to match the Whole River. **So, after many years of disaster the white men began to live in a truce with the river.**

—GEORGE R. STEWART

Not *every* paragraph you will write will have a topic sentence, though the practice of including a focusing sentence in each paragraph is a good one. In some cases, the topic sentences may be omitted entirely without violating unity. *But it should always be possible to summarize a paragraph's central idea or thought in a single sentence.* For instance, although the following student paragraph has no topic sentence, the central idea might be summarized thus: "The long school day at the medieval University of Paris demanded much from the students."

TOPIC SENTENCE LEFT IMPLIED

Classes at the medieval University of Paris began at 5 a.m. First on the agenda were the ordinary lectures, which were the regular and more important lectures. After several ordinary lectures and a short, begrudged lunch hour, students attended extraordinary lectures given in the afternoon. These were supplementary to the ordinary lectures and usually given by a less important teacher, who may not have been more than fourteen or fifteen years old. A student would spend ten or twelve hours a day with his teachers, and then following classes in the late afternoon, he had sports events. But after sports, the day was not over. There was homework, which consisted of copying, recopying, and memorizing notes while the light permitted. Nor was there much of a break. Christmas vacation was about three weeks, and summer vacation was only a month.

If your papers are criticized for disunified paragraphs, you should certainly make a conscientious effort to write a clear topic sentence for each of your paragraphs. Similarly, you can often clarify an assigned reading by locating and underlining the topic sentences for the paragraphs that confuse you. The great value of the topic sentence for the reader and writer alike is its function in focusing on the main idea and in giving the paragraph direction.

3. Length of Paragraph

The principle that governs paragraph length is the *reader's convenience*. If each sentence is a separate paragraph, the reader will be unable to see the groupings the writer has in mind. Pages consistently cluttered by short, underdeveloped paragraphs scatter the reader's attention. If, on the other hand, there are too many sentences in the paragraph, the reader will be unable to see the subdivisions of the material clearly. Paragraphs that run consistently to more than a page are little better than no paragraphing at all, since the reader is forced to make the subdivisions of material for himself.

Ordinarily, then, a paragraph should consist of more than one sentence but less than a page. But note that paragraphs vary considerably in length in different kinds of writing. In formal, scientific, or scholarly writing they are sometimes as long as 250 words. In ordinary magazine articles the average length is about 150 words. In newspapers the average is 50 words or less. Good questions to ask yourself are: "Should any of my paragraphs be written as two, for clarity?" and "Are there any noticeably short paragraphs so closely related that they should be combined?" Consider the following student paragraphs, which have been fragmented in ways that often occur in undergraduate writing.

Disunified

1. This afternoon, the beach takes me away from myself. I gaze out over the huge expanse of ocean, stretching out in the distance, getting darker and darker until it meets the powder blue sky. Staring along the fuzzy dark line where sky and ocean meet, I wonder if anyone is out there, drifting aimlessly across the sea.

2. After a moment or so, I shift my eyes to a group of about two dozen sailboats that are clipping through the water about a hundred yards off shore. The owners apparently belong to a club, because each boat has the same brightly colored red, white, and blue striped sail.

3. Looking closer still, I see the white crested breakers pushing several body-surfers up the beach. Though the surfers stop, the pale, blue-green water continues to slide across the wet sand, eventually engulfing a nearly completed sand castle.

4. The young architect building the castle can't be much older than five, but he doesn't sulk or cry. Instead, he just trudges up the beach to a spot where the water can't reach him and begins another project.

Paragraphs Combined for Unity

This afternoon, the beach takes me away from myself. I gaze out over the huge expanse of ocean, stretching out in the distance, getting darker and darker until it meets the powder blue sky. Staring along the fuzzy dark line where sky and ocean meet, I wonder if anyone is out there, drifting aimlessly across the sea. After a moment or so, I shift my eyes to a group of about two dozen sailboats that are clipping through the water about a hundred yards offshore. The owners apparently belong to a club, because each boat has the same brightly colored red, white, and blue striped sail. (Paragraphs 1 and 2 combined)

Looking closer still, I see the white crested breakers pushing several body-surfers up the beach. Though the surfers stop, the pale, blue-green water continues to slide across the wet sand, eventually engulfing a nearly completed sand castle. The young architect building the castle can't be much older than five, but he doesn't sulk or cry. Instead, he just trudges up the beach to a spot where the water can't reach him and begins another project. (Paragraphs 3 and 4 combined)

With the combining of the paragraphs, the essay gains unity. The reader can now easily follow the thematic movement of (1) what is seen on the water, and (2) what is seen on the shore. With this gain in unity, the reader more easily feels *how* "This afternoon, the beach takes me away from myself." In fact, the four paragraphs could be joined into one unified whole—as indeed they were in the original. But either way, as one paragraph or two, the materials are tighter and better focused.

The student who wrote the following composition did not build it up painfully by adding one paragraph to another; rather, he conceived of the experience as a unified and coherent one, with movement and continuity. Nevertheless, the subject was obviously far too long to appear as a single paragraph, so he located the phases he wished to emphasize and made these his paragraphs. His paper illustrates how unity helps continuity.

I Surrendered

Social order, it is said, can only be maintained through the restriction and prohibition of our often whimsical impulses (taking off from school or work, swimming nude, open sex), and we find ourselves inhibited by a civilization that was supposed to ensure our well-being. Parents, the law, and public opinion condition us to keep the lid tightly clamped on our drives for free and outward expression of inner needs: we are made to stop and evaluate our actions and thoughts and to feel guilty when they are not acceptable. And because this guilt often makes us tense and ill-at-ease, we give up and submit. This is what I understand Freud to be saying in *Civilization and Its Discontents,* and this is what I learned to be the melancholy fact when I went hitchhiking up the West Coast with my sleeping bag and thoughts of "doing my own thing."

My hitchhiking trip with a white friend from Long Beach to Canada was plagued by social pressure even before it began. Two weeks before we started, reports over the news about hitchhikers being axed in their sleeping bags, as well as drivers being robbed, beaten, or killed, did not make our trip sound like a good idea to my family. My family was also concerned that reports like these make drivers hesitant of stopping for anyone unless they have a gun under the seat. That was just the beginning, though. I could have handled the fears others had for me, but the guilt I was made to feel was harder to cope with.

My brother-in-law and I had a long discussion about the dangers of hitchhiking. The list was a frightening one that included the possibility I might be hassled and jailed by the police or be robbed and stranded. I felt quite guilty about running off and frolicking around while everyone worried about me, and this guilt took some of the pleasure—the thrill, day-to-day suspense, and excitement—out of the trip and made me wary.

My brother-in-law and I also discussed the fact that very few blacks hitchhike in the live-on-the-road manner I was about to, which means sleeping in forests, communes, or in freeway shrubbery, or going into strange towns and meeting all kinds of people. He suggested that if tension in any given situation forced a serious racial confrontation, my friend would surely turn to the safe side and against me. This kept me wondering all through the trip, and to my dismay, kept me looking for hints of racism in him, which took some of the pleasure out of the trip. It also made me feel guilty for suspecting him. My brother-in-law and I also talked about the fact that, instead of hitchhiking, I should be working to pay for college. Feeling all this guilt, and sensing the concern of my parents, I still set out with my friend.

We carefully heeded (out of fear) California's policy on hitchhiking. Hitchhiking is illegal, but the law is not usually enforced if the hikers stay on the curb. We had no problems at all until just south of San Luis Obispo, where we were searched for weapons. There we were insulted by a pair of California Highway Patrol officers while they went over us. Among the many insults was the one directed at me, asking me who I was going to rape next. But, knowing how public opinion would side with the police if we retaliated, we kept our mouths closed. We knew that if the police reported subduing a couple of wandering, violent hippies, then the stereotype of the hippie (shiftless young bums begging for food and for money to buy drugs with) would justify the police in the public's view and set people's minds at ease. So we checked our natural impulse to fight back, but we were angry with ourselves for having to do so. We felt guilty for not standing up for our rights.

Even with that episode behind us, the rest of the trip didn't bring me the pleasure I'd hoped for. The possible presence of dope in the cars of the young people who picked us up made me uneasy. But not my friend. He indulged heavily in marijuana all the way up the coast whenever he could get some. I knew that if we were arrested for dope it would go on my record, damage my chances in the future, and hurt my family badly. I would be ashamed and guilt-ridden. I was very worried about the presence of dope around me, even back in the deepest woods near Eureka, California. There, at one in the morning, my friend and another hiker who joined up with us smoked as much marijuana as they could hold. I was fearful that a band of night-roaming vigilantes would swarm on us and take us away. In Canada itself, I felt guilty the very first time I got in line for a feed-in. I was overly self-conscious because the food was paid for by Canadian taxpayers and was meant for needy people. We had enough money to buy food.

It now seems that everything we did, beginning with the very thought of hitchhiking, was meant to prove we weren't as trapped as the people we left behind. But when it came to the wild, free expression of inner drives, I couldn't throw off the wet blanket of society. I couldn't even go skinny dipping in the Russian River because there were people around and I was afraid of what they might think if I stripped. We loved Canada and its forests, but we came back. Even though the air and water were like nectar in comparison to that of Los Angeles, we came back to the smog and noise and people. We discarded the forests, rivers, and meadows for the benefits and security of our social surroundings. I surrendered.

—Samuel Reece

4. Short Paragraphs

To call attention to an important shift in the line of thought, or to emphasize a crucial point, you may occasionally want a very short paragraph. Sometimes, a short paragraph will serve both these purposes. In any case, such paragraphs should be used *sparingly*. Notice in the following example that the student might have joined his short paragraph of rhetorical emphasis to either of the other paragraphs. He chose instead to make the two sentences into a separate paragraph and thus to stress the importance of his early training and the shock he was to receive.

TURNING POINT STRESSED

. . . I know from personal experience the truth of Erich Fromm's criticism that the American male is forced to repress his feelings. Our society does tend to suspect emotional outbursts in a man as signs of "abnormality." From childhood onward, I was taught to "control" my emotions. I was told constantly that good little boys don't cry; they act like big strong men. The little boy who fell off his tricycle and got up with a smile was admired and recommended as a model to be emulated by the rest of the tricycle set. Nor were feelings of pain the only emotion I was encouraged to suppress. Anger, hostility, envy, and melancholy were all taboo, and this training was almost impossible to resist.

> By the age of thirteen, I was a true believer in this Spartan code. It was at this age that I was first startled into doubting it.
> My uncle had been ill but had kept this fact secret from. . . .

Short paragraphs are also used for dialogue. *In a narrative, any direct quotation, together with the rest of a sentence of which it is a part, is paragraphed separately.* The reason for this convention is to make immediately clear to the reader the change of speaker.

IDENTIFIED SPEAKERS PARAGRAPHED SEPARATELY

> "But 'glory' doesn't mean 'a nice knock-down argument,' " Alice objected.
> "When *I* use a word," Humpty Dumpty said, in a rather scornful tone, "it means what I choose it to mean—neither more nor less."
> "The question is," said Alice, "whether you *can* make words mean so many different things."
> "The question is," said Humpty Dumpty, "which is to be master— that's all."
>
> —LEWIS CARROLL

This same convention is usually observed in cases where the speaker is not named each time.

UNIDENTIFIED SPEAKERS PARAGRAPHED SEPARATELY

> "Hello," she said. "Are you awake?"
> "Where have you been?"
> "I just went out to get a breath of air."
> "You did, like hell."
> "What do you want me to say, darling?"
>
> —ERNEST HEMINGWAY

However, a short quoted speech that is closely united with the context is sometimes included in a paragraph of narration:

SHORT DIALOGUE INCLUDED

> Now and then Mr. Bixby called my attention to certain things. Said he, "This is Six-Mile Point." I assented. It was pleasant enough information but I could not see the bearing of it. I was not conscious that it was a matter of any interest to me. Another time he said, "This is Nine-Mile

Point." Later he said, "This is Twelve-Mile Point." They were all about level with the water's edge; they all looked alike to me; they were monotonously unpicturesque. . . .

—Mark Twain

Exercise 1

Select one of the following statements. Use it as the topic sentence for a unified paragraph.

1. Students often learn more from each other than they do from their classes.
2. Beginnings are more exciting than endings.
3. Most of us have more prejudices than we realize.
4. A slogan such as "Progress is our most important product" is misleading because progress is an attitude toward achievement, not the achievement itself.
5. Those who can, do; those who cannot, administer.

Exercise 2

Choose one of the following exercises and write a unified paragraph based on it.

1. Try to capture the mood and feeling of a specific place that meant a great deal to you in your childhood—a room, a park, a field, whatever.
2. Try to catch the mood and feeling of a specific and repeated experience that meant a great deal to you in your childhood—a holiday, an occasion with the family, a private ritual of your own, whatever.
3. Try to catch the mood and feeling of a specific place or experience that you frequently seek out at present.

Exercise 3

In the following selections find and mark the topic sentence. Be prepared to explain why your choice is the most complete summary or statement of the paragraph's idea.

Imagine a society, no matter how ideal in other respects, where word and gesture could never be counted upon. Questions asked, answers given, information exchanged—all would be worthless. Were all statements randomly truthful or deceptive, action and choice would be undermined from the outset. There must be a minimal degree of trust in communication for language and action to be more than stabs in the dark. This is why some level of truthfulness has always been seen as essential to human society, no matter how deficient the observance of other moral principles. Even the devils themselves, as Samuel Johnson said, do not lie to one another, since the society of Hell could not subsist without trust any more than others.

—SISSELA BOK

Disease from contaminated food or beverages was very common a few generations ago, and nutritional deficiencies were almost the rule. Now laboratories check on the safety of what we eat and drink. Furthermore, the nutritional requirements of man are now well known, and in the Western World, at least, we have the means to satisfy them. But all this theoretical and practical knowledge does not guarantee that nutrition will not present problems in the immediate future, even assuming that economic prosperity continues. On the one hand, modern agriculture and food technology have come to depend more and more on the use of chemicals to control pests and to improve the yields of animal and plant products. The cost of food production would enormously increase without these chemicals, and for this reason their use is justified. Unfortunately, however, and despite all care, several of them eventually reach the human consumer in objectionable concentrations. As more and more substances are introduced in agriculture and food technology every year, it will become practically impossible to test them all with regard to long-range effects on human health, and the possibility of toxic reactions must be accepted as one of the inevitable risks of progress.

—RENÉ DUBOS

Even if now attenuated and largely metaphorical, the diction of war resides everywhere just below the surface of modern experience. American football has its two-platoon system, and medical research aspires to breakthroughs. One says, "We are bombarded with forms" or "We've had a barrage of complaints today" without, of course, any sharp awareness that one is recalling war and yet with a sense that such figures are somehow most appropriate to the modern situation. The word *crummy*, felt to apply to numerous phenomena of the modern industrial environment ("This is a crummy town"), is a Great War [1914–18] word, originally meaning itchy because lousy. And there is *lousy* itself, without which, it sometimes seems, modern life could hardly be conducted. Before the war *keepsake* was the English word for a small thing kept for remembrance; after the British had lived in France for so long, the word became *souvenir*, which has now virtually ousted *keepsake*. Popular discussion of economics relies heavily on terms like *sector* ("The public vs. the private sector"), and the conduct of labor politics would be a very different thing without the military jargon (like *rank and file*) which it appropriated from the war.

—Paul Fussell

In many ways, we break down children's convictions that things make sense, or their hope that things may prove to make sense. We do it, first of all, by breaking up life into arbitrary and disconnected hunks of subject matter, which we then try to "integrate" by such artificial and irrelevant devices as having children sing Swiss folk songs while they are studying the geography of Switzerland, or do arithmetic problems about rail-splitting while they are studying the boyhood of Lincoln. Furthermore, we continually confront them with what is senseless, ambiguous, and contradictory; worse, we do it without knowing that we are doing it, so that, hearing nonsense shoved at them as if it were sense, they come to feel that the source of their confusion lies not in the material but in their own stupidity. Still further, we cut children off from their own common sense and the world of reality by requiring them to play with and shove around words and symbols that have little or no meaning to them. Thus we turn the vast majority of our students into the kind of people for whom all symbols are meaningless; who cannot use symbols as a way of learning about and dealing with reality; who cannot understand written instructions; who, even if they read books, come out knowing no more than when they went in; who may have a few new words rattling around in their heads, but whose mental models of the world remain unchanged and, indeed, impervious to change. The minority, the able and successful students, we are very likely to turn into something different but just as dangerous: the kind of people who can manipulate words and symbols fluently while keeping themselves largely divorced from the reality for which they stand; the kind of people who like to speak in large generalities but grow silent or indignant if someone asks for an example of what they are talking about; the kind of people who, in their discussions of world affairs, coin and use such words as megadeaths and megacorpses, with scarcely a thought to the blood and suffering these words imply.

—John Holt

Exercise 4

The following selection was originally written as six paragraphs. Try outlining it, first. Then indicate where, in your opinion, the five divisions should be made and be able to give reasons for your choice. In dividing the selection, try to find topic sentences for your paragraphs.

To begin to understand economic development we must have a picture of the problem with which it contends. We must conjure up in our mind's eye what underdevelopment means for the two billion human beings for whom it is not a statistic but a living experience of daily life. Unless we can see the Great Ascent from the vantage point of those who must make the climb, we cannot hope to understand the difficulties of the march. It is not easy to make this mental jump. But let us attempt it by imagining how a typical American family, living in a small suburban house on an income of six or seven thousand dollars [in 1963], could be transformed into an equally typical family of the underdeveloped world. We begin by invading the house of our imaginary American family to strip it of its furniture. Everything goes: beds, chairs, tables, television set, lamps. We will leave the family with a few old blankets, a kitchen table, a wooden chair. Along with the bureaus go the clothes. Each member of the family may keep in his "wardrobe" his oldest suit or dress, a shirt or blouse. We will permit a pair of shoes to the head of the family, but none for the wife or children. We move into the kitchen. The appliances have already been taken out, so we turn to the cupboards and larder. The box of matches may stay, a small bag of flour, some sugar and salt. A few moldy potatoes, already in the garbage can, must hastily be rescued, for they will provide much of tonight's meal. We will leave a handful of onions, and a dish of dried beans. All the rest we take away: the meat, the fresh vegetables, the canned goods, the crackers, the candy. Now we have stripped the house: the bathroom has been dismantled, the running water shut off, the electric wires taken out. Next we take away the house. The family can move to the tool-shed. It is crowded, but much better than the situation in Hong Kong, where (a United Nations report tells us) "it is not uncommon for a family of four or more to live in a bedspace, that is, on a bunk bed and the space it occupies—sometimes in two or three tiers—their only privacy provided by curtains." But we have only begun. All the other houses in the neighborhood have also been removed; our suburb has become a shantytown. Still, our family is fortunate to have a shelter; 250,000 people in Calcutta have none at all and simply live in the streets. Our family is now about on a par with the city of Cali in Colombia, where, an official of the World Bank writes, "on one hillside alone, the slum population is estimated at 40,000—without water, sanitation, or electric light. And not all the poor of Cali are as fortunate as that. Others have built their shacks near the city on land which lies beneath the flood mark. To these people the immediate environment is the open sewer of the city, a sewer which flows through their huts when the river rises."

—Robert L. Heilbroner

4b

Effective Paragraphs

How can paragraphs be made effective? Although we cannot enumerate all the possibilities, we do have a couple of standards for testing paragraph effectiveness—*development* and *coherence*. We also have some useful techniques and models to help us write more effective paragraphs and to help us rewrite weak ones. A word of explanation about these techniques and models is needed.

We often use these methods quite unconsciously because we understand the material we're working with. To put it another way, what happens in the paragraph—the shape and form it assumes—is often determined by the subject itself. If we are analyzing the kinds of tapes and records students buy, we quite naturally classify; if we are discussing the choice between two jobs or professions, we will probably compare and contrast them. In short, in the words of the American architect Louis Sullivan, "Form follows function." These methods can help us revise and reorganize ineffective paragraphs, or suggest ways of handling materials when we are not sure how to proceed. Readers expect (usually unconsciously) to see the methods observed, and may be confused if the pattern is violated without apparent reason—for example, if the paragraph jumps confusingly back and forth in time or from one location to another. These methods are often most valuable when we are revising a rough draft, a defective section, or an unsatisfactory paper. For most of us, who are not born writers, it is during revision that we have our best chance to improve a paper.

1. Paragraph Development

Although its central idea may be clear, an undeveloped paragraph may be brief, general, thin, or dull. Developing a paragraph requires that the writer take time to see clearly and say accurately what his or her generalities signify. It means filling out the bare statement with specific detail. It certainly does not mean padding out a simple statement or repeating the same idea in different words. Unless the writer shows how his generalities apply in detail to particular cases, how his conclusions differ from someone else's, or what specifically has led him to his view, the reader remains uninformed and unpersuaded. Undeveloped paragraphs are among the most common and most irritating weaknesses in student writing. In this student essay, concerned with small groups of freshmen meeting their advisors and having dinner together, notice the thinness of the paragraphs:

> Mr. Miller was not what I had expected of a faculty member. He was not over fifty years old. He was not wearing thick glasses. He was, in contrast, about twenty-six, rather athletic looking, and a very interesting conversationalist, not only in his own field, but in every subject we discussed.
>
> My classmates, most of whom I had not met before, were also a surprise. There were no socially backward introverts, interested only in the physical sciences, as I had feared. I found instead some very interesting people with whom I immediately wanted to become friends. Some were interested in sports, some in hobbies, some in card games, and all in sex. Each individual had something to offer me.
>
> The Millers did a marvelous job of preparing the dinner. We did a marvelous job of eating it. However, the real purpose of the dinner was to become acquainted with at least two of our faculty members and about ten of our fellow students. In this endeavor we were also quite successful, for the discussions begun during the meal lasted for a long time after and, as a matter of fact, some of them were continued the next day.
>
> This year's advisor dinner was very rewarding and I believe it should remain a tradition. The students really get to know each other, and a few of the faculty are pleasantly surprised.

A reader might well wonder why the dinner should be continued as a tradition. Nothing the writer says carries real conviction because nothing is developed concretely. These paragraphs raise more questions than they answer: (1) Why should the writer have expected the faculty to resemble his caricature of them as ancient, nearsighted bores? (2) What was Mr. Miller's "field" and what did he talk about as a "very interesting conversationalist"? (3) What "sports," "hobbies," and "card games" was the writer so pleased to discover he shared in common with his classmates? (4) If the meal was so memorable, what was it and how many servings did he have? If it wasn't important, why give two vague sentences to it? (5) What was talked about so enthusiastically and "for a long time after" the meal?

The writer has substituted jargon (the pretentious phrasing "very interesting conversationalist," "socially backward introverts"), vague generalities ("some were interested in sports, some in hobbies, some in card games"), and unexplained events (the dinner discussion) for specific detail. The paragraphs are not developed; they merely repeat the same idea unconvincingly—that the advisor's dinner was a good chance to discover that faculty and students were in some vague way "interesting" and "rewarding," not what the writer "had expected."

Concrete diction cuts out fuzziness and gives a paper sharpness and depth. Consider these sentences: "The Millers did a marvelous job of preparing the meal. We did a marvelous job of eating it." Do they mean that the Millers barbecued two dozen hamburgers and tossed a spicy bean salad for a delicious buffet meal on paper plates? Or do they mean that the Millers gave a sit-down dinner, complete with white linen, silver setting, and candlelight, and served roast turkey, hot rolls, and two vegetables? Either of these alternatives is better than the empty generality of the original. A buffet dinner for thirteen people implies a relaxed host and hostess, students going back for several helpings, and comfortable informality. A sit-down dinner for thirteen people implies a busy host and hostess, reserved freshmen, hushed requests for the gravy, and long, earnest discussion as the coffee lingers in cups and the candles melt. Whatever the case was, specific wording would help the reader *see* the event and prepare him for the writer's conclusion about it.

To get specific detail by specific wording, writers think in concrete images to recall and *re*-create the taste, touch, sound, and sight as clearly as possible. In doing so, writers are trying to give the reader as much relevant information as they can. For example, in the following two versions of the same paragraph the student has improved the second by more complete information. Her revision is not much longer than the original but it tells far more. It is the choice of words, not the number of words, which creates an image. The boldface passages indicate the places where she has made her major changes.

Vague Original

Though the air was **uncomfortable**, the sand was **soothing** and warm, and I dug a **hole** into it and piled it up **until it half-covered** me from the air. I sat there, shivering in the **air**, until the sand **began falling away** from me. I tried to **bury my legs** again, but the sand **was dry and it would not stay in place.** I **tried to find** damp sand near me, but in a short time it also dried out and **wouldn't stay in place.** So I rested **for a while** and watched the sea rise and fall and the various objects it threw onto the beach. **Seaweed** and **other things** were washed up, then carried back in a regular rhythm.

Revision for Detail

Though the air was **cold**, the sand **felt soft** and warm, and I dug a **damp trough** in it and piled it up around my **legs until I had a body only from the waist up.** I sat there, shivering in the **cool mist**, until the sand began **to crumble** down around me. I tried to **gather it back up** on my legs, but it **had dried** and **kept slithering down again in little shifting rivers. I dug with my hands beside me** until I came to damp sand which I piled on my legs, but in a short time it too **dried and slipped away.** So I rested **my head on my knees** and watched the sea rise and fall **and rise and fall, bringing with it,** to the beach, something new each time: a **loop of rust-colored** seaweed, **a shell, a rock, a small jellyfish. And falling away**, it would **often take with it** what it had **just brought.**

Notice that the writer has done more than make the diction specific. She has developed her paragraph by adding extra detail and slowed down the tempo of the narrative. She has tried to make the reader see and feel what happened.

Developing a paragraph requires that a writer give content to generalities by using *relevant* details and illustrations. These details may be found in particular actions, sensory impressions, objects, processes. But they must be *selected*, not merely inventoried. Details become boring—mere padding—when the writer confuses quantity with quality. If, for example, an American student has been asked by his Polish correspondent what a "drugstore" is, the American should not try to explain it by listing every type of cold tablet, sleeping pill, foot powder, lipstick, face cream, hair remover, shaving lotion, cigarette, stale candy, and garish paperback it sells. But neither should he content himself by saying that a drugstore fills prescriptions and sells medical supplies and cosmetics. The correspondent can get this broad definition from a dictionary. The American might begin with such a definition and then suggest, through selected details, that "medical supplies" *range* from cough syrups through pink bandages and that cosmetics *range* from green fingernail polish through perfumed hair rinses. Without trying to be exhaustive, he would try to suggest the odd variety and specialization of items covered by the general terms "medical supplies" and "cosmetics."

DEVELOPMENT BY DETAIL

If your instructor comments that your paragraphs are inadequately developed, you can do several things. First, *examine* the paragraph or paragraphs carefully for all vague generalities, needlessly abstract words, and clichés, and *underline* them. For instance:

> When they are young, children are free and can be themselves. They are protected from nature's hardships by our modern-day society and by our complex technology. They only have to keep out of trouble. Mostly, they are free to do whatever they want. But as they get older, they have more and more duties and responsibilities put upon them. They begin to lose their freedom and become conformists.

Such phrases as "When they are young" may be changed to "Before they start elementary school"; "free and can be themselves" to "playful, spontaneous, and imaginative"; "protected from nature's hardships" to "protected from hunger, disease, and the weather." Underlining may also reveal that certain generalities, if they mean anything at all, are untrue or need extensive qualification: Do children who bike to school, who roam where they wish afterward, and who spend time in the evenings with their friends really "lose their freedom and become conformists"? Or, to take a very different view, is it true that our "modern-day society" or our "complex technology" "protect" a ghetto child from rats, crime, poverty, sickness, and dilapidated firetraps?

Many undeveloped paragraphs result from a writer's failure to distinguish between fact and opinion. Did the writer of the paragraph about children ever bother to ask what factual basis he had for his opinions? He assumes as self-evident that young children lose their identity and freedom as they grow up. But is it true to say that a child of three or four has a wider range of choices or a more clearly defined individuality than a child of nine or eleven? Clearly, in handling topics of any complexity, writers need to examine their underlying assumptions and to question the external evidence and authority for their views. If they take the time to do this, they are more likely to spot the flaws in their own generalizations and to discover how much *more* there is to be said.

Another useful device is making a list of the concrete images, details, and examples you want to include. One way is outline form:

1. Drama in Robert Frost's Imagery
   A. Natural settings
      —For example, a boy climbing to top of birch tree
   B. Domestic settings
      —For example, wife crouching on stairs in "Home Burial"

If you find this method too mechanical, at least jot down the specific items that can *illustrate* and *deepen* your generalizations. In the footnotes to the following example, notice how the writer has visualized the concrete details to give the generalizations some real content:

> Working as a door-to-door magazine salesman in and around St. Louis last summer gave me more than just extra spending money. It gave me a chance to meet types of people[1] I might otherwise never have known, and some practical experience[2] I am glad I had.
>
> *The last two generalizations could stand expansion.*
>
> [1] Young wives of construction workers living in trailers, retired jazz musicians and newsstand operators living in boarding houses, electronic engineers in suburbs.
> [2] How to keep temper when insulted, how to walk through a neighborhood not showing fear, how to size up a person's tastes by the way he keeps lawn or TV show he's watching.

An excellent way to get depth is to practice building up examples that contribute to the dominant idea or impression, the topic sentence. Cutting is usually easy, and you can always thin out in revising. In the following student paragraph, notice how skillfully the writer has picked his details to show why he remembers an attic that would only seem dirty and uncomfortable to an adult, and notice how he builds up these details.

Building up Details to Support a Thesis

The attic was the third floor of an old Victorian house, one of those countless look-alike monstrosities of towers and porches and trim. **To the adult eye, the attic was dirty and uncomfortable, but to the boy it was a sanctuary.** The attic always had that sneezy smell of twenty-year-old newspapers just shuffled; and its roof arched clear down to the floor at the four corners so that the boy had to play near the middle of the room. And the floor had a thick layer of—not exactly dust, not exactly dirt—dry, yet slick gray pollen that filters out of old wooden rafters. On the floor the boy had his Lionel trains and build-it-yourself brick houses and farms—but they were merely strategic positions and crucial points of supply which he, as General, and his army defended against the Enemy. The whole floor was occupied with troops marching at the slope or resting in position. Here, all bundled up in a jacket, he used to spend his dark winter evenings directing his men. He sometimes even played up here in the summer, when it was so hot his face would turn prickly red and he had to worry about the hard, black wasps knocking at the window sills. Here he would set up Gettysburg with some paper-paste mountains he had molded or trap the Enemy on an isthmus, using the rough-finished chimney as a barrier.

Notice that this method of development by specific detail moves from the general to the particular—that is, deductively. (We shall look at some other methods shortly.) Many effective paragraphs have this pattern of organization:

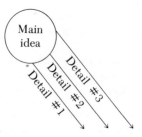

In the following paragraph, Swift attacks two hundred years of European exploration and colonizing with an extended bitter example supporting the irony of his opening and closing statements.

Illustration Supporting Ironic Comment

But I had another reason which made me less forward to enlarge his Majesty's dominions by my discoveries. **To say the truth, I had conceived a few scruples with relation to the distributive justice of princes upon those occasions.** For instance, a crew of pirates are driven by a storm they know not whither, at length a boy discovers land from the topmast, they go on shore to rob and plunder, they see an harmless people, are entertained with kindness, they give the country a new name, they take formal possession of it for their King, they set up a rotten plank or stone for a memorial, they murder two or three dozen of the natives, bring away a couple of more by force for a sample, return home, and get their pardon. Here commences a new dominion acquired with a title by **divine right**. Ships are sent out with the first opportunity, the natives driven out or destroyed, their princes tortured to discover their gold, a free license given to all acts of inhumanity and lust, the earth reeking with the blood of its inhabitants: and this execrable crew of butchers employed in so pious an expedition is a **modern colony** sent to convert and civilize an idolatrous and barbarous people.

—JONATHAN SWIFT

OTHER METHODS OF PARAGRAPH DEVELOPMENT

There are many ways of developing paragraphs, and each has its advantages. One of them, development by *specific detail*, has already been considered. In actual practice, writers are apt to employ a combination of methods; a few of the most useful are worth illustration and analysis.

The first of these methods is development by *definition*. Here, a writer limits the range of a term's application. In this kind of development, the writer uses a number of sentences to tell the reader what the key term or terms signify. A few words about definitions are in order here.

In formal logic, a term is defined by referring it to a general class (or genus)—that is, by classifying it—and then distinguishing it from others in the general class it belongs to. To take a simple example, one might begin by *classifying* a pen as a "writing instrument." However since the class "writing instrument" also includes pencils, one would have to differentiate a pen by continuing

". . . writing instrument that makes use of a hard point and a colored fluid."

term		class	differentiation
Pen	is	a writing instrument	making use of a hard point and colored fluid.
Pencil	is	a writing instrument	with a core of solid-state material like graphite inside a wooden or plastic case.

A description of the object can include all kinds of details—the pencil has a chewed end, used to cost five cents, peels in bits of yellow paint—but these details are irrelevant to the definition of the term. Similarly, examples do not constitute a definition, although they can certainly help to clarify a definition. To say that a Dixon Ticonderoga No. 2 Soft is an example of a pencil is not the same as specifying what the meaning of the term "pencil" is.

Much of the time a writer can successfully define technical terms or concrete words by using an appositive construction.

Definition by Apposition

The X-ray showed a crack in the **tibia, or shinbone.**

Please analyze the importance of the **denouement—the final unraveling or outcome of the plot**—in *Lord Jim.*

Tonight the moon will be in **apogee, that is, at the point in its orbit farthest from the earth.**

Sometimes, however, especially when dealing with complex or highly abstract terms, a writer will need a fuller definition. He may spend several paragraphs, not just one, in defining the term if the term is crucial to a long essay or research paper. To do so, he should observe certain principles.

First, avoid circular definitions. "Democracy is the democratic process" and "An astronomer is one who studies astronomy" are circular definitions. When words are defined in terms of themselves, no one's understanding is improved.

Second, avoid long lists of synonyms if the term to be defined is an abstract one. When a paper begins, "By education, I mean to give knowledge, develop character, improve taste, draw out, train, lead," the reader knows he is in for the shotgun treatment. The writer has indiscriminately blasted a load of abstract terms at the reader, hoping one will hit.

Third, avoid loaded definitions. Loaded definitions do not restrict key terms but make an immediate appeal for emotional approval. A definition beginning "By abortion I mean ruthless, outright murder of the helpless" is loaded with pejorative connotation. Conversely, "By abortion I mean the absolute and unquestionable right of a woman to control over her own body" is heavy with favorable emotional connotation. Such judgments—for that is what they are—can be vigorous conclusions to a discussion, but they invite argument, not clarification, when offered as definitions.

The following student paragraph illustrates the process of definition. The writer first classifies Sarah Woodruff and Clarissa Dalloway as belonging to the class of people having "certain heroic qualities." She then clarifies and limits the term "heroic" by rejecting one set of meanings (control and domination) and choosing another (sensitivity, endurance, independence). To further limit the concept, the writer then discusses how each character is "heroic."

Definition by Distinction

The central characters in John Fowles's *The French Lieutenant's Woman* and Virginia Woolf's *Mrs. Dalloway* are women who embody certain heroic qualities that set them apart from what one character calls "the great niminypiminy flock of women in general." These two women, Sarah Woodruff and Clarissa Dalloway, are not heroic in the traditional masculine, aggressive sense of the word. They do not seek to control or to dominate but to cultivate a sensitivity, to endure, and to remain free of masculine narrow-mindedness. They possess a power that allows them to remain open to the compelling vitality of life. Their heroism is their ability to be responsive to reality, to feel even if it entails suffering and uncertainty; and this heroism spurs others on to live in the presence of life, with all its beauty and terror. Sarah is a free woman, and through her sensitivity, forbearance, and courage, she liberates Charles, a man caught in the petrifying forces of Victorian society, preoccupied with duty and piety. Clarissa Dalloway's radiant, vital presence at her party, a ritual of community, helps to liberate her guests from their shells of individual solitude and memory. It is in this sense and these ways that they are heroic.

The following example by a well-known writer will illustrate how extended definitions are formulated, developed, and put to use. Notice that E. M. Forster begins by comparing story and plot; and then, having defined plot as "a narrative of events, the emphasis falling on causality," he illustrates the term "plot" and restricts its application even further.

> Let us define a plot. We have defined a story as a narrative of events arranged in their time-sequence. **A plot is also a narrative of events, the emphasis falling on causality.** "The king died and then the queen died" is a story. "The king died, and then the queen died of grief" is a plot. The time-sequence is preserved, but the sense of causality overshadows it. Or again: "The queen died, no one knew why, until it was discovered that it was through grief at the death of the king." This is a plot with a mystery in it, a form capable of high development. It suspends the time-sequence, it moves as far away from the story as its limitations will allow. Consider the death of the queen. If it is in a story we say "and then?" If it is in a plot we ask "why?" That is the fundamental difference between these two aspects of the novel. A plot cannot be told to a gaping audience of cave-men or to a tyrannical sultan or to their modern descendant the movie-public. They can only be kept awake by "and then—and then—." They can only supply curiosity. But a plot demands intelligence and memory also.
>
> —E. M. Forster

A second method of development is by *subdivision* and *classification*. Here the writer enumerates and distinguishes the main aspects of a topic, either as an introduction to a further discussion or for identification. The material can vary in subject matter—the major kinds of job opportunities in a community, the legal requirements a candidate must fulfill, the types of people one meets while working. The writer's concern should be to keep the features or classifications distinct.

There are "X" types of. . . .

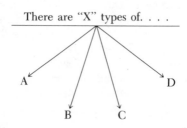

Subdivision and Classification

The distinctions I am making among **three** different kinds of culture—**postfigurative**, in which children learn primarily from their forebears, **cofigurative**, in which both children and adults learn from their peers, and **prefigurative**, in which adults learn also from their children—are a reflection of the period in which we live. Primitive societies and small religious and ideological enclaves are primarily **postfigurative**, deriving authority from the past. Great civilizations, which necessarily have developed techniques for incorporating change, characteristically make use of some form of **cofigurative** learning from peers, playmates, fellow students, and fellow apprentices. We are now entering a period, new in history, in which the young are taking on new authority in their **prefigurative** apprehension of the still unknown future.

—Margaret Mead

A third method is development by *comparison* or *contrast*. Here, a writer stresses likenesses or differences. To be effective, the paragraph should state the main point of the comparison early and should be organized so that the reader does not have to jump back and forth from one subject to another. Joseph Wood Krutch makes the point of the contrast very clear at the beginning of the following example:

Contrast

Sociologists talk a great deal these days about "adjustment," which has always seemed to me a defeatist sort of word suggesting dismal surrender to the just tolerable. The road runner is not "adjusted" to his environment. He is triumphant in it. The desert is his home and he likes it. Other creatures, including many other birds, elude and compromise. They cling to the mountains or to the cottonwood-filled washes, especially in the hot weather, or they go away somewhere else, like the not entirely reconciled human inhabitants of this region. The road runner, on the other hand, stays here all the time and he prefers the areas where he is hottest and driest. . . .

—Joseph Wood Krutch

One special type of comparison is *analogy*, discussed at length in Chapter 11. As a method of illustration, analogy can simplify and clarify complex relationships. In the following student paragraph, for example, the writer was faced with the problem of showing how the characters in William Faulkner's short story "Spotted Horses" could continue to admire and tolerate a man who continually fleeced them. To solve this problem, the student used the apt analogy of a game of pool with Willie Hoppe, for many years the world champion.

Analogy for Characterization

"That Flem Snopes," says the narrator. "I be dog if he ain't a case now." The townspeople had respect for a good horse trader and Flem Snopes was that. Since money was of grotesque importance to these people who had to dig for every penny, they admired a man who could come by it easily and cleverly. Ironically, when Flem skinned someone of his last nickel and kept the fact to himself, the people would interpret Flem's silence as sheer modesty, while the victim laughed off as hopeless any thought of retribution. **Their admiration and toleration of Flem is not hard to understand. It was like a game of pool** in which you lose so decisively to Willie Hoppe that you feel no bitterness— merely a sense of pride and awe at having played the master at all. After Willie has beaten you and quietly taken off the stakes, you admit sheepishly to others you were licked before you started and put the cue back on the rack instead of taking it into some dark alley to wait for Willie. Most people didn't even try to beat the time-honored master, Flem Snopes, at his game of swindling.

Professional writers often try to make difficult technical or abstract ideas concrete through analogy, and they take care, while developing their paragraphs, to be sure the reader understands that the analogies are illustrations, not proof. In developing the following paragraph, for instance, Lincoln Barnett calls his analogy "this little fable."

Analogy for Description

The distinction between Newton's and Einstein's ideas about gravitation has sometimes been illustrated by picturing a little boy playing marbles in a city lot. The ground is very uneven. An observer in an office ten stories above the street would not be able to see these irregularities in the ground. Noticing that the marbles appear to avoid some sections of the ground and move toward other sections, he might assume that a [semi-magnetic] "force" was operating which repelled the marbles from certain spots and attracted them toward others. But another observer on the ground would instantly perceive that the path of the marbles was simply governed by the curvature of the field. In this little fable Newton is the upstairs observer who imagines that a "force" is at work, and Einstein is the observer on the ground, who has no reason to make such an assumption. Einstein's gravitational laws, therefore, merely describe the field properties of the space-time continuum. . . .

—LINCOLN BARNETT

A fourth method is development by *cause* and *effect*. Here, the writer stresses the connections between a result or results and the preceding events. The writer may begin with the causes or with the effects, but in either case he raises the question of connections and makes it the basis for his paragraph development.

$$
\begin{array}{ccc}
A & & C \\
\downarrow & & \uparrow \\
B & \text{or} & B \\
\downarrow & & \uparrow \\
C & & A
\end{array}
$$

Causes and Effects Linked

Here is one of the most familiar forms of the vicious circle of poverty. The poor get sick more than anyone else in the society. That is because they live in slums, jammed together under unhygienic conditions; they have inadequate diets, and cannot get decent medical care. When they become sick, they are sick longer than other groups in society. Because they are sick more often and longer than anyone else, they lose wages and work, and find it difficult to hold a steady job. And because of this, they cannot pay for good housing, for a nutritious diet, for doctors. At any given point in the circle, particularly when there is a major illness, their prospect is to move to an even lower level and to begin the cycle, round and round, toward even more suffering.

—MICHAEL HARRINGTON

Often, cause-and-effect paragraphs are the basis for a whole paper. The first paragraph may raise the question of causes, the second paragraph eliminate some alternatives, the third focus on the remaining possibilities. Or the first paragraph may state the effect, the second raise the question, and the remaining ones analyze the cause or causes. Since the pattern of cause and effect is so important, the following student essay is given in its entirety to show this method of development. The essay concerns the function of Old Hilse, a character in Gerhart Hauptmann's play *The Weavers*, a dramatization of a revolt by impoverished Silesian weavers in central Europe during the 1840s. The writer's central question is "Why is Old Hilse even in the play?" Her answer is a persuasive demonstration of *how* Old Hilse changes our understanding of the play—the effect he has upon us.

Causes and Effects in Sequence

Why Old Hilse?

If one were to examine the contribution of Old Hilse to the plot of *The Weavers*, one would be hard put to find any excuse for his being in the play. He neither alters the course of the main action nor initiates any new actions. His speeches to the main characters are unheeded. He does not join the rebel weavers nor does he come to the defense of the manufacturers. He remains neutral in the battle, in no way affecting its outcome. His only connection with the action of the play is to be an unintentional and all-but-unnoticed casualty.

What Old Hilse does not *cause or influence*

Then why are his unheeded lines ever spoken? Why is this character brought into the play at all?

Focusing question

The play begins with a dispute between the younger weavers and the manufacturer's buyer, builds up the weavers' discontent with their poverty and fatigue, and reaches a climax with their open rebellion. It roars toward what we hope will be its triumphant conclusion. But it runs head on into Old Hilse. Here is a man whom we fully expect to jump on the bandwagon, or at least act as a dramatic counterpoint by siding with the manufacturers. But Old Hilse just states his contempt for this particular uprising, reiterates his belief in duty, and goes back to his daily weaving. For a moment the rapidly moving

Old Hilse's action—his refusal to join the rebellion—and its

picture of a community in revolt is frozen. The logic that has been leading up to the great truth of why all the weavers must kill all the owners is stopped just short of a final conclusion. The almost cornily beautiful victory of good over evil, already foreshadowed in the impoverished mass's sacking of a manufacturer's estate, falters. Old Hilse, the most respected weaver, the one most representative of simple devotion to weaving, will not join the rebellion.

immediate effect on our involvement in the plot

In a moment the machine starts to rumble again. The drunken and possessed leaders of the rebellion rush out of Hilse's house to battle the government troops. The plot starts up again. **But the reader left behind begins to question the rebels.** Why won't Old Hilse join? Why does his refusal, although not altering the plan of the rebellion one bit, alter the meaning of it so greatly? Hilse is certainly not afraid. He is a wounded veteran of a much greater war. As he starts to talk about that war, the rebellion raging outside begins to shrink. It is nothing to him. What's more, it is nothing to anyone except those who are inside of it. **Suddenly the story of the young weavers battling for their rights and the older ones gradually joining them becomes a pathetic example of the pattern we see in the papers almost daily, the local rebellion. This is Hilse's contribution.** He is the only character who stands far enough outside the battle to see it as the futile effort it is, not as the glorious rebellion that the other weavers think it is. He has seen it all before. He can even predict jail terms for the leaders. **Hilse takes *us* far enough from the story to see it clearly.** Hilse, who is nothing to the plot's outcome, is everything to its meaning: he makes the plot change from a story in which we are as personally wrapped up as the characters

Further effects on the reader—the meaning(s) of Old Hilse's choice

Initial statement of what Old Hilse does cause—our seeing the plot in a new perspective

Full summary and strong restatement of Old Hilse's function—final

> into a dismal pattern of the universality of re-   *answer to "Why*
> volt born by suffering and hunger, which is   *Old Hilse?"*
> doomed to be led astray by its own excesses,
> and thus defeated.

Some cause-and-effect paragraphs, such as the preceding ones, are primarily persuasive. Their purpose is to make the reader feel the forcefulness of the writer's conclusions, or at least see the *grounds* for those conclusions. Other cause-and-effect paragraphs, like Harrington's on "the vicious circle of poverty," are primarily explanatory. Their purpose is to make a reader see a series of causal links and the necessary results. Chapter 11 discusses the principles underlying cause-and-effect reasoning in some detail.

Depending on the nature of the material, a writer may use any *combination* of the methods just discussed to develop a paragraph adequately. The following paragraph has been pulled apart to show how its topic is developed by means of definition, contrast, and example.

Topic   I never have much confidence in people who talk a great deal about "their image" or "so-and-so's image": they make me wonder if they even care about what the real thing is.

Definition   By image, I don't mean an accurate copy or truthful likeness. I mean, rather, the same thing that PR types, bureaucrats, and political managers too often mean: a counterfeit, a phony projection, a manipulated picture intended to give the illusion of actuality.

Contrast   In daily situations where actual performances can be judged and experienced firsthand, rather ordinary ones like house painting or plumbing, no one spends much time worrying about the image of the performer. These performances are very different from the rigged ones on TV: either the walls are smoothly rolled and the faucets are fixed, or they aren't; the painter or plumber is competent or not so competent. But in some parts of our society, we are not even supposed to think about the reality as long as the image is "good."

Example   Recently, while watching a talk show, I was struck by one guest, a candidate for office, who kept harping on our need for "the image of strong leadership." The more he dwelled on his opponent's failure to project such an image, the more I wondered what policies the speaker stood for, what he would do if elected. And when he defended his expensive media blitz as part of "getting my image across" to the voters . . . .

In summary, a well-developed paragraph gives readers as much information as they need for a full understanding of the point. To help yourself write well-developed paragraphs, try to

1. Use concrete diction, which helps your readers see and feel the object or event, and select your details so that there is no doubt as to what they illustrate.

2. Revise underdeveloped paragraphs, identifying trite or vague generalities, distinguishing the opinions that need fuller explanation and evidence, and making a list of the details and examples to be included.

3. Determine whether a particular method of paragraph development, such as by definition or by contrast, best suits your immediate ends or whether a combination of methods will be necessary.

A good paragraph is a "bounding line" which encloses its own distinct material. The phrase belongs to the artist and poet William Blake: "The great and golden rule of art, as well as of life, is this: That the more distinct, sharp, and wiry the bounding line, the more perfect the work of art. . . . How do we distinguish the oak from the beech . . . one face or countenance from another, but by the bounding line and its infinite inflexions and movements? . . . Leave out this line, and you leave out life itself: all is chaos again."

Exercise 5

(Exercises 5 and 6 are for practice in working with concrete detail and diction.)

Pick one of the following topics and write two paragraphs about it. Make the diction of your first paragraph as vague, general, and trite as you can. Then, still describing the same event, make the diction of your second paragraph as concrete and clear as you can.

A man shaving sleepily with a dull razor
A student trying to stay awake in the front row
A teacher who cannot sit still or stay in one place
A man or woman shopping for clothes

Exercise 6

List six or eight details that you could use in describing one of the following subjects. Then organize the details into a well-developed paragraph.

Subway or bus passengers after midnight
The amusement section of a fair or carnival
A public swimming pool on a hot day
A college dining room at noon
A large crowd at a disco
People watching monkeys at the zoo

Exercise 7

(Exercises 7 through 12 are for practice in working with different methods of paragraph development. Your instructor may ask you to develop one or more of your choices into paragraphs.)

Pick one of the following and list several details you could use in developing a paragraph by specific detail.

A lazy roommate
A dull movie
An annoying lecturer
A successful party
An ideal campsite
A persistent salesperson
A spoiled child

Exercise 8

In a short paragraph for each, define any two of the following terms. Be sure to distinguish each term from other terms which are sometimes used as loose synonyms for it. For example, if you were to pick the term "chuckle," you would need to differentiate it from terms like "giggle" and "laugh."

a. Pond
b. Coupe
c. Violin
d. Pantomime
e. Rage
f. Bowl
g. Macadam
h. Biscuit

Exercise 9

Choose one of the following terms and define it in a paragraph or two.

a. Ecology   d. Propaganda
b. Jock   e. Women's Liberation
c. Lobbyist   f. Fundamentalism

Exercise 10

Pick one of the following and list the main categories you would use in developing a paragraph by subdivision. Then write the paragraph.

The traits of a goof-off
The traits of a good talker
The best ways to study ineffectively
The kinds of movies students prefer

Exercise 11

Pick one of the following. List the main points you would use in developing the paragraph by comparison and contrast (or analogy). Then write the paragraph.

Dating in high school and dating in college
Arguing and discussing
Living at college and living at home
What is meant by the expression "mathematics is a language"

Exercise 12

Pick one of the following and develop it in one or more paragraphs of cause and effect.

Why I have been uncertain about my major
Why teenage marriages often fail
How a bull session can clarify one's thinking
How cigarette companies sell their product to teenagers

Exercise 13

This exercise is designed for practice in analyzing the methods of paragraph development used by professional writers. For each of the paragraphs below, identify the method or combination of methods used by the writer. Pick out the topic sentence (or make up one if there is none) and study each paragraph carefully to see what are its main points and what kind of evidence or detail is offered in support.

Snobbery is not the same thing as pride of class. Pride of class may not please us but we must at least grant that it reflects a social function. A man who exhibited class pride—in the day when it was possible to do so—may have been puffed up about what he was, but this ultimately depended on what he *did*. Thus, aristocractic pride was based ultimately on the ability to fight and administer. No pride is without fault, but pride of class may be thought of as today we think of pride of profession, toward which we are likely to be lenient.

Snobbery is pride in status without pride in function. And it is an uneasy pride of status. It always asks, "Do I belong—do I really belong? And does he belong? And if I am observed talking to him, will it make me seem to belong or not to belong?" It is the peculiar vice not of aristocratic societies which have their own appropriate vices, but of bourgeois democratic societies. For us the legendary strongholds of snobbery are the Hollywood studios, where two thousand dollars a week dare not talk to three hundred dollars a week for fear that he will be taken for nothing more than fifteen hundred dollars a week. The dominant emotions of snobbery are uneasiness, self-consciousness, self-defensiveness, the sense that one is not quite real but can in some way acquire reality.

—LIONEL TRILLING

All of the disconnector virtues—courage, perseverance, rectitude, chastity, ambition, honor, dutifulness, self-discipline, temperance, purity, self-reliance, impartiality, incorruptibility, dependability, conscientiousness, sobriety, asceticism, spirituality—are ecologically unsound. All express the same arrogant assumption about the importance of the single individual in society and the importance of humanity in the universe. To imagine that it matters (except to those in immediate contact with him) whether or not a man is righteous, holy, or self-actualized is the height of pomposity.

The opposite virtues—cowardice, distractibility, sensuality, inability to complete tasks or resist temptations, partiality, dependency, inconsistency, corruptibility, and so on—are humble virtues. They express humanity's embeddedness in a larger organic system—a system that has its own laws and justice. As such they ultimately have higher survival value than the disciplines since they serve to reconnect the individual with his or her environment. This is not to say that the arrogant virtues should be extirpated from the human repertory. We need only recognize the *price* of the disconnector virtues.

—PHILIP SLATER

I suppose that obvious things are the hardest to define. Everybody thinks he knows what a story is. But if you ask a beginning student to write a story, you're liable to get almost anything—a reminiscence, an episode, an opinion, an anecdote, anything under the sun but a story. A story is a complete dramatic action—and in good stories, the characters are shown through the action and the action is controlled through the characters, and the result of this is meaning that derives from the whole presented experience. I myself prefer to say that a story is a dramatic event that involves a person because he is a person, and a particular person—that is, because he shares in the general human condition and in some specific human situation. A story always involves, in a dramatic way, the mystery of personality. I lent some stories to a country lady who lives down the road from me, and when she returned them she said, "Well, them stories just gone and shown you how some folks *would* do," and I thought to myself that that was right; when you write stories, you have to be content to start exactly there—showing how some specific folks *will* do, *will* do in spite of everything.

—FLANNERY O'CONNOR

When I was first out of college, learning to hold my liquor and trying to enchant the world, I used to *do* The Attitudes at parties. Most anyone could sing old songs, but my skill in pantomime was acknowledged as special and antic, though my pick-up audiences, like my family, never believed in me. I like to think I am the only living person who can perform this lost art form. All the gestures of life boiled down, jelled to a routine and practiced first to the right side of Mrs. Holton's living room, then to the left: Calling (hand cupped to the mouth), Looking (hand over the eyes), Hearing, Greeting, Farewell, then into the deeper emotional material: Rejection, Fear, Love (both open and guarded variety), Laughter (head tossed, eyes dancing) and my favorite, Sorrow. Sorrow was posed with the head sagged, eyes covered with one drooping arm while the other was thrust back in limp Despair.

—MAUREEN HOWARD

It is seldom that an English judge or magistrate does not at least wince or yawn when a psychiatric opinion is being read; often he speaks his mind. This is a favourite. "It is not going to hurt your victim any the less to know that you knocked her down because of some complex or other." True. Just as it is not going to hurt any the less if what knocked her down had been a falling branch or brick. We no longer think of cutting down the tree or burning down the house; we've become quite rational towards inanimate things. The tree may need a prop; those bricks may need more mortar; the hooligan may need some treatment or another kind of life. The chief difference is that we know more about roofs and trees; men and women being of course more complex, and we much less willing to learn.

—Sybille Bedford

4c

Paragraph Coherence

Within every paragraph the sentences should be arranged and linked in such a manner that readers can easily follow the thought. It isn't enough for readers to know what each sentence means; readers must also see how each sentence is related to the one that precedes it and how it leads into the one that follows it. The connections may be clear enough to the writer but not at all clear to readers: incoherence means that the relationships have not been shown, not that they don't exist. Coherence is *continuity* within and between paragraphs. The means of securing continuity are, first, the arrangement of sentences in a logical order and, second, the use of special devices such as the repetition of key words to link sentences.

1. Logical Order of Ideas

Although a topic sentence will help give focus to a paragraph, you need a consistent pattern of organization within the paragraph to ensure continuity. The particular pattern will depend on the kind of material that is to go into the paragraph. The four patterns to be discussed include chronological order, spatial order, deductive order, and inductive order.

The pattern most often used for narrating personal experiences, summarizing steps in a process, and explaining historical events and movements is *chronological order*—the arranging of events in an orderly time sequence. If the time sequence of a narrative is unclear or disorderly, incoherence can result. Diagrammed, chronological order means

$$A \rightarrow B \rightarrow C \rightarrow D, \textit{not } C \rightarrow A \rightarrow D \rightarrow B.$$

For instance, in revising the following paragraph for greater coherence, the writer placed her motives first [1] and then arranged the rest of the paragraph in an orderly chronological sequence—routine [2], first week on the job [3], following weeks on the job [4], conclusion at the summer's end about the value of interesting work [5]. (The brackets and numbers have been added here for illustration.)

PATTERNED CHRONOLOGICALLY

In early June 1980, I took a job as a waitress. [1] My motives at the time were strictly financial: I had been attracted by local fables of the generous tips left by tourists who were quick and easy on the draw with credit cards, and I thought I would earn some fast money toward college expenses. [2] My routine was the regular one: take orders, carry food, clean up the mess on the table, and repeat—eight hours a day, six days a week. During that first week [3], I could only stumble home after a day's work, take a cold shower, and fall into bed. Even when I had become accustomed to the routine [4], I never had any trouble distinguishing between the drudgery of that noisy, hot restaurant where the air-conditioning never worked and the relaxation which came naturally but too briefly with the leisure of a cool evening and chilled beer. By the end of the summer [5], I had firmly resolved never to take another job unless the work itself was interesting and the working conditions were decent.

An important pattern of organization is *spatial order*, useful for many kinds of description. This pattern helps provide coherence by arranging visual details in some consistent sequence—from left to right, right to left, east to west, west to east, from the distant to the near, or from the near to the distant. If the writer moves haphazardly from one place to another, this randomness produces an incoherent pattern. Diagrammed, spatial order can mean

$$
\begin{array}{l}
A \\
\downarrow \\
B \\
\downarrow \quad \text{or} \quad A \to B \to C \to D, \text{ or their opposites.} \\
C \\
\downarrow \\
D
\end{array}
$$

It can also mean

$$A \nearrow B \searrow C$$

or

$$A \rightarrow B$$
$$\downarrow$$
$$D \leftarrow C$$

and variations thereof.

In the following student paragraph (set in memories of Iowa and Missouri), the writer begins with the trees on the edge of the lawn, moves to the lawns themselves, and quietly climaxes with the houses and garages toward the back of the properties.

PATTERNED SPATIALLY

There were trees back in that other world. They lined the streets and gave shade, and in autumn the leaves that covered the streets and lawns were raked in big piles and burned. Most of the lawns weren't worth uncovering. People didn't take care of them much. The thick bladed grass didn't look cut but just flattened and uneven, and it grew up around the trees and at the edges stuck out over the sidewalk, and there were brown spots, the earth sometimes showing through. Those lawns fit the houses, though. There were big houses, and old—two stories high with an attic and a cellar, and of wood siding. Cool, gray cement steps, often of blistered wood, led to a porch sometimes enclosed in screen, but there were no picture windows, only small ones. The one-car garage, with a door that swung open and had small, dirty window panes in it, was usually separate from the house. These houses looked peaceful—lazy in the summer and snug in the winter. They smelled rather strange inside and had worn, patterned rugs on wooden floors and worn sofas and china cabinets, kitchens with cracked and yellowed linoleum and gas stoves, and bath tubs with legs and rubber stoppers. In that other world, they had been home.

A paragraph laid out in *deductive order* makes a well-known logical structure. This pattern of organization is one that moves from a general statement to the particular details that support or explain it. Diagrammed, deductive order can mean the following:

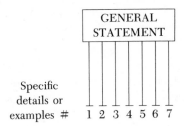

If details are scattered throughout the paragraph, the reader may be left with a blurred memory of miscellaneous information. The original of the following paragraph began with a clear general statement—"The Roman Empire expanded because the Romans were great organizers as well as fine builders and engineers"—but the paragraph jumped from bridges and roads to language and religion, from language and religion to law and citizenship, from law and citizenship to the training of soliders, from the training of soldiers back to bridges and roads. To make the paragraph coherent, the student revised it by dividing it into two paragraphs and grouping his ideas accordingly.

PATTERNED DEDUCTIVELY

The Roman Empire expanded because the Romans were great organizers as well as fine builders and engineers. When they conquered a territory, they systematically tried to make it a willing part of the Empire. They brought Roman law and the promise of Roman citizenship and they introduced Latin as a common language. Sometimes they recruited and trained native men to become Roman soldiers, as in the case of the members of the German tribes who became part of the Praetorian Guard, the Emperor's personal soldiers. But they did not try to change all of the religious beliefs and social customs of the conquered people. They did not, for example, try to compel the Egyptians to accept the Roman gods.

Moreover, when the Romans conquered a territory, they constructed key cities and highways to consolidate their military and financial power in the colony. London, for instance, was built as a military depot and trade center. The excellent roads and bridges built by Roman engineers to the main administrative city gave the Romans good

● control over the surrounding countryside. A few of these bridges and roads in France and Italy are still in use today.

Another pattern for organizing paragraphs is arrangement by *inductive order*. The inductive paragraph is organized with the details at the beginning and in the middle, and with an ending that is a summary or generalization, usually the topic sentence. Diagrammed, inductive order means the following:

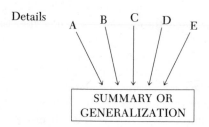

The inductive pattern is the complementary counterpart of the deductive; some of the preceding deductively arranged material about the Romans might just as easily have been arranged and more fully developed in this pattern:

PATTERNED INDUCTIVELY

Roman roads were built on a solid stone base and paved with flat rocks. They were crowned on the top and ditched along the sides for drainage. They were designed to run in almost straight lines and to go over hills, not around them. Roman armies used them as military highways—ten to twenty feet wide—to move legions rapidly and to supply them adequately. These roads led to and from key administrative cities such as London, originally built as a depot and trade center, and gave the Romans good control over the surrounding countryside. In Britain alone, a great series of roads radiated from the southeast to all parts of the island. **Thanks to these superbly designed roads linking cities and ensuring rapid troop movement, the Romans could hold conquered territory and expand the Empire.**

2. Special Devices for Coherence

The other means of achieving coherence include the use of transitional words, the use of linking pronouns, the repetition of key words, and the use of parallel structure. Usually, experienced writers employ *all* these means, and they are not much interested in the label attached to the method they use. Instead, they are concerned to achieve coherence accurately and gracefully. But here it will be helpful to discuss separately each technique available to you for improving paragraphs that lack coherence. What happens when the available means are not fully employed can be seen in the following paragraph:

Disjointed

> In Tillie Olsen's story "I Stand Here Ironing," a young woman attempts to love and help her oldest daughter, Emily. The mother's own problems and responsibilities prevent her. The mother was young. Her husband abandoned her. She was forced to work. This separated her from Emily. Emily had to be left with others, and the mother lost touch with her. The mother was able to find a new husband. She was soon forced to concentrate on her other children. Her other daughter, Susan, is the most notable example. Susan became everything Emily was not. Susan was blonde, pretty, quick, and articulate. Emily was dark, slow, and sickly. The mother looks back with guilt. She says, "I was a young mother, I was a distracted mother."

Although it has unity and development, the paragraph generally lacks coherence because the writer too often leaps and jumps erratically from one sentence to the next, as reading aloud will make especially clear. Revised by slight rephrasing and the addition of connecting words, the paragraph becomes easier to follow:

More Coherent

> In Tillie Olsen's short story "I Stand Here Ironing," a young woman attempts to love and help her eldest daughter, Emily, **yet her own** problems and responsibilities prevent her from fulfilling **these goals. As a young mother, abandoned by her husband,** she was forced to work, **separating her from her daughter. Forced to leave** Emily with others, the mother lost touch with her. **Although** the mother was able to find a new husband, she was soon forced to concentrate on her other children, **most notably** her other daughter, Susan. Susan became everything Emily was not—blonde, pretty, quick, and articulate. Emily was dark, slow, and sickly. **Looking back in guilt,** the mother says, "I was a young mother, I was a distracted mother."

In the revised passage, *the writer is no longer thinking in single sentences only.* Instead, he has looked for the continuity among his ideas and for the most accurate means of showing this continuity in each case.

Transitional words and phrases serve to indicate different relationships. Here is a list of relationships and appropriate transitional words:

1. Result or consequence: *hence, consequently, as a result, therefore.*

2. Comparison or contrast: *similarly, likewise, however, on the other hand, yet, still, nevertheless.*

3. Example or illustration: *as an illustration, for example, specifically, for instance.*

4. Additional aspects or evidence: *moreover, furthermore, also, too, next, besides, in the first place, first.*

5. Conclusion or summary: *in conclusion, to sum up, to conclude, in short.*

Notice the careful use of transitional words in the following passage:

RELATIONSHIPS INDICATED

Past and future are two time regions which we commonly separate by a third which we call the present. **But** strictly speaking, the present does not exist, **or** is at best no more than an infinitesimal point in time, gone before we can note it as present. **Nevertheless** we must have a present; **and so** we get one by robbing the past, by holding on to the most recent events and pretending that they all belong to our immediate perceptions. If, **for example,** I raise my arm, the total event is a series of occurrences of which the first are past before the last have taken place; yet I perceive it as a single movement executed in one instant of time.
—CARL BECKER

Sentences also may be connected by linking pronouns that have clear antecedents. This technique is an effective way of avoiding needless repetition. Notice in the following example how Henry James substitutes "it" for "symbolism" and later for "this suggestion" and how he uses the phrase *"this* suggestion" to point back to the entire preceding sentence.

LINKING PRONOUNS

In *The Scarlet Letter* there is a great deal of symbolism; there is, I think, too much. It is overdone at times, and becomes mechanical; it ceases to be impressive, and grazes triviality. The idea of the mystic A which the young minister finds imprinted upon his breast and eating into his flesh, in sympathy with the embroidered badge that Hester is condemned to wear, appears to me to be a case in point. *This* suggestion should, I think, have just been made and dropped; to insist upon it, and return to it, is to exaggerate the weak side of the subject. Hawthorne returns to it constantly, plays with it, and seems charmed by it; until at last the reader feels tempted to declare that his enjoyment of it is puerile.

—HENRY JAMES

Paragraph coherence is also maintained *by the repetition of key words* that are related to a central idea. In the following passage, notice the key words *darkness, deep sea,* and *blackness* and the words related to them by contrast such as *sunlight, red rays,* and *surface*:

KEY WORDS REPEATED

Immense pressure, then, is one of the governing conditions of life in the **deep sea; darkness** is another. The unrelieved **darkness** of the **deep waters** has produced weird and incredible modifications of the **abyssal** fauna. It is a **blackness** so divorced from the world of the **sunlight** that probably only the few men who have seen it with their own **eyes** can visualize it. We know that **light fades out rapidly with descent below the surface**. The **red rays** are gone at the end of the first 200 or 300 feet, and with them all the **orange and yellow warmth of the sun**. Then the **greens** fade out, and at 1,000 feet only a **deep, dark brilliant blue** is left. In **very clear waters** the **violet rays** of the spectrum may penetrate another thousand feet. Beyond this is only the **blackness** of the **deep sea**.

—RACHEL CARSON

Continuity can also be sustained by *parallel structure*, which calls attention to similar ideas. This coordination of equally important ideas is often useful with introductory or summary paragraphs, although its use is by no means confined to such paragraphs. In the following example, the first paragraph is taken from the beginning of a chapter, the second from near its conclusion.

PARALLEL STRUCTURE

To "become a pueblo" **meant to adopt** many of the ways and political forms and ambitions of townspeople. **It meant to accept** the tools, leadership, and conceptions of progress which were then being offered to the villagers of Yucatan by the leaders of Mexico's social revolution. **It required** the inhabitants **to give up** some of the isolation which was theirs in the remote and sparsely inhabited lands that lay apart from the goings and comings of city men. In future they would be a part of the political and economic institutions of Yucatan, of Mexico, and—though of course they would not have put it so—of the one world that was then in the making.

· · ·

Chan Kom had attained its loftiest political objective. **It had become** the head of its own municipality. **It had made** itself into a pueblo, a community of dwellers—some of them—in masonry houses. **It had** a municipal building, with a stone jail; a school building, also of masonry; a masonry church—and a masonry Protestant chapel. **It had** two gristmills and four stores. **It had** two outdoor theatres and a baseball diamond.

—ROBERT REDFIELD

Notice how the parallel structure in the first three sentences of the second paragraph restate what it meant for Chan Kom to achieve its "loftiest political objective." Notice how the parallel structure in the last three sentences of the second paragraph lists equally important features in a "community of dwellers." And notice how the parallel structure of the second paragraph harks back to the parallel structure of the first paragraph—from what Chan Kom "had attained" back to what "it required" to become a pueblo.

If the paper is to read smoothly, the reader must be able to see the *connections between the paragraphs* as well as the relationships within a paragraph. Even though a paragraph is well constructed in itself, it may fail to be an integral part of the paper. Indeed, from the reader's viewpoint, it is more important that a paragraph should carry him along from one point to the next than that it should be a little masterpiece in itself. Aside from the short transitional paragraphs discussed earlier, the main devices for providing coherence among paragraphs are the same as those for providing coherence within a paragraph—transitional words, linking pronouns, key words repeated, and parallel structure.

Probably more important than any of these devices is the *arrangement* of the material so that a paragraph ends with some reference to the idea that is to be taken up next. In the following example, taken from Turner's "The Significance of the Frontier in American History," notice how continuity is sustained by the progression of the argument:

CONTINUITY BY ARRANGEMENT OF MATERIAL AND FOCUSED THESIS

. . . Up to our own day [1893] American history has been in a large degree the history of the colonization of the Great West. The existence of an area of free land, its continuous recession, and the advance of American settlement westward, explain American development [thesis].

Behind institutions, behind constitutional forms and modifications, lie the vital forces that call these organs into life and shape them to meet changing conditions. The peculiarity of American institutions is the fact they have been compelled to adapt themselves to the changes of an expanding people—to the changes involved in crossing a continent, in winning a wilderness. . . . [omission of the rest of a long paragraph]

In this advance, the frontier is the outer edge of the wave—the meeting point between savagery and civilization. . . . [omission of the rest]

The American frontier is sharply distinguished from the European frontier—a fortified boundary line running through dense populations. The most significant thing about the American frontier is that it lies at the hither edge of free land. . . . [omission of the rest of the paragraph]

In the settlement of America we have to observe how European life entered the continent, and how America modified and developed that life. . . . The frontier is the line of the most rapid and effective Americanization. . . . [rest of paragraph suggests how, and concludes] And to study this advance, the men who grew up under these conditions, and the political, economic and social results of it, is to study the really American part of our history.

—FREDERICK JACKSON TURNER

Exercise 14

Pick an aspect of a subject you know well and jot down about a dozen nouns or noun phrases connected with it—for example, hard wax, soft wax, backache, shammy, clean rags, car washed, shady spot, lots of time. Then arrange the items in a logical order, discarding any that won't fit, and write a coherent paragraph from your outline.

Exercise 15

Pick one of the following topics. Then write two separate paragraphs about it in which you try to develop the same idea each time but use a different pattern of organization for each paragraph.

The pleasure of being a good tennis player (or poker player, or dancer, or whatever)
The most effective way to put things off without feeling guilty
The most offensive commercial on TV
How to make your advisor (or teacher) remember your name
How to keep your temper in a traffic jam

Exercise 16

Analyze the paragraphs you have written for Exercise 15 to determine what specific devices you have used most frequently for coherence.

Exercise 17

Compare the rough draft and the final version of one of your papers to determine how much you revised for coherence. If you made changes, were they to improve the order used (for example, making time sequence clearer), to supply more specific links, or to sharpen up the thrust of the whole argument? Or were they a combination of these?

Exercise 18

For the following paragraphs, identify the pattern of organization and the specific transitional devices used in each.

When we are children, though, there are categories of films we don't like—documentaries generally (they're too much like education) and, of course, movies especially designed for children. By the time we can go on our own we have learned to avoid them. Children are often put down by adults when the children say they enjoyed a particular movie; adults who are short on empathy are quick to point out aspects of the plot or theme that the child didn't understand, and it's easy to humiliate a child in this way. But it is one of the glories of eclectic arts like opera and movies that they include so many possible kinds and combinations of pleasure. One may be enthralled by Leontyne Price in "La Forza del Destino" even if one hasn't boned up on the libretto, or entranced by "The Magic Flute" even if one has boned up on the libretto, and a movie may be enjoyed for many reasons that have little to do with the story or subtleties (if any) of theme or character. Unlike "pure" arts which are often defined in terms of what only they can do, movies are open and unlimited. Probably everything that can be done in movies can be done some other way, but—and this is what's so miraculous and so expedient about them—they can do almost anything any other art can do (alone or in combination) and they can take on some of the functions of exploration, of journalism, of anthropology, of almost any branch of knowledge as well. We go to the movies for the variety of what they can provide, and for their marvelous ability to give us easily and inexpensively (and usually painlessly) what we can get from other arts also. They are a wonderfully *convenient* art.

—PAULINE KAEL

Biologists used to entertain themselves by speculating as to what would happen if, through some unthinkable catastrophe, the natural restraints were thrown off and all the progeny of a single individual survived. Thus Thomas Huxley a century ago calculated that a single female aphis (which has the curious power of reproducing without mating) could produce progeny in a single year's time whose total weight would equal that of the Chinese empire of his day.

Fortunately for us such an extreme situation is only theoretical, but the dire results of upsetting nature's own arrangements are well known to students of animal populations. The stockman's zeal for eliminating the coyote has resulted in plagues of field mice, which the coyote formerly controlled. The oft repeated story of the Kaibab deer in Arizona is another case in point. At one time the deer population was in equilibrium with its environment. A number of predators—wolves, pumas, and coyotes—prevented the deer from outrunning their food supply. Then a campaign was begun to "conserve" the deer by killing off their enemies. Once the predators were gone, the deer increased prodigiously and soon there was not enough food for them. The browse line on the trees went higher and higher as they sought food, and in time many more deer were dying of starvation than had formerly been killed by predators. The whole environment, moreover, was damaged by their desperate efforts to find food.

—RACHEL CARSON

What man most passionately wants is his living wholeness and his living unison, not his own isolate salvation of his "soul." Man wants his physical fulfillment first and foremost, since now, once and once only, he is in the flesh and potent. For man, the vast marvel is to be alive. For man, as for flower and beast and bird, the supreme triumph is to be most vividly, most perfectly alive. Whatever the unborn and the dead may know, they cannot know the beauty, the marvel of being alive in the flesh. The dead may look after the afterward. But the magnificent here and now of life in the flesh is ours, and ours alone, and ours only for a time. We ought to dance with rapture that we should be alive and in the flesh, and part of the living, incarnate cosmos. I am part of the sun as my eye is part of me. That I am part of the earth my feet know perfectly, and my blood is part of the sea. My soul knows that I am part of the human race, my soul is an organic part of the great human race, as my spirit is part of my nation. In my own very self, I am part of my family. There is nothing of me that is alone and absolute except my mind, and we shall find that the mind has no existence by itself; it is only the glitter of the sun on the surface of the waters.

So that my individualism is really an illusion. I am part of the great whole, and I can never escape. But I *can* deny my connections, break them, and become a fragment. Then I am wretched.

What we want is to destroy our false, inorganic connections, especially those related to money, and re-establish the living organic connections, with the cosmos, the sun and earth, with mankind and nation and family. Start with the sun, and the rest will slowly, slowly happen.

—D. H. LAWRENCE

4d

Economizing: Writing Under Pressure

Sometimes, we don't have the time to plan, write, and revise with the leisure or the space to amplify, develop, and document with the fullness we would prefer. Pop quizzes, short-answer essays, the hour-long test with three questions to be covered, the one-page critique of a book or three-page comparison of two books—these examples should remind us of limits often imposed. In this context, economizing means working intelligently to one's best advantage within such restrictions. And because the paragraph, *not* scattered sentences or an outline, is the usual form expected of the writer, it helps to know certain relevant principles and techniques for working under pressure—for the efficient use of limited time and space.

A few preliminary qualifications about these principles and techniques follow. First, none of them are substitutes for having thought about and mastered the material; they will not conceal the fact that a writer has little to say, given ten minutes or two hours, one page or ten. Second, although some of these aids may seem obvious or general, *that* is their value. Because they are obvious, they are often ignored or forgotten; because they are general, they can be applied to a variety of writing situations. Third, although they may seem like formulas, that also is a value: while being learned, they may help give confidence; once mastered, they can be modified by experience.

1. Focusing

To describe the process of collecting one's self and getting into focus, the Quakers speak of "centering down." That is what you have to do, fast, when writing examinations—the model we use here. The first basic principle is to be *sure* you understand the topic or question. Read it through slowly and carefully. If you don't understand what is called for, ask the instructor or T.A. Your doubts or bewilderments may be shared by other students. Further, in reading the topic, attend to the verb that tells you what you are required to do:

Explain   = *spell out* the reasons, causes, connections.
Analyze   = *break up*, separate, segment into parts, steps, phases, sections, causes.
Compare   = *Place side by side* and *point out* significant similarities, differences, or both.
Summarize = *Reduce*, abbreviate to the major aspects, features, events, arguments without distortion.
Evaluate   = *Judge*, take a position on the merits of, adequacy of, reasons for or against, consequences of.

But what about *discuss*, that open-ended verb so often used for exam questions and short papers? Broadly, *discuss* means to open up, reflect on, show that you know about and have thought about your subject. Sometimes, the context makes clear what is called for. If you are in doubt, try turning the command into a question *in order to discover which analytic skill is necessary.* To take a few examples:

1. Discuss the believability of the last chapters in *Huck Finn* = *How* believable are the last chapters of Huck Finn? = *Evaluate.*

2. Discuss the major therapies in the treatment of autistic children = *What are* the major therapies in the treatment of autistic children? = *Summarize* and *Compare* and *Contrast.*

3. Discuss the significant changes in Hester Prynne's attitude toward her sin in *The Scarlet Letter* = *What are* the major changes? = *Analyze.*

If you are asked to compare two characters in a novel, a mere description, which only outlines each, will not do: you are asked to bring prominent similarities or differences, or both, together—to highlight these features. So, also, if you are asked to analyze or evaluate a plot, don't give a summary. One of the most common failures in essay answers is the writer's stating what happened without interpretation, without making connections or shaping an argument—the summary that all too often runs: "This happened and this happened and that was the result, so thus and such also happened and . . . ."

The second principle is to plan your answer before starting. Except for brief quizzes, you *always* have at least a few minutes to think before writing; take them. Strategies for planning answers vary: some students jot down an informal outline; others simply list key terms, phrases, names, or details and then look for a pattern or case (a form of jotting); still others reflect, work out a thesis, a case to argue, and then dive in. Any of these techniques is valuable. The point is to get *inside* the topic *before* writing, so that you don't use up half your time in desperate false starts or chewing on your pen and vaguely wondering what to say. By planning, you not only center down; you also make yourself a searcher in pursuit of an answer instead of remaining a spectator waiting for something to happen.

2. Writing

Even in pressure situations, when things are going well—the examples coming easily, the connections emerging, the topic itself deepening in interest—your pen barely keeps up with your thoughts. But what about the times when you realize that you are drifting, getting far away from the topic, off on a tangent? You can, of course, try to twist your argument back to the question, but that often distorts both your analysis and the topic itself. The first principle, in such cases, is to *stop*, go back to the original topic, and start again. Even if your second attempt is incomplete, most teachers prefer that to the irrelevant or tangential answer. They can see, from what you have crossed out and from the fresh beginning, that you were at least headed in the right direction. Start with a new outline, thesis, or list of items: to some extent you can make up for lost time.

The second dilemma you may face at times concerns examples: what kind? how many? how thoroughly discussed? First, unless asked to give all examples, be selective, not exhaustive. Pick the most telling or typical ones. For instance, if you were discussing Huck Finn's essential decency, his humaneness, you couldn't list all cases—the novel is full of them—but you could focus on his growing awareness of how much he cares for Jim and on his resolve to help Jim escape, and you could point out the risks Huck takes to help the Wilks girls. Perhaps other examples interest you more—Huck's shock at the feud or pity for the tarred-and-feathered Duke and King, despite their treachery. Whatever the case, *limit* your choices to a few pointed ones.

Second, *do* something with your evidence. Merely mentioning an example or two in a sentence or two is not enough: until you show by concrete development how the example applies, how it makes your point, *how it fits the terms of the question*, you have no depth. For instance, if you were discussing why German and Japanese car manufacturers have taken over a significant part of the American market, you couldn't merely drop the names Volkswagen and Toyota. What about them—better engineering? quicker anticipation of the demand for small cars and flexibility in planning and retooling? lower cost to the customer because of gas economy and cheaper production costs? better marketing and servicing? Any or several of these may be relevant. However, until you specifically discuss, say, what is better in the engineering of a major foreign model, you haven't done anything with your evidence or answered the question "Why?"

Finally, when finished, take a few minutes to proofread, not just skimming for obvious errors but considering changes in wording, insertions, occasionally even the renumbering of paragraphs. You haven't really finished until you turn the bluebook in; after that, it's too late.

3. The Précis

Most of the techniques for economizing on wording are taken up elsewhere, particularly in Chapters 5, 6, and 7 on sentences and in Chapter 9 on diction. Chapter 12, on the long paper, also contains some useful tips on note-taking and the ways to boil down data and long quotations. One technique for condensing long paragraphs into short ones deserves comment here.

The *summarizing note*, especially the type called a *précis*, is the most useful and versatile way to record your reading. The précis is a brief, accurate condensation which preserves only the main ideas of the material summarized. It omits digressions, rhetorical flourishes, illustrative details or anecdotes, and stylistic niceties in the original and prunes it down by about two-thirds. When we write a précis, however, we do not string together excerpts from the original or jot down disconnected notes. Rather, we try to record in our own words the ideas we understand to be the basic ones. We may use a few key phrases from the original, provided that we carefully distinguish them by quotation marks, but our main purpose is to master the original, find its core of meaning, and state this in our own words.

Often, in taking notes for a paper, you may wish to make a précis of a long paragraph, or several. To do so, read the paragraph carefully, noting its topic sentence and the sequence in which the basic ideas are taken up. Then read it again, this time making sure you have omitted no major qualifications or connections. Then write a brief, fair summary of these basic ideas and compare your summary with the original, making necessary changes. Précis writing requires practice, but once learned, it is an excellent way of mastering and preserving material for papers or reviewing.

In the following examples, note the four numbered sets of parentheses in the original source material; these numbered sets correspond with the four numbered sentences in the first summarizing note. Also observe the boldface key phrases in the original source material and the way they are carried over or paraphrased in the first summarizing note; this is the essence of précis writing: isolating the *key* ideas and relationships and reducing them to a bare, accurate summary of the original. In comparing the first summarizing note with the final précis, note how four sentences have been condensed to three by the tightening up of relationships and even more direct wording. The original of 229 words has been reduced to 68 words, then 59. The one key phrase retained from the original in both summaries is "moral equivalent of war."

ORIGINAL SOURCE MATERIAL

#1 (The immediate aim of **the soldier's life is,** as Moltke said, **destruction** and nothing but destruction; and whatever constructions wars result in are remote and non-military. **Consequently the soldier cannot train himself to be too feelingless** to all those usual sympathies and respects, whether for persons or for things, that make for conservation). #2 (**Yet the fact remains that war is a school of** strenuous life and **heroism;** and, being in the line of aboriginal instinct, is **the only school** that as yet is **universally available.**) #3 (But when we gravely ask ourselves whether this wholesale organization of irrationality and crime be our **only bulwark against effeminacy,** we stand aghast at the thought, and think more kindly of ascetic religion. One hears of the mechanical equivalent of heat. **What we now need** to discover in the social realm is **the moral equivalent of war: something heroic that will speak to men as universally as war** does, **and yet will be as compatible with** their **spiritual selves as war** has proved itself to be **incompatible.**) #4 (I have often thought that in the old **monkish poverty-worship,** in spite of the pedantry which infested it, there might be something **like the moral equivalent of war** which we are seeking. May not **voluntarily accepted poverty** be "the strenuous life," **without the need of crushing** weaker people?)
—WILLIAM JAMES

FIRST SUMMARIZING NOTE

#1 A soldier's purpose is destruction and he must therefore harden himself completely. #2 Yet war does train men in heroism and is the only such training now generally available. #3 What is needed to prevent softness is a "moral equivalent of war" whose heroism has war's universal appeal but which lacks war's destructive and brutalizing effects. #4 Perhaps the monk's vow of voluntary poverty is an analog of this needed equivalent.

FINAL PRÉCIS

Although war demands soldiers who can harden themselves to destroy unfeelingly, it does train men in heroism and is the only such training now generally available. The world needs a "moral equivalent of war" with war's universal appeal but without its destructive and brutalizing effects. Perhaps the monk's voluntary vow of poverty is an analog of this needed equivalent.

5

CONSTRUCTING SENTENCES

5a

Elements of a Sentence

We all know that a sentence in grammar is a series of spoken or written words which forms the grammatically complete expression of a single thought. On the page such a unit of discourse begins with a capital letter and ends with the appropriate end punctuation mark. Spoken aloud, the sentence is marked by voice inflection and pauses, the longest of which signals its completion. We have a well-developed, intuitive sense of the sentence because we have been hearing and speaking and writing and reading them most of our lives.

In English this grammatical term also names a judicial pronouncement. If we look up the word in the *Oxford English Dictionary*, that historian of our language, we find that "sentence" is one of those words that has contracted over the centuries: it had more meaning in Shakespeare's time than it has in ours. Some of these meanings, such as "opinion" and "way of thinking," are listed in the dictionary as obsolete and are not available to contemporary writers. Nevertheless, they point the way back to the Latin origin of the word, *sentire*, to feel, to be of the opinion, to perceive, to judge. The word *sentence* shares the same root as sensation and sense, and appropriately so, for the construction of a sentence, even the simplest two-word kind, requires sensing and thinking, perceiving and judging. Good sentences are written by a vigilant observer with the courage to judge and the passion to declare.

Such confident declaration comes from an understanding of how the English sentence works. Like most highly functional constructions, the sentence is complicated, perhaps at times bewildering, but always interesting in its varieties and patterns and possibilities. An analysis of sentence structure begins with a classification of words on the basis of how they function in the sentence. Such classification is called PARTS OF SPEECH—a term that happily reminds us that grammar has something to do with listening to the human voice. There are eight parts of speech.

A *noun* names a person, place, idea, or thing	student, city, justice, rope
A *pronoun* stands in place of a noun	I, they, that, anyone
An *adjective* defines, limits, modifies, or describes a noun or pronoun	small, ugly, Victorian, bright
A *verb* expresses action, existence, or occurrence	wrote, lived, happen, build
An *adverb* modifies a verb, an adjective, or another adverb	gingerly, very, ever, quickly
A *preposition* usually precedes a noun or a pronoun, called the object of the preposition, and shows its relationship to another word in the sentence	out, from, in, by, under
A *conjunction* connects words, phrases, and clauses to coordinate and to subordinate	and, or, nor, but, since, after, because, if
An *interjection* interrupts the rhythm of the sentence to express feeling	ah, alas, please, oh

Some words—for example, *and* and *if*—function only as one part of speech. Many, however, with little or no inflection, can be a noun or a verb, an adjective or an adverb.

I dream of Jeannie.	(verb)
Jeannie's dream was prophetic.	(noun)
She looked dreamy.	(adjective)
He gazed dreamily.	(adverb)

Because of their flexibility, it is sensible not to classify words absolutely as nouns or verbs but to study the way they work in sentences. Words have four functions in sentences: to name things, to assert things, to modify (describe, identify, limit) other words, and to connect parts of a sentence. Groups of words may have the same function as single words. Such groups are called phrases or clauses.

class	function	types
Substantive	to name	nouns, pronouns, infinitives, gerunds
Predicative	to assert	verbs
Modifier	to describe, limit, qualify	adjectives, adverbs, participles
Connective	to join elements	conjunctions, prepositions

Infinitives, gerunds, and participles are verbals, that is, verbs that function as other parts of speech. They will be discussed more fully later in the chapter.

Sentences ask questions or answer them, issue commands or requests, express strong feeling, and, most often, make statements. The SYNTAX of the sentence, its arrangement of words, tells us immediately what kind of a sentence it is.

What a ridiculous assignment!	Exclamatory
Write the paper.	Imperative
Are you writing the paper?	Interrogative
I have written the paper.	Declarative

Although questions and commands, used discreetly, and the very occasional exclamation can add variety to a composition, most written sentences will be declarative statements.

1. Subject and Predicate

Every sentence contains a subject, expressed or implied, and a predicate. The SUBJECT names something or someone; the PREDICATE makes an assertion about the subject.

subject	predicate
Horses	sweat.
Men	perspire.
Ladies	glow.
My grandmother	distinguishes these three words.
My first language lesson	came from her.

The subject is usually a noun or a pronoun, although it may be a phrase or a clause. The predicate may contain a number of different words used in different ways, but the essential part of the predicate is a verb, a word that asserts. While the subject of a sentence may be implied—*Listen!* or *Watch out for falling rocks*—a series of words without a verb is not a sentence.

2. Modifiers

The kernel English sentence is two words: a subject and a verb.

Grandmother spoke.

Although effective for their very spareness, such sentences are rare in writing. We usually need to limit or define or otherwise qualify the subject and the verb for clarity and precision.

My articulate, southern grandmother spoke clearly and frequently.

The adjectives *articulate* and *southern* define particular qualities of the subject, *grandmother*, while the adverbs *clearly* and *frequently* describe how and how often she spoke. Such words or groups of words, which may be attached to almost any part of the sentence, are called MODIFIERS. Although modifiers usually describe, they also indicate how many (*three* books, *few* readers), which one (*this* pencil, *the* pen, *my* brush), or how much (*very* clearly, *half* read, *almost too* late).

Modifiers are divided into two main classes, ADJECTIVES and ADVERBS, which correspond to those respective parts of speech. Words that modify nouns, pronouns, or gerunds (verbs acting as nouns) function as adjectives; words that modify verbs, adjectives, or other adverbs function as adverbs.

Very hungry people seldom display good table manners.

In this sentence, *hungry*, *good*, and *table* are adjectives, describing what kind of people and manners. *Very* is an adverb since it modifies the adjective *hungry*; *seldom* is an adverb modifying the verb *display*.

Adjectives and adverbs have different forms to indicate RELATIVE DEGREE. In addition to the regular, or "positive," form (*slow, comfortable, slowly*), there are the COMPARATIVE and SUPERLATIVE DE-

GREES (*slowest, most comfortable, most slowly*). The examples illustrate the rule: adjectives with more than two syllables form the comparative and superlative degrees by the words *more* and *most*, instead of the suffixes *-er* and *-est*. All adverbs ending in *-ly* use *more* and *most* to indicate degrees of comparison.

3. Identifying Subject and Verb

To understand how a sentence works, we must be able to distinguish its parts and to see how they function in relation to one another. Such an analysis begins with identifying the subject and the verb. Look first for the verb: a word or group of words that states an action or happening or an existential fact. Some forms or tenses of a verb are phrases, including one or more AUXILIARY VERBS: I was hired, I have been hired, I had taken, He will have taken. Verbs that do not add *-ed* to form the past tense are called IRREGULAR VERBS. We must remember their PRINCIPAL PARTS—*write, wrote, written; sing, sang, sung*—to use them correctly.

> I **handed** him my paper.
>
> The professor **wrote** comments all over the page.
>
> I **had** simply **tried** to explain my grandmother's passion for accuracy.
>
> We **will have written** ten essays by the end of the term.

Some verbs, called LINKING (or COPULATIVE) VERBS, connect the subject with a noun or an adjective that predicates something about the subject. The most common linking verb is *to be (is, were, am, are)*. Other linking verbs include *seem, appear, look, become, grow, smell, taste, sound, turn, feel*.

> She **is** a good stylist.
>
> His argument **seemed** logical.
>
> There **were** reasons for disagreement.
>
> She **sounded** angry.

Once we have located the verb, we can ask the question: "Who or what did this?" The answer is the subject, which, stripped of its modifiers, is the simple subject. *Who* sounded angry? *She* did.

What seemed logical? The *argument.* Notice that in the third sentence the verb is *were.* Because *there* comes at the beginning of the sentence, we may mistake it for the subject. But if we question the verb, we cannot ask, "What *were* for disagreement," but "What were *there* for disagreement," and the answer is *reasons,* which is the subject.

This method of identifying the subject is especially helpful when the normal order of the sentence is inverted (that is, when the subject comes after the verb).

Half a mile away **rose** the spires of the cathedral.

"No," **said** the man firmly.

What rose half a mile away? The answer is the subject, "spires."
Who said "no?" The answer is the subject, "man."

In a sentence that asks a question, the subject often follows some form of the verb *have* or *be,* or a form of an auxiliary verb.

verb	subject	
Have	you	the time?
Is	he	qualified?

auxiliary	subject	verb	
Have	you	read	this novel?
Did	she	write	it?
May	they	borrow	it?

	auxiliary	subject	verb
What kind of story	did	he	tell?

In an imperative sentence the subject is not expressed. Since a command or request is addressed directly to someone, that person need not be named.

	subject		verb	
	(	)	Come	in.
	(	)	Return	the books no later than Monday.
Please (		)	take	these books to the library.

Since we can make one assertion about several persons and things, a sentence may have several nouns as its subject. Such a construction is called a COMPOUND SUBJECT.

compound subject	
The trees and plants	were dying.
Jane Austen, George Eliot, and Emily Brontë	are my favorite novelists.

Similarly, we can make several assertions about one subject. Such a construction is called a COMPOUND PREDICATE.

She **wrote, revised, copied,** and **proofread** the manuscript.

Exhausted, she **went** to bed and **slept** for twelve hours.

Exercise 1

Expand the following kernel sentences by adding one-word modifiers. Include words that describe and limit and those that specify how many and how much and which one. Be ready to classify the modifiers as adjectives or adverbs.

1. Trees grow.
2. The car runs.
3. People vote.
4. Prices rose.
5. Vocalists sing.

Exercise 2

Pick out the simple subjects and the verbs in the following sentences. Note that either the subject or the verb may be compound.

1. After locking the door, the flight attendant sat down at the rear of the plane.
2. Invisible to us, the pilot and copilot were checking the instruments.
3. Signs warning passengers not to smoke and to fasten their seat belts flashed on.
4. Directly beneath the signs was a door leading to the pilot's compartment.
5. Altogether there were about sixty passengers on the plane.
6. In a few moments the plane moved, slowly at first, and then roared into life.
7. After taxiing out to the airstrip, the pilot hesitated a moment to check the runway.

8. Then with a sudden rush of speed the plane roared down the runway and gradually began to climb.
9. Below us, at the edge of the airport, were markers and signal lights.
10. The football field and the quarter-mile track enabled me to identify the high school.

4. Complements

So far we have concentrated on the subject and verb—the bare roots of all statements. You noticed, certainly, that in many of the examples used to illustrate points about subjects and verbs and the modifiers that define and limit them, there was a sentence element which was not identified but which was crucial to the structure. Such a word or group of words that completes the sense of the predicate is called a COMPLEMENT. Simple sentences, then, fall into three basic patterns.

Subject–Verb

Subject–Verb–Complement

Subject–Linking Verb–Complement

Some verbs do not require any further words to complete their assertion. Such verbs are called INTRANSITIVE VERBS.

The mourners sat in the pews.

Grandmother died.

All those at the funeral wept copiously.

Copiously, you will recognize from its inflected ending, does not complement or complete the verb *wept*, but modifies it by stating how much. *Wept*, however, can have a complement, as in the following sentence.

I wept copious tears.

Here *wept* functions as a TRANSITIVE VERB, that is, one followed by an object that completes the predicate.

The minister delivered a stirring eulogy.

Minister and *delivered* provoke in the reader the perfectly natural question "what?" And the answer is the complement, *eulogy*.

The commonest type of complement is the direct object of a transitive verb. The DIRECT OBJECT is a noun or a pronoun or a phrase or a clause that completes the verb by naming what the subject acts upon.

subject	verb	direct object
My uncle	wore	a black suit.
The neighbors	sent	flowers.

The easiest way to identify a direct object is to name the simple subject and verb and then ask the question "what?" My uncle wore *what?* The answer, *suit,* is the direct object of the verb *wore.*

Direct objects, like subjects and verbs, may be compound.

subject	verb	direct object
The florist	delivered	sprays of forsythia, bunches of violets, and a wreath of spring flowers.

In addition to the direct object, certain verbs (usually involving an act of giving or telling) may take an INDIRECT OBJECT, a complement that receives whatever is named by the direct object.

The flowers gave the family solace.

What did the flowers give? *Solace* is the direct object. Who received the solace? *Family* is the indirect object—the receiver of what is named by the direct object. The same meaning can be expressed by a phrase beginning with *to* or *for:*

The flowers gave solace to the family.

He offered me his handerchief.

He offered his handkerchief to me.

I wrote her an elegy.

I wrote an elegy for her.

Direct and indirect objects are called OBJECT COMPLEMENTS. A SUBJECT COMPLEMENT follows a linking verb and completes the predicate by giving another name for the subject or by describing the subject.

My grandmother was the mayor of our town.

Mayor cannot be called the direct object of the verb since it is merely another name for *my grandmother,* and it can be made the subject of the sentence without changing the meaning. "The mayor of our town was my grandmother." To appreciate the difference between object and subject complements, change the verb:

My grandmother scolded the mayor.

The direct object, *mayor,* now names a person other than the subject, one who is acted upon by *my grandmother.* Making *mayor* the subject of this sentence changes the meaning considerably. A noun that serves as a subject complement of a linking verb is called a PREDICATE NOUN. Linking verbs may also be completed by an adjective that describes the subject. Such a subject complement is called a PREDICATE ADJECTIVE.

The mayor was attractive and popular.

Attractive and *popular* describe the subject, *mayor,* but instead of being directly attached to the noun ("an attractive, popular mayor"), they are joined to it by the linking verb *was* and become predicate adjectives. Keep in mind the fact that a subject complement follows a linking verb, an object complement follows a transitive verb, and that the subject is always in the nominative case, the object in the objective case. Thus: It is *I;* it is *he;* it is *she.* It bothered *them;* it troubles *me.*

5. Phrases

A PHRASE is a group of two or more words that functions in the sentence as a single word but does not have a subject and a verb of its own. Phrases may be named for the kind of word around which they are constructed—prepositional, participial, gerund, or infinitive. Or they may be named by the way they function in the sentence—as adjective, adverb, or noun phrases. Phrases are a common and useful means of modifying.

Carrying banners and flowers, a group **of schoolchildren** marched **at the funeral.**

The first phrase, a participial one, modifies the subject, *group,* which is also modified by the second phrase, which is prepositional. The last prepositional phrase modifies the verb, *marched.*

PREPOSITIONAL PHRASES

A PREPOSITIONAL PHRASE consists of a preposition joined to a noun or a pronoun which is called the object of the preposition. Such phrases usually modify nouns or verbs, and they are described accordingly as adjective or adverb phrases.

	adjective		adverb
The leader	of the band	swayed	in the sun.
The walk	from the church to the cemetery	lasted	over an hour.

VERBALS AND VERB PHRASES

A VERBAL is a form of the verb that does not function as a verb but as some other part of speech. It is important to distinguish verb forms ending in *-ing* and *-ed* when they function as part of the verb, as in "I was turning around," from when they function as adjectives to modify a noun, as in "a turning point" or "a turned ankle." A verbal that modifies a noun is called a PARTICIPLE. Note that a participle may be in the past or in the present tense—"a *used* car with *splitting, worn* upholstery."

A verb form that functions as a noun is called a GERUND: "Writing is his passion." In this sentence, *writing* is the subject of the sentence. Gerunds may also be used as the objects of verbs or of prepositions.

object of verb	object of preposition
He loves **writing**	and amuses himself by **scribbling dull verses.**

A third type of verbal is the INFINITIVE, the present form of the verb preceded by the preposition *to*: to write; to scribble. Infinitives are frequently used as nouns—as subject or object of the verb.

subject	object
To publish was his ambition, but he forgot **to enclose** his manuscript.	

Since they are verb forms, participles, gerunds, and infinitives may take objects and they may be modified by adverbs or by prepositional phrases. A verbal with its modifier and its object, or subject, makes up a verbal phrase and functions as a single part of speech, but it does not make a full statement.

Participial Phrase **Moved by the spirit of her life and the dignity of her death,** my friend proposed that the town build a monument to my grandmother.

Here the participle "moved," modified by a prepositional phrase, describes "my friend."

Gerund Phrase **Selecting an inexpensive and appropriate site** took considerable time.

Here the phrase—gerund, object, and the modifiers of the object—is the subject of the sentence.

Infinitive Phrase The task required us **to walk for hours.**

The infinitive has a subject, "us," and a modifying prepositional phrase, "for hours."

ABSOLUTE PHRASES

An ABSOLUTE PHRASE is a group of words that has a subject but no verb and is not grammatically connected to the rest of the sentence. The subject of an absolute phrase is frequently followed by a participle.

The site having been selected, we met to choose a sculptor.

A tree, **all things considered,** is a better monument than a statue.

His brow creased with anger, his hands clenched on the table, the chairman insisted on having his way.

He being in this frame of mind, we decided to postpone the vote.

The subject of an absolute phrase may also be followed by an adjective or a prepositional phrase:

She recounted the incident, **her voice angry, her face pale, her eyes tearful.**

We listened quietly, **our hearts in our mouths.**

We left the room, **all hopes of a peaceful settlement in shambles.**

Because absolute phrases are formed by the suppression of connecting elements—prepositions ("*with* our hearts in our mouths") or subordinating conjunctions and the finite verb ("*when* all things *are* considered")—they have a toughness and economy that can be a virtue in writing. Moreover, the emphasis given to verbals in many absolute constructions lends vitality to the sentence. They are invaluable for rigorous subordination and for lively descriptive writing.

APPOSITIVE PHRASES

An APPOSITIVE is a noun, or noun substitute, added to explain another noun. "My grandmother, *the mayor*, was the subject of controversy all her life." Appositives with their modifiers make up phrases, since they function as a unit to give further information about a noun.

> The memorial she wanted, **a grand magnolia tree**, now stands in the center of town.

> The townspeople, **wise and practical citizens**, made the decision, **a radical one for that time and place.**

Appositives, like absolute constructions, compress connections by eliminating words. The last sentence could have been written, "The townspeople, who were wise and practical citizens, made the decision, which was a radical one for that time and place," with a considerable loss of punch.

6. Clauses

A CLAUSE is a group of words that contains a subject and a predicate and which makes a statement. Except for elliptical questions and answers, every sentence must contain at least one clause.

INDEPENDENT AND DEPENDENT CLAUSES

Although all sentences must contain a clause, not all clauses are sentences. Some clauses, instead of making an independent statement, serve only as a subordinate part of the main sentence. Such clauses, called DEPENDENT (or subordinate or relative), perform a function like that of adjectives, adverbs, or nouns. INDEPENDENT CLAUSES, on the other hand, can stand alone as complete sentences. They provide the framework to which modifiers, phrases, and dependent clauses are attached in each sentence. Any piece of connected discourse is made up of a series of independent clauses.

"She heard the news" is a clause because it has a subject, *she*, and a verb, *heard*. It is an independent clause because it is complete in itself and can stand alone as a sentence. "When she heard the news" is also a clause because it has a subject and a predicate, but it is a dependent one. The addition of the word "when" creates a condition of incompleteness or dependency. Any reader will expect to be told what happened when she heard the news.

dependent clause	independent clause
When she heard the news	she was delighted

Dependent clauses are usually connected to the rest of the sentence by RELATIVE PRONOUNS (*who, which,* or *that*) or by SUBORDINATING CONJUNCTIONS such as *while, although, as, because, if, since, when,* or *where.* The terms "relative" and "subordinating" remind us that clauses introduced by these words are not self-sufficient: they are related or subordinated to the main or independent clause of the sentence. Written separately, they are fragments. Dependent clauses function like parts of speech. They can be subjects and objects (like nouns), and (like adjectives and adverbs) they can be modifiers.

NOUN CLAUSES

A NOUN CLAUSE functions as a noun in a sentence. It may be a subject or a complement in the main clause, or the object of a preposition or of a gerund.

Noun clause as subject of the sentence

That she was considered for the position at all is remarkable.

Noun clause as direct object of the verb

She said that she would accept only under certain conditions.

Noun clause as object of the preposition

We will give the job to whoever is best qualified.

Noun clause as object of a gerund

We do best for ourselves by asking what we can do for others.

ADVERB CLAUSES

An ADVERB CLAUSE is a dependent clause used to modify a verb or an adjective or an adverb in the main clause.

Adverb clause modifying a verb

I work whenever I feel like it.

Adverb clause modifying an adjective

The work was more difficult than I had anticipated.

Adverb clause modifying an adverb

We completed the project sooner than we expected.

ADJECTIVE CLAUSES AND RELATIVE PRONOUNS

An ADJECTIVE CLAUSE is a dependent clause used to modify a noun or a pronoun.

Adjective clause modifying a noun

He showed us his library, which includes the first editions of Dorothy Sayers.

Adjective clause modifying a pronoun

He, who was the last to know of the plans, was the first to object.

Adjective clauses are usually introduced by relative pronouns, which serve both as pronouns and as subordinating conjunctions. Here's how they work.

Dorothy Sayers wrote many books; the books were widely read.

This sentence consists of two independent clauses, but it would be more idiomatic to substitute a pronoun for the second "books."

Dorothy Sayers wrote many books; they were widely read.

If, instead of using the pronoun *they*, we substitute the relative pronoun *that*, the second clause becomes dependent, and the sentence itself becomes more tightly subordinated.

Dorothy Sayers wrote many books that were widely read.

"That were widely read" no longer will stand as an independent sentence. Joined to the first clause, it functions as an adjective, modifying "books."

The relative pronouns *who* (and *whom*), *which*, and *that* always have two functions: they serve as subordinating conjunctions, connecting dependent clauses to independent ones, but they also function like nouns, as subject or complement in the dependent clause. Often, relative pronouns can be omitted: "She is a person I cherish." But just as often, they need to be expressed. "He thought to be educated we should read good books" is awkward, but "He thought that to be educated we should read good books" is not.

5b

Types of Sentences

Sentences are traditionally classified, according to their structure, as simple, compound, complex, and compound-complex.

1. Simple Sentences

A SIMPLE SENTENCE consists of one independent clause with or without modifying words or phrases but with no dependent clauses attached.

          subject   verb
Simple Harvey   despaired.

              modifying phrase   subject   verb
Simple Nervously biting his fingernails,   Harvey   despaired

          modifying phrase
of ever learning grammar.

          modifying phrase
Simple Nervously biting their fingernails,

          compound subject
Harvey and his girlfriend, Zelda,

              modifying phrase
puzzled once more by the red correction marks on their papers,

         compound predicate with modifying phrase
despaired of ever learning the fine points of grammar and
longed for the simple beauty of differential calculus.

Obviously, simple sentences can be quite elaborate as the subject or the verb is modified with verbals and appositives. Still, such sentences can be reduced to a simple kernel and, as such, are limited in expressing complicated ideas or showing the relation of one idea to another. Simple sentence following simple sentence leads to tedious writing at best, at worst to what in writing is called a "primer style." The straightforward thrust of the simple declaration should be modulated by the careful use of other types of sentences.

2. Compound Sentences

The COMPOUND SENTENCE consists of two or more independent clauses joined by a coordinating conjunction or by a semicolon.

	independent clause		independent clause
Compound	He wrote for hours,	and	his hunger vanished.

	independent clause	independent clause
Compound	His style was graceful;	his sentences were lively and varied.

Compound   independent clause
His roommate left the shower running,   but

independent clause
he did not notice.

The compound sentence has the advantage of balance and antithesis. Skillfully used, it creates parallelism and coordination.

3. Complex Sentences

The COMPLEX SENTENCE contains one independent clause and one or more dependent clauses, which express subordinate ideas.

       dependent clause
Complex   Because he was tired and hungry and discouraged,

       independent clause
he did not want to rewrite the paper.

	independent clause	dependent clause
Complex	Ideas for writing come	when we least expect them.

	independent clause	dependent clause
Complex	Still, he put pen to paper,	while his roommate sang in the shower.

The complex sentence has the advantage of flexibility; it can be arranged to produce a variety of sentence patterns and to indicate subtle relationships between ideas. It also provides selective emphasis, since the subordination of dependent clauses throws the weight of the sentence on the main clause. Complex sentences are indispensable to expository writing, which is the most common in college courses, and an understanding of when and how to subordinate is fundamental to constructing effective sentences.

4. Compound-Complex Sentences

When a compound sentence contains one or more dependent clauses, the whole is described as a COMPOUND-COMPLEX SENTENCE.

Compound-Complex

independent clause
He was surprised

dependent clause
when the water rose above his tennis shoes,   but

independent clause
he went on writing.

Compound-Complex

dependent clause
Although he was drenched to the bone,

independent clause
he typed up the paper,   and

dependent clause
while his roommate bailed out the room,

independent clause
he read the manuscript with damp but cheerful satisfaction.

5c

Standard Sentence Patterns

The basic pattern of the English sentence, as we have seen, is subject-verb-complement.

S	V	C
She	wrote	the book

Many of our written sentences—and most of our spoken ones—with variously placed modifying phrases follow this typical line. It is forthright, clear, and predictable. Practiced writers, aware of how this pattern can be altered, sometimes reverse subject and complement; reverse complement and verb and eliminate the subject altogether; begin the sentence with the main idea; conclude the sentence with the main idea. Writing that is interesting to read explores all possible sentence patterns for emphasis, for rhythm, and for variety and the surprise of change of pace.

1. Active and Passive Voice

Most of the time we speak and write in the active voice:

> She wrote the book.
>
> He read and reviewed the book.
>
> The critics praised it.

A verb is in the ACTIVE VOICE when the grammatical subject of the sentence is the one who does the action of the predicate. *Who* wrote the book? (*she* did); who read and reviewed it? (*he* did). Occasionally, we want to emphasize that which is acted upon, so we place the complement in the subject position:

> Her book was nominated for the Pulitzer Prize.
>
> Only exceptional books are chosen.

In these sentences the doer of the action—nominating, choosing—is unknown or irrelevant to the statement being made. To write "A jury nominated her book for the Pulitzer Prize" is to place undue emphasis upon an anonymous group of people to the detriment of "her book," which the sense of the sentence seems to insist is more important and, therefore, should occupy the important subject position. The thrust of the statement, of course, could make "jury" of more interest than "her book": "A hastily selected jury, which later was accused of favoritism, nominated her book for the Pulitzer Prize." Here the sense of the sentence puts the emphasis firmly on "jury," so it is in the subject position and the verb is in the active voice. Note that in the noun clause ("which . . . favoritism"), where the fact that the committee was charged is more consequential than who made the charge, the verb is in the PASSIVE VOICE.

There is no right or wrong use of the passive or the active voice. The conventions of scientific and technical writing dictate frequent use of the passive voice, since it is the experiment and not the performer of the experiment that is significant:

> A cubic centimeter of water was added to the solution, and the test tube was heated. The experiment was conducted under adverse conditions, and the results were considered worthless.

In most writing the doer of the action is important, and the sentence should declare who she or he is. Because passive constructions are formed by the past participle and a form of the verb "to be," the predicate is more wordy than a predicate in the active voice. The performer of the action must be mentioned in a prepositional phrase—"by me," "by the committee"—which adds to the number of words in the sentence. Overuse of the passive voice can lead to wordy, flabby assertions:

Weak	Classics like *Middlemarch* will always be appreciated by readers.
Weak	The question "Who ever reads an American book?" was asked by an English critic in the nineteenth century.
Weak	The "Book of Love" was written by whom?

Translated into the active voice, these sentences are concise and forceful.

Strong	Readers will always appreciate classics like *Middlemarch.*
Strong	"Who ever reads an American book?" an English critic asked in the nineteenth century.
Strong	Who wrote the "Book of Love"?

Another hazard of passive constructions is the DANGLING MODIFIER.

Dangling   Having read everything on the subject and having conducted
a number of experiments, the paper on the "Book of Love"
was finally begun.

The adjective phrase that begins the sentence has no subject to modify. Obviously, "the paper" did not read or conduct experiments, although that is literally what the sentence says. Rewriting the sentence in the active voice and naming the subject of the action eliminates the flaw.

Correct   Having read everything on the subject and having conducted
a number of experiments, I finally began the paper on the
"Book of Love."

A good style is a blend of the active·and passive voice, with the active voice predominating. Some statements seem to demand passive constructions:

The game **was cancelled** because of rain.

After much debate, the measure **was defeated.**

Grades **will be posted** at ten o'clock.

In these sentences the object rather than the agent of the action requires emphasis, and the passive voice is appropriate. Be alert during revisions for the inadvertent, vague passive—the voice that is shirking the responsibility of judging and making, often on the basis of little evidence, some rather grand assumptions. "It has been decided that," "it is known," "agreement has been reached," "it was thought" are constructions that should be challenged with the question, *by whom?* The introduction of the agent of the action into the sentence may result in sharper thinking and more exact phrasing.

Vague   It was thought that the world's natural resources were in-
exhaustible.

Clear   Only a handful of the relatively few people who considered the
question thought that the world's natural resources were in-
exhaustible.

2. Loose and Periodic Sentences

A LOOSE SENTENCE puts the main idea first and adds qualifications and supplemental information at the end.

> I began to keep a journal when I discovered that my life was interesting, my dreams colorful, and my thoughts rather remarkably profound.

The major assertion, "I began," initiates the sentence with an independent clause; additional information follows in the dependent clause beginning, "when."

A PERIODIC SENTENCE suspends the main point until all the subordinate details have been mentioned.

> When I discovered that my life was interesting, my dreams colorful, and my thoughts rather remarkably profound, I began to keep a journal.

The sentence begins with the dependent clause, which gives reasons for and explains the main assertion *before* stating what that assertion is. The periodic sentence is usually suspenseful and conclusive, since the weight of the statement falls on the long-awaited predication.

We generally speak in loose sentences, making a statement and then adding, almost as afterthoughts, reasons and qualifications for what we said. Loose sentences are more characteristic of contemporary prose, and our feeling that some writing sounds "old-fashioned" often comes from our uneasiness with the long, periodic sentences favored by many writers in the past. Because they are artful and deliberate, such sentences give writing the effect of thoughtful arrangement. Placed strategically after a series of loose sentences, the periodic sentence, surprising the reader by reversing the expected pattern, makes an emphatic impression.

Once again, no one can prescribe when to use a loose sentence, when a periodic one. Learn which is which and analyze your style to see what type you favor. If you almost always write loose sentences, strengthen the periodic muscle with exercise, even if at first such sentences feel awkward. Your writing will be the better for it.

Exercise 3

Pick out the subjects and verbs in the following sentences. Identify direct objects, indirect objects, predicate nouns, and predicate adjectives.

1. As a wedding present, my uncle gave us a picture.
2. It was an original sketch by Dufy.
3. The technique was interesting, since Dufy had used only a few simple lines.
4. It seemed an early work, according to a friend to whom I showed it.
5. We hung it in the living room and it looked good.
6. I wrote my uncle a note and thanked him for the picture.
7. We enjoyed it for several months, until my friend told us its value.
8. Then we worried about burglars, and we wrote my uncle again asking if he would give us a less valuable picture.

Exercise 4

a. Pick out the phrases in the following sentences. Identify them as preposi-tional, participial, gerund, infinitive, or appositive, and be ready to describe their function in the sentence.

1. On Tuesday I came home expecting to drive my car, a shiny new convertible, into the garage.
2. To my surprise, I found a ditch between the street and the driveway.
3. A crew of workers had begun to lay a new water main along the curb.
4. Hoping that I would not get a ticket for overnight parking, I left the car in the street in front of the house.
5. For three days a yawning trench separated me from my garage.
6. Finding a place to park was difficult, since all the neighbors on my side of the street were in the same predicament.
7. By Friday the workers had filled up the ditch, but my car, stained with dust and dew, looked ten years older.
8. I had to spend the weekend washing and polishing it.
9. My wife, a strong advocate of justice, suggested sending the city a bill for the job.
10. My refusal convinced her that men are illogical, improvident, and eas-ily imposed upon.

b. Find the simple subject and verb of each clause in the following sen-tences. Point out the main clauses and the dependent clauses, and be prepared to state the function in each sentence of each dependent clause.

1. The movie director who did much to perfect the one-reel Western as a distinct genre was D. W. Griffith.
2. Shortly after he had entered movies in New York, Griffith achieved immediate success with his first film, which he directed in 1908.
3. Between 1908 and 1913, while he was directing Westerns, Griffith con-

tinually worked with techniques which, though they had been introduced by others, were developed and refined by him.

4. Griffith was delighted by the Western because it offered opportunities
   for spectacle and scope.

5. He found that the Western was an ideal genre in which to experiment
   with close-ups and with cross-cutting, the techniques he employed to
   build narrative suspense.

6. Some critics have pointed out that Griffith was more interested in
   dramatic situations which lent themselves to lively visual treatment
   than he was in the details of plot or conventional justice.

7. He would willingly let the villains go free whenever he felt the dramatic situation warranted it.

8. The close-up of the outnumbered settlers grimly hanging on and the
   panoramic view of the battle seen from afar were characteristic Griffith
   shots.

9. In 1915, Griffith produced *The Birth of a Nation*, the first great spectacle movie.

10. It made use of many of the techniques he had developed while he was
    making one-reel Westerns.

Exercise 5

*Classify the following sentences as simple, compound, complex, or com-
pound-complex. Identify the subject, verb, and complement, if any, of
each clause. Describe the function of each dependent clause.*

1. When Renaissance physicians began to study human anatomy by
   means of actual dissection, they concluded that the human body had
   changed since the days of antiquity.

2. Galen, an ancient Greek physician, was generally accepted as the authority on anatomy and physiology.

3. His theory of the four humors, blood, phlegm, bile, and black bile, was
   neat and logical, and authorities had accepted it for centuries.

4. Similarly, his account of the structure of the human body, revised by
   generations of scholars and appearing in many printed editions, was
   generally accepted.

5. If dissection showed a difference from Galen's account, the obvious
   explanation was that human structure had changed since Galen's time.

6. One man who refused to accept this explanation was Andreas Vesalius,
   a young Belgian physician who was studying in Italy.

7. Asked to edit the anatomical section of Galen's works, Vesalius found
   many errors in it.

8. Galen's statement that the lower jaw consisted of two parts seemed wrong to Vesalius, who had never found such a structure in his own dissections.

9. He finally concluded that Galen was describing the anatomy of lower animals—pigs, monkeys, and goats—and that he had never dissected a human body.

10. When he realized that Galen could be wrong, Vesalius began a study that came to be recognized as his major work: a fully illustrated treatise on the human body based on actual observation.

6

REWRITING SENTENCES

a Sentence Unity
b Concise Sentences
c Parallel Structure

When we begin to write it is important to put down ideas as rapidly as they come to mind so that we do not lose one thought, one detail in the rush that often accompanies the creative process. Or, if we are temporarily blocked, it is helpful to free-associate on paper, to nudge the mind toward the unobstructed flow of words. At this preliminary stage of writing it doesn't matter whether or not sentences are well shaped or even shaped at all. Fragments and fused sentences may sprawl on the page; mixed constructions and problematic parallelism may reveal the mind of the writer trying out the logical relationship of ideas. Such is the crude material with which every writer then sits down to the hard work of revision.

"Rewriting," the novelist Henry James said, "is rethinking." Perhaps this is why it is so difficult, for rethinking demands that we examine every statement to see if it is saying exactly what we want it to say. Few sentences will survive this rigorous scrutiny intact. Testing what we think about a topic, we grope for words and stumble over structures, but in rethinking we cross out and rearrange, shift parts, add and cut, polish and hone to make each sentence coherent, concise, and unified.

6a

Sentence Unity

A well-organized sentence makes a main point and produces a single effect. It can contain many details if the subordinate relationship of them to the major idea is made clear by the grammatical structure. Here are the details that a good writer gathered into one clear and efficient sentence:

The barber's pole originally represented an arm or leg wrapped in bandages. Barbers were also the surgeons in those days. The jars of colored water in a chemist's shop represented the medicines and elixirs offered for sale. Three gold balls are the traditional sign of a pawnbroker. They originally indicated the shop of a banker or moneylender. Most villagers in those days could not read. The signs indicated where these essential services could be found.

Here is the final product:

The barber's pole (originally intended as a limb swathed in bandages), the chemist's coloured jars, the banker's three gilt balls, were marks of identification for those (and they were most of the village) who could not read.

—Louis Kronenberger

A sentence is not a container designed to hold all the available information on a subject, although some sentences read as if their authors had that impression:

The earliest known examples of sculpture date from the Old Stone Age, which was more than 20,000 years before the time of Christ and is sometimes called the Paleolithic Period, making sculpture one of the oldest arts known to man, many pieces of ancient sculpture having been found in caves or old burial grounds in various parts of the world.

The main point of this sentence seems to be the great antiquity of the art of sculpture. The following sentence stresses that idea and subordinates or eliminates all other details.

Improved   Sculpture is one of the oldest arts known to man: the earliest examples, found in caves or burial grounds, go back to the Old Stone Age, more than 20,000 years ago.

It is common to lose sight of the main point in first-draft sentences and to allow unrelated ideas to intrude. Good rewriting requires the elimination of everything that does not contribute to the point being made.

Disunified   The critical response to *Wuthering Heights*, which was written in 1847 and which, like many another classic, has been relegated to the shelves of young adult fiction, changed radically when Charlotte Brontë, who wrote *Jane Eyre* and three other novels, revealed that her sister, Emily, was the author.

The present treatment of *Wuthering Heights* in libraries may or may not be related to the change in critical response. Another sentence, perhaps even another paragraph, should make that point clear. Although it is interesting information that Charlotte Brontë wrote four novels, it is not relevant to the main idea of the sentence, which is how critics changed their minds about a novel once they discovered that it had been written by a woman and not a man, as Brontë's pseudonym, Ellis Bell, had led them to believe.

> Unified   The critical response to *Wuthering Heights* changed radically when Charlotte Brontë revealed that her sister, Emily, was the author.

A sentence should be to the thought it expresses as a map is to the terrain it describes. Often in unsuccessful sentences the relationship between two ideas is obscured or only implied by the structure. The reader of such a sentence fails to see connections and gets lost, much as the reader of a faulty map does.

> Obscure   Being from Honolulu, I am not used to putting on a parka and putting up an umbrella the minute it starts raining.

The sentence suggests the interesting if unintended generalization that all people living in Honolulu are averse to parkas and umbrellas, which would be difficult, even pointless to prove. The writer has omitted a logical step in the cause-and-effect relationship, which the rewritten version includes:

> Clear   Since I come from Honolulu, where the rains are warm and refreshing, I am not used to putting on a parka and putting up an umbrella the minute it starts raining.

A writer can also assume connections that the sentence should make explicit:

> Obscure   Maturing faster because of parents' divorcing does not hold true in all cases, and a child may become timid and insecure.

The causal relationship between a child's shock at divorce and his or her emotional maturity needs to be clearly stated.

> Clear   The shock of a divorce may contribute to the maturity of a child or retard that maturity by making the child timid and insecure.

1. Excessive Detail

Some sentences are very long, some short, some of moderate length. A sentence should be constructed to hold compactly what it has to say in as many words as it needs to say it.

> When the cry for woman's suffrage was first heard, there was immediate opposition to it, which continued for a long time until men finally began to realize that women were entitled to the vote, and in 1920 the Nineteenth Amendment was ratified.

This sentence tries to say too much about the beginning of the woman's suffrage movement, opposition to it, continued opposition, gradual change of public opinion, and the ratification of the Nineteenth Amendment. It should be broken down into at least two sentences.

> When the cry for woman's suffrage was first heard there was immediate opposition to it, and this opposition continued for a long time. Gradually, however, men realized that women were entitled to the vote, and in 1920 the Nineteenth Amendment was ratified.

2. Primer Sentences

Earlier we described the habitual use of simple, declarative sentences as "primer style." The term is derived from the primer books that taught us how to read in the early grades. Most of us can still chant by heart, "See Dick throw the stick to Spot. Spot is chasing the stick. Run, Spot, run!" Seldom do such naive patterns turn up in college writing, but some apprentice writers have the tendency to rely on short, uncomplicated sentences that put every detail and idea in a main clause. But all ideas and facts are not of equal weight, and the structures we choose should reflect this disparity. Less important elements should be put into subordinate constructions—dependent clauses, participial phrases, or appositives. Ideas of equal importance should be put into coordinate constructions.

3. Coordination and Subordination

The prefixes of these two important grammatical terms explain the different sort of ordering each construction provides: *co* (same) and *sub* (under) *ordinare* (to arrange in order). Coordinate arrangements express equality, sameness, or balance by means of the coordinating conjunctions, *and, but, or, for, nor.* Subordinate arrangements express inequality among sentence parts and rank these parts in relation to each other by means of such subordinating conjunctions as *since, when, unless, because, while.* The term *subordination* also refers to all those sentence elements—phrases, clauses—which modify by tucking into the sentence additional, elaborating information.

Many sentences deftly combine coordination and subordination.

> Since we must and do write each our own way, we may during actual writing get more lasting instruction not from another's work, whatever its blessings, however better it is than ours, but from our own poor scratched-over pages.
>
> —EUDORA WELTY

This is a complex sentence, which, with the use of the subordinating conjunction *since*, subordinates the opening, dependent clause as the explanation of the independent clause that follows. Within this diagonal frame the writer has placed a number of coordinate or balanced or horizontal elements.

```
must
      and
do                      write
not from      another's work
                        whatever its blessings
                        however better it is
but from      our own
                        poor
                        scratched-over pages
```

Readers feel a sense of balance and equity when they read such a sentence and (better still for the writer) the inclination to agree with it.

4. Faulty Subordination and Coordination

The more a writer practices, the more the habits of coordination and, especially, subordination become easy, even automatic. There are, however, hazards along the way to finding the best arrangement in words for our thoughts. The coordinate or subordinate constructions we select must be suitable to the ideas they are expressing. If not, the reader will sense a discrepancy between the subject of the sentence and its form. We must be careful not to coordinate elements that are not equal to each other, thus leaving the reader with a false sense of parity between ideas.

> **Faulty** In English courses we had to learn many rules of grammar, and few of these rules are taken seriously today.

The writer of this sentence is hedging on the important question of what these two ideas have to do with one another. One or the other deserves more emphasis, which can be shown through subordination.

> **Correct** In English courses we had to learn many rules of grammar, **few of which are taken seriously today.**
>
> **Correct** Few of the rules **that we had to learn in English courses** are taken seriously today.

Each of these sentences subordinates in a different direction, but each avoids the mistake of the first sentence, which implied, with the coordinator *and*, that the ideas are balanced. Equally distracting is the sentence that ranks its main idea in a subordinate position as a dependent clause or a modifying phrase.

> **Faulty** Ruth Benedict is the author of *Patterns of Culture*, in which she praises the Zuñi Indians for their ceremonial life and its cooperative attitude toward the natural world.

That Benedict wrote a book, *Patterns of Culture*, is clearly not the main idea of this sentence, but the predication of the independent clause implies as much. What she does in the book is the important idea of the statement, and the sentence should be phrased to reveal that.

> **Correct** In her *Patterns of Culture*, Ruth Benedict praises the Zuñi Indians for their ceremonial life and its cooperative attitude toward the natural world.

The title of the book is subordinated in the introductory phrase to the important assertion, which is that Benedict praises a certain manner of life.

The context finally determines which ideas are important and which are by-the-way. A personal narrative might well subordinate otherwise significant facts to the experience of the writer.

> I read yesterday that George Eliot, who created some of the most powerful women characters in literature, didn't much like women herself. Gwendolyn Harleth in *Daniel Deronda,* that frightening portrait of a strong-willed, but vain and self-absorbed woman, reminded me of myself and my constant need to look in a mirror. If George Eliot came into a party I was attending, would she want to sit down on the couch beside me?
>
> —Student Journal

A more formal analysis of Eliot's characters, of her attitudes toward women in fiction and in life, would require the subordination of personal experience to judgments about the writer and the work.

> George Eliot, who didn't much like women herself, created some of the most powerful women characters in literature. Gwendolyn Harleth in *Daniel Deronda* is the portrait of a strong-willed, but vain and self-absorbed woman, like me, who constantly needs to be assured by her reflection in the mirror.

The initial phrasing of a statement may bury the real subject in a subordinate part of the sentence. After discovering in the first or second draft what the purpose and thrust of your essay is, go over each sentence to see if the real subject is the grammatical subject.

> We can readily see how fame was achieved by Chief Joseph of the Nez Percé Indians whose famous surrender statement—"I will fight no more forever"—proves that language does not have to be grammatical to be eloquent.

The real subject of this sentence is Chief Joseph and his statement; the real predicate is "proves." As the sentence stands, however, "we" is the subject and "can see" is the predicate. The independent clause that begins this sentence is simply a windy windup to what the writer finally manages to say in the last subordinate clauses. The sentence should begin where it ends.

> The famous statement by Chief Joseph of the Nez Percé Indians—"I will fight no more forever"—proves that language does not have to be grammatical to be eloquent.

Overuse of the passive voice often leads to a false subject, which can make the sentence confusing as well as wordy.

Confusing   The changes that **had been made** in the conservation bill by the Committee **were accepted** by the Senate, which voted to pass the bill.

One can hardly tell what happened here. Who did what? The real subject is "the Senate"; what it did was to pass a bill, and the sentence should be written accordingly.

Clear   The Senate passed the conservation bill as amended in committee.

Beginning a sentence with "There is . . ." or "It is . . ." is a common idiomatic construction.

Correct   There is no reason to doubt his honesty.

"There" is an introductory word; the grammatical subject is "reason."

Correct   It is true that he had been drinking at the time.

In this idiomatic construction, "it" anticipates the actual grammatical subject, the clause "that he had been drinking." The writer uses this construction to imply that a concession is being made.

Used unnecessarily or simply as a means of filling up the page, this idiom can lead to awkward, weak, and repetitious sentences.

Weak   It was to no avail that I made an effort.

Weak   It was in the year 1909 that Selma Lagerlöf became the first woman to receive the Nobel Prize for Literature.

Weak   There are a large number of people who still read her novels.

Emphasizing the subject of the sentence results in these brisk versions.

Strong   My effort was useless.

Strong   In 1909 Selma Lagerlöf became the first woman to receive the Nobel Prize for Literature.

Strong   Many people still read her novels.

Exercise 1

Revise the following sentences by putting the main ideas in main clauses and less important ideas in subordinate clauses. Be prepared to explain why you have chosen certain ideas as the main ones and to explain the form of subordination you have used.

1. An especially big wave rolled in, when I finally managed to get my line unsnagged.
2. Nellie Sachs, co-winner with the Israeli writer S. Y. Agnon of the Nobel Prize for Literature in 1966, fled Nazi Germany in 1940.
3. The ocean was choppy, causing the fishermen to have little luck and to return to the pier disappointed.
4. The population of Latin America, ranging from Indians who live as their ancestors did hundreds of years ago to highly educated women and men in the modern cities such as Buenos Aires and Rio de Janeiro, is varied.
5. He was trying to kill a bee inside the car, driving off the road as a result.
6. Contact lenses are worn next to the eyeballs and have advantages over ordinary glasses, since contact lenses are invisible, are kept unfrosted by the eyelids, and correct faulty corneas.
7. The horse came to the first jump, where he stumbled and threw Janet off.

Exercise 2

Revise the following sentences by subordinating the less important ideas. Be prepared to explain the choices you make and the form of subordination you have used.

1. The potter must roll the clay out on a flat surface, and a surface that the clay will not stick to.
2. Five hundred citizens were too many to meet at one time, and so instead the Council was divided into ten smaller groups.
3. The job was interesting, and the pay was good, but finally I decided not to accept it and I regretted my decision later.
4. Gertrude Stein and Hemingway were contemporaries, and Stein was one of the first to recognize Hemingway's genius as a writer.
5. Scientists are continually developing new photographic equipment, and now they have devised ways of photographing planets as far away as Saturn by rockets that relay the pictures back to Earth.
6. I got the note from my parents, and I gave it to my teacher, but he just scowled at me, but finally he said I could take the afternoon off.

Exercise 3

Revise the following student sentences by eliminating the excessive subordination.

1. In 1666 when he sent a beam of white light through a glass prism which broke the beam up into bands of colored lights which resembled a rainbow, Isaac Newton showed that what we normally think of as white light is actually made up of light that consists of different colors, a discovery that revolutionized the science of optics, which was in its infancy before Newton.

2. When I bought my parrot from the pet store on the Mall, where I had visited several times and spent hours gazing at the cages because I so badly wanted a bird of my own, I was so excited that I could hardly contain myself as I rushed home to begin training him from the booklet which I had also bought at the store.

3. At the beginning of the story, which takes place in Sicily at some unknown time in the past, Verga makes us realize that the main character is called "La Lupa," which means the wolf, because the villagers are superstitious people who believe in the devil and other evil forces that can take human form.

Exercise 4

Revise the following sentences to improve their unity. Be prepared to explain the changes you have made.

1. I usually enjoyed an appointment with my dentist, and she would make me feel good because she complimented me on my teeth.

2. The swimming pool was intended for college students only, but is now open to townspeople as well.

3. The train was late, causing me to miss my appointment and lose the client.

4. The picture that won first prize was in water color. It was an abstract painting. Most people criticized it, but the judges liked it.

5. The first book I consulted lacked an index, and next I tried an almanac.

6. The Greek word *papyros* originally meant thin sheets of paper made from a certain Egyptian reed, from which we have borrowed our modern word *paper* and which now means any kind of writing material.

7. The United Nations, which was founded in San Francisco more than thirty-five years ago when many of the major diplomats of the world were there, has increased greatly in size, many of the new members being the small nations which have recently gained their independence.

8. Freud grew up in Vienna, doing some of his most creative psychoanalytic research in that city.

9. There were about ten women out for field hockey, and we only had four weeks before our first match, so we worked very hard to get in

condition, but three of our best players caught the flu and so we didn't do well against our opponents.

10. The match burned his fingers. He tried to light his pipe in the wind, and he dropped it on the ground when he burned himself.

6b

Concise Sentences

Waste in writing, as in anything else, dilutes, weakens, demoralizes. A sentence that spills more words on the page than its sense justifies pollutes a reading environment that is already littered with verbiage. Wordiness in student writing is often caused by the requirements of an assignment—write 250, 500, 1,000 words—a mandate that seems to emphasize quantity rather than quality. Teachers, however, do not want to read unnecessary words any more than students should want to write them. When you begin to write, forget about the suggested length of the paper. Concentrate, rather, on getting the best effect from the fewest words.

There is a difference, of course, between brevity and conciseness. Brevity is not always a virtue; conciseness always is. Any statement can be made brief by omitting detail, but details are often essential and must be included. Concise writing states the necessary details without wasting words.

Brief The market dropped.

Concise The stock market fell fifteen points today, the sharpest decline in seven years.

Wordy By the time trading stopped on Wall Street, the stock market had fallen down fifteen points, which was significant because it was the sharpest decline since a similar drop seven years ago.

Wordy constructions flourish in free-writing and in first drafts as we find out what we want to say and the most efficient means of saying it. No harm is done if we can recognize what is deadwood and ruthlessly cut it away. Phrases used in casual speech as fillers between thoughts are as unconscious as clearing one's throat, but, like the distracting noises made during a recording, they should be erased in editing. Here are some common examples of deadwood in writing:

in today's society	it is thought to be true that
proceeded to	at this point in time
it is my opinion that	it is my intention to discuss
in this day and age	let me say that
in conclusion I will say	the point I have been making is
what I am trying to say is	a person by the name of
in the field (or area) of	

Answering a young man's question about how to become a good stylist, the English writer Sydney Smith once said, "You should cross out every other word. You have no idea what vigor it will give your style." The advice, though exaggerated, makes a fine point. In revising, writers should cross out every word that is not essential to what they are saying. Look at the following student sentence and note how many words are simply filling up space.

> Just recently, a man by the name of Alexander Solzhenitsyn addressed the graduation class at Harvard University with an unconcealed and overt attack on life in America today, and claimed that we are spoiled and pampered and debilitated to the point of weakness, and that as individuals we lack the courage of our convictions and moral strength.

"Recently" does not need the intensive "just." To name is to assert that this is "a man by the name of." "Unconcealed" and "overt" mean virtually the same thing, and the writer might well ask whether "attack" needs either of these modifiers, since it would be difficult in a graduation address to secretly attack a way of life. "Debilitated" means exactly what the superfluous prepositional phrase following it says. "Courage of our convictions" is trite, and what, the scrupulous stylist might question, is the difference between that phrase and "moral strength"?

Rethinking this sentence begins with finding the subject and the predicate and determining whether or not they are the main assertion. "A man" is the subject; "addressed and claimed" is its compound predicate. Is the fact that a man addressed the graduating class the important idea, or is it rather what this address *did*, which was to attack the complacency of Americans? Even with Solzhenitsyn restored to the subject position, the sentence still claims that he "addressed" the class "with an attack," a predication that, upon examination, doesn't make much sense. The student, hesitant to make a judgment, has disguised what should be the verb of the sentence as a noun, the object of the preposition "with." Beginning the sentence with the new subject-verb kernel "Solzhenitsyn attacked" will enable the writer to cross out everything that does not contribute to that assertion.

> Recently, in an address to the graduating class at Harvard, Alexander Solzhenitsyn, the exiled Soviet writer, attacked life in America, claiming that we are spoiled and pampered and that we lack moral strength.

The writer decided that the compound predicate of the original was not appropriate, since the new verb "attacked" is stronger than "claimed." "Claimed" in the revised sentence becomes the participle "claiming," which retains the energy of the verb but now functions as a modifier. The fifty-six words of the original sentence have been trimmed to the thirty-three of the rewritten one, even with the added detail "exiled Soviet writer," which the student, considering the audience and the context, decided was necessary.

1. Redundant Phrases and Clauses

The word REDUNDANCY, cherished by teachers and editors, means "overflowing"; words that carelessly repeat what has already been said are redundant. Readers are seldom misled by such writing, but they are certainly bored and irked by it.

Wordy   When the poet writes in his poem that the character was never "odd in his views," he means to imply that the man was a conformist, accepting the standards of his society in all aspects.

Concise   When the poet writes that the character was never "odd in his views," he implies that the man was a conformist.

Much redundant phrasing results from spelling out the meaning of a word that can and should stand alone. "Conformist" means "accepting the standards of society."

Wordy   Over the years, she became suspicious that she was being exploited by people who wanted to take advantage of her and use her.

Wordy   The criticisms I will make are major ones which ought to be given careful consideration because of their importance.

> Wordy   We like to be appreciated and admired for our talents **which we possess** and we hope to be praised for our achievements **that we have attained as individuals.**

In the last sentence the writer wasted nine words defining the pronoun "our." Some other redundant phrases include:

attractive **in appearance**	red **in color**
connected **up** with	refer **back** to
expert **in the field of**	repeat **again**
the reason **why**	several **in number**
our modern society **of today**	retangular **in shape**
at this point **in time**	the reason **is because**

2. Unnecessary Repetition

REPETITION is not necessarily a flaw in writing. In fact, as you will see in the discussion of parallel structure, writing that gracefully repeats phrases and words pleases the ear and reminds the reader of what is being said. However, unnecessary repetition sounds awkward and looks cumbersome.

> Wordy   The question **of** who is to be considered needy is **a** hard **question** to answer.

> Concise   The question who is to be considered needy is hard to answer.

> Wordy   If one examines the **story** carefully, **one** will find that the hidden symbolism in the **story** makes the **story** stand for something more than **one** first found in the **story.**

> Concise   If one reads the story carefully, one will discover a symbolism that deepens it.

The rewritten sentences are leaner, stronger, more muscular; in concise prose, as in a well-trained body, every part is in prime working condition.

6c

Parallel Structure

The human eye and the human ear lean toward balance and harmony. We like matchings and pairs, equity, pattern, and order. Once a major chord is struck in a piece of music, we expect to hear it again, just as we appreciate looking at surfaces where planes and colors complement one another. In writing, this ordering of like element with like element is called PARALLELISM or PARALLEL STRUCTURE. Sound parallel structure balances word with word, phrase with phrase, subordinate clause with subordinate clause. Read the following sentence slowly as if you were saying it aloud:

> The cunning and attractive slave women disguise their strength as womanly weakness, their audacity as womanly timidity, their unscrupulousness as womanly innocence, their impurities as womanly defencelessness; simple men are duped by them, and subtle ones disarmed and intimidated. It is only the proud, straightforward women who wish, not to govern, but to be free.
>
> —G. BERNARD SHAW

The first independent clause of Shaw's compound sentence states its subject and predicate simply. The phrases functioning as the direct objects of the verb (*What* do these slavish women disguise?) have exactly the same construction because they are grammatical equals. Since they are coordinate and could be connected by the conjunction *and*, they are in parallel construction.

However, the parallelism of Shaw's stylish sentence does not end there. In the independent clause following the semicolon, "simple men" are balanced against "subtle ones." "Duped," "disarmed," and "intimidated" form a series. The two clauses of the sentence are themselves constrasted in parallel fashion. The active voice of the first clause ("disguise") is balanced against the passive verbs of the second ("are *duped* . . . *disarmed* and *intimidated*"). The voices are perfectly appropriate to the aggression of the first clause, the passivity of the second.

The brisk second sentence parallels the direct objects of the verb in the adjective clause following "women"—the infinitives "to govern" and "to be free"—by means of the correlatives "not . . . but." Moreover, the series of adjectives ("cunning and attractive"), which defines the subject of the first clause ("slave women"), parallels that which describes the "women" of the second sentence ("proud, straightforward"). Shaw ingeniously suggests the inequality between the two types of women by replacing "and," which connects the first set of adjectives, with the comma of the second. A new rhythm is established. The sentence seems to stride away from the thick luxuriance of its predecessor as if to contrast, by a slight alteration in parallel structure, the langour of the manipulative women with the vigor of the women who would be free.

Parallel structure both compares and contrasts, affirms ("both . . . and") and negates ("neither . . . nor") by putting sames or opposites in similar constructions. Perhaps the fact that we have two eyes, two legs, two sides of the brain, two hands ("on the one hand . . . on the other") accounts for our pleasure when elements are balanced and our irritation when they are askew. Whatever the reason for our attraction to equality and balance, parallelism is indispensable in good writing. Here are some guidelines for fashioning parallel sentences.

1. Coordinating Conjunctions

All sentence elements joined by the coordinating conjunctions *and, or, nor, for, but* should be in like grammatical structures. Balance nouns with nouns, phrases with phrases, clauses with clauses.

Faulty   He likes to read all the books he can lay his hands on and writing whenever the mood hits him.

The reader is jarred by the faulty parallelism of the infinitive "to read" with the gerund "writing." Rewriting them as the same part of speech creates parallel structure.

Parallel   He likes to read all the books he can lay his hands on and to write whenever the mood hits him.

Parallel   He likes reading all the books he can lay his hands on and writing whenever the mood hits him.

Faulty   Students in composition classes are taught to read with attention and that coherent essays must be written.

The conjunction *and* connects an infinitive phrase and a subordinate clause beginning with *that*—structures that are certainly not parallel.

Parallel   Students in composition classes are taught to read with attention and to write coherent essays.

The sentence could be phrased to emphasize the parallelism even more.

> **Parallel** Students in composition classes are taught to read with attention and to write with coherence.

Sometimes a part of the sentence that should be parallel to another part is so far away that the writer forgets to balance.

> **Faulty** I try to stay awake in English class, fortifying myself with coffee, pinching myself at intervals, hanging by my fingernails on the professor's every word, but still falling asleep.

The *but* must be followed by an independent clause, to balance the one beginning the compound sentence.

> **Parallel** I try to stay awake in English class, fortifying myself with coffee, pinching myself at intervals, hanging by my fingernails on the professor's every word, but I still fall asleep.

2. Elements in a Series

Every element in a series should be parallel to every other element.

> **Faulty** I concluded that she was intelligent, witty, and liked to make people uncomfortable.

The first two elements are adjectives; the second is a predicate—a verb with an infinitive phrase as a complement. The imbalanced series can be mended by making all three elements adjectives:

> **Parallel** I concluded that she was intelligent, witty, and malicious.

Or the sentence can be rewritten by inserting another *and* to make clear which elements parallel which.

> **Parallel** I concluded that she was intelligent and witty and that she liked to make people uncomfortable.

3. Repetition of Words

Often we need to repeat a conjunction, preposition, or other preceding word to make a parallel construction clear.

> **Faulty** My adviser told me that I spent far too much time worrying about what was expected of me and I needed more confidence in myself.

Parallel	My adviser told me **that** I spent far too much time worrying about what was expected of me **and that** I needed more confidence in myself.
Faulty	Because she had been teaching for twenty years and she could remember being a student herself, I listened to her advice.
Parallel	**Because** she had been teaching for twenty years and **because** she could remember being a student herself, I listened to her advice.

If a preceding word is omitted, the sentence can be quite misleading.

Faulty	The vineyard is often visited by tourists who sample the grapes and connoisseurs of wine.
Parallel	The vineyard is often visited **by** tourists who sample the grapes **and by** connoisseurs of wine.

4. Correlatives

Some conjunctions, called correlatives, occur in pairs: *either . . . or, neither . . . nor, not only . . . but also, both . . . and.* Be sure to place the first correlative so that the construction that follows will parallel the construction after the second correlative.

Faulty	William Blake is not only famous for his poetry, but also for his illustrations.

"Not only" is followed by the adjective "famous" with a prepositional phrase modifying it. "But also" is followed by a prepositional phrase. Thus the two are not parallel. In the rewritten version "not only" is placed where it belongs.

Parallel	William Blake is famous **not only** for his poetry, **but also** for his illustrations.
Faulty	He either is a liar or a remarkably naive person.
Parallel	He is **either** a liar or a remarkably naive person.
Faulty	The legislature hoped both to raise taxes and stimulate business.

Placing "both" after "to" would make the two verbs parallel, but it would produce an awkward split construction: "to both raise . . . ." A smoother sentence would result from adding another "to."

Parallel The legislature hoped **both to** raise taxes and **to** stimulate business.

5. Subordinate Clauses

A subordinate clause, which is not parallel to the main clause, should not be connected to it by *and* or *but*.

Faulty She is a woman of strong convictions and who always says what she thinks.

The clauses can be put in proper relationship to one another either by omitting the coordinating conjunction:

Correct She is a woman of strong convictions, who always says what she thinks.

or by writing two subordinate clauses and connecting them with *and*:

Parallel She is a woman who has strong convictions and who always says what she thinks.

Sentences with faulty parallel structures such as the following often show up on first drafts. They are easily mended.

Faulty In the middle of the sleepy village is a statue dating from 1870 **and which** shows General Lee on horseback.

Parallel In the middle of the sleepy village is a statue **which** dates from 1870 **and which** shows General Lee on horseback.

Faulty He appeared before the committee with a long written statement, **but which** he was not allowed to read.

Parallel He appeared before the committee with a long written statement **but he** was not allowed to read it.

The relative *which* clause is rewritten as the main clause and the elements are parallel.

6. Sequence of Ideas

Elements that are parallel in structure should also be parallel in sense. Used carelessly, a parallel construction can lead to an illogical series or an awkward sequence of ideas.

Faulty   Her slumping business, her many friends, and even her husband Sam could in no way offer her a chance to find the happiness she had known while in college.

The three items are not parallel in meaning. A woman might reasonably be expected to find a chance for happiness in those closest to her, her friends and her husband. She would hardly be expected to find happiness in a "slumping business."

Correct   Her friends and even her husband Sam could in no way offer her a chance to find the happiness she had known while in college.

Faulty   During her last year in law school, she rose to the top of her class, worked on the legal review, and broke her engagement the day after graduation.

The last element in this sequence is not logically parallel to the others.

Parallel   During her last year in law school, she rose to the top of her class and worked on the legal review. The day after graduation she broke her engagement.

Exercise 5

One way to alert yourself to wordy sentences is to write them deliberately. For each sentence in the following exercises, give yourself 5 points if you succeed in making it wordier without adding anything to the meaning. Perfect score 100.
a. Pad out each of the following sentences by using the passive.
   1. The women's volleyball team won all of its home games last season.
   2. Lock all doors and leave the keys at the desk.
   3. The Valley String Quartet decided to hold extra rehearsals during the week and agreed to postpone other activities.
   4. She cut the wood with her ax.

5. Some college students choose medicine as a career as early as the beginning of their sophomore year.

b. *Pad out each of the following sentences by adding dead phrases or clauses.*
   1. Many writers dislike personal publicity because the lionizing keeps them from their work.
   2. The apartment rooms were small, boxlike, and painted in a hideous green.
   3. The City Council agreed to work with the Board of Education to determine the principles for zoning schools and homes.
   4. In 1960, Kennedy won by a very small plurality.
   5. Sometimes I study from 8 P.M. to 2 A.M.

c. *Pad out each of the following sentences by using the verb* to be *and a clumsy complement to replace the precise verb.*
   1. I like musical comedies and I collect record albums of them.
   2. David Riesman, author of *The Lonely Crowd,* thinks many Americans lack a firm sense of individuality.
   3. Mrs. Spaulder lives in Cincinnati but practices law in the suburbs.
   4. Distance bicycling requires stamina and ten gears.
   5. He has given up cigarettes and now he feels better.

d. *Pad out each of the following sentences by expanding the modifiers into phrases and clauses.*
   1. A *mano* is a hand stone for grinding corn in a large hollowed stone *metate.*
   2. A biographer lacks the artistic freedom of a novelist because the biographer cannot invent her characters or move them about as she pleases.
   3. Since Paul was tired when he took the Civil Service examination, he missed several easy questions and did poorly on familiar topics.
   4. A number of educational theories and practices still regarded as dangerously "modern" and "progressive" date back to Rousseau.
   5. If my mother, born in the Kentucky backwoods, had stayed there and spoken only with her childhood friends, she would never have had to change her speech habits; only when she moved north and began associating with teachers and business people did she realize how much people scorned her grammar and pronunciation.

Exercise 6

Reduce the wordiness in the following student sentences. Be prepared to explain your changes.

1. It is my intention to be affiliated with some large automobile manufacturer in connection with sales of cars and accessories.
2. There are all too many instances of condemnation of a person by other human beings before "sufficient knowledge" has been found.
3. I was especially interested in going to the University of Southern California because of the fact that it was near home.
4. Respect is the individual's personal ability to be aware of another person's unique individuality.
5. Owing to the fact that quick action was taken by this employer, a major crisis was averted.
6. He is often thought to have a lack of responsibility; hence, he is not trusted to any great extent by those who know him.
7. I am now very sorry that I didn't find reading a meaningful and worthwhile experience when I was younger.
8. The reason that Lincoln kept in close contact with his generals by writing them letters was that he felt that he was responsible as commander-in-chief for the running of the war.

Exercise 7

Identify the cause of faulty parallelism in each of the following sentences and make the needed correction.

1. Applicants for the position must be United States citizens, willing to work abroad, and qualify under security regulations.
2. In the remedial reading clinic he learned how to coordinate his eye movements, how to scan for information, and how frequent reviewing for key ideas helps.
3. The opera's opening performance was spirited, colorful, and with many people attending.
4. During the summer, they planned to hitchhike along Route 40, to stop at interesting places, and take sidetrips whenever they felt like it.
5. Joan of Arc was either regarded as a patriotic martyr or a crazed fanatic.
6. The flasks were difficult to fill, not only because their necks were narrow but also they were slippery and hard to hold.
7. The bumper crop of rice neither helped the farmer nor were the customers helped.
8. At the campground we met a Mr. Osborn from somewhere near San Francisco and who had his whole family with him.
9. And on these hunting trips, Sam teaches the boy when to kill and when not to, ability, patience, and endurance.

10. If you get ambitious, you might even shoot nine holes of golf from your new four-cylinder golf cart, or with your neighbor go bowling at that new air-conditioned alley, or you might even go and play miniature golf.

7

REVISING SENTENCES

After rethinking and rewriting the sentences of the first draft, the writer comes in composition to the important step of revision. Revision is "seeing again." It is a task best accomplished a day or two after the rewritten manuscript is put aside, allowed to settle and to separate itself from the writer's hand. When we revise, we are trying to see where in our writing a phrase is misleading, where a shift in point of view or in tense might confuse the reader. Rewriting is mostly for the benefit of the writer, who thinks, argues, connects, persuades, and whose every sentence should reflect accurately the thought and the judgment behind it. In revision we have the reader chiefly in mind. Whatever we find that will distract, annoy, or bewilder those persons who will read our manuscript must, through revision, be eliminated or changed.

7a

Pronoun Reference

A pronoun is a substitute for a noun. The noun that it stands for is called the ANTECEDENT because it goes (*cedere*) before (*ante*) the pronoun. As you read over your sentences with an eye to revising them, examine every pronoun to make sure there is no confusion as to what its antecedent is.

1. Ambiguous Reference

When persons of the same sex are mentioned in the sentence, there can be confusion about which one the pronoun refers to:

Unclear   The novelist Virginia Woolf assured her sister Vanessa, who
            was a painter, that she was a great artist.

*We cannot be sure whether or not Woolf was assuring her sister that
she (Woolf) or Vanessa was a great artist.*

Correct   The novelist Virginia Woolf told her sister Vanessa, who was a
            painter, "You are a great artist."

Do not use a pronoun in such a way that it might refer to either of
two antecedents. If there is any possibility of doubt, revise the
sentence to remove the ambiguity.

Unclear   In *Nostromo* Conrad's style is ironic and his setting is highly
            symbolic, so that it sometimes confuses the reader.

Does "it" refer loosely to Nostromo, *Conrad's style, his setting, or to a
combination of these? Banishing the pronoun from the sentence, the
writer is forced to say exactly what he or she means.*

Correct   Conrad's ironic style and highly symbolic setting in *Nostromo*
            sometimes confuse the reader.

Correct   In *Nostromo*, Conrad's style is ironic, and his highly symbolic
            setting sometimes confuses the reader.

*Each of the sentences is now clear and each is saying something differ-
ent from the other.*

2. Remote Reference

A pronoun too far away from its antecedent may cause misreading.
Either repeat the antecedent or revise the sentence.

Unclear   Each sonnet in the sequence "Sonnets from an Ungrafted
            Tree" tries to describe her attempts to rekindle a dead flame
            and to ignite the passion she and her husband had once had
            for each other and how they all come to end at the same point
            at which they started.

The "theys" of the last part of the sentence are meant to refer to
"attempts," but between that word and the pronoun are "flame"
and "passion" and "she" and "her husband." The reader is not to
be blamed for thinking that they all "came to end at the same
point at which they started." In revising, the writer repeated the

noun and tightened up the wording of the last clause of the sentence.

Correct   Each sonnet in the sequence "Sonnets from an Ungrafted Tree" describes her attempts to rekindle a dead flame and to ignite the passion she and her husband once had for each other; each shows, too, how *these attempts* failed the moment they began.

Sometimes the noun to which a pronoun refers cannot logically be its antecedent.

Incorrect   The Tzotzil Indians are only nominal Catholics, using its symbols and adapting them to the traditional Mayan religion.

The antecedent of "its" has to be inferred from the noun "Catholics," which means people who belong to a church and not the institution itself with its symbols and names.

Correct   The Tzotzil Indians are only nominal Catholics, using the symbols and the names **of the Church** and adapting them to the traditional Mayan religion.

Make sure the pronoun is not placed next to a word that cannot possibly be its antecedent.

Incorrect   The botanist told us the plants' names which were all around us.

Clearly, names were not sprouting out of the ground, which is what the sentence says.

Correct   The botanist told us the names of the **plants that** were all around us.

3. Broad Pronoun Reference: *this, that, which*

In speech we often use the relative pronouns, *this, that,* or *which* to refer broadly to the idea of the preceding clause or sentence. In writing, however, such loose pronoun reference can be misleading or confusing. If the preceding clause contains a noun that might also be mistaken for the antecedent, the reference may be ambiguous as well. If there is any doubt in your mind about whether or not the reader may wonder what is the word or phrase to which a *this*, a *that*, or a *which* refers, revise the sentence to eliminate the pronoun or to give the pronoun a definite antecedent.

Unclear   The beginning of the book is more interesting than the conclusion, which is unfortunate.

On first reading, the pronoun *which* seems to refer to *conclusion*, even though conclusions are not usually described as fortunate or unfortunate. The writer wants the *which* to refer to the whole idea of the main clause, but the noun at the end gets in the way. Revised, the sentence might read:

Correct   Unfortunately, the beginning of the book is more interesting than the conclusion.

The pronoun has been eliminated and the sentence is crisper for it. In the following sentence, the *which* is being made to stand for more than it can clearly express.

Unclear   In the eighteenth century, more and more land was converted into pasture, which had been going on to some extent for several centuries.

The inclusion of a noun in the revised version to name again what the *which* is referring to both defines and reiterates the idea.

Correct   In the eighteenth century, more and more land was converted into pasture, **a process which** had been going on to some extent for several centuries.

The vague pronoun reference has been cleared up by adding *process*, a noun that summarizes the idea of the main clause and gives the pronoun *which* an antecedent.

The pronoun *this* should not be used as the beginning word in a sentence that follows another sentence of great length and complication.

Unclear   She was so blinded by her desire that she disregarded the fact that the small flame would soon die out, and nothing would be left to burn but the wood which was too wet to burn. **This** does not mean that she wanted to accept this fate.

To begin to revise the second concise but confusing sentence, the writer should ask: this *what*? That she was so blinded? That she disregarded the fact? That the small flame would soon die? That nothing would be left to burn but the wet wood? Even *this* used demonstratively, "this fate," is unclear, since we are not sure whether the fate refers to the woman's or to the fire's. The revision depends on what the writer means.

> Correct   Such blindness, however, did not mean that she wanted to accept the extinguishing of the flame.

> Correct   This disregard, however, did not mean that she wanted to accept the fact that her marriage was over.

4. Indefinite Use of *it, they, you*

English contains a number of idiomatic expressions using the impersonal pronoun *it*: "It is hot," "It rained all day," "It is late." The pronoun *it* is also used clearly in sentences like "It seems best to go home at once," in which *it* anticipates the real subject, *to go home at once*. Avoid, however, the unexplained *it*, the *it* that needs a clear antecedent and has none.

> Unclear   Lewis Thomas, author of *Lives of the Cell*, is a physician and writer who spends his spare hours practicing **it**.

> Correct   Lewis Thomas, author of *Lives of the Cell*, is a physician who spends his spare hours practicing writing.

The indefinite use of *they* is always vague; it can sound childish or paranoid.

> Unclear   If intercollegiate sports were banned, **they** would have to develop an elaborate intramural program.

Who, the writer should rigorously ask, are *they*? And answer by revising the sentence:

> Correct   If intercollegiate sports were banned, **each college** would have to develop an elaborate intramural program.

Watch out for the vague, accusatory *they*, which can swell to dark proportions.

Unclear At registration they made us line up on the outside of the gymnasium and wait until they called the first letter of our last names; they made some of us stand in the rain for hours.

Be exact in describing the event and in assigning responsibility:

Correct At registration we had to line up on the outside of the gymnasium and wait until a monitor called the first letter of our last names; some of us had to stand in the rain for hours.

The indefinite use of the pronoun *you* to refer to people in general is widespread in conversation: "Joan Didion writes that some people think that if you have pins in your underwear you haven't got self-respect." Formal usage still prefers the impersonal pronoun *one* to *you*, although some translations into that pronoun sound somewhat ludicrous:

In her essay "Self-Respect" Joan Didion writes that some people think that if one has pins in one's underwear one hasn't got self-respect.

If the *one* pronoun seems stilted, try casting the sentence in other words:

In her essay "Self-Respect" Joan Didion writes that some people think that pins in underwear and self-respect are mutually exclusive.

Overreliance on the broad *you* pronoun creates a point of view that alienates the reader from the writer.

Self-respect is your sense of pride, your confidence, and your acknowledgement of your own worth; it can be measured in your respect for others and for yourself, whether you're throwing a football or taking a test.

5. Awkward Use of *his or her*

English has no singular pronoun to refer to both male and female persons. One would logically and in accordance with reality follow a noun like "student" or "human being" with "his or her" or even "his/her" to indicate that these categories include members of both sexes. Some people feel that to write "Each student is responsible for his/her books" is awkward, and some people feel that even "his or her books" is repetitious.

In the past it has been accepted that the masculine pronoun can stand for both sexes: "Each student is responsible for his books," just as *man* has been understood to mean the human race, including both men and women. Recently, however, writers and publishers have begun to eliminate discriminatory language practices— words or constructions that may reflect the dominance of the male in history. Women argue, with justice, that they are being ignored when a writer uses *his* to refer to both men and women, and many feel that terms such as *congressman* or *policeman* help to perpetuate the false assumption that these positions are occupied only by men.

To avoid such misrepresentation, substitute alternative terms with no indication of gender: *member of congress, representative* or *senator, police officer.* The plural pronouns *they, their, them* and neutral terms such as *one, person, people* may also be used.

Students are responsible for their books.

People in England like unchilled beer. (Rather than "The Englishman likes his beer unchilled.")

In England one usually drinks unchilled beer.

A problem arises with the use of indefinite pronouns such as *each, every, any, some,* and their compounds, *somebody, anyone,* which are singular, take singular verbs, and must have singular pronouns refer to them. In conversation, we generally say "Everybody should bus their tray," since we mean all of us, and all of us is more than one. The conventions of English require that in edited writing *everybody* be followed by *he* or *she.* Once again *she or he* or the visibly spliced pronoun *s/he,* which some publishers have recently adopted, will, in most cases, be the more accurate designation. Whatever alternative you choose, consider your audience. If your readers will be alienated by *he/she,* use *he* to refer to both sexes. If your audience will feel excluded by such usage—and, remember, in a college English class women often comprise more than half of the population—find a suitable pronoun form with which all of you will feel comfortable. If you wish to draw attention to the problem and to alert your readers to how ingrained language habits are, try using *she* to refer to the indefinite pronoun. If nothing else, the reading of your paper should generate a lively response.

Exercise 1

Revise the following sentences to correct the ambiguous reference of pronouns.

1. The runner lunged toward the tape, threw out his chest, and snapped it.
2. In the course of the argument, Jack told his father that he needed a new car.
3. It wouldn't hurt people to read about criminals because they live in a different kind of world and they don't have to follow their example.
4. Both parents were there when the twin brothers graduated together, and we couldn't help noticing how happy they were.
5. Under Roosevelt's leadership, the Democratic party, which had not really been united under one president for some years, came together effectively for a time. Historians tend to agree that this was a case of the right man at the right moment.
6. The hives buzzed with activity, and the beekeeper covered himself with netting before going after the honey and then motioned for us to follow at a distance. It was about fifty feet away.
7. In Joyce's novel, he delights in complex puns and in playing with words.
8. The spider gently shook the strands of his web as he scurried toward the fly and the moth. Although they were barely visible, they were obviously strong.
9. Engineering is the profession that applies scientific knowledge to the building of such things as bridges, harbors, and communication systems. This is my ambition.
10. Ethics must not be understood to be the same thing as honor because this is not the case.
11. When there is no harmony in the home, the child is the first to feel it.
12. Most of the students at the work camp were inexperienced, and many of them had never seen raw poverty before, but on the whole they were up to it.
13. It says in the brochure that in England they drink tea instead of coffee.
14. Fielding's *Shamela* successfully used farcical incident and character development as tools for his satire in the novel.
15. Since the white settlers held the Indians to be of no significant value,

they regarded their rights as equally nonexistent. This is exemplified by several incidents in Kroeber's account.

7b

Dangling Modifiers

A modifier, you will recall, is a word or phrase that functions in the sentence to modify, that is, to limit, qualify, or restrict another word or group of words. If there is no word or group of words in the sentence for the modifier to qualify or limit, the modifier is said to DANGLE, as in the following sentence.

Dangling Having eaten our lunch and waited an hour to digest our food, the lake felt cool and pungent on that first hot afternoon of summer.

The literal syntax of this sentence states that the lake, well fed and well digested, felt cool on a summer afternoon. Of course, that is not what the writer meant, but the subject the modifying phrase is intended to limit—"we" or "the picnikers" or "the class of eighty-four"? (there is no way of knowing)—is not in the sentence. "Lake," then, is the only possible body, even if it is of water, for the participial phrase "having eaten our lunch and waited an hour to digest our food" to modify.

Almost all dangling modifiers occur at the beginning of the sentence, and almost all result from carelessness or oversight. Once detected, they can be mended in either of two ways.

1. By supplying the noun or pronoun that the phrase logically modifies.

modifier

Correct **Having eaten our lunch and waited an hour to digest our food,**
word modified
we plunged into the lake, which was cool and pungent that first hot afternoon of summer.

2. Or by changing the dangling construction into a complete clause:

Correct After we had eaten our lunch and waited an hour to digest our food, we swam, that first hot afternoon of summer, in the cool and pungent lake.

1. Dangling Participial Phrases

Participial phrases are verbal modifiers that function in the sentence as adjectives do. Like adjectives, they should be placed next to the words they modify.

Dangling Analyzing Joan Didion's style, her essay seemed to me to be cool, detached, and uncommitted to purpose or point of view.

It is unlikely that an essay will analyze the style of the author who wrote it, but that, in effect, is what this sentence says. The writer has tossed off the participial phrase without examining its function in the sentence. Perhaps this was meant:

Correct Analyzing Joan Didion's style, **I discovered** that the writing, especially in this essay, was cool, detached, and uncommitted to purpose or point of view.

Sometimes a dangling participial phrase indicates that the writer has not thought the idea through to its logical subordinate structure.

Correct After I analyzed Joan Didion's style, I discovered that the writing, especially in this essay, was cool, detached, and uncommitted to purpose or point of view.

Dangling modifiers at the end of a sentence are less frequent than those at the beginning, but they are often confusing and always awkward.

Dangling The mountains were snow-covered and cloudless, flying over the Rockies.

Correct Flying over the Rockies, we saw snow-covered, cloudless mountains.
OR:

Correct When I flew over the Rockies, the mountains were snow-covered and cloudless.

2. Dangling Gerunds

A gerund is a verb form ending in *-ing* that is used as a noun. A gerund phrase dangles when the subject of the gerund is not apparent to the reader.

Dangling   After explaining my errand to the guard, an automatic gate swung open to let me in.

Obviously, a gate cannot explain an errand to a guard or to anyone else. There is nothing in the sentence to indicate who is doing the explaining.

Correct   After explaining my errand to the guard, I drove through the automatic gate, which had opened to let me in.
OR:

Correct   After I had explained my errand to the guard, an automatic gate swung open to let me in.

Often dangling gerunds result when the gerund functions as the object of a preposition, and the grammatical subject of the main verb would not be the subject of the gerund were the gerund to take a subject.

Dangling   In writing a term paper, notes should be carefully entered on 3 × 5 cards.

The subject of the main verb "should be entered" is "notes," which could not possibly be the subject of "writing."

Correct   In writing a term paper, one (or *we* or *the writer*) should carefully enter notes on 3 × 5 cards.

3. Dangling Infinitives

An infinitive is a verb preceded by the word *to*, and is said to dangle when the subject of its action is not expressed.

Dangling   To be considered for college, the aptitude test must be taken.

Correct   To be considered for college, a student must take the aptitude test.

This faulty construction is similar to the dangling gerund. Its revision is equally simple.

Always look carefully at an infinitive phrase to make certain that *who* is doing the action is clearly expressed.

Dangling   To develop a lively writing style, all kinds of sentence structures should be used.

Correct   To develop a lively writing style, the writer should use all kinds of sentence structures.

"Sentence structures" are not going to develop "lively writing styles" as the faulty sentence claims, but writers are, and the sentence should make that agency clear.

4. Dangling Elliptical Clauses

Sometimes we omit the subject and main verb from a dependent clause and write *while going* instead of *while I was going*, or *when a child* instead of *when he was a child*. Such shorthand phrasing results in an elliptical clause which is perfectly acceptable as long as its subject is made clear in the rest of the sentence. If the subject of an elliptical clause is not stated, the construction may dangle.

Dangling   When six years old, my grandmother died.

Dangling   At the age of six, my grandmother died.

Correct   When I was six years old, my grandmother died.

In both faulty sentences, the implied subject of the elliptical clause, "I," is omitted. The addition of the subject and verb eliminates the dangling modifier and, unlike the other two, makes sense.

The implied subject of the elliptical clause can be the subject of the main clause. If so, that subject status should be made clear.

Dangling   While hitting high E, a white wine glass was shattered by the tenor.

Correct   While hitting high E, the tenor shattered a white wine glass.

Dangling   Do not add the beans until thoroughly soaked.

Correct   Do not add the beans until they have been thoroughly soaked.

Dangling modifiers are common problems in student writing for two related reasons: first, the English language does not have an expression like the German *Man* or the French *on* that functions as an indefinite pronoun. Its closest equivalent, *one*, sounds stuffy and stiff. *You* is too narrow a pronoun; *we* too sweeping. Sensing this lack in the language, the apprentice writer lapses into the passive voice and forgets that the verbal phrase with which he or she began the sentence now has no suitable noun for the phrase to modify.

Awareness of how a sentence is put together is the beginning of the solution, as it is for most writing problems. The writer who continues to have difficulty with dangling modifiers should make it a practice to write every sentence in the active voice. Such a writer should also learn to identify verbals and know how they function in the sentence. Once we understand the pattern that leads to dangling modifying phrases, we can revise sentences so that there is no confusion about who is doing what to whom. And when we spot such a sentence as

> Dangling   Revising my paper, the passive voice was discovered to be the culprit responsible for dangling modifiers.

we can revise it to read:

> Correct   Revising my paper, I discovered that the passive voice was the culprit responsible for dangling modifiers.

5. Permissible Introductory Expressions

Some verbal phrases, such as *to begin with, judging from past experience, considering the situation, granted the results,* or *to sum up,* have become well established and need not be attached to any particular noun.

> Judging from past experience, he is not to be trusted.
>
> Granted the results, what do they prove?
>
> To sum up, all evidence suggests that the decision was a fair one.

An absolute phrase should not be confused with a dangling modifier. Such a phrase consists of a participle with a subject (and sometimes a complement) grammatically unconnected with the rest of the sentence and usually telling when, why, or how something happened.

> His mind preoccupied with his marital problems, William forgot his lunch date with the chancellor.
>
> The dinner for the new athletic director started late, the guest of honor having been caught in the five o'clock traffic.

Exercise 2

Revise the following sentences to eliminate the dangling modifiers.

1. When waiting for the dentist, every sound from the office is nerve-wracking.
2. After correcting my original calculations, the problem was finally solved.
3. Having seen Beckett's *Waiting for Godot,* my attitude toward modern drama has changed completely.
4. The directions were clear, and my trouble could have been prevented, if followed correctly.
5. After hurrying to answer the phone, the operator told the woman the other party had hung up.
6. In order to see the comet in detail, a small telescope was set up in the backyard.
7. The zoning petition was widely supported, after having canvassed many people in the neighborhood and stirred up concern about the proposed high-rise apartment building.
8. Being covered with plastic, I did not expect the car seats would be cool, having sat in the hot parking lot for several hours.
9. At last able to earn my car insurance, my parents allowed me to buy my own car.
10. Although tired and out of practice, the last set of the tennis match was too much of a personal challenge for me to resist.

7c

Misplaced Modifiers

Modifiers dangle when there is no word or group of words within the sentence for them to modify. A modifier is misplaced if it is not close to the word it is intended to modify. In English, word order is crucial to meaning. Adjectives, adverbs, and phrases or clauses that function as modifiers are placed close to the words they are intended to limit or define:

She read **quickly** and **carelessly** the **printed** notice **that came in the mail.**

The difference that the placement of a modifier makes in a sentence becomes clear if we observe what happens in the following sentence when the adverb *only* is moved about:

The notice said **only** [said **merely**] that clients were invited to see the exhibit on the third floor.

The notice said that **only** clients [clients **alone**] were invited to see the exhibit on the third floor.

The notice said that clients were invited **only** [invited for the **one** purpose] to see the exhibit on the third floor.

The notice said that clients were invited to see the exhibit on the third floor **only** [the third floor **alone**].

Many modifying phrases and clauses can be moved around to various positions in the sentence. An introductory clause, for example, can be shifted from the beginning of a sentence to the middle or the end.

Whatever the public may think, I am sure that Picasso will be remembered as one of the greatest artists of our times.

I am sure, **whatever the public may think,** that Picasso will be remembered as one of the greatest artists of our times.

I am sure that Picasso will be remembered as one of the greatest artists of our times, **whatever the public may think.**

This freedom, however, has its dangers. Movable modifiers may be placed so as to produce misreadings or real ambiguities. Unlike the dangling modifier, which cannot logically modify any word in the sentence, the misplaced modifier may seem to modify the wrong word or phrase in the sentence:

Misplaced   She wrote the full story of her harrowing escape from memory.

Unless the writer meant the rather unlikely statement that the author was freed from her own memory, the sentence should read:

Correct   She wrote from memory the full story of her harrowing escape.

To avoid the appearance of rather grotesque images on your paper, put modifying phrases as close as possible to the nouns they modify.

Misplaced   Peacefully nibbling on the lawn, Jim found his pet rabbit.

Correct   Jim found his pet rabbit peacefully nibbling on the lawn.

Misplaced   Broken down, rusty, and out of gas, she abandoned the car on the country road.

Correct	She abandoned the car, which was broken down, rusty, and out of gas, on the country road.

Be especially careful that adverbs are placed exactly where they belong in the sentence.

Misplaced	He scolded the student for cheating **severely**.
Correct	He **severely** scolded the student for cheating.
Misplaced	I have followed the advice **faithfully** given by the manual.
Correct	I have **faithfully** followed the advice given by the manual.

1. Squinting Modifiers

Modifiers are said to squint or to look two ways at once when they are placed so that they might refer to either a preceding word or a following word in the sentence.

Squinting	The child who lies **in nine cases out of ten** is frightened.
Correct	**In nine cases out of ten,** the child who lies is frightened.
Squinting	The tailback who injured his knee **recently** returned to practice.
Correct	The tailback who **recently** injured his knee returned to practice.
Correct	The tailback who injured his knee returned **recently** to practice.
Squinting	He searched around and found an old bus schedule **that was out of date** in the drawer.
Correct	He searched around and found in the drawer an old bus schedule **that was out of date.**

The placement of the noun clause gives the impression that only in the drawer is the bus schedule out of date. Placing the prepositional phrase next to the verb it modifies makes for a precise and clear sentence.

2. Split Constructions and Infinitives

It is best not to separate the parts of tight grammatical constructions. The insertion of a modifier between the parts of a verb phrase or an infinitive can give the reader an awkward jolt.

Split	The operator told him that he **should,** if he expected to get his call through, **place** it soon.
Correct	The operator told him that he **should place** his call soon if he expected to get it through.
Split	I, more than the rest of the class, have been in a panic since the term paper was assigned.
Correct	More than the rest of the class, I have been in a panic since the term paper was assigned.

SPLIT INFINITIVES—that is, infinitives with a modifier between the *to* and the verb (**to personally supervise**)—may be awkward, especially if the modifier is long.

Awkward	I should like to, if I ever get the chance, take a trip to Reno.
Correct	I should like, if I ever get the chance, **to take** a trip to Reno.

Frequently, however, an adverb fits naturally between the two parts of an infinitive:

Correct	Some young couples regard children as a nuisance, but as they grow older they begin **to actually look** forward to having a family.

If the modifier is moved and the sentence reads ". . . but as they grow older they actually begin to look forward . . .," the emphasis is slightly changed and the stress the adverb receives in the original sentence is lost.

Exercise 3

Revise the following sentences to correct misplaced words, phrases, and clauses.

1. He wore a ring on his right finger which was made of topaz.
2. The film about the life of the sea otter that I saw downtown was very interesting.
3. She wrote her book on surfing in Kansas.
4. We camped in a small shelter near the edge of the cliff that had not been used for months.
5. Bread that rises rapidly too often will have a coarse texture.
6. The dean told me I could return to school in a high rage.
7. He was hit by a rotten egg walking back to his apartment one night.

8. Wild and primitive, with hidden snags and rapids on one side, jungle and savage natives on the other, danger is ever present.

9. I promised during the evening to call her.

10. Often she would spend hours on the edge of the beach watching her small son build a sand castle with half-closed eyes.

Exercise 4

Revise the following sentences to correct the split constructions.

1. At the end of the period we were told to promptly hand in our blue-books.

2. The pharmacist told her she should, since she needed the medicine in such a hurry, have the doctor phone in the prescription.

3. The term *reactionary* can be applied to political, social, or economic (or a combination of the three) beliefs.

4. After nicking a submerged rock, the canoe began to slowly but steadily leak and to gradually settle deeper in the water.

5. She told him to for heaven's sake shut up.

7d

Confusing Shifts

Shifts in sentence structure lead to confusion. If the first clause of a sentence is in the active voice, the second clause should not be in the passive voice unless there is a good reason for the change. Similarly, a sentence that begins in the present tense should not lapse into the past tense halfway through, and one that starts with the first person *I* point of view should not shift to *you.* Consistency in mood, tense, voice, and person results from sharp revision. Watch out for shifty sentences.

1. Confusing Shifts of Voice or Subject

A shift from the active to the passive voice almost always involves a change in subject. Such a shift in voice makes a sentence doubly awkward.

> **Awkward**   After **I** finally **discovered** an unsoldered wire, the **dismantling** of the engine **was begun.**

Correct   After I finally discovered an unsoldered wire, I dismantled the motor.

The subject of this sentence shifts from the "I" of the dependent clause to the "dismantling" of the independent one; the voice shifts from active in the first clause to passive in the second. The sentence would be logically consistent if both verbs were in the passive voice: "After an unsoldered wire was found, the motor was dismantled." But the passive voice is not required by the sense of the sentence. Reinstating "I" as the subject of the independent clause produces subject and voice consistency.

Confusing shifts from the active to the passive voice can also lead to questions of agency.

Awkward   He left the examination after his answer **had been proofread**.

Correct   He left the examination after he **had proofread** his answer.

The passive second clause of the faulty sentence leaves us with the puzzling question of who proofread the answer. The translation into the active voice of the correct sentence reinstates the subject and tells who performed the action.

2. Confusing Shifts of Person or Number

A common—and, to the reader, annoying—shift in inexperienced writing is from the third person (*he, she, they, one*) to the second person (*you*). Another common shift is from a singular number (*a person, one, he*) to a plural (*they*). The inconsistencies usually occur when the writer has little or no sense of audience. Having no particular individual in mind as a listener, such a writer speaks in vague platitudes to an even vaguer anybody or everybody. The result is fuzzy, vapid writing with no focus.

Awkward   When **one** tries hard enough, **you** can do almost anything.

Correct   When **you** try hard enough, **you** can do most anything.

Correct   When **one** tries hard enough, **one** (or **she** or **he**) can do most anything.

Correct   When **we** try hard enough, **we** can do most anything.

The first revision, although consistent, illustrates the limitations of the second-person point of view. The speaker is not included in the generalization, and the responsibility for the statement seems to fall upon the reader—the *you* who is being told what he or she thinks and does. The second revision introduces the rather stilted tone occasioned by the use of *one*, and creates the problem of whether to use *she* or *he* as its referent. The third revision is an inclusive, generous point of view which gathers the voice of the writer as well as the audience into its assertion.

A shift in number from singular to plural confuses the reader and results in faulty pronoun agreement.

Shift　　When **a person** gets an early start, eats a vitamin-packed breakfast, and jogs ten miles to school, **they** work efficiently.

Correct　When **a person** gets an early start, eats a vitamin-packed breakfast, and jogs ten miles to school, **he** (or **she**) works efficiently.

Shift　　**Anyone** who follows this regimen will discover that **they** feel one hundred percent better.

Correct　**Anyone** who follows this regimen will discover that **she** (or **he**) feels one hundred percent better.

Shifts in number and person often indicate that the writer is unsure of his or her perspective on the subject matter.

Shift　　I tried this regimen yesterday morning and found a snag: when **someone** gets to school, where do **they** put **their** sweaty clothes?

Correct　I tried this regimen yesterday morning and found a snag: when **I** got to school **I** didn't have any place to put **my** sweaty clothes.

One of the disciplines of writing, especially at the revision stage, is to settle firmly on one point of view. Writers should be aware of the difference point of view makes, and they should select the person—singular or plural; first, second, or third—with care. Once selected, that point of view should remain consistent throughout the paper.

3. Confusing Shifts of Mood or Tense

A sentence should end in the same mood with which it begins. If the opening mood is an order or a command, the sentence is imperative and should not shift without good reason to the indicative mood.

Shift   First, locate the library on the campus map; then you should find the card catalog and the reference section.

Correct   First, locate the library on the campus map; then find the card catalog and the reference section.

The first clause is an order, a command addressed in the imperative mood to an understood *you*. The second clause, which is a statement giving advice, is in the indicative mood. The revision puts both clauses in the imperative mood.

A sentence that begins in the past tense should not change to the present tense.

Shift   I **stood** on the starting block and **looked** tensely at the water below; for the first time in my life I **am** about to swim the fifty-yard freestyle in competition.

Correct   I stood on the starting block and **looked** tensely at the water below; for the first time in my life I **was** about to swim the fifty-yard freestyle in competition.

Correct   I **stand** on the starting block and look tensely at the water below; for the first time in my life I **am** about to swim the fifty-yard freestyle in competition.

Remember that it is a convention to use the historical present in writing about literature: "Hamlet stabs Laertes," "Isak Dinesen writes about South Africa." Be careful not to lapse by habit into the past tense; keep the historical present consistent.

Shift   At the beginning of the *Divine Comedy*, Dante **finds** that he has strayed from the True Way into the Dark Wood of Error. As soon as he **realized** this, Dante **lifted** his eyes in hope to the rising sun.

Correct   At the beginning of the *Divine Comedy*, Dante **finds** that he has strayed from the True Way into the Dark Wood of Error. As soon as he **has realized** this, Dante **lifts** his eyes in hope to the rising sun.

Exercise 5

Correct the shifts in voice, person, number, mood, or tense in the following sentences.

1. After I finished planting my garden, the seeds were watered daily.
2. The matinee was enjoyed by all the children because they saw two monster films.
3. A person can always find something to criticize if they look hard enough.
4. In the school I attended, you had just five minutes between classes, and that was not enough time for most of us.
5. Don't ride the clutch; you should keep your left foot off the pedal.
6. Because he was so naive, Candide listens to almost anybody he meets.
7. Parson Adams went to London to try to sell his sermons and finds out that people are neither kind nor generous; he does not worry about taking money with him because he thought that people would be hospitable to him.
8. Thus, in *The Way of All Flesh,* Butler is telling his readers to look ahead; he tells them not to be caught without knowing what is going on around you.
9. Of course, knowing how to use one's leisure is also important, but I do not think that it is up to the college to more or less arrange your social life, as many colleges do.
10. Fifty years ago, your house was the center of your everyday life; today, we Americans practically live in our cars.

7e

Mixed Constructions

We designate as mixed constructions those sentences that begin in one way and end in another. For example, we may start a sentence with a modifying phrase, leading the reader to expect a substantive that it will modify. But instead of a noun the reader finds a verb, so that the modifying phrase becomes the subject of the sentence.

Mixed   By requiring citizens to regulate their thermostats is one way to conserve our energy supply.

Correct   By requiring citizens to regulate their thermostats, we can conserve our energy supply.

Correct   Requiring citizens to regulate their thermostats is one way to conserve our energy supply.

In the first revision, the prepositional phrase at the beginning of the sentence is given a subject, *we,* to modify. In the second revision the preposition *by* is dropped and the construction becomes a gerund phrase, subject of the verb *is*.

1. Dependent Clauses Used as Subjects and Complements

A dependent clause, by definition, stands beside an independent clause for support. Using a dependent clause as the subject or the complement of a verb can produce a badly mixed construction.

Mixed   Because they installed solar heating when they remodeled their house made their fuel bills lower.

Correct   Because they installed solar heating when they remodeled their house, their fuel bills were lower.

Correct   Installing solar heating when they remodeled their house made their fuel bills lower.

The first revision subordinates dependent to independent clause by means of the complex sentence construction. In the second revision the gerund phrase is the subject of the verb *made*.

Mixed   The reason their fuel bills were lower is because they installed solar heating when they remodeled their house.

Correct   Their fuel bills were lower because they installed solar heating when they remodeled their house.

Correct   The reason their fuel bills were lower is that they installed solar heating when they remodeled their house.

The first revised sentence, the most efficient of the three, crisply subordinates effect to cause with the complex sentence. The second, like the faulty sentence, is wordy, but it is grammatically correct. A "that" clause, because it functions as a noun, can be the complement of the verb *is*. A dependent clause beginning with *because* does not function as a noun and cannot be the complement of the verb *is*.

Common to speech, "the reason . . . is because . . ." construction is both redundant and wordy. *Reason* means *because*. The most energetic revision of such constructions is achieved by dropping "the reason."

Mixed   The reason her sentences improved is because she stopped using wordy constructions.

Correct	Her sentences improved because she stopped using wordy constructions.

2. Adverbial Clauses Used as Nouns

A frequent cause of mixed constructions is the illogical use of *when* or *where* as part of the complement of *is*—the "is when" or "is where" habit.

Incorrect	One **thing** that keeps me from driving my car to the grocery store **is when** I think of waiting in line for hours at the gas station.
Correct	One **thing** that keeps me from driving my car to the grocery store **is** the **thought** of waiting in line for hours at the gas station.
Correct	I don't drive my car to the grocery store when I think of waiting in line for hours at the gas station.
Incorrect	**Symbiosis is where** dissimilar organisms live together in a mutually advantageous partnership.
Correct	**Symbiosis is a state** where dissimilar organisms live together in a mutually advantageous partnership.
Correct	**Symbiosis is the** mutually advantageous **partnership** of dissimilar organisms living together.

The faulty sentences are mixed constructions that link a noun with an adverbial clause. They are revised by retaining the *is* verb and linking the noun with a noun or an adjective (or with groups of words that function like nouns and adjectives) or by dropping the *is* and subordinating dependent to independent clause.

3. Idiomatic Comparisons

In making comparisons, use the same idiom throughout the sentence.

Incorrect	The amateur typist will find erasable paper easier to type on than on bond.
Correct	The amateur typist will find erasable paper easier to type on than bond.
Correct	The amateur typist will find it easier to type on erasable paper than [to type] on bond.

Exercise 6

In the following student sentences, analyze the constructions that have been mixed and revise the sentences.

1. Since cheating in schools instigates distrust on so large a scale that I think all people caught cheating should be punished as a lesson to all.
2. Because Joyce's stories are written with the greatest skill makes each and every character come alive before the reader's eyes.
3. In the container is where the experiment takes place.
4. For college students, I feel that teaching assistants who read papers for the professors are really a disadvantage to the student.
5. It would be hard for me to say what the outlook on life a person with this disease would have.
6. In choosing the class play, we found small reading groups much easier to work with than with the whole committee together.
7. In my high school, which is rated as one of the best in the state, it is my opinion that it was much too easy.
8. As the volume of sound increases in the earphones, the nearer the submarine is approaching.
9. In my study of campus slang, to get an A on a test or in a course is where you "ace" it.
10. Of course, if I decide to become an engineering major doesn't mean that it is too late to change later on.
11. By defining the term "socialism" accurately will save us argument.
12. When waiting for the mail on the day a check from home is expected is very frustrating.

7f

Incomplete Constructions

Do not omit words and expressions necessary for grammatical completeness.

Incorrect	The very sound of the poem gives the feeling fleeting light and life.
Correct	The very sound of the poem gives the feeling of fleeting light and life.
Incorrect	Like Hamlet, he pondered the question being or not being.
Correct	Like Hamlet, he pondered the question of to be or not to be.

1. Incomplete Verb Forms

When the two parts of a compound construction are in different tenses, the auxilary verbs should usually be fully written in so that their meanings will be clear.

| Incorrect | Language **has** and always **will be** a profitable subject in a college curriculum. |
| Correct | Language **has been** and always **will be** a profitable subject in a college curriculum. |

When there is no change in tense, part of a compound verb can be omitted:

| Correct | Information will be sent to all students who have signed up for the Education Aboard program and [who have] paid the fee. |

In sentences where the predicate is the linking verb *to be*, the verb must agree with its subject in number.

| Incorrect | He **was lecturing** and the students **taking notes.** |
| Correct | He **was lecturing** and the students **were taking** notes. |

The plural "students" requires the plural auxiliary "were."

2. Idiomatic Prepositions

English idiom requires that certain prepositions be used with certain adjectives and verbs; we say, for example, "interested *in*," "aware *of*," "devoted *to*." We expect others "to agree *with*," or "to object *to*," or even "to protest *against*" our plans. Use the proper idiomatic preposition with each part of a compound construction. Your dictionary will help you learn which is the right preposition.

Incorrect	He was **oblivious** and **undisturbed by** the noise around him.
Correct	He was **oblivious to** and **undisturbed by** the noise around him.
Incorrect	No one could have been more **interested** or **devoted to** her constituents than Senator Chong.
Correct	No one could have been more **interested in** or **devoted to** her constituents than Senator Chong.

3. Incomplete and Inexact Comparisons

In comparisons, do not omit words necessary to make a complete idiomatic statement.

Incorrect   She is as witty, if not wittier, than her brother.

Correct   She is as witty as, if not wittier than, her brother.

Correct   She is as witty as her brother, if not wittier.

If we delete the "if not wittier" interjection in the faulty sentence, it becomes apparent that the statement says "She is as witty than her brother," which makes no sense.

Incorrect   Leonardo Da Vinci had one of the greatest, if not the greatest, minds of all time.

Correct   Leonardo Da Vinci had one of the greatest minds, if not the greatest mind, of all time.

No one, not even Leonardo, can have "the greatest minds." Comparisons should be complete, logical, and unambiguous.

Incorrect   His expectations were more modest than his sister.

Correct   His expectations were more modest than those of his sister.

Correct   His expectations were more modest than his sister's.

A sister may be modest, but it is unlikely that the comparison was intended by the writer. That his sister had expectations, too, is made clear in each of the revisions.

Incorrect   The food here costs no more than any other restaurant in town.

Correct   The food here costs no more than [it does] at any other restaurant in town.

Avoid the illogical use of *than* or *any.*

Incorrect   For many years the Empire State Building was taller than any building in New York.

Correct   For many years the Empire State Building was taller than any other building in New York.

"Any building in New York" includes the Empire State Building, and a building cannot be taller than itself.

Make sure the reader can tell what is being compared with what.

Incorrect	Claremont is farther from Los Angeles than Pomona.
Correct	Claremont is farther from Los Angeles than Pomona **is**.
Correct	Claremont is farther from Los Angeles than **it is** from Pomona.

In the two revisions, both terms of the comparison are completely fillled in, and there is no ambiguity about what is being compared.

Many commercials and advertisements make claims that rest on incomplete comparisons. Both the student of language and the consumer should challenge ungrammatical and empty statements.

Incorrect	Philsoc Gas gives more and better mileage for the dollar.

We should ask, more and better than what? Than a team of mules? Than another kind of gasoline? If so, which one?

Incorrect	Buy the bigger, crunchier, crisper, better-tasting breakfast cereal.
Incorrect	More bounce to the ounce!
Incorrect	The smaller, more convenient calculator.

Again: Than what?

If clearly indicated by the context, the standard of comparison need not be specified:

Correct	Boulder Dam is big, but the Grand Coulee Dam is bigger.

Note that the words *so, such,* and *too* when used as comparatives are completed by a phrase or clause indicating the standard of comparison.

Correct	I am **so** tired **that I could drop**. I had **such** a small breakfast **that** I was starving by noon, and when we stopped for lunch, I was **too** tired **to eat**.

Exercise 7

Revise the following sentences by filling out the incomplete or illogical constructions.

1. The waters of the South Pacific are at least as blue as the Aegean Sea.
2. Disneyland is as large, if not larger, than any other amusement park in the country.

3. The Hondas and Yamahas weigh less and are cheaper.
4. My father complained that his income tax was higher than last year.
5. The distributor was cleaned and the points adjusted.
6. Vale did some of her best work and learned a great deal from her high school history teacher.
7. Because of their climate and soil, Florida and Texas raise more citrus than all the states put together.
8. According to our map of Arkansas, Fort Smith is farther from Little Rock than Pine Bluff.
9. As your Class Secretary, I have and will continue to send you all the news that I receive about the class of '81.
10. Trying to analyze my good points and weaknesses made me a happier and secure person.

Exercise 8

The following student sentences contain faults discussed in the preceding chapter on coherence—faulty parallelism, faulty reference of pronouns, dangling and misplaced modifiers, confusing shifts, and mixed and incomplete constructions. Identify the causes of faulty coherence in each sentence, and then revise the sentence.

1. Entering the door, after walking up several steps made of concrete, there is a police officer sitting behind the desk, who will gladly give you any needed information.
2. The politician has dinners given, circulars printed, and attends rallies.
3. If someone knows that a certain person is a "cheat," they wouldn't want to be around them and they wouldn't trust him.
4. By the way she tells the story is indication enough of how Mansfield feels.
5. I found Charlie Macklin to be the closest thing to perfection, but at the same time still being human, than any other I have either read about or known in real life.
6. Pulled through a broken window with pieces of glass scattered about, a passing motorist rescued a woman in her home early this morning, which was blazing.
7. One advertisement shows a washing machine "growing" before our eyes to be ten feet tall, and in a different commercial for soap portrays a giant in your washer who labors to clean your clothes.
8. Some occupations in which following directions might not be important are where a person is an artist, a potter, a novelist, or some other creative artist.

9. Although surprising to students, this writer feels that in most questionable cases, the uncertainty of science should be presented for what it is.

10. While personally finding nothing to recommend Marx's system, it is fitting to examine him in order to see how and why so many people have believed in it.

11. He certainly didn't look like a man of my father's age and he certainly didn't have a particle of dignity that I so commonly associated with my father of having.

12. Paul has different ideas about schooling than the school principal.

13. Just because our campus radio station plays so much popular music is no reason for the college to cut its funds.

14. The Lilliputians are much more like the human race than the giants.

15. After being locked in the cabin about two hours, our first roll call of the evening took place.

8

CHOOSING WORDS

8a

Choosing a Voice

Each year, we buy thousands of books that claim to help us know ourselves better. We sign up for courses and programs advertising a path to self-discovery. Finding ourselves is a topic of conversation on all the talk shows we watch and listen to. Clearly, we want to find out who we are, and just as clearly, it isn't easy for us to know.

We are tempted to imitate the quirks of baseball players, television stars, and political candidates; we take on the mannerisms of those with whom we work and study. In all this copying there is little opportunity for us to recognize ourselves. It is equally difficult for us to write with our own voice, when so many attractive voices beckon. We imitate in our writing the talk of television personalities, government officials, newspaper editors, and our friends and neighbors.

Our difficulty is complicated by the fact that our language, like our behavior, comes from a public stock. We cannot invent a new language or a new system of habits: nobody would understand us. Yet the symbols that limit us also empower us to say what we can and be who we are. We must find our identity by choosing, from the habits and language we see and hear around us, that which pleases us most and fits our goals best. Perhaps Ezra Pound was thinking of such appropriations when he said, "Bad poets imitate; good poets steal."

It is hard to decide what to make your own, but an important first step is to be aware that you make the decisions. According to

Socrates, the unexamined life is not worth living; when you examine your voice in your writing, you discover how many of your choices have been made for you by your thoughtless habits or those of others. Sometimes, on the other hand, you are surprised by the strength of your beliefs. You find that you have something you want to say and that you want to say it with clarity and feeling and power. The composition of a letter to someone you love or the declaration, under pressure, of a value you believe in can move you to choose your words carefully, to change the order of your sentences, to revise and write again until you feel certain that what you have written will move another person. In such a creative act you can almost hear your voice in the words on the page and see the look of recognition on the face of the person you are addressing. Moments like this are rare, but they produce the best writing, and the best is always rare.

We would all like to re-create our discovery of ourselves in writing and apply it to everything we write. But rarely is composition so intense as to require all your commitment. You need to examine each moment of insight so that you can bring even to routine assignments a human concern. If you resolve to be personally committed to any act of writing, to care about what you say and how you say it, such involvement will compel you to write vigorously and well. Writing becomes mechanical and inhuman only if you fail to listen to your voice and to the imagined voice of your listener.

Writing as Dialogue

Writing begins as dialogue. It is one person speaking to another about something of importance to both. We write because we wish to extend the one-to-one relationship—where all communication begins—to a larger number of persons for a longer time. We write because we learn new things to say and new ways of saying them. As you become literate and learn the language of written discourse, your audience widens, your knowledge of the world and its history deepens, and your awareness of self expands. Your writing skills must grow in complexity and scope if they are to keep pace with this maturing experience.

In spoken dialogue, your facial expression, gestures, and tone of voice determine to a great extent the way your audience responds to what you say. The pitch, volume, and pace of your speech tell your audience whether you are serious or mocking, authoritative or questioning—in short, how you feel about your subject matter. In writing, you must translate these physical and auditory signals into visual symbols so that the eyes of your audience will hear the tone of your voice.

One of the pleasures of learning to write well is the discovery that you have a number of writing voices and that the more proficient you become as a stylist, the more voices you have at your disposal. On one occasion you may speak from the authority of personal experience; on another as the questioning investigative reporter or the reasonable observer who gathers and evaluates evidence. Your written tone of voice can vary from ironic to wry, formal, elegant, funny, passionate, casual, or grim.

Before you can write consistently with any voice, you must know exactly how you feel about the topic. You must try to say what you think, not what you think someone else (usually the teacher) wants to hear. Instead of abandoning your personal voice, you must write with a lively sense of self. The reader must be convinced that you know exactly what you want to say and that you consider it important.

Such confident writing demands self-examination. Part of self-examination is the process of self-discovery in jotting and free-writing. Another part is your response to your reading. As you go through a book, get involved in an active exchange of ideas with the author. Take notes on a separate sheet of paper. Summarizing comments will map areas of the material that you find important. Question marks and exclamation points help to start an argument with the author. Comments such as "That's right" or "Garbage!" may help you discover what you think and where you stand.

You examine more than your opinions when you try to find your voice. If the constituents of your identity are those bits of behavior that you have admired and imitated, the constituents of your voice are the things that bad poets have imitated and good poets stolen: words.

You have imitated, usually without thinking, the language of your parents and peers, of the media and public personalities. Now you want to "steal" words—but from whom? Which ones? How will you know their value? Your best sources are those places where language is used most accurately: in the works of thoughtful writers and in the dictionary. You need to enter into a dialogue with those writers who are speaking to you, who reward you when you examine their meaning. Many writers, among them Benjamin Franklin, Robert Browning, Alexander Pope, Eldridge Cleaver, Virginia Woolf, and John Stuart Mill, report that they began to find a voice in imagined conversations with earlier writers.

8b

Using the Dictionary

You cannot enter into a decent conversation with these writers—or with any others—unless you begin where they began, with a curiosity about words. If you were to study Alexander Pope's writing, you might be puzzled by many of his words. You would find that some of his language, like the American double-eagle or half-penny of the nineteenth century, has gone out of currency.

This should not surprise you. Like all languages, English is continually changing. New words are added as names are required for new inventions, discoveries, and ideas: *laser, meson, transistor, cybernetics, apartheid.* Old words acquire new meanings as they are used in new ways: *half-life* (physics), *snow* (television), *software* (computers), *cartridge* (high-fidelity recording). Some old words disappear as the need for them vanishes; a whole vocabulary dealing with horse-drawn vehicles is on its way out. Words gain or lose prestige: *strenuous* and *mob* are now standard words, although they were once considered slang. *Negro,* once considered a neutral word, has taken on bad connotations and is now widely replaced by *black.*

A dictionary is an attempt to record the current uses and meanings of words. Although many people believe that a dictionary tells them what a word *ought to* mean or how it *should be* used, a modern dictionary tries to be an accurate and objective record of what is actually being said and written. It discriminates among the current meanings of a word and tries to indicate the ways in which each is used. Since words and constructions differ in prestige value, a conscientious lexicographer will also try to record the current status of words, usually by labels such as Dialectal or Regional, Obsolete or Archaic, Informal, Colloquial, Nonstandard, or Slang.

A good dictionary can be a trustworthy aid in your dialogue with a writer or with those who will read your writing. Large, unabridged dictionaries include a history of the meanings of words, biographical and geographical data, guides for pronunciation, spelling, and punctuation, and a variety of other useful information. The large dictionaries in established widespread use in most college libraries include the following:

The Oxford English Dictionary, 13 volumes and 4 supplements (in progress), Oxford University Press, New York, 1933, 1972, 1976. (This is the standard historical dictionary of the language; it traces and illustrates the development of each word from its earliest appearance to the present.)

Webster's New International Dictionary of the English Language, Second Edition, G. & C. Merriam Co., Springfield, Mass., 1954.

Webster's Third New International Dictionary, Unabridged: The Great Library of the English Language, G. & C. Merriam Co., 1976. (This dictionary gives few usage labels.)

The Random House Dictionary of the English Language, New York, 1973.

Webster's New Twentieth Century Dictionary of the English Language, Second Edition, New York, 1975.

Unabridged dictionaries are invaluable for occasional reference, but more practical for the student are the following abridged desk dictionaries. All are reliable, but some instructors may have preferences, which they will indicate.

The American Heritage Dictionary of the English Language, Houghton Mifflin Company, Boston.

Funk & Wagnalls Standard College Dictionary, Harper & Row, New York.

The Random House College Dictionary, New York.

Webster's New Collegiate Dictionary, G. & C. Merriam Co., Springfield, Mass.

Webster's New World Dictionary, William Collins Publishers, Inc., Cleveland, Ohio.

1. Abbreviations and Symbols

To use a dictionary effectively, you must understand the abbreviations and symbols it uses. These are explained in its introductory section. Here are entries from four collegiate dictionaries.

---

spelling & syllabication   *etymology*
   ↓   ↓

¹im·ply (im plī′) *vt.* -plied′, -ply′ing [ME. *implien* < OFr. *emplier* < L. *implicare*, to involve, entangle < *in-*, in + *plicare*, to fold < IE. base **plek-*, to plait, wrap together, whence Gr. *plekein*, to braid: cf. FLAX] **1.** to have as a necessary part, condition, or effect; contain, include, or involve naturally or necessarily [drama *implies* conflict] **2.** to indicate indirectly or by allusion; hint; suggest; intimate [an attitude *implying* boredom] **3.** [Obs.] to enfold; entangle –**SYN.** see SUGGEST

                                                          ↑
                                                 usage label

---

pronunciation   *part of speech*   *meanings*
   ↓   ↓   ↓

²im·ply (im·plī′) *v.t.* ·plied, ·ply·ing **1.** To involve necessarily as a circumstance, condition, effect, etc.: An action *implies* an agent. **2.** To indicate or suggest without stating; hint at; intimate. **3.** To have the meaning of; signify. **4.** *Obs.* To entangle; infold. –**Syn.** See INFER. [< OF *emplier* < L *implicare* to involve < *in-* in + *plicare* to fold. Doublet of EMPLOY.]

   –**Syn. 1.** *Imply* and *involve* mean to have some necessary connection. *Imply* states that the connection is casual or inherent, while *involve* is vaguer, and does not define the connection. **2.** *Imply, hint, intimate, insinuate* mean to convey a meaning indirectly or covertly. *Imply* is the general term for signifying something beyond what the words obviously say; his advice *implied* confidence in the stock market. *Hint* suggests indirection in speech or action: our host's repeated glances at his watch *hinted* that it was time to go. *Intimate* suggests a process more elaborate and veiled than hint: she *intimated* that his attentions were unwelcome. *Insinuate* suggests slyness and a derogatory import: in his remarks, he *insinuated* that the Senator was a fool.

full discussion of synonyms

---

inflected forms

³**im·ply** (ĭm-plī′) *tr. v.* **-plied, -plying, -plies. 1.** To involve or suggest by logical necessity; entail: *His aims imply a good deal of energy.* **2.** To say or express indirectly; to hint; suggest: *His tone implied a malicious purpose.* **3.** *Obsolete.* To entangle. –See Synonyms at **suggest.** –See Usage note at **infer.** [Middle English *implien, emplien,* from Old French *emplier,* from Latin *implicāre,* infold, involve, IMPLICATE.]

³© 1979 by Houghton Mifflin Company. Reprinted by permission from *The American Heritage Dictionary of the English Language.*

---

⁴**im·ply** im-′plī *vt* **im·plied; im·ply·ing** [ME *emplien,* fr. **MF** *emplier,* fr. L *implicare*] **1** *obs:* ENFOLD, ENTWINE **2:** to involve or indicate by inference, association, or necessary consequence rather than by direct statement <rights ~ obligations> **3:** to contain potentially **4:** to express indirectly <his silence *implied* consent>
syn see SUGGEST **ant** express

↑   ↑   ↑

synonym   *antonym*   *illustration of use*

---

⁴By permission. From *Webster's New Collegiate Dictionary* © 1980 by G. & C. Merriam Co., Publishers of the Merriam-Webster Dictionaries.

2. Information Found in a Dictionary

SPELLING AND SYLLABICATION

When more than one spelling is given, the one printed first is usually to be preferred. Division of the word into syllables follows the conventions accepted by printers.

PRONUNCIATION

A key to the symbols used to indicate pronunciation of words is usually printed on the front or back inside cover of the dictionary. Some dictionaries also run an abbreviated key to pronunciation at the bottom of each page or every other page. Word accent is shown by the symbol (′) after the stressed syllable or by (′) before it.

PARTS OF SPEECH

Abbreviations (explained in the introductory section of the dictionary) are used to indicate the various grammatical uses of a word: for example, *imply, v.t.* means that *imply* is a transitive verb. Note that some words can be used as several different parts of speech. *Forfeit*, for example, is listed first as a noun, and its various meanings in this use are defined. Then its meaning when used as an adjective is given, and finally its meaning as a transitive verb.

INFLECTED FORMS

Forms of the past tense and past and present participles of verbs, the comparative or superlative degree of adjectives, and the plurals of nouns are given whenever there might be doubt as to the correct form or spelling.

ETYMOLOGY

The history of each word is indicated by the forms in use in Middle or Old English, or in the language from which the word was borrowed. Earlier meanings are often given.

MEANINGS

Different meanings of a word are numbered and defined, sometimes with illustrative examples. Some dictionaries give the oldest meanings first; others list the common meanings of the word first.

USAGE LABELS

Descriptive labels, often abbreviated, indicate the level of usage: Archaic, Obsolete, Colloquial, Slang, Dialectal, Regional, Substandard, Nonstandard, and so on. Look up the meanings of these words in the dictionary you use. Sometimes usage labels indicate a special field rather than a level of usage: for example, *Poetic, Irish, Chemistry*. If a word has no usage label, it may be assumed that, in the opinion of the editors, the word is in common use on all levels; that is, it is *Standard English*. Usage labels are often defined and illustrated in the explanatory notes in the front of a dictionary. Check yours; it is important to understand how the labels are used.

SYNONYMS

In your imagined conversation with writers or readers, you want to be precise. Yet many words have nearly identical or closely related meanings and often need careful discrimination to indicate the precise denotation of each. A full account of the distinctions in meaning among synonyms (for example, *suggest, imply, hint, intimate,* and *insinuate*) may be given at the end of the entry for the basic word, or cross references to its synonyms may be provided.

Exercise 1

In looking up the meanings of words, try to discover within what limits of meaning the word may be used. Read the definition as a whole; do not pick out a single synonym and suppose that this and the word defined are interchangeable. After looking up the following words in your dictionary, write sentences that will unmistakably illustrate the meaning of each word.

anachronism	innocuous	precocious
eminent	materiel	sinecure
fetish	misanthropy	sophistication
hedonist	nepotism	taboo
imminent	philanthropy	travesty

Exercise 2

Look up each of the following words in the Oxford English Dictionary, *in an unabridged dictionary, and in an abridged one, and write a report showing how the larger volumes explain the use of each word more discriminatingly and clearly than the smaller one does. State the exact title, the publisher, and the date of each dictionary.*

Bible	Christian	court	idealism
catholic	color	evolution	liberal

Exercise 3

How may the etymologies given by the dictionary help one to remember the meaning or the spelling of the following words? (Note that when a series of words has the same etymology, the etymology is usually given only with the basic word of the series.)

alibi	insidious	privilege
capitol	isosceles	sacrilegious
cohort	magnanimous	sarcasm
concave	malapropism	subterfuge
denouement	peer (noun)	thrifty

Exercise 4

Most dictionaries put abbreviations in the main alphabetical arrangement. Look up the following abbreviations and be ready to state in class what they mean.

at. wt.	colloq.	Ens.	K.C.B.	LL.D.	PBX
CAB	e.g.	ff.	l.c.	OAS	Q.E.D.

Exercise 5

Consult the dictionary for the distinction in meaning between the members of each of the following pairs of words:

neglect—negligence	instinct—intuition
ingenuous—ingenious	nauseous—nauseated
fewer—less	eminent—famous
admit—confess	criticize—censure
infer—imply	increment—addition

Exercise 6

In each sentence, choose the more precise of the two italicized words. Be able to justify your choice.

1. Many in the class were *disinterested, uninterested* and went to sleep.
2. His charming innocence is *childlike, childish.*
3. The problem is to assure the farm workers *continuous, continual* employment.
4. She is *continuously, continually* in trouble with the police.
5. I am quite *jealous, envious* of your opportunity to study in Europe.
6. She is so *decided, decisive* in her manner that people always give in to her.

7. If we give your class all of these privileges, we may establish *precedents, precedence* which are unwise.
8. She always makes her health her *alibi, excuse* for her failures.

Exercise 7

Find the precise meaning of each word in the following groups, and write sentences to illustrate that meaning.

1. abandon, desert, forsake
2. ludicrous, droll, comic
3. silent, reserved, taciturn
4. meager, scanty, sparse
5. knack, talent, genius
6. anxious, eager, avid

8c

Considering Your Audience

In spoken dialogue, you can see whether or not other people understand what you are saying, whether they approve, when they object. As a writer, alone with your thoughts and your typewriter, you must imagine how the audience will react to what you write. To do this, try to visualize your intended audience. Will your readers be older, younger, or about the same age as yourself? What do they know about the subject matter—more or less than you do, or about as much? Is the audience of the same race, religion, or sex as you are? What is your own feeling toward such an audience: affection, distrust, anxiety, fellowship? You need to decide whom you want to reach before you can select the appropriate voice for making contact with them.

Some writers find it helpful to visualize a specific member of the audience they are addressing. While in the British Museum reading a book entitled *The Natural Inferiority of Women*, Virginia Woolf began to draw a picture of the kind of man she imagined the author to be. To her surprise she found that her sketch of the angry author also revealed her own anger, and she was able to trace its source: "the professor's statement about the mental, moral, and physical inferiority of women." "One does not like," she continues, "to be told that one is naturally the inferior of a little man—I looked at the student next to me—who breathes hard, wears a ready-made tie, and has not shaved this fortnight."

To her surprise, Woolf discovered that the assumption of inferiority which had blinded the professor to his anger against women revealed her own anger against men. In coming to terms with her feelings, she gained the rhetorical advantage; the book she subsequently wrote, *A Room of One's Own*, is an exemplar of modulated tone. Only when we are in control of our feelings and ourselves can we control the responses of others.

Good writers can adapt to a number of audiences. You make such adjustments of tone and style every day. If you are explaining a bridge to a small child, you don't use the vocabulary of a structural engineer. If you are speaking to a stranger, you don't use slang or obscenity or the familiar dialects that you use with close friends or family members. The person who is sincerely trying to communicate, rather than impress or confound, makes every effort to find the language appropriate to the audience.

In the writing course you can assume, unless otherwise instructed, that the students and the instructor constitute your audience. Most teachers, when they read student papers, try to exemplify the informed and questioning mind that should be the result of a university education. Keep such an audience in mind, but remember also that your classmates, though of your generation, may represent geographic areas and cultures different from your own. Becoming aware of these different provinces and comparing them with your own provincial outlook will help you to discover the assumptions you bring to your writing and the prejudices your audience brings to its reading.

Part of the task of writers is learning to anticipate the objections of an audience. In reading fiction or watching a play, we willingly suspend disbelief, as Coleridge says, but in reading exposition or argument, we seldom do. In fact, the tension generated by our unspoken objections contributes to the excitement we discover in expository discourse. "Prove it . . . , show me . . ." we insist in conversation. As writers, we try to imagine when the audience will begin to look incredulous or skeptical, and then to do something about it.

You must also always be alert for signs of a listener's boredom. While the sound of one hand clapping may be the ultimate of Zen enlightenment, the sound of one voice droning on and on is apt to put a listener to sleep. You must keep in mind that your audience is distracted by a number of things—perhaps the inclination to read something else—or the disinclination to read at all. If you care about your audience, you must be careful to keep them interested, and you do this best when you yourself are interested in the subject.

Don't hesitate to bring your own biases to bear on the topic. Prod the topic with questions. How do I, as a young person, or a black, or a pre-law student, or a man, or a southerner—a poet, a gambler, a Buddhist, a hopeless romantic or a confirmed skeptic—feel about the problem of ecology? How does my personal history—the fact that my grades are lousy but my love life good, that I like to swim and hike and want to own a car, that I like to be alone at times and crowded together with people at others—how does all this affect my attitude toward water and trees, toward babies and oil wells, solar energy, condominiums, and plastics? What sort of objections would someone have if I advocated the banning of the internal combustion engine? What sort of objection would I have if someone stole my car? What sort of evidence might convert either of us to the other's point of view? Every topic is potentially controversial, and controversy is always interesting.

To sum all this up, you should speak in one of your own natural voices, not in the inhuman abstractions of the bureaucrat. And you should always keep your intended audience in mind and try to make reading pleasant and comprehension easy for them.

Exercise 8

Observe your instructors and your classmates in the courses you are taking. How much do the instructors rely on body language or gesture to convey information as they lecture or lead discussions? How much information does the "audience" (the class) reveal through body language? How attentive is the instructor to this language? Be prepared to translate into words your interpretation of these gestures.

Exercise 9

Analyze the point of view from which this chapter is written. Is it consistent or does it change; if so, where and why? What tone does the point of view (or points of view) convey? Is the tone appropriate to the audience and to the subject matter?

Exercise 10

Make a list of your own assumptions about the following topics and of the objections you would anticipate on the part of the intended audience.

TOPIC	AUDIENCE
The right of women to obtain an abortion.	The trustees of a Catholic hospital.
The legalization of marijuana.	High school seniors.
The vitality of the institution of marriage and the family.	Your parents in a letter.
The abolition of the combustion engine.	Stockholders of General Motors.
The necessity for National Health Insurance.	American Medical Association.
Prohibiting the distribution of birth control devices.	Membership of the Planned Parenthood Association.
Public control of television programming	President of a major TV network.

Try to visualize these audiences. Draw a picture of a representative member of that audience. What does the picture tell you about your feelings for the audience and for the subject matter?

Exercise 11

How would you make the following topics interesting?

The equal distribution of funding to female and male athletic programs in colleges and universities

Violence and sex in the contemporary cinema

The grading system as an obstacle to education

The selling of nuclear arms to foreign countries

Racial prejudice in high school

The patient's right to determine in terminal cases when medical assistance should be stopped

Do prisons rehabilitate criminals?

Should foreign languages be required courses in elementary schools?

The enforcement by local governments of air pollution regulations

Mandatory spaying of cats and dogs

Exercise 12

A Danish theologian, Søren Kierkegaard, made notes in his Journal *for writing a novel about a madman which began in the third person and*

ended in the first. Try a similar experiment on any topic in which you begin a paragraph in the third person singular and end in the personal "I." What happens as the point of view shifts?

8d

Using the Language of Your Audience: Levels of Usage

As you can see, your consideration for your audience includes more than anticipating and sharing their concerns. You also need to address them in a language they are likely to understand and accept. Your own judgment is one guide. In addition, every good dictionary tells you the context in which the use of a word is appropriate, its level of usage.

1. Standard English

STANDARD ENGLISH includes the great majority of words and constructions that native speakers would recognize as acceptable in any situation or context. All words in a dictionary that are not specifically labeled are, in the judgment of the editors, Standard English and acceptable for general use. However, a good many words and constructions have, for various reasons, a more limited use, and these are commonly labeled in dictionaries. For example, words used in some sections of the country but not in all, such as *carry* in the sense of "escort to a dance or party," will be labeled REGIONAL or DIALECTAL. If the usage is more localized, such as *arroyo* (a dry gully), the word will be labeled *Southwestern U.S.*, or *New England*, or whatever. Other labels explain words still found in books but no longer in common use, such as OBSOLETE (for example, *deer* used in the sense of "any animal," as in Shakespeare's "Rats and mice and such small deer") or ARCHAIC (very old but preserved for historical or poetic reasons, such as *olden*).

In addition to such geographic or temporal limitations on word use, most people feel that certain kinds of language, or certain dialects, have more or less prestige because of the people who use them. In the past, the language of the educated upper class was thought of as Good English, and all other dialects or levels were ignored or condemned as incorrect, ungrammatical, or illiterate. To the modern linguist, all the dialects spoken by different groups in American society are equally valid varieties of English, but they are not always appropriate in serious public writing.

In a country where many people are trying to improve their position in an open society, differences in prestige among dialects need to be pointed out. The usual way to do this in a handbook is to attach Usage Labels to words that are limited in some way. This handbook, in addition to regional and temporal labels, tries to indicate levels of acceptability by using the following labels: STANDARD (acceptable in formal and informal use), FORMAL, INFORMAL (or general), COLLOQUIAL, SLANG, and NONSTANDARD. The overlapping of various levels and labels (in capital letters) can be seen in the following diagram.

Levels of Usage

Edited English	{ FORMAL INFORMAL (general)	Not Labeled
Spoken English	{ COLLOQUIAL SLANG NONSTANDARD	Labeled

Notice that Edited English, the main concern of this handbook, is not labeled in most dictionaries. Accordingly, any word that *is* labeled in your dictionary should be used sparingly, if at all, in public writing.

Sharp lines cannot always be drawn between the levels indicated by these labels, but relative differences are clear. *Fatigued* and *exhausted* are more formal than *tired*, which in turn is more formal than *bushed* (Colloquial) or *pooped* (Slang). *Fatigued* seldom occurs in speech and is usually found only in technical or poetic writing. *Tired* is acceptable in any spoken or written context. *Bushed* would be used mainly in familiar conversation or in writing among friends. The slang term *pooped* would seldom appear in serious writing, and then only for its shock value or its slightly comic effect.

As we have seen, levels of usage, like the language itself, undergo changes from generation to generation. Such changes have been especially rapid in recent decades. During the past fifty years, the center of Edited usage has moved away from the Formal level toward the Informal. Especially in magazines and newspapers, good writers are more apt to use colloquialisms and even slang rather than risk the stilted pomposity of Formal English in a commonplace context. Many once-forbidden words are coming up in the world, too. *Ain't* used to be universally regarded as Nonstandard; today, though it is generally disapproved even in informal writing, some dictionaries label it Nonstandard only when it is used to mean "has not" or "have not," as in "I ain't got any." As a result of a campaign by the advertising industry, *like* is now widely used as a conjunction ("like a cigarette should"; "tell it like it is"), though recent dictionaries continue to label this usage Nonstandard or Colloquial. It seems likely that, eventually, this use of *like* will be generally acceptable, despite the distaste of purists. Meanwhile, if your dictionary indicates by a usage label that a word is limited in its use, you will do well to keep that word out of your serious writing—that is, an article for a college magazine (unless you are trying for some special effect), a term paper, or a letter of application.

We have said that the basic principle of good usage is to fit the level of your language to the situation and to the expected reader. Formal English is for formal occasions, such as commencement or a funeral, or for official personages, such as college presidents in their public speech and writings. You would not be apt to use the noun *gripe* in a commencement address, an obituary, or a letter to the President. Conversely, language suitable for a letter of application might be inappropriate in the locker room or in a poker game. In making such discriminations, your own sense of the language, aided in doubtful cases by the dictionary, will have to serve you. But before your dictionary can help you with such problems, you must study the meaning of the labels it uses. The labels used in this handbook are explained below.

2. Formal English

FORMAL ENGLISH appears in scholarly or scientific articles, formal speeches, official documents, and any context calling for scrupulous propriety. It makes use of words and phrases, such as "scrupulous propriety," which nobody would use in speech and which would seldom appear in ordinary writing. As another example, consider the word *scrutinize*. This is a perfectly good word that everyone knows, but its use is almost entirely limited to formal written English, and even there it is not common. It is apt to give a bookish flavor to ordinary writing, and it is almost never used in speech. (Try to imagine yourself handing a friend a piece of writing with the request "Scrutinize this.") Formal English also includes technical language—the specialized vocabularies used in such professions as law, medicine, and the sciences. Technical language can be very precise and economical, but it is Greek to the ordinary reader and out of place in most Edited English. A good general rule is to use formal or technical language as we wear best clothes—only on special occasions.

3. Edited English

EDITED ENGLISH is the written language of books from reputable publishers, good magazines, and many newspapers. It is defined, not merely by choice of words, but by generally accepted conventions of spelling, punctuation, grammatical patterns, and sentence structure. In this section, we are considering Edited English primarily as it is reflected in choice of words. But the general purpose of all the rules laid down in this handbook is to enable you to write Edited English, the normal means of official communication in the professions and in the upper levels of business and industry.

Authorities, it must be admitted, often differ among themselves. Many handbooks, including this one, deplore the use of *contact* as a verb meaning "to get in touch with." Theodore Bernstein of the *New York Times*, though he dislikes the usage, admits in *The Careful Writer* that it is a useful verb and "will undoubtedly push its way into standard usage sometime." The most recent editions of three leading dictionaries differ widely: one accepts the usage, with no label, as standard English; one gently reproves it as an "Americanism"; the third labels it *Informal* and disapproves its use in Edited English.

Faced with such disagreement, what practical conclusion can we draw? If you use *contact* as a verb and someone challenges it, you can of course defend yourself by citing *Webster's New Collegiate Dictionary*, which makes no objection to it. But being challenged is a nuisance, and your defensive explanations are seldom convincing. If the main purpose of your writing is to get something said, don't use words that are likely to be challenged or that need lengthy defense.

4. Colloquial English

COLLOQUIAL ENGLISH means, literally, conversational English. Everyone's language is more casual and relaxed among friends than in public speech or writing. Colloquial expressions are part of Standard English, since everyone uses them, but they may be jarringly out of place in formal contexts or in serious writing. Examples are phrases such as *rock hound,* to *get away with* something, or a *square deal,* or a word such as *sure* in the sense of "certainly" (I sure would like . . .). When words and constructions are labeled *Colloquial* (some dictionaries use *Informal* for the same purpose), you should consider their possible effects on a reader before writing them. If in doubt, look for an accepted synonym.

5. Nonstandard English

The label NONSTANDARD indicates the wide variety of usages not accepted by most college-educated readers: misspellings, unconventional punctuation, illiterate grammatical constructions, and certain widely heard expressions that educated people have qualms about writing. Examples are words such as *nowheres, hain't,* especially in double negative constructions like "I hain't got none," and constructions such as *he don't,* or *of* for *have* in sentences like "I would of gone. . . ." Expressions labeled *Nonstandard* have no place in serious Edited English, except in direct quotation.

6. Dialect

A DIALECT is a form of the native language spoken in a particular region of the country or in a large geographical area by a particular group of persons. Its vocabulary and grammatical structures often differ from Standard English, which is the dialect of prestige and power in the United States. Within the region or among the group, however, the dialect may be more prestigious than Standard English. Dialect words are often colorful and vigorous: *varmint, poke, blood, polecat, da kine, foxy, streak-o-lean, talk story, branch water.* Some dialects, such as that in the Southeast, retain words from the early settlers—*reckon, yonder*—and echo grammar that was in use before Latin rules were imposed on English syntax. There's no question about what the dialect phrase "it don't bother me none" means, even though double negatives were banished from Standard English in the eighteenth century. Black Dialect retains the "be" verb in its aspectual sense, as a state of being, a form now lost to Standard English. "I be working when he be bothering me" is not the same sentence as "I am working when he bothers me," its Standard English approximation. An important distinction is lost in translation.

Often people create dialects in order to speak to one another. Black Dialect began as a means of communicating among slave traders (who were not always English), English slave owners, and persons sold into slavery who spoke a number of African languages. The pidgin dialect of Hawaii came about when persons from radically differing language families—the Tagalogs of the Philippines, Portuguese, Hawaiians, Japanese, Chinese—needed to communicate as they worked under English overseers side by side in the cane fields. The dialect is characterized by the absence of features that give English speakers difficulty: prepositions, tenses of verbs, articles. Because the dialects are spoken, the many inflections of English are not needed. Neither Black Dialect nor Hawaiian Pidgin consistently obeys the agreement rule. Students who are bi-dialectal, that is, fluent in Standard English and a dialect, are wise to be aware of those areas where their spoken and written voices conflict; they should proofread scrupulously to make sure they have followed the conventions of Edited English.

7. Regional English

The label REGIONAL refers to usage that is considered reputable in certain areas of the country but has not gained nationwide acceptance. These words are not necessarily nonstandard in the regions where they are found, and sometimes they are useful additions to the local vocabulary. But for general college writing, they should not be used when equivalent words in national currency are available. Some examples of regional words are *crack grass* for *crabgrass*, *monkeychop* for *chipmunk*, *you all* to refer to one person, *eastworm* or *angle dog* for *angleworm*.

8. Slang

SLANG is the label given to words with a forced, exaggerated, or humorous meaning used in extremely informal contexts, particularly by persons who wish to set themselves off from the average, respectable citizen.

To call a man whose ideas and behavior are unpredictable and unconventional *a kook* and to describe his ideas as *for the birds* or *way out* apparently satisfies some obscure human urge toward irreverent, novel, and vehement expression. Some slang terms remain in fairly wide use because they are vivid ways of expressing an idea that has no exact standard equivalent: *stooge, lame duck, shot* of whiskey, a card *shark*. Such words have a good chance of becoming accepted as Standard English. *Mob, banter, sham,* and *lynch* were all once slang terms. It is quite likely that, eventually, useful slang words, such as *honkytonk* and *snitch*, will be accepted as standard colloquial English.

A good deal of slang, however, reflects nothing more than the user's desire to be different, and such slang has little chance of being accepted into the language. Newspaper columnists and sportswriters often use a flamboyant jargon intended to show off their ingenuity or cleverness. For centuries criminals have used a special, semisecret language, and many modern slang terms originated in the argot of the underworld: *gat, scram, squeal,* or *sing* (confess), *push* (peddle). Hippies and rock musicians have developed a constantly changing slang which seems intended to distinguish the user as a member of a select group or inner circle.

Whatever the motive behind it, slang should be used with discretion. Its incongruity in a sober, practical context makes it an effective way of achieving force and emphasis.

Acceptable Slang   His book is so intelligently constructed, so beautifully written, so really acute at moments—and so *phony.*

But most slang terms are too violent to fit comfortably into every-day writing. Furthermore, slang goes out of fashion very quickly through overuse, and dated slang sounds more quaint and old-fashioned than Formal English. *Tight* has worn well, but *boiled, crocked, fried,* and *plastered* may soon be museum pieces.

The chief objection to the use of slang is that it so quickly loses any precise meaning. Calling a person a *fink*, a *square*, or a *creep* conveys little more than your feeling of dislike. *Cool* and *crummy* are the vaguest kind of terms, lumping all experience into two crude divisions, pleasing and unpleasing. Try to get several people to agree on the precise meaning of *square* and you will realize how vague and inexact a term it is. The remedy is to analyze your meaning and specify it. What exactly are the qualities that lead you to classify a person as a *square* or a *weirdo?*

If, despite these warnings, you must use slang in serious writing, do it deliberately and accept the responsibility for it. Do not attempt to excuse yourself by putting the slang term in quotation marks. If you are ashamed of a slang term, do not use it.

Exercise 13

With the aid of a dictionary and your own linguistic judgment (that is, your ear for appropriateness), classify the following Standard English words as Formal, Informal, or Colloquial.

1. crank, eccentric, [a] character
2. hide, sequester, ditch
3. irascible, cranky, grouchy
4. increase, boost, jack [up the price]
5. decline, avoid, pass [up]
6. pass [out], faint, swoon
7. necessity, [a] must, requirement
8. inexpensive, [a] steal, cheap
9. snooty, pretentious, affected
10. room, domicile, pad

Exercise 14

For each of the following Standard English words supply one or more slang terms and, to the best of your ability, judge which are so widespread that they have already begun to creep into highly informal writing (for example, letters to friends, college newspaper columns) or seem likely to do so in the near future.

Example: to become excited [to be turned on by, slang]

1. money
2. to relax
3. a skilled performer
4. to be going steady or to be in love
5. failure
6. to tell off
7. pleasant or enjoyable
8. to play a part
9. liquor
10. to ignore or disregard
11. complaint
12. a dull person
13. unconventional person
14. to be unfairly treated
15. puzzling

Exercise 15

Pick five or six slang terms widely used around campus and ask at least five people to define the meaning of each term in Standard English. Write the results and your conclusions.

From your use of the dictionary to help you determine the meaning and level of usage of words, you will develop a large, active vocabulary that you can use confidently in writing as well as passively in reading.

9

SHARPENING YOUR WORDING

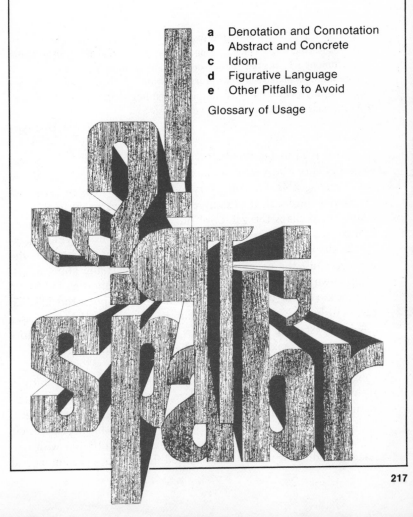

> The great archetypal activities of human society are all permeated with
> play from the start. Take language for instance—that first and supreme
> instrument which man shapes in order to communicate, to teach, to
> command. Language allows him to distinguish, to establish, to state
> things; in short, to name them and by naming them to raise them into
> the domain of the spirit.
>
> —JOHAN HUIZINGA

Language is a link between self and other: in playing with language,
we experience the world; in sharpening our words, we make the
world manageable. Our discovery of these powers begins early and
unselfconsciously. If, for example, we move back to our childhood
games (or perhaps the games of our parents and friends), we may
rediscover these powers. We may live once again in the child's jeer-
ing or shame of "Tattle-tale, tattle-tale,/ Stick your head in the
garbage pail"; the ritual oath of "Cross my heart and hope to die/
Drop down dead if I tell a lie"; or the gleeful celebration of "Made
you look, you dirty crook,/ Stole your mother's pocketbook!" We
distinguish the "tattle-tale" (What naming could be more specific?); we establish our laws ("Cross my heart"); we state the victory
of "Made you look." We communicate, teach, command.

But, looking back, it appears that we did more. We twisted our
tongues with "She sells seashells by the seashore"; mocked authority with "Teacher, teacher, I declare/ I spy a hole in your underwear"; and counted off with "One potato, two potato, three potato,
four." We *tested* words for their sounds, their shock value, their
rhythmic combinations. In playing (often very intently) with language, we did not merely master the different ways of naming and

therefore of making the world inhabitable; we learned that the emotional colors, the sounds, and the contexts of particular words belong to their meaning as much as a deep, insistent voice belongs to the Siamese cat or the horny rings of warning belong to the rattlesnake. We learned a fundamental lesson about diction, or word choice: that different words not only name different realities but that the ways they name are as curious and as complicated as the reality itself.

We may even have sensed dimly that each word has a long history behind it, a fascinating ancestry of origins, of slowly changing meanings, of curious and forgotten uses as well as current, living ones—in short, an etymology. For instance, the word *diction* is derived from the Latin *dicere*, to say, and ultimately from the Indo-European root *deik*, to show or to point out, as its kinship with the Latin word for finger, *digitus*, and the English *digit* reveals. We point forward to things we don't know the names for. Words point backward to their roots and growth, if only we choose to look. Whether it is hybrid or pure stock, domestic or foreign, plant, flower, or weed, part of a word and its essence lies in its ancestry. To know the root or roots of a word is to know something valuable about its heredity.

One of the complex ways by which words gain their power to name is through their past. Some of the other ways will be discussed in this chapter: *the more you become sensitized to and experiment with these various ways,* the greater the precision *in your naming.* ("Sharpening words" may suggest the imagery of grinding an axe, a fitting picture if meaning were only logs to be split by forceful blows and keen steel; the image might just as well refer to more delicate wood carvings. Or, to discover another meaning, the image might suggest the sharpening of taste, learning to discriminate among and to savor words as if they were wines.)

Granted, no word can ever duplicate the reality of the thorn that pierces our thumb, the sunset that moves us to silent joy, or the turbulence of first infatuation. Recognizing this limitation of language, however, writers who are attentive to diction achieve precision and depth by selecting words that most nearly approximate their thoughts and feelings. For it is only through words on the printed pages—not the blank spaces above or below them—that one is understood in writing. Too often the complaint "You *know* what I meant" or "You *know* what I'm saying" is really the hurry of someone who cannot be bothered—someone too much in a rush to learn about words.

The first, most elementary principle is the following: we draw on the names of those things and events that are the most important to us. The Eskimos have a rich vocabulary to discriminate among the colors, degrees of wetness, and textures of different kinds of snow. Americans have a similar vocabulary for cars (How many types and makes can you name? What beyond the Silver Cloud, Aspen, Lotus, Chevette, Rabbit, each a current, separate model, not to mention the Edsel, Pierce-Arrow, Hupmobile, and others of the past? Each model named is another reality.) The corollary of this principle is that the more we develop our ability to name, the greater is our ability to *discover* and *specify* meanings. To do this, we need a large, active vocabulary that we can use confidently in writing as well as in reading; good writers own, paw through, and wear out their dictionaries.

Begin, then, by looking up both the meanings and pronunciation of the unfamiliar words you come across in reading and those that seem familiar but which you cannot define. Jot them down on a slip, a matchbook cover, or a paper napkin, if necessary. Keep a vocabulary notebook and try these words out in conversation and writing. You may falter or blunder, just as you might in learning a new dance step with a new partner. Becoming acquainted with a new word, like learning a new dance, demands the willingness to stumble at first as we learn its expressive possibilities and the appropriate occasions for its use. But taking the risk is the only way of learning, and the confidence gained with practice soon wipes out the memory of an occasional word circled in red pencil on a returned manuscript.

9a

Denotation and Connotation

The first of the complex ways that words name is by their denotations and connotations. Their DENOTATIONS are their most literal meanings. For instance, to take a stark example, *body, corpse,* and *cadaver* can all have the same denotation—a dead human being. CONNOTATIONS, on the other hand, are a word's overtones, echoes, emotional colorings, and associations. Thus we would hardly speak of going to a funeral home to view the *corpse* of a friend, let alone the *cadaver*. *Body* is the most intimate in its connotations, expressing the sad acknowledgment that someone we care for is no longer *there* and that those familiar features will soon be gone forever: the word, in this context, connotes a commonly shared grief over an irrevocable reality. By contrast, *corpse* and *cadaver* connote the coldly impersonal, the anonymous, the institutional, as when police officially speak of finding an unknown corpse in a field or when medical students speak of dissecting a cadaver.

The connotation of each word must be appropriate to the context. For instance, *to compliment* and *to flatter* may denote the same action—giving praise to another person—but note the differences in their connotations. Usually, *to compliment* (or *compliments*) is used in the context of generous, justified praise given publicly or freely: "I'd like to compliment you on (or pass on a compliment about) your performance." Occasionally, it may suggest doubts—"I'm not sure he deserved all the compliments," or "I don't want to compliment her for simply doing her job"—but in these cases the *context* ("not sure," "don't want to," "simply doing her job") makes our uncertainty clear. We are not sure the connotations apply.

To flatter (or *flattery*) connotes excess, even deception. Sometimes it may be harmless enough, as when we speak of "a photographer who flatters his subjects," or innocent, self-admitted smugness as when we say, "I flatter myself that . . . ." More often, though, it connotes gratifying vanity, favor-seeking, blandishments. Still, if forced to choose between being called a *flatterer* and an *applepolisher*, most of us would probably elect the former. The context in which *apple-polishing* is used is unmistakable: blatant insincerity and favor-seeking which are obvious to everyone, except perhaps the recipient. Such slang is always powerfully connotative.

Not all connotations are pejorative, of course, not by any means. *Kindness, compassion, thoughtfulness; strength, fortitude, guts; witty, amusing, funny; vitality, liveliness, vigor; to comfort, to console, to solace; religious, devout, reverent*—in each of these groupings, the words denote more or less the same thing but have different connotations. (Would you speak of Lincoln's "strength" or "guts" in issuing the Emancipation Proclamation?) Even with these and similar words, however, context determines appropriateness.

In short, context—the relevant *environment* of speaker, audience, and subject—is all. Consider the shifting contexts in the following: "I am slender; you are thin; he is skinny." To determine appropriateness, try testing words *aloud*. Good abridged desk dictionaries (see Chapter 8) will also help; they frequently discuss the differences in connotations among terms that have similar denotations. Pocket dictionaries and thesauruses, insofar as they merely list rough synonyms without distinction, can be quite misleading. A heightened sensitivity to connotation and denotation is essential for all effective speaking and writing.

One final word: many connotations stem from deep, often unconscious associations that we have. When, for example, the poet Phyllis Thompson concludes a poem "When I die, I will turn to bone/ like these. And dust of bone. And then, like God,/ to stone," she draws on these associations in rhyming "bone" and "stone": hardness, dryness, gray-whiteness, inertness. Drawing on equally deep but different associations, Andrew Marvell three centuries ago praised "a green thought in a green shade." He knew very well that readers of English after his lifetime would bring to the phrase associations of grass, trees, growth, life, tranquility. These associations often reveal our most elementary hopes, desires, experiences, and fears. For instance, the campaign of American blacks to replace certain negative connotations of *black* with positive ones of power and beauty has been a conscious one by users of the language to alter the ways in which we respond to words. The history of linguistic change is, among other things, the history of oppressed peoples striving to change the associations—and often the words—we live by in order to make their world more inhabitable.

9b

Abstract and Concrete

If you can describe clearly without a diagram the proper way of making this or that knot, then you are a master of the English tongue

—H. Belloc

The second of the complex ways that words name is by their abstractness and their concreteness. Words that name *specific*, tangible things are concrete; words that designate general qualities, categories, or relationships are abstract. A general term like *food* is a name for a whole group of specific things: tomato soup, fried chicken legs, chilled lettuce and alfalfa sprouts, sliced apples, cheesecake, and so forth. Note that *abstract* and *concrete* are relative, not absolute terms. Using S. I. Hayakawa's well-known model, we may speak of going up the "ladder of abstraction":

1. The tree *Charter Oak* which exists at the atomic and subatomic level, incredibly complex and changing;

2. The tree *Charter Oak* that we experience, not the word but only the limited number of features our nervous system selects from the complex reality;

3. The word *Charter Oak* itself, which is the name we give the particular perceived object but which is not the object itself, already tremendously simplified;

4. The word *oak*, which stands for what $Charter\ Oak_1$ and oak_2, oak_3, etc. share in common—in short, thousands of oaks of different ages, sizes, conditions, etc.;

5. The word *tree*, which stands for the traits we have abstracted that oaks, palms, pines, etc. share in common and which, of course, omits much, much more;

6. The word *plant*, which includes any living organism that cannot move voluntarily and usually makes its own food by photosynthesis—trees, flowers, bushes, etc.;

7. The word *organism*, which includes any living thing;

8. And so on up the ladder, as far as we choose to go.

The point, then, is not just that "abstractness" and "concreteness" are relative as terms, but also that general words as well as specific ones are necessary. For certain subjects or in certain contexts, we have to generalize, abstract, deal in whole categories. And *at its own level of generality* such prose can have great precision. The English philosopher John Stuart Mill, writing on "The Subjection of Women" in the late 1860s, is as intelligible to us now as he was to his contemporaries because of such precision:

For what is the peculiar character of the modern world—the difference which chiefly distinguishes modern institutions, modern social ideas, modern life itself, from those of times long past? It is that human beings are no longer born to their place in life, and chained down by an inexorable bond to the place they are born to, but are free to employ their faculties, and such favorable chances as offer, to achieve the lot which may appear to them most desirable. Human society of old was constituted on a very different principle. All were born to a fixed social position, and were mostly kept in it by law, or interdicted from any means by which they could emerge from it.

He continues, with the same forceful generalities, to argue that what is becoming true for the men of Western Europe and America should also be true for women. Discussing the slaveries that have vanished and "The Subjection of Women," which still remains, he is necessarily well up "the ladder of abstraction": long historical periods and change, abuses of one half of humanity, and the huge social costs are all part of his argument.

But even writers as skillful as Mill is at this "rung" come down the ladder because abstract terms at some point (preferably sooner rather than later) *have* to be given the substance of concreteness by comparisons or examples. In the following passage, for instance, Jonathan Swift makes us see and feel what the term *war* meant in the eighteenth century:

And being no stranger to the art of war, I gave him a description of cannons, culverins, muskets, carabines, pistols, bullets, powder, swords, bayonets, battles sieges, retreats, attacks, undermines, countermines, bombardments, sea-fights; ships sunk with a thousand men, twenty thousand killed on each side; dying groans, limbs flying in the air, smoke, noise, confusion, trampling to death under horses' feet; flight, pursuit, victory; fields strewed with carcases left for food to dogs, and wolves, and birds of prey; plundering, stripping, ravishing, burning and destroying. . . . I assured him that I had seen them blow up a hundred enemies at once in a siege, and as many in a ship, and beheld the dead bodies drop down in pieces from the clouds, to the great diversion of all the spectators.

The abstract term *war* is translated into the realities it too often obscures: massive cruelty, pain, and dying—pieces of human bodies dropping "from the clouds, to the great diversion of all the spectators."

This passage from Swift should suggest why teachers of writing urge their students to be specific, to be concrete. Too often students write in vague generalities that seem to have no reference to the world of anyone's experience. Yet when we are learning a language we begin with that world; we ask for the names of what we see, hear, smell, touch, taste: red, thunder, burning, smooth, salty. While the best writing moves gracefully from abstract to concrete and back from particular to general, most of us are prone to sacrifice the sharp and concrete for the colorless abstraction. Consider the following:

Vague and General	For dinner we had some really good food.
Specific	For dinner we had barbecued steaks and sweet corn.
Vague and General	She liked to argue about controversial subjects.
Specific	She liked to argue about politics and religion.
More Specific	She liked to argue about God's existence and the merits of socialism.

Paragraphs—even entire papers—that settle for "really good food" and "controversial subjects" are dull to read and thin in content because only the most shallow of broad surfaces is being glanced at; no real thought is taking place because, like an unfocused camera, the writer is not registering anything in particular.

Chapter 4 discusses several of the ways by which you can revise vague paragraphs and suggests means of noting the details to be used in giving depth to generalities. In reworking sentences, remember that a specific statement often requires no more space than a vague one, yet it can communicate much more information:

Vague	One member of my family has recently begun his professional career.
Concrete	Last week my brother Ken joined the law firm of Bailey, Harney, and Johnson.

To sum up, you will achieve only as much reality in your papers as your words actually name; you may find that the effort to think concretely takes time and imagination, but it's the only way you have of discovering your meaning.

9c

Idiom

Still another of the complex ways that words name is by *idiom,* an expression peculiar to the language, not explainable by the principles of logic or the ordinary meaning of individual words. Idioms, in short, are arbitrary, as when we say *make out* (succeed), *make up* (reconcile), and *make do* (be satisfied with). They are as fixed as the Spanish "Hace frío" ("It's cold"), which literally and unaccountably to one learning the language translates as "It makes cold."

In English, we rely on prepositions to indicate subtle but essential relationships. To take a stand *on* an issue, to be *in* a quandary, *out* of luck, *off* your rocker—these idiomatic expressions make a kind of spatial sense as figures of speech: we can, if we stop to visualize it, imagine standing *on* an issue, defending our point of view, planting our feet firmly on an ideological turf we call our own. Some verbs require prepositions that are arbitrary and unexplainable. How can persons who are learning English and know the words *take, in, up, down,* and *over* deduce the meaning of the following: *take in* (comprehend), *taken in* (fooled), *take up* (begin to do something), *take down* (humiliate), *take over,* and *overtake?* They can't, any more than they could figure out the differences among *put up with* (tolerate), *put on* (assume), *put away* (deposit, renounce), and *put down* (suppress). Each of these idioms has to be learned separately. Here are some idiomatic uses of prepositions:

> abide **by** a decision
> agree **with** a person; **to** a proposal; **on** a procedure
> argue **with** a person; **for** or **about** a measure
> angry **at** or **about** something; **with** a person
> compatible **with**
> correspond **to** or **with** a thing; **with** a person
> differ **from** one another in appearance; differ **with** a person in opinion
> independent **of**
> interfere **with** a performance; **in** someone else's affairs
> listen **to** a person, argument, or sound; listen **at** the door
> with regard **to** or **as** regards

stand **by** a friend; **for** a cause; **on** an issue

superior **to**; better **than**

wait **on** a customer; **for** a person; **at** a place; **in** the rain; **by** the hour

Idiom demands that certain words be followed by infinitives, others by gerunds. For instance:

infinitive	gerund
able to go	capable of going
like to go	enjoy going
eager to go	cannot help going
hesitate to go	privilege of going

If two idioms are used in a compound construction, each idiom must be complete.

Incomplete	He had no love or confidence in his employer.
Complete but awkward	He had no **love for,** or **confidence in,** his employer.
Improved	He had no love for his employer and no confidence in him.
Incomplete	I shall always remember the town because of the good times and the friends I made there.
Complete	I shall always remember the town because of the **good times I had** and the **friends I made** there.

9d
Figurative Language

The last broad category to be discussed is that of FIGURATIVE LAN-GUAGE. When we speak figuratively, we speak nonliterally: we compare one quite distinct thing with another for some quality we think they have in common, or identify one thing by another in terms of a common quality. Figurative language is a complex and powerful means of creating, showing, or limiting relationships. Thus, when we speak of costs being "cut," of price "gouging," or of a state "draining" its taxpayers, we are using metaphors; so, too, when we speak of a "head" on the beer, the "hands" of a clock, or the "heart" of the subject; so also when we speak of "losing our shirt," "covering" a subject, or "building up" expectations. Of course, a merchant charged with price "gouging" has not, in fact, taken a chisel and scooped grooves on his customers any more than we have made a chest incision and inspected the right auricle and right ventricle when we speak of "getting to the heart of the subject." These metaphors, *dead metaphors*, are economical and precise: price "gouging" says how we feel when we think we have been defrauded (we speak of the "chiseler"); "getting to the heart of the subject" names our intent to discover the source of its life, the vital center.

A METAPHOR is, then, a direct comparison of two things on the basis of a shared quality. The word *metaphor* is itself a buried metaphor since it means *to transfer or carry across*: when we compare, we are carrying a trait from one thing to another as if over a bridge or road. Metaphor says that one thing is another: "All the world's a stage"; "Snow *blanketed* the ground"; "The road of excess leads to the palace of wisdom." A *dead metaphor* has, so to speak, become so common in usage that it has lost its life, its capacity to startle us with the appositeness of the comparison; but it is not really "dead," only moribund, and can be brought back to life, as when we complain: "The beer was all head and no body."

Metaphor is one of the most powerful causes of linguistic growth, change, and vitality. To speak of large, expensive, inefficient automobiles as "gas-guzzlers," a sharp decline in the value of currency and a sharp rise in prices as "runaway inflation," or citizens receiving inadequate services for their money as "the public's being shortchanged"—to employ these and other metaphors that have come into general use is to be conveniently brief, exact, and vivid. Language is always vitally metaphoric because our realities—our hopes, desires, circumstances, and fears—change. The relevant issue is not whether metaphors are employed but whether they pinpoint accurate relationships, or whether they are forced, mixed, or trite. We shall return to these abuses later.

One final, positive word about metaphors, and some advice: begin to feel their presence; make a practice of discovering them not only in nouns (the *heart* of the subject) but also in verbs. Such verbs (and nouns) give nourishment in ways that the junk food of need-lessly abstract phrasing never can—the difference between saying "Cut out the deadwood" and "Avoid repetitious or unnecessary phrasing." American English has been wonderfully rich fare for our writers, as the following passage from *Huck Finn* (verbs italicized) may suggest:

> When you got to the table you couldn't go right to eating, but you had to wait for the widow to *tuck* down her head and *grumble* a little over the victuals, though there warn't anything the matter with them—that is, nothing only everything was cooked by itself. In a barrel of odds and ends it is different; things *get mixed* up, and the juice kind of *swaps* around, and the things *go* better.

Granted, Twain's prose is in a dialect that only a gifted writer could imitate; but the presence of metaphor here is clear enough. In more Standard English, F. Scott Fitzgerald's metaphors deepen the vision of Long Island and America as a lost Eden at the end of *The Great Gatsby*:

> Most of the big shore places were closed now and there were hardly any lights except the shadowy, moving glow of a ferryboat across the Sound. And as the moon rose higher the inessential houses *began to melt away* until gradually I became aware of the old island here that *flowered* once for Dutch sailors' eyes—a fresh, green *breast* of the new world. Its vanished trees, the trees that had *made way for* Gatsby's house, had once *pandered in whispers* to the last and greatest of all human dreams; for a transitory enchanted moment man must have *held his breath* in the presence of this continent, compelled to an aesthetic contemplation he neither understood nor desired, face to face for the last time in history with something commensurate to his capacity for wonder.

Other types of figurative speech—techniques for making an image—include simile, analogy, and allusion. As comparisons, these sometimes tend to be more self-conscious and formal than metaphors, though they also can be forced or become trite. A *simile* uses the words *like* or *as* to state a comparison:

Simile   "I sensed a wrongness around me, *like* an alarm clock that has gone off without being set." (Maya Angelou)

Simile   ". . . her tepid, sluggish nature, really sluggish *like* something eating its way through a leaf." (Katherine Anne Porter)

Simile a muddy sow which would "stretch out and shut her eyes and wave her ears whilst the pigs was milking her, and look *as* happy *as* if she was on salary." (Twain's Huck, again)

A comparison can be extended into an *analogy*, which not only illustrates a point but also suggests an argument or point of view. (Chapter 4 discusses the use of analogy in building paragraphs; Chapter 11, their uses and abuses in reasoning). Consider, for instance, Mary Ellman's startling analogy between astronauts and pregnant women:

> The astronaut's body is as awkward and encumbered in the space suit as the body of a pregnant woman. It moves about with even more graceless difficulty. And being shot up into the air suggests submission too, rather than enterprise. Like a woman being carted to a delivery room, the astronaut must sit (or lie) still, and go where he is sent. Even the nerve, the genuine courage it takes simply not to run away, is much the same in both situations—to say nothing of the shared sense of having gone too far to be able to change one's mind.

In an ALLUSION the comparison is made between some present event, situation, or person and an event or person from history or literature. Usually, the allusion is a brief reference to something the reader is assumed to know, as when journalists allude to a recent scandal as "another possible Watergate." Sometimes the writer may employ several allusions, as when Adrienne Rich says of a woman who reads about women in books written by men:

> She finds a terror and a dream, she finds a beautiful face, she finds La Belle Dame Sans Merci, she finds Juliet or Tess or Salome, but precisely what she does not find is that absorbed, drudging, puzzled, sometimes inspired creature, herself, who sits at a desk trying to put words together.

A sense of audience should determine what allusions, if any, are appropriate. There is no point in throwing away allusions or in alienating your readers by appearing to be more knowledgeable than they. An allusion can deepen the meaning of a statement for those who recognize the comparison, but the statement should still make perfectly clear sense without it.

And what of the abuses of figurative language, especially metaphors and similes? In "Politics and the English Language," George Orwell writes: "Modern writing at its worst does not consist in picking out words for the sake of their meaning and inventing images in order to make the meaning clearer. It consists in gumming together long strips of words which have already been set in order by someone else, and making the results presentable by sheer humbug." Much of the time these "long strips of words" are the tritest of metaphors and similes. No thought is involved, no feeling evoked; thus we get *the man in the street*, whose *home is his castle*, whose wife is *the little woman* and *knows her place is in the home*, along with the son who is *a chip off the old block;* this is *the All-American family* lucky to live in the *land of opportunity*, *working like the devil* to keep the *cancer of communism from our shores*, and generally preventing others from *undermining the foundations*. Ludicrous? Yes, it is, but only when the plastic phrasing is strung out this way. Here is a typical list of such clichés:

abreast of the times	live from hand to mouth
acid test	more than meets the eye
agony of suspense	other side of the coin
all boils down to	out in the cold
as luck would have it	poor but honest
beat a hasty retreat	proud possessor of
bitter end	quick as a flash
bolt from the blue	reigns supreme
breathless silence	rotten to the core
checkered career	slow but sure
cool as a cucumber	straight from the shoulder
deep, dark secret	tempest in a teapot
depths of despair	trials and tribulations
doomed to disappointment	undercurrent of excitement
few and far between	uphill battle
gone off the track	walking on air
green with envy	water under the bridge
growing by leaps and bounds	wave of optimism
heave a sigh of relief	wended their way
hit the nail on the head	work hand in hand
in this day and age	worth its weight in gold
jumping on the bandwagon	young in spirit
last but not least	youthful glee

Forced figures of speech often begin in dead metaphors and end in clichés.

> Forced   I was so eager for people to like me that I would take any position they wanted and bend over backward to please them.
>
> *Here, the dead metaphor "take any position" has led the writer to the cliché of "bend over backward" and into an image that strains visual and conceptual belief.*

Mixed figures usually occur when writers have stopped thinking about the *logical and visual sense* of what they're saying. Used deliberately, they make their point by comic incongruity; for example:

"Whenever he saw a spark of genius, he watered it."

OR

"The early bird gets the worm—but who wants the worm?"

Most of the time they are confused, bizarre, or both.

> Mixed   He was saddled with a sea of grass-roots opinion that his campaign workers had ferreted out for him.
>
> Mixed   The southern states, being completely agricultural, hinged around the barn.
>
> Mixed   She penetrated the impervious gaze of her challenger.
>
> *One can no more "penetrate an impervious gaze" than "be saddled with grass-roots opinion" that others have "ferreted out"—except, perhaps, in the world of Monty Python.*

9e

Other Pitfalls to Avoid

For the most part, we have been emphasizing the complex ways that words name, in order to improve your prose. Writing that is puffy with abstractions, flabby with clichés, or thin and undeveloped requires new exercises: more climbing down the ladder of abstractions, as well as up, more agile play with connotations, more striving for concreteness. We have concentrated primarily on nouns and verbs because they are the best conditioners; they *do* the most basic naming.

Words also have complex ways of confusing, obscuring, and deceiving. Misleading connotations, unidiomatic expressions, and mixed metaphors exemplify some of the means by which we can go awry; there are others. In illustrating these other ways, we will necessarily be saying, "Don't, don't." What we intend to *affirm* continually is the fact that the disciplined writer, the one who truly loves and considers words, will not, out of sheer pleasure in respect for them, want to use them carelessly. As you read, try to recall where we began—with that childlike delight, awe, and mastery that increase as we learn to communicate, teach, and command. Recalling something of that playfulness is about as close as we will ever come to the "naming day in Eden."

1. Weak Verbs

One way in which writing goes awry—never really even gets started—stems from the needless use of weak verbs. Anemic writing results when, rather than using a vigorous verb, we connect subject and complement with the verb *to be.* Such verbs, called *linking* (or *copulative*) verbs, also include *become, seen, appear, remain,* and others. We cannot, of course, write without linking verbs, especially when indicating logical equivalents:

> Yoruk doctors, with extremely rare exceptions, were women—all their great doctors were women.
>
> —THEODORA KROEBER

> *The linking verb "were" functions as an equal sign in mathematics and is appropriate to Kroeber's sentence.*

Acceptable in speech, the phrase "the reason is because" weakens written assertions. Don't waste words: "The reason I like the play is because Nora walks out the door." Be assertive: "I like the play because Nora walks out the door."

Make your verbs work. Good writers enliven their observations by selecting sharp verbs and by using verbals as modifiers. Consider these sentences from an essay by the black poet Langston Hughes:

> Let the blare of Negro jazz bands and the bellowing voice of Bessie Smith singing Blues penetrate the closed ears of the colored near-intellectuals until they listen and perhaps understand. Let Paul Robeson singing Water Boy, and Rudolph Fisher writing about the streets of Harlem, and Jean Toomer holding the heart of Georgia in his hands, and Aaron Douglas drawing strange black fantasies cause the smug

Negro middle class to turn from their white, respectable, ordinary books and papers to catch a glimmer of their own beauty.

The verbs that make the assertion of the statement, *let, penetrate, listen, understand, cause,* and the infinitives, *to turn, to catch,* are reinforced by the continual action of the participles, *bellowing, singing, writing, holding,* and *drawing.* Even the nouns *blare* and *glimmer* contribute to the energy of the passage, since in other contexts they function as verbs and carry those active connotations with them.

Occur, took place, prevail, exist, happen, and other verbs expressing a state of affairs have legitimate uses, but they are often colorless, tossed in merely to complete a sentence.

Weak	In the afternoon a sharp drop in the temperature occurred.
Stronger	The temperature dropped sharply in the afternoon.
Weak	Throughout the meeting an atmosphere of increasing tension existed.
Stronger	As the meeting progressed, the tension increased.

Linking verbs completed by an adjective or participle are usually weaker than concrete verbs.

Weak	He was occasionally inclined to talk too much.
Stronger	Occasionally he talked too much.
Weak	In some high schools there is a very definite lack of emphasis on the development of a program in remedial English.
Stronger	Some high schools have failed to develop programs in remedial English.

Unnecessary use of the passive voice also produces weak sentences (see Chapter 5).

2. Wordiness and Euphemisms

Wordiness and euphemisms also blur the horizon of clear meaning. Writing that is needlessly repetitive has a strained, awkward effect. If handled carefully, however, repetition can be effective:

The really important question is: "What does the *composer* start with; where does he begin?" The answer to that is, "*Every composer* begins with a *musical idea*—a *musical idea*, you understand, not a mental, literary, or extramusical *idea*."

—Aaron Copland

Copland emphasizes his declaration by repetitions intended to make his meaning unmistakable. Often, however, repetition is cumbersome:

Awkward   Probably the next problem that confronts parents is the problem of adequate schooling for their children.

There is no reason for emphasizing "problem" and no excuse for clumsily echoing its sound in the cautious "probably."

Improved   The parents' next problem is finding adequate schooling for their children.

Read your writing aloud to catch offenses to the ear which are elusive to the eye. Alliteration and other repetition of sounds, functional in poetry, are rarely suited to expository prose.

Unsuitable   Henderson set some kind of record by sliding farther on the slippery slope than anyone else had slid.

Intensives, such as *really, very, so, much,* which may give emphasis to conversation, weaken written language. They are often coverups for the fact that the writer lacks a vocabulary with a wide range of emphatic words. Why settle for *really angry* when there are *enraged* and *furious,* for *so happy* when there are *joyful, delighted, cheerful,* for *very bad* when there are *wicked, detestable, rotten, vile?* Every time you are tempted to dump a "really" before a word, look that word up in a good college dictionary and try to discover a word that will convey the meaning you want in all its intensity.

Often when we want to avoid harsh facts we resort to a particular kind of circumlocution, the EUPHEMISM. The Greek word means "good speech," but euphemisms seldom are good for writers. Too often they are cosmetics to cover up painful realities. To avoid facing the finality of death people have always used euphemisms: *passed on* or *passed, gone west, met his Maker, gone to her reward.* The *dear departed* rests in his casket in the *slumber room,* often having been *prepared* by the *funeral director,* who today is likely to preside at a *memorial service* instead of a funeral. Ultimately, the *loved one* is not buried but *laid to rest,* not in a graveyard but in the

Valley of Memories. Such sentimental wordiness is intended to comfort the bereaved by pretending that death is sleep, but its effect is one of stilted insincerity. There is no need, however, to go to the opposite extreme and speak ill of the subject. *Croak* and *kick the bucket,* while brisk and salty, are no closer to the fact of dying than *wrestled with the Angel of Death and was vanquished.*

3. Jargon and Pretentious Diction

Once again, Orwell: "The great enemy of clear language is insincerity." Sincerity implies candor, trust, unaffectedness. Jargon and pretentious diction mislead and boast. They are the most morally objectionable ways of using language, short of outright lying.

There are two kinds of jargon: the technical language used by certain professionals and the empty generalities that are the bluff of the insincere or incompetent writer. Here, we are *not* concerned with the inevitabilities of technical language: even handbook writers and readers need terms like *dangling modifier, comma splice,* and *faulty subordination* to name specialties of the trade. We are concerned, rather, with the ponderous, wordy, inflated prose that obscures the obvious. This is the jargon we object to; this is the language of bureaucrats, publicists, politicians, college professors, and students when they hope the inflation of their prose will raise the commonplace to the sublime.

Our minds are befogged every day by phrases like *capability factor, career potential, divergent lifestyles, culturally disadvantaged, socio-personal development, decision-making process, social interaction, protective reaction strike, holistic learning procedures, methodologies, technical implementations, fundamental value structures.* We cannot easily escape from this publicized network of confused language, but if we learn to recognize the stylistic flavor of jargon, we may avoid it in our own writing. Jargon words are, by and large, abstract rather than concrete, and contain more than one syllable (as if the jargon writer assumed that the addition of a syllable would add weight to the word). Jargon words are often nouns masquerading as verbs: *concretize, finalize, interiorize.* Sometimes nouns are turned into adverbs or adjectives by the addition of the suffix *-wise: languagewise, subjectwise, moneywise, weatherwise.* Jargon is best deflated by a translation into clear English:

A corollary of reinforcement is that the consequences of responding may be represented exhaustively along a continuum ranging from those that substantially raise response likelihood, through those that have little or no effect on response likelihood, to those that substantially reduce response likelihood. An event is a positive reinforcer if its occurrence or presentation after a response strengthens the response. Sometimes good grades, words of praise, or salary checks act as positive reinforcers. An object or event is a negative reinforcer if its withdrawal or termination after a response strengthens the response. Often bad grades, shame, or worthless payments act as negative reinforcers. The above notion sounds complex and difficult to apply but is indeed extremely simple.

The relatively plain English of the third and fifth sentences contrasts vividly with the puffy syllables, the awkward constructions, the straining adverbs and unclear substantives that clutter the rest of the paragraph. What the writer wants to say is, as he notes, fairly simple, though abstract:

> The psychological principle of reinforcement means that the likelihood of a learned response is increased if a person is rewarded for responding correctly. Good grades, words of praise, or salary checks act as positive reinforcers. Bad grades, shame, or worthless payments are negative reinforcers in that a response is strengthened only if such consequences are eliminated.

In addition to being obscure and tiresome, jargon, when it conceals or distorts the reality it describes, can be dangerous, even deadly. The phrase *anti-personnel detonating devices* obscures the chilling reality of bombs that kill men, women, and children. Similarly, the deviousness of official statements like "The U.S. cannot foreclose any option for retaliation" distracts us from the protest we might register had the writer said what he meant: "The U.S. will use nuclear weapons if necessary."

Pretentious diction, like the pretentious person, is stiff, attitudinizing, phony—in short, a bore. Our diction becomes pretentious if we always choose the polysyllabic word over the word of one syllable, a Latinate word when an Anglo-Saxon one will do, flowery phrases in place of common nouns and verbs. Writing should be as honest and forthright as plain speech. And since we have the opportunity to revise and edit what we write, it should be even more economical, direct, and to the point.

Sometimes, ordinary words seem inadequate to carry the weight we want our thoughts to have, so we encumber statements with ornate language:

A perusal of the tomes penned by the ancient bards can influence the lifestyles and existential patterns of our future.

The sentence is saying little more than "the study of ancient books can teach us how to live," but the pompous and wordy language is out of proportion to the statement it makes.

Occasionally, we lapse into pretentious diction in an attempt to give our prose a lofty or poetic tone. To protect yourself against this, read your writing aloud to a classmate. If he or she looks uncomfortable or laughs at the wrong places or seems annoyed by the tone, examine the diction of your paper for phony phrases, for words that don't sound like you.

Be wary of words that dress up simple facts: *inebriated* for *drunk, utilize* for *use, institution of higher learning* for *college* or *university, purchase* for *buy, charisma* for *popularity* or *appeal, profitable enterprise* for *money-maker.* As you consult your college dictionary in order to develop your vocabulary, note the fine distinctions among synonyms and listen to the sounds of the words to judge whether they will strike your reader as counterfeit or genuine.

Exercise 1

Pick one or two words that interest you (nouns, verbs, adjectives, and adverbs are your best bet) and consult the Oxford English Dictionary in your library. The OED (its familiar title) is the indispensable reference for anyone curious about our language: it gives a word's first known appearance in print, its changing uses (with historical examples), and the fullest record we have of its connotations and denotations. Write a full paragraph in which you (1) note the word's primary shifts in meaning, (2) analyze these shifts for some common principle, logic of associations, or consistency in figurative use that runs throughout, and (3) indicate what you take to be its primary connotations and denotations now.

Exercise 2

With the help of a dictionary (and perhaps a dictionary of Roman and Greek mythology) discover the concrete particular in which each of these abstract words originated. Write a brief explanation of why and how you think some of these words came to mean what they mean today.

cereal	cupidity	hackneyed	panic
chapter	erotic	infant	paradise
comma	genius	language	surgery

Exercise 3

Choose three words that have similar denotations: for example, to please, to gratify, to delight; concerned, involved, committed; fame, celebrity, stardom. *Then write a paragraph on the differing connotations of each word, and compose a sentence or two to show how the word is used in context.*

Exercise 4

Choose four concrete nouns and take them up three or four rungs on "the ladder of abstraction," beginning above the atomic and subatomic rung.

Exercise 5

Choose four abstract nouns (for example, wealth, humanity, art) *and take them down four or five rungs on "the ladder of abstraction."*

Exercise 6

Analyze the following paragraph from a memo distributed by a Communications Department. Is it jargon and why? What clichés or submerged figures of speech can you find? Do they conflict with one another? Translate the paragraph into Standard English if you can, and if not, be prepared to say why.

All courses (process or outcome) in the University system that are judged to contain written or oral communication goal statements should constitute a set of courses from which a student must select some number. This client-oriented marketplace approach to core requirements is a solution. Enrollment determines which courses will survive and which will not. However, academic tradition is rife with distrust of student judgment; and it can result in a self-fulfilling prophecy where faculty compete in playing to the "house" because they are convinced that ultimately only those who do will survive. This solution is usually condemned without trial.

Exercise 7

Analyze the following student paragraphs for clichés, pretentious diction, jargon, and so on. Translate the paragraphs into Standard English if you can, and if not, be prepared to say why.

Henry

As human beings, each of us grows and benefits in some way from ordinary experience each day. For the past five years I have sought a higher understanding of human attitudes, especially those of a positive nature, and of the mental processes which underlie and reinforce them. By listening to people, I have gained much wisdom; by seeking out those who have much to share, I have grown. I have begun the arduous but satisfying search for maturity.

One individual who has given me special insights is Henry. A married, older person who has had much experience in diverse walks of life, he is a special person. One day he joined a group of us after classes while we were sitting on the grass. I immediately felt his desire to communicate some special aspect of his life—something that was preoccupying him very deeply.

Henry began to relate the experience of his recent separation from his wife. It bothered me at the time that someone with such an understanding nature as his would have such a deep personal problem, and I questioned him regarding the reasons for his trouble. At the time I was involved in a personal relationship and wanted our communications to be open. What Henry told me became one of the most valuable teachings of my life. He told how he and his wife had stopped making a conscious effort to work at their relationship. Their life had become a burden and a sorrow.

My own relationship has grown into a beautiful experience, but it is one I have to work at and strive to improve. Henry made me realize that we have to lose our selfishness. I feel that I have matured, and we have grown together, and I am a better person for it. Today is the first day of the rest of my life.

Exercise 8

Analyze the diction of the following sentences for exactness, connotation, figures of speech. Be prepared to discuss what words would more effectively express what the writer was trying to say.

1. Thus the young athletes are the workhorses that made the ends of the budget meet to form a vicious circle.

2. Our balloons of egotism filled with the air of freshman knowledge were soon to be pricked by the pinpoints of self-awakening.

3. As the town grew, the theater obtained a foothold in the hearts of the citizens.

4. This is the Achilles' heel of their position. For once a set of ideas are ruled fair game for witch-hunters, Pandora's box has been opened, and there is no ending.

5. Drinking seems to have its claw in the economy of San Francisco.

6. Our tariff wall will continue to be an unsurmountable obstacle until we throw a span across the ebb to link the rest of the world to our industrial growth.

7. Poring through *Paradise Lost* was like wading in deep water.

8. A good education is the trunk for a good life for it is the origin of all the branches which are your later accomplishments.

9. His immaturity may improve with age.

10. The basic objective of the indoctrination program is to build strong class spirit and to weed out those who are leaders in the class.

11. Darwin's *Origin of Species* began an epic of materialism.

12. Margaret Mead's book had a great success because Americans are grossly interested in sex.

13. I flitted away my first three years in college.

14. Jefferson and Madison were two of the most prolific characters our nation produced at that time in history.

15. The reason I like Christina Rosetti's *Goblin Market* is because it shows how love between sisters triumphs over the prowess of darkness.

16. Because he did not follow the code, he was blandished from society.

17. He was a male shogunist pig.

18. She succeeded in deleting her flaw and, in doing so, became a stronger, ursine being.

19. In Tillie Olsen's story, "Help Her to Believe," the mother paradoxically loves her child but has to farm it out to a day-care center.

20. Sarty does not realize that his father is the noose around his neck until Sarty gets his feet planted firmly on the ground to stop his mutation into a passive being.

Exercise 9

On the basis of sound association and of your knowledge of words, make an educated guess as to the lexical meaning of the following archaic words. Then look up the words in Charles MacKay's Lost Beauties of the English Language. *If you arrived at a meaning different from that listed in MacKay, explain the reasons for your definition.*

crambles (n)	roaky (adj)
flathers (n)	sculsh (n)
glunch (v)	skime (v)
jugbitten (adj)	slive (v)
mazle (v)	slodder (n)
mirkshade (n)	sloom (v)
overword (n)	snurl (v)
pleach (v)	suckets (n)
prog (v)	tartle (v)
quillet (n)	ugsome (adj.)

Exercise 10

Write a short essay or prepare a class discussion using examples from your own experience in which you defend or deny the truth of this Confucian maxim: "If language is incorrect, then what is said is not meant. If what is said is not meant, then what ought to be done remains undone."

GLOSSARY OF USAGE

This Glossary discusses only the more commonly misused words in student prose. In recommending that you observe rules of usage, no one is suggesting that you abandon your natural speech for what may to your taste seem stilted. But remember that written language is selective. It is the cultivation of that which grows wild and natural in our speech. Teachers of language, like practiced gardeners, tend to be conservationists. Before becoming annoyed with what may seem to you petty complaints, consider that your teacher and the editors of handbooks and dictionaries are attempting to preserve distinctions that you may not be aware of. Roger Sale devotes a number of pages in his book *On Writing* to a concept that will be lost should the distinction between *disinterested* and *uninterested* not be preserved. Rather than decide that the difference in prefixes is inconsequential, read the entry in this chapter and then read his argument. The choice of whether or not to observe standards of usage is yours, but the choice should be an informed and prudent one.

a, an   Indefinite articles. *A* is used before words beginning with a consonant sound, *an* before words beginning with a vowel sound. Before words beginning with *h*, use *an* when the *h* is silent, as in *hour*, but *a* when the *h* is pronounced, as in *history*.

above   Colloquially used as an adjective: "The above remarks." In writing, this usage should be confined to legal documents.

accept, except   Different verbs which sound alike. *Accept* means "to receive," *except* "to leave out."

I *accepted* the diploma.

When assigning jobs, the dean *excepted* students who had already worked on a project.

adapt, adopt   To *adapt* is to change or modify to suit a new need, purpose, or condition.

Man can **adapt** to many environments. The movie was **adapted** from a novel.

To *adopt* something is to make it one's own, to choose it.

The couple **adopted** a child. Our club **adopted** "Opportunity knocks" as its motto.

adverse, averse   Often confused, but important to distinguish. *Adverse* means "antagonistic" or "unfavorable."

Adverse weather forced postponement of the regatta.

*A*verse means "opposed to"; only sentient beings can be *averse*.

She **was averse** to sailing under such conditions.

affect, effect   Words close in sound and therefore often confused. *Affect* as a verb means "to influence." *Effect* as a verb means "to bring about."

Smoking **affects** the heart.

How can we **effect** a change in the law?

As a noun, *effect* means "result."

One **effect** of her treatment was a bad case of hives.

The noun *affect* is a technical term used in psychology.

aggravate   Means "to intensify" or "to make worse."

The shock **aggravated** his misery.

Colloquially, it means "to annoy," "irritate," "arouse the anger of."

ain't   A nonstandard contraction of *am not, is not* or *are not.* Not to be used in formal writing.

all ready, already   Not synonyms. *All ready* refers to a state of readiness.

The twirlers were **all ready** for the half-time show.

Already means "by or before the present time."

Has the game **already** started?

all right Unlike the pairs of words in the preceding and following entries, *all right* stands alone. There is no word *alright*, although many people, misled by the existence of *altogether* and *already*, assume that there is.

all together, altogether *All together* refers to a group with no missing elements.

If we can get our members *all together*, we can begin the meeting.

Altogether means "completely."

You are *altogether* mistaken about that.

allude, refer To *allude* is to make an indirect reference.

Did her letter *allude* to Sam's difficulties?

To *refer* is to call attention specifically to something.

The instructor *referred* us to Baudelaire's translations of Poe.

allusion, illusion, delusion An *allusion* is a brief, indirect reference.

Anyone who speaks of "cabbages and kings" is making an *allusion* to *Alice in Wonderland*.

An *illusion* is a deceptive impression.

He enjoyed the *illusion* of luxury created by his imitation Oriental rugs.

A *delusion* is a mistaken belief, implying self-deception and often a disordered state of mind.

She fell prey to the *delusion* that she was surrounded by enemy agents.

among, between *Among* always refers to more than two.

He lived *among* a tribe of cannibals.

Between is used to refer to two objects or to more than two objects considered individually.

The scenery is spectacular *between* Portland and Seattle.

The governors signed the agreement *between* all three states.

amoral, immoral Anything *amoral* is outside morality, not to be judged by moral standards.

The behavior of animals and the orbits of the planets are equally *amoral*.

Anything *immoral* is in direct violation of some moral standard.

Snatching an old lady's purse is generally considered to be an *immoral* act.

amount, number *Amount* is used as a general indicator of quantity; *number* refers only to what can be counted.

An immense *amount* of food was prepared for the picnic, but only a small *number* of people came.

anxious, eager *Anxious* refers to worry about the future.

He was *anxious* about the outcome of his exam.

Eager indicates hopeful excitement.

She was *eager* to meet her relatives from Ohio.

but Often used colloquially in such idioms as "I can't help but think." In writing "I can't help thinking" is preferred. If the nonstandard expression "I don't know but what he wants to do it" leads to confusion (does he or doesn't he?), it should be avoided in speech, too.

can, may In formal speech and in writing, *can* is used to indicate ability, *may* to indicate permission.

If you *can* open that box, you *may* have whatever is in it.

In informal questions, *can* is often used even though permission is meant.

Can I try it next? Why *can't* I?

censor, censure To *censor* something (such as a book, letter, or film) is to evaluate it on the basis of certain arbitrary standards to determine whether it may be made public.

All announcements for the bulletin board are *censored* by the department secretary.

Censor is often used as the equivalent of "delete."

References in the report to secret activities have been *censored.*

Censure means "to find fault with," "to criticize as blameworthy."

Several officers were *censured* for their participation in the affair.

compare to, compare with, contrast with   *Compare to* is used to show similarities between different kinds of things.

Sir James Jeans *compared* the universe *to* a corrugated soap bubble.

Compare with means to examine in order to note either similarities or differences.

Compare this example *with* the preceding one.

Contrast with is used to show differences only.

Contrast the life of a student today *with* that of a student in the middle ages.

concur in, concur with   *Concur in* refers to agreement with a principle or policy.

She *concurred in* their judgment that the manager should be given a raise.

Concur with refers to agreement with a person.

She *concurred with* him in his decision to give the manager a raise.

contact   The use of *contact* as a verb meaning "to get in touch with" has gained wide acceptance, but a more exact term such as *ask, consult, inform, meet, see, telephone,* or *write* is generally preferable.

continual, continuous   The first is widely used to indicate an action that is repeated frequently, the second to indicate uninterrupted action.

We heard the *continual* howling of the dog.

The dog kept a *continuous* vigil beside the body of his dead master.

data, phenomena, criteria   Latin plural, not singular forms, and so used in formal writing. But the use of *data* (rather than *datum*) with a singular form is widespread.

These **data** have been taken from the last Cenus Report.

Criteria and *phenomena* are always plural. The singular forms are *criterion* and *phenomenon.*

Scientists encountered a **phenomenon** that could not be evaluated under existing **criteria.**

different from, different than   *Different from* is always acceptable usage.

College is **different from** what I had expected.

Different than is not acceptable.

dilemma, problem   A *dilemma* is a choice between two equally distasteful alternatives.

We faced the **dilemma** of paying the fine or spending three days in jail.

A *problem* is wider in meaning, referring to a difficulty or a question that must be solved.

The United States must soon resolve the **problem** of guaranteeing an energy supply for the 1980s.

disinterested, uninterested   *Disinterested* means "unbiased," "impartial." *Uninterested* means "without any interest in," or "lacking in interest."

Although we were **uninterested** in her general topic, we had to admire her **disinterested** treatment of its controversial aspects.

due to   In writing, *due to* should not be used adverbially to mean *because of.*

Colloquial

I made many mistakes, **due to** carelessness.

Preferred in Writing

I made many mistakes **because of** carelessness.

Due to is an adjective and usually follows the verb *to be:* His illness was *due to* exhaustion.

each other, one another   When two individuals are involved in a reciprocal relationship, *each other* is used.

My sister and I respected *each other.*

When more than two individuals are mutually related, *one another* is appropriate.

The sheep rubbed up against *one another* in the chill.

either, neither   As subjects, both words are singular. When referring to more than two, use *none* rather than *neither.*

Either red or pink is appropriate.

I asked Leahy, Mahoney, and another Irishman, but *none* of them was willing.

enthused   Either as a verb (he *enthused*) or adjective (he was *enthused*), the word is strictly colloquial. In writing, use "showed enthusiasm" or "was enthusiastic."

equally as good   A confusion of two phrases: *equally good* and *just as good.* Use either of the two phrases in place of *equally as good.*

Their TV set cost much more than ours, but ours is *equally good.*

Our TV set is *just as good* as theirs.

-ess   Feminine ending acceptable in such traditional words as *waitress, actress, hostess.* But many persons object to *poetess, authoress, sculptress* as patronizing and demeaning. Unless an *-ess* word has a long history and you are sure there are no objections to its use, it is best to avoid it.

etc.   Avoid the vague use of *etc.;* use it only to prevent useless repetition or informally to represent terms entirely obvious from the context.

Vague   The judge was honorable, upright, dependable, *etc.*

Preferred   The judge was honorable, upright, and dependable.

Standard   Use even numbers like four, eight, ten, *etc.*

Avoid *and etc.,* which is redundant.

expect   Colloquial when used to mean "suppose," "presume": I *expect* it's time for us to go.

Preferred   I *suppose* it's time for us to go.

factor   Means "something that contributes to a result."

Industry and perseverance were *factors* in her success.

Avoid using *factor* to mean vaguely any thing, item, or event.

Vague   Ambition was a *factor* that contributed to the downfall of Macbeth.

Since *factor* includes the notion of "contributing to," such usage is redundant as well as vague and wordy.

Preferred   Ambition contributed to the downfall of Macbeth.

farther, further   In careful usage *farther* indicates distance; *further* indicates degree and may also mean "additional." Both are used as adjectives and as adverbs: *a mile farther, further disintegration, further details.*

faze, phase   *Faze* is a colloquial verb meaning "to perturb," "to disconcert." *Phase* as a noun means "stage of development" (a passing *phase*); as a verb it means "to carry out in stages." Be wary of *phase in* and *phase out*, which have the ring of jargon.

fewer, less   *Fewer* refers to number, *less* to amount. Use *fewer* in speaking of things that can be counted and *less* for amounts that are measured.

Fewer persons enrolled in medical schools this year than last.

Less studying was required to pass chemistry than we had anticipated.

flaunt, flout   Commonly misspelled, mispronounced, and, therefore, confused. *Flaunt* means "to exhibit arrogantly," "show off."

He *flaunted* his photographic memory in class.

Flout means "to reject with contempt."

They *flouted* the tradition of wearing gowns at graduation by showing up in bluejeans.

flunk   Colloquial for *fail*. In formal writing, I *failed* (not *flunked*) the test.

former, latter   Preferably used to designate one of two persons or things. For designating one of three or more, write *first* or *last*.

get, got, gotten *Get to* (go), *get away with*, *get back at*, *get with* (something), and *got to* (for *must*) are widely used in speech but should be avoided in writing. Either *got* or *gotten* is acceptable as the past participle of *get*.

good An adjective. Should not be used in formal writing as an adverb meaning "Well."

Colloquial She plays tennis *good*.

Standard She plays tennis *well*. She plays a *good* game of tennis.

had have, had of Nonstandard when used for *had*.

Nonstandard If he *had have* (or *had of*) tried, he would have succeeded.

Standard If he *had* tried, he would have succeeded.

had ought Nonstandard as a past tense of *ought*. The tense of this verb is indicated by the infinitive that follows.

He *ought to go;* she *ought to have gone*.

hanged, hung When *hang* means "to suspend," *hung* is its past tense.

The guard *hung* a black flag from the prison to signal the execution. When *hang* means "to execute," *hanged* is the correct past tense.

After the flag was *hung*, the prisoner was *hanged*.

hardly, barely, scarcely Since these words convey the idea of negation, they should not be used with another negative.

Nonstandard We *couldn't hardly* see in the darkness.
We *hadn't barely* finished.

Standard We *could hardly* see. We *had barely* finished.

hopefully Although widely used in speech to mean "it is to be hoped," or "I hope" (*Hopefully*, a check will arrive tomorrow), the adverb *hopefully* is used in writing to mean "in a hopeful manner":

They spoke *hopefully* of world peace.

imply, infer *Imply* means "to suggest" or "hint"; *infer* means "to reach a conclusion from facts or premises."

His tone **implied** contempt; I **inferred** from his voice that he did not like me.

insupportable, unsupportable Often confused, but not synonymous. *Insupportable* means "unable to be endured."

The noise of the bulldozers during the lecture was **insupportable**.

Unsupportable means "not capable of support."

The building program, though imaginative, is financially **unsupportable**.

inter, intra As a prefix *inter* means "between" or "among": *international, intermarry; intra* means "within" or "inside of": *intramuscular, intramural.*

irregardless A nonstandard combination of *irrespective* and *regardless.*

Regardless (or **irrespective**) of the minority opinion, we included the platform in the campaign.

its, it's Often confused. *Its* is the possessive form of *it.*

My suitcase has lost one of **its** handles.

It's is the contracted form of *it is* or *it has.*

It's a good day for sailing.

It's been a month since I mailed the check.

kind, sort Colloquial when used with a plural modifier and verb: *These* kind (or *sort*) of books *are* trash.

Standard **This sort** of book **is** trash.
      These kinds of books **are** classics.

In questions, the number of the verb depends on the noun that follows *kind* (or *sort*).

What kind of **book is** this?
What kind of **books are** these?

kind of, sort of   Colloquial when used to mean "rather."

Colloquial   I thought the lecture was *kind of* dull.

Standard   I thought the lecture was *rather* dull.

Also colloquial when followed by *a* or *an*:

What *kind of a* house is it? It is *sort of a* castle.

Preferred in Writing

What *kind of* house is it?

It is *a sort of* castle.

latest, last   *Latest* means "most recent"; *last* means "final."

I doubt that their *latest* contract proposal represents their *last* offer.

lay, lie   Often confused. *Lay* is a transitive verb meaning "to put" or "place" something. It always takes an object. Its principal parts are *lay, laid, laid*. *Lie* is intransitive; that is, it does not take an object, and means "to recline" or "to remain." Its principal parts are *lie, lay, lain*. When in doubt, try substituting the verb *place*. If it fits the context, use some form of *lay*.

Present Tense   I *lie* down every afternoon.

Past Tense   I *lay* down yesterday after dinner.
I *laid* the paper by his plate two hours ago.

Perfect Tense   I *have lain* here for several hours.
I *have laid* the paper by his plate many times.

let's   Contraction of *let us*. In writing, it should be used only where *let us* can be used.

Colloquial   *Let's don't* leave yet. *Let's us* go.

Standard   *Let's not* leave yet. *Let's* go.

liable, likely, apt   In careful writing, the words are not interchangeable. *Likely* is used to indicate a mere probability.

They are *likely* to be chosen.

Liable is used when the probability is unpleasant.

We are *liable* to get a parking ticket.

Apt implies a natural tendency or ability.

She is *apt* to win the musical competition.

like The use of *like* to introduce a clause is widespread in informal English, especially that used by advertising agencies. In edited writing, *as, as if,* and *as though* are preferred.

Colloquial   This rose smells sweet, **like** a flower should.

Standard   This rose smells sweet, **as** a flower should.
        This perfume smells **like** roses.

However, don't always avoid *like* in favor of *as,* or you may end up in ambiguities.

As Lady Macbeth, she was disturbed by the sight of blood.

Does the writer mean "in the role of Lady Macbeth" or "similar to Lady Macbeth"?

literally Means "precisely," "without any figurative sense," "strictly." It is often inaccurately used as an intensive, to emphasize a figure of speech: I was *literally* floating on air. This makes sense only if one is capable of levitation. Use the word *literally* with caution in writing.

loan, lend Traditionally, *lend* is a verb, *loan* a noun, but *loan* is also used as a verb, especially in business contexts.

The company **loaned** us money for the down payment.

most As a noun or adjective, *most* means "more than half."

Most of us plan to go to the dance.

Most people admire her paintings.

As an adverb, *most* means "very."

His playing was **most** impressive.

Most is colloquial when used to mean "almost," "nearly."

Colloquial

Most everyone was invited.

Preferred in Writing

Almost everyone was invited.

myself Correctly used as a reflexive: I cut *myself,* sang to *myself,* give *myself* credit. Colloquial when used as an evasive substitute for *I* or *me.*

Colloquial

My brother and *myself* prefer coffee.

She spoke to my brother and *myself*.

Preferred in Writing

My brother and *I* prefer coffee.

She spoke to my brother and *me.*

of   *Could of, may of, might of, must of, should of,* and *would of* are slurred pronunciations for *could have, may have, might have, must have, should have,* and *would have;* they are nonstandard in writing.

off of   A colloquial usage in which *of* is superfluous.

Colloquial

Keep *off of* the grass.

Preferred in Writing

Keep *off* the grass.

outside of   Correct as noun: He painted the *outside of* the house. Colloquial as a preposition: He was waiting *ouside of* the house. Omit the *of* in writing. Nonstandard as a substitute for *except for, aside from.*

part, portion   A *part* is any piece of a whole; a *portion* is that part specifically allotted to some person, cause, or use.

We planted beans in one *part* of our garden.

She left a *portion* of her estate to charity.

party   Colloquial when used to mean "person," as in "The *party* who telephoned left no message." Write *person.*

percent   In formal writing use *percent,* or *per cent,* only after a numeral—either the spelled-out word (six) or the numerical symbol (6). The sign (%) is used only in strictly commercial writing. The word *percentage,* meaning "a part or proportion of a whole," is used when the exact amount is not indicated.

A large *percentage* were Chinese.

Thirty-one *percent* were Chinese.

principal, principle   As a noun, a *principal* is the head or leading figure in an institution, an event, or a play.

The *principals* in the negotiations were Henry Kissinger and Le Duc Tho, who later shared the Nobel Peace Prize.

Used as an adjective, *principal* refers to a leading feature or element in a group.

The *principal* types of telescopes are the refracting and the reflecting, or Newtonian, telescope.

A *principle* is a rule.

The main *principle* in skiing is to keep on one's feet.

real   Colloquial when used for "very." Write *very* hot, not *real* hot.

reason is because, reason why   Both of these expressions are wordy. Eliminate *is because,* or *why,* or *the reason is.*

Wordy   The *reason* we came *is because* we knew you needed help.

Concise   We came *because* we knew you needed help.

regarding, in regard to, with regard to, in relation to, in terms of   These windy phrases are usually dispensable. Replace them with concrete terms.

Wordy   *With regard to* grades, she was very good.

Concise   She *got* very good grades.

Reverend   In formal writing should be preceded by *the* and followed by a title or full name, or both.

The Reverend Mr. (or **Dr.**) Carter preached.

The Reverend Amos Carter led the march.

The widely used form *Reverend Amos Carter* is deplored by usage panels but accepted by the clergy. The use of *the reverend* as a noun, to mean "a clergyman," is strictly colloquial.

sarcasm   Not interchangeable with *irony. Saracastic* remarks, like *ironic* remarks, convey a message obliquely, but sarcasm contains the notion of ridicule, of an intention on the part of the writer to wound. Only persons can be *sarcastic*, while both persons and events can be *ironic*.

The sergeant inquired **sarcastically** whether any of us could tell time; it was **ironic** that his watch turned out to be ten minutes fast.

sensual, sensuous   Both words refer to impressions made upon the senses. Their connotations, however, are widely different. *Sensual* most often carries unfavorable connotations. It is applied primarily to the gratification of appetite and lust.

Sensual delights are often considered inferior to spiritual pleasures.

Sensuous, on the other hand, is used literally or approvingly of an appeal to the senses (the *sensuous* delight of a swim on a hot day), and can even refer to such abstract appeals as those found in poetry.

Milton's **sensuous** imagery calls upon sight, touch, and even smell to form the reader's impression of Eden.

set   A transitive verb meaning "to put" or "place" something. It should be distinguished from *sit*, an intransitive verb.

Present Tense	I *sit* in the chair. I *set* the book on the table.
Past Tense	I *sat* on the chair. I *set* the book on the table.
Perfect Tense	I *have sat* in the chair. I *have set* the book on the table.

shall, will   The distinction is rapidly fading, although many grammarians still conjugate the verb as *I shall, you will, he will, we shall, you will, they will.* Most writers, however, now use *will* throughout. *Shall* may still be used for emphasis (He *shall* be heard); since it is less common than *will*, it has a formal tone. See page 414.

should, would   Generally interchangeable in modern American usage, though they formerly followed the pattern of *shall* and *will*. Each word does, however, have some special uses. *Should* substitutes for "ought to" (He *should* go on a diet); *would* for "wanted to" (He could do it if he *would*). *Should* indicates probability (I *should* be finished in an hour); *would* indicates custom (He *would* always call when he got home).

so, such   Avoid using *so* and *such* as vague intensifiers: I am *so* glad; I had *such* a good time. The full forms, which should always be used, are *so . . . that, such . . . as.*

I was *so* glad to find that print *that* I bought copies for all my friends.

Such a good time *as* that is worth repeating.

some   Colloquial when used as an adverb meaning "somewhat" (I am *some* better today) or when used as an intensifying adjective (That was *some* dinner).

Preferred in Writing

I am *a little* (or *somewhat*) better today.

That was *an excellent* dinner.

sure   Colloquial when used for "certainly, "surely," as in "He *sure* can play poker."

that, which   *That* is largely used to introduce restrictive clauses, which limit or define the antecedent's meaning and are not set off by commas.

The law *that* gave women the right to vote was passed in 1920.

Which is used to introduce nonrestrictive clauses, which do not limit or define the meaning of the antecedent. Nonrestrictive clauses are always set off by commas.

The 19th Amendment, *which* gave women the right to vote, was passed in 1920.

The amendment is already identified by number; the clause "which gave women the right to vote" merely gives additional information.

Often the antecedent will be identified in a preceding sentence, in which case the clause is still nonrestrictive.

The 19th Amendment gave women the right to vote. This amendment, *which* was passed in 1920, marked the entry of women into party politics.

toward, towards   Interchangeable. *Toward* is more common in America, *towards* in Britain.

transpire   In formal writing, where the word properly belongs, it means "to become known." It is colloquial in the sense of "happen," or "come to pass."

try and   Often used for "try to," but should be avoided in writing. I must *try to* (not *try and*) find a job.

unique   Adverbs such as *rather, more, most, very* are colloquial when used to modify *unique*. Since the word means "being the only one of its kind," no thing can be more (or less) unique than another.

This copy of the book is **unique.**

This copy of the book is **very rare.**

up   Do not add a superfluous *up* to verbs: We opened *up* the box and divided the money *up*. Write: We opened the box and divided the money.

very, much (with past participles)   A past participle that is felt to be a part of a verb form, rather than an adjective, should not be immediately preceded by *very* but by *much, greatly,* or some other intensive. A past participle that can be used as an adjective may be preceded by *very*.

Colloquial

He was **very** admired by other students.

He was **very** influenced by the teacher.

Preferred in Writing

He was **very much** admired by other students.

He was **greatly** influenced by the teacher.

He was a **very** tired boy.

wait on   Colloquial for *wait for*.

ways   Colloquial in such expressions as *a little ways*. In writing, the singular is preferred: *a little way*.

where . . . to, where . . . at Colloquialisms whose prepositions are redundant or dialectal.

Colloquial

Where are you going **to**? **Where** is he **at**?

Preferred in Writing

Where are you going? **Where** is he?

who, whom (For the choice between these forms, see the section on Case, page 405.)

-wise Commercial jargon when attached to nouns in such combinations as *taxwise, languagewise, timewise, moneywise*. To be avoided in serious writing.

would have Colloquial when used in *if* clauses instead of *had*.

Colloquial

If he **would have stood** by us, we might have won.

Preferred in Writing

If he **had stood** by us, we might have won.

write-up Colloquial for a description, an account, as in "a *write-up* in the newspaper."

you, one *You* is not acceptable in formal prose. Replacing *you* with *one* often creates prose that is formally correct, but stiff. Rewrite, usually with *we* or a general noun such as *Americans*.

Colloquial   *You* can't do that in Baltimore.

Formal   *That* is not allowed in Baltimore.
            No one can do that in Baltimore.

10

SEEING THE PAST: THE HISTORICAL CONTEXT

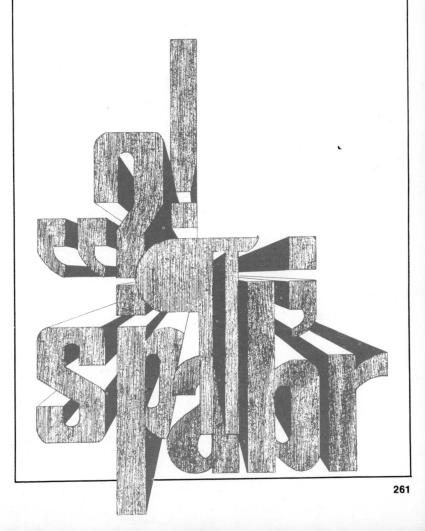

As you write, you learn to recognize two dimensions of your situation: deciding what you have to say and communicating that decision clearly to your audience. Few of us reflect much about the third dimension of our writing, the historical context. We do not imagine that a thousand years from now anyone will read our writing, much less study it. Quite likely, the anonymous author of *The Battle of Maldon* (ca. A.D. 1000) little imagined that we would be studying his work or that his language would alter so radically that our reading it would become primarily a task of translation, even though our language has its roots in his.

An awareness of roots enriches both our reading and our writing. In some cases, we cannot understand an author at all without a sense of the history of words. When Samuel Johnson mentions "a nice distinction," he means a close, not a pleasant one. In other cases, our historical awareness of a word brings to mind its past and its life. When we see the word *girdle* in these lines of Matthew Arnold's,

> The Sea of Faith
> Was once, too, at the full, and round earth's shore
> Lay like the folds of a bright girdle furled.
>
> —"DOVER BEACH"

we may think of a modern corset, but also of a Biblical belt which ties up loose robes and allows freer action. We can then see Arnold's choice as one suggesting both restraint and freedom. Because this meaning has its roots in the King James version of the Bible, it strengthens our sense of a Biblical faith that is lost. We may never see the word *girdle* again without thinking of a Biblical meaning or of Arnold's use of it. In fact, we could now hardly write the word without some echo of these uses in mind.

Understanding the history of a word gives us power over its connotations, makes us more careful in our diction, and sharpens our sense of participation in the life of our language. The same is true of our understanding of the history and variety of language. We form possessives to singular nouns by adding an apostrophe and the letter "s." A seventeenth-century gentleman would have written (and perhaps said), "a man his hat" or "a house his window," expressions that may seem to us as quaint and clumsy as a dinosaur. Yet we recognize in them the ancestors of our own means of showing possession, and feel the past of our language a bit more deeply.

Any living language, like a biological organism, is undergoing constant, gradual change. The English we know and use today is only one stage in a long, presumably endless, process of gradual development. Everyone who has read Chaucer knows that his English was different from ours, and if we go back another five centuries, we find a still different stage of English—so different from that used today as to be unintelligible to all but the scholar.

Here is a sentence written by King Alfred about the year 880. It concerns the *hors-hwael*, "horse-whale," or as we say today, "the whale-horse," or *walrus*:

> Hīe habbath swīthe aethele bān on hiora tōthum, ond hiora hȳd bith swīthe gōd tō sciprāpum.

All but two of these words are in common use today, but they have changed so much over the centuries as to be unrecognizable to most of us.

We might guess at the archaic verb-ending *-eth* and translate two words as "haveth" and "be-eth"—that is, *have* and *be*. A linguist who knew the facts of grammatical and phonetic change in English could interpret *bān* as "bone," *tōthum* as an old plural form of *tooth*, *hȳd* as "hide" (skin), *gōd* as "good," and *sciprāpum* as "ship-ropes." He would recognize *aethele* as akin to German *edel*, meaning "noble," and *swīthe* as an intensive, like *very*. If we know that *hīe* and *hiora* correspond to *they* and *their*, and that some prepositions have changed their meanings if not their written forms, we can translate:

They have a very noble bone in their teeth (that is, tusks), and their hide (rawhide) is very good for shipropes.

Historical linguistics is concerned with the principles of change from one stage of a language to another. Linguistic evolution is gradual: phonetic change proceeds by the accumulation of slight variations in sound which may hardly be noticed by the people who make them. Today many people pronounce "going to" as "goin to" or "gawn ta" or even "gonna"* without being aware of these differences. Similarly, in the past the sound of English words varied slightly from speaker to speaker, or from place to place, and an increment of small changes has brought about the difference between King Alfred's English and Chaucer's, and between Chaucer's and our own. There were other kinds of change as well: new words were borrowed, old words disappeared, spellings varied, meanings shifted. But phonetic change—that is, change in the sound of the language—is basic for a linguist.

Phonetic changes are often regular enough to be generalized into principles. Old English *rāp* (pronounced to rhyme with Modern American English *top*) became something like "rawp" in Chaucer's day and has become *rope* in our own time. If you say these three words in front of a mirror, you will notice that the vowel in *top* is made with the mouth spread wide toward the sides. To pronounce "rawp" you will move your lips so that your open mouth is in the shape of an approximate square. To pronounce *rope* you round your lips into a still smaller opening, even protruding your lips a little. This account is oversimplified, but it suggests a kind of principle: the change from old English *rāp* to Modern English *rope* involves progressive rounding of the mouth. The principle can be checked by looking at similar words; Old English *bān*, *rād*, *hām*, and *stān*, have become Modern English *bone*, *road*, *home*, and *stone* by the same principle of progressive rounding.

---

*The spellings used here to indicate different pronunciations of "going to" illustrate some shortcomings of the English alphabet. There are no letters to indicate unmistakably the vowel sounds we have tried to suggest by "gawn ta." Linguists have provided such symbols [gɔn tə], and enough others to indicate fairly accurately all the sounds used in English. For any serious study of linguistics, learning a phonetic alphabet is indispensable.

Some of the consonants have also changed, and the changes can often be described by phonetic principles. A number of English consonant sounds can be arranged in pairs according to the way they are formed. The tongue is held in approximately the same position for pronouncing s and z; the difference in sound depends on whether our vocal cords vibrate to produce the voiced z or we whisper the voiceless s. Here are some other examples:

voiced	voiceless
b	p
d	t
g	k
v	f

A change from a voiced consonant to its voiceless counterpart is fairly common, and we can find many instances in the history of English of the opposite change, from voiceless to voiced. (Notice the difference, which is not indicated by the spelling but can be heard, between the s in *house* and the s in *houses*.) But there is no simple explanation for a change from a voiceless s to a g, nor from a d to an f, and in fact such changes have seldom if ever occurred in the history of English. Phonetic change seems to occur only along what a geologist would call "natural lines of cleavage." These natural lines in language can often be explained by a careful study of the mechanisms of speech.

Historical linguists in the nineteenth century noticed that there are marked similarities between some English words and words with the same meaning in other European languages. Consider, for example, English *mother*, Old English *modor*, Dutch *moeder*, German *mutter*, Celtic *mathair*, Latin *mater*, Greek *meter*, and Lithuanian *moter*. Such similarity can hardly have been accidental, and it raised some questions. Were these words all variants of a common original? If so, what was the original?

By comparing thousands of related words in different languages, historical linguists could note some relationships: Latin is more like Greek than like Dutch; Dutch is more like English than like Russian. Romance languages (for example, French, Spanish, Italian) have many close similarities, and since it can be shown historically that the Romance languages have evolved from dialects of Medieval Latin, it seems likely that other European languages have evolved as descendants of a single very ancient language. This hypothesis is now supported by so much circumstantial evidence that it is almost universally accepted by linguists. The original parent language is called Indo-European, since some of its branches are spoken in Iran and northern India as well as in Europe. No record of Indo-European remains, because the people who spoke it had not invented a writing system. But comparative linguists have worked out a good many of the principles of phonetic change operating in the Indo-European languages and have reconstructed many words of the parent language.

Data from other sciences have contributed to our knowledge of the location and way of life of this hypothetical Indo-European people, and linguistic research has helped the historian. For example, since a good many widely separated languages in the family have similar words for *salmon, turtle, honey,* and *beech* tree, it is a fair assumption that the parent language had these words and that the speakers were acquainted with these things. The geographic limits of these animals and plants can be determined: the turtle did not live north of Germany; the beech tree did not grow naturally much to the east of the Vistula River in Poland; the line marking the occurrence of the honeybee can be drawn on a map.

Somewhere within these boundaries, in the fourth millennium B.C., the Indo-European tribesmen lived as small farmers, who kept cows for milk, knew and used the wheel, and were organized into patriarchal families. Paul Thieme locates the original homeland of the Indo-Europeans on the Baltic coast, between the Vistula and the Elbe rivers, in what is now East Germany and Poland. Other linguists have placed it farther east and south, in what is now the Ukraine. But there is general agreement that the original homeland was in central Europe rather than in Asia.

During the third millennium the tribes began migrations which took them east to Persia (present-day Iran) and India, south to Italy and Greece, north to Scandinavia, and west to Spain and the British Isles. As they separated, they developed their own dialects, which eventually became the separate languages of the Indo-European family.

The changes that, over the centuries, produced the branch of the Indo-European family to which English belongs are often regular enough to be described in general "laws." For example, it can be shown that the Germanic languages (English, Dutch, German, Scandinavian, and some others) all went through a regular change of consonants in the first millennium B.C., whereas other Indo-European languages, such as Greek, Latin, or Sanskrit, preserved for the most part the original consonants. In the Germanic languages, an original Indo-European voiced *b* became the voiceless *p*. Latin *labia* preserves the original *b*, but English *lip* shows the change to *p*. Similarly, Latin *turba* (crowd, group) keeps the original Indo-European consonants, but English *thorp* (village) shows, among other things, the shift of *b* to *p*.

Turba and *thorp* are thus related by being descended from a common Indo-European root, and they are called *cognates*. Words that are borrowed by one language from another usually do not show the phonetic changes that distinguish the Germanic languages from their Indo-European brothers and sisters. For example, we have borrowed the Latin stem of *turba* directly into English in such words as *turbid*, *turbulent*, and *disturb*. Borrowings are relatively recent; cognates go back to the early stages of each language. The words for *mother* listed on page 265 are presumably all cognates, descendants of a common Indo-European ancestor which probably sounded something like "mah-tár." Within historical times we have borrowed *maternal* and *matron* from Latin and Old French.

The following lists show other changes that make up the Germanic Consonant Shift, often called "Grimm's Law." The Indo-European consonants are represented here by roots of Latin and Greek words, instead of less familiar words from Sanskrit or Lithuanian. After each root, some English words borrowed from Latin or Greek are added in parentheses to indicate the meaning. Since they are borrowings, they preserve the original Indo-European consonants.

Indo-European *d*	becomes	Germanic *t*
ed- (*edible*)		eat
dic- (*dictate, diction*)		teach

Indo-European *g*	becomes	Germanic *k*
gen- (*generate, genus*)		kin
ager ("field," as in *agriculture*)		acre

Indo-European *p*	becomes	Germanic *f*
pyr (*pyre, pyrotechnics*)	.	fire
pullus (*pullet, poultry*)		fowl
Indo-European *t*	becomes	Germanic *th*
tu (*second person pronoun*)		thou
frater (*fraternal*)		brother
Indo-European *k*	becomes	Germanic *h*
cornu (*cornet, cornucopia*)		horn
canis (*canine*)		hound

With a little knowledge of Greek and Latin roots, some ingenuity, and a good dictionary, a student will be able to find other examples of the Germanic Consonant Shift and of borrowed words that preserve the original Indo-European consonants.

Exercise 1

Look up the etymologies of the following pairs of words, keeping in mind the Germanic Consonant Shift.

1. canine, hound
2. domestic, tame
3. gusto, choose
4. intrude, threaten
5. octopus, eight, foot

6. peril, fear
7. pedal, foot
8. piscatorial, fish
9. subjugate, yoke
10. tension, thin

The Indo-European family includes almost all of the languages of Europe, from Scandinavia to Greece, from Russia to Ireland, and some of the languages spoken in Armenia, Iran, and northern India. Among the latter, Sanskrit is especially important to the linguist because it is the oldest recorded Indo-European language, appearing first in the *Vedas*, ancient religious books of India written down in the second millennium B.C.

There are many other language families in the world, but the only important non-Indo-European languages in Europe are Finnish and Hungarian, which belong to the Finno-Ugric family. Basque, spoken in the Pyrenees along the border between France and Spain, is a linguistic mystery; it has no known relatives and may be a lone survivor of the lost Iberian languages spoken in the Late Stone Age throughout southern Europe.

The Germanic tribes who invaded Great Britain in the fifth century came from the low country around the base of the Danish peninsula. They conquered all of the island except Scotland and Wales and imposed their Germanic dialects on the Celts who survived the invasion. (Celtic languages still persist in Scotland, Wales, Ireland, and the Breton peninsula in France.) Old English, as the Anglo-Saxon dialects of the invaders are now called, was not written down until after the arrival of Christian missionaries from Rome in the year 597. Like their modern counterparts the world over, these missionaries wrote down the language of the natives in the Roman alphabet, and they taught English monks to write and make translations. In so doing, they rendered a great service to historical linguistics, for they provided us with the earliest specimens of the English language.

To this Old English language stock, a great many words borrowed from other languages have been added. Some Latin words used for place names in the first century, when the Roman legions established army posts throughout the island, have remained on the map. Most conspicuous is the Latin word for "camp," *castra*, which frequently appears in place names like Lancaster, Winchester, Worcester, and the like. More Latin words were borrowed when Christianity was introduced into England, and since the Renaissance, a great many Latin and Greek words, especially those dealing with education, law, and science, have been borrowed, sometimes by way of French. In the following sentence, all italicized words are of Latin origin.

> Today the *curriculum* of our *educational institutions—elementary, secondary,* and *collegiate—is administered* by *deans, superintendents, coordinators,* and *principals* as well as *professors* and other *faculty members.*

The traditional fields of study often have Greek names: *geography, theology, economics, physics, psychology, mathematics, philosophy, botany.* Modern physics has taken Greek roots to form such words as *thermodynamics, atomic, cyclotron, electronics, gamma ray,* and *proton.*

French words were borrowed in increasing numbers after the Norman Conquest, especially in the thirteenth and fourteenth centuries. A famous passage in Scott's *Ivanhoe* reminds us that language can reflect differences in social class. The Saxon serfs in *Ivanhoe* used English words for the animals they tended: *ox, cow, sheep, swine.* Their Norman overlords had little need for the names of the animals but were interested in the end product; they used French words for the different kinds of meat that appeared on their tables: *beef, veal, mutton,* and *pork.*

French words make up the largest part of the borrowed words in our everyday vocabulary, but the English-speaking peoples have borrowed words from almost every language they have come in contact with. *Sky* and *happy* and *window* come from Scandinavian; *flannel* and *whiskey* from Celtic; *tub, yacht,* and *pump* from Dutch; *pretzel, kindergarten,* and *hamburger* from German. From Italian come words like *balcony, piazza,* and *umbrella,* as well as many terms used in music and art. Spanish has contributed *cigar, alligator, mosquito,* and many words used in the American Southwest, such as *canyon, rodeo, lariat,* and *mesa.* From Hebrew have come *camel* and *sabbath;* from Arabic, *algebra* and *sugar* and *alcohol.* Many words for fruits and flowers come from Persia: *peach* and *orange, tulip* and *lilac;* and we have borrowed *tea* and *mandarin* from China, *kimono* and *tycoon* from Japan, *pajama* and *bungalow* from India, and *gong* and *gingham* from Malaysia.

Exercise 2

In a good dictionary, look up the ultimate origin of the following borrowed words:

1. alkali	8. lute
2. alligator	9. Negro
3. amethyst	10. potato
4. bamboo	11. skipper
5. calico	12. skunk
6. cherub	13. stirrup
7. isolate	14. syrup

Since Old English times, the language with its borrowed additional vocabulary has changed steadily. Englishmen have apparently always had a tendency to telescope and shorten words—a tendency that today sometimes reduces *extraordinary* from six syllables to three: "extráwdnry." Old English *hlāf-weard* (literally, "loaf-guard") meant the leader of a tribe; *hlāf-dige* (literally, "loaf-kneader") meant a woman. Both words were shortened in Middle English to *loverd* and *lavedi,* and they have been further shortened in Modern English to *lord* and *lady.*

Many changes in the form of words fall into regular patterns like that already mentioned in the change from Old English *rāp* to *rope*. A pattern of vowel changes, very common in German, where it is called *umlaut*, also appears in Old English and has produced such pairs of words as *man* and *men*, *strong* and *strength*, *blood* and *bleed*, *goose* and *geese*, *full* and *fill*, *mouse* and *mice*. Voiceless consonants tend to become voiced when they occur between vowels: contrast *house* and *houses*, *bath* and *bather*, *wife* and *wives*. Especially in the vicinity of vowels, a *k*-sound may become palatalized to *ch*, as in *chill* (compare *cool*), Greenwich (compare *Berwick*), and Winchester (compare *Lancaster*). Palatalization also distinguishes verb from noun in *bake* and *batch*, *speak*, and *speech*, *stick* and *stitch*. Other forms of palatalization account for pairs like *skirt* and *shirt*, *gard(en)*, and *yard*, *drag* and *draw*.

Initial *k* disappeared before an *n*, and *w* before an *r*, though we still preserve a record of the earlier pronunciation in modern spelling: *knee*, *know*, *knight*; *wrap*, *wreck*, *wrong*. Inflectional endings, once as common in English as in Latin, have mainly eroded away. In King Alfred's time there were still three different declensions of the noun, and one of them had six different forms, illustrated in *stan*, *stanes*, *stane*, *stanas*, *stana*, *stanum*. Today *stone* has only two phonetic forms, *stone* and *stones*, though in spelling we distinguish two more, *stone's* and *stones'*. The inflection of verbs has been similarly simplified, and we have given up entirely the old inflection of adjectives. The final *e*'s that trouble students trying to read Chaucer aloud are vestigial remnants of earlier inflectional endings. Today their only function is to indicate the pronunciation of the preceding vowel, as in *hate* compared with *hat*, or *site* with *sit*.

The constant erosion of word endings has increased the importance of word order in modern English. In a highly inflected language such as Latin, the function of a word in the sentence (subject, object, and so on) is indicated mainly by case endings. One can write "puer puellam amat" or "puellam amat puer" without changing the meaning of the sentence. As long as a reader knows that *puer* (boy) is in the nominative case and that adding an *m* to *puella* (girl) makes the case of the noun objective, he will translate the sentence correctly as "boy loves girl."

In English, lacking case endings for nouns, we indicate the function by the position of the noun. If it precedes the verb, it is the subject; if it follows the verb, it is usually the object. There is a great difference in meaning between the sentence "Boy loves girl" and the inverted sentence "Girl loves boy." Pronouns still show a case distinction between *I* (subject) and *me* (object), between *he* and *him* or *she* and *her*. But even so, we usually put *I* before the verb and *me* after it. In modern English word order is functional in more subtle ways than simply indicating case; precise degrees of emphasis or tone can be conveyed by the position of a word or phrase, as the sections on sentence unity in Chapter 6 demonstrate.

Exercise 3

The second word in each of the following pairs shows a change in form. What phonetic principles explain the various changes? Look for changes in sound, not in spelling.

1. calf, calves
2. dike, ditch
3. food, feed
4. kirk, church
5. long, length
6. louse, lousy
7. proud, pride
8. stink, stench
9. tug, tow
10. use (noun), usable

Exercise 4

Look up in a good dictionary the Old English forms of the following words, and note the consonant sounds that have been dropped in Modern English.

1. eye
2. leap
3. loud
4. lee
5. nil
6. rack (and ruin)
7. retch
8. ring

Just as the spoken forms of words change by slow degrees over a long period of time, so do the meanings of words. Old English *hlāf-weard* must once have meant something like "loaf-keeper" (compare modern *breadwinner*), but along with the change in form to *lord* there has been a considerable change in meaning. Such semantic changes do not follow regular principles, but one can often trace the psychological connections between the different meanings of a word. *Head* means, basically, a part of the body. But it is easy to see how this meaning was extended, as a kind of metaphor, in such phrases as "head of lettuce," "head of a pin," "come to a head," "headmaster," "newspaper headline," "head on a glass of beer," "headwaters," and "headland." Latin *candidatus* originally meant "dressed in white"—that is, in one's best toga. Since aspirants for public office dressed in white, *candidate* has come to mean a person seeking office, but the original idea of whiteness has disappeared entirely. English *hearse* came, through Old French, from Latin *hirpex*, a rake or harrow. When it first appeared in English it meant a frame with candles on which a coffin was placed. The frame with candles sticking up around the edge looked like a primitive harrow. Later the meaning changed to a device for carrying a coffin and eventually to the leading Cadillac in a funeral procession.

Some meanings are expanded, or generalized. *Gossip* originally had the fairly specific meaning of "god-parent," but it became generalized to any talkative person, and eventually to what he or she said. *Barn* at first meant a place for storing barley. *Manuscript* originally meant "written by hand," but since the invention of the typewriter, the word has been expanded to mean an author's typed or written copy, as distinguished from a printed version. By the same kind of change, some airplanes can now "land" at sea.

Other words become more specialized in meaning. In Shakespeare's time, *deer* still meant any kind of wild animal ("Rats and mice and such small deer"), but today it means only one kind. *Starve* meant "to die" in Chaucer's time: the little boy in the Prioress's Tale "starved" of a cut throat. Today the word means to die from lack of food, or even just to be very hungry.

A few words that once had a derogatory meaning have become complimentary terms. *Shrewd* used to mean harmful or malicious, from the supposedly poisonous small animal called a shrew. Today a good many people would be pleased to be described as "shrewd." Similarly, *knight* once meant a servant boy, and only under the feudal system did the word acquire its present honorific sense.

A great many words have undergone the opposite change. *Hussy* is a contraction of Old English *huswif*, "house wife," and originally had none of its present depreciatory sense. *Wanton* and *lewd* once meant simply undisciplined or untaught. A *knave* was once merely a boy, a *boor* was simply a farmer, and a *villain* a farm laborer at a villa or village.

Folk etymology—a bad guess as to the meaning or origin of a word—may cause a change in the form of a word. *Crayfish* (American and Irish *crawfish*) comes from a misunderstanding, and hence misspelling, of Middle English *crevis*. A *penthouse* represents an English misunderstanding of Old French *apentis*, from Latin *appendix*, "an addition to." *An umpire* was originally *a nompere* (Old French *nonper*, not one of a pair of contestants), but the *n* of the original word was taken by the English to be the last letter of the article *an*.

Exercise 5

Look up the etymologies of the following words and try to account for the changes in meaning.

1. adder (snake)
2. auger
3. belfry
4. bishop
5. bridegroom
6. can (as in *ashcan*)
7. churl
8. cretin
9. marshal
10. newt
11. pretty
12. shrive
13. volume
14. wiseacre

Even a brief look at the history of English shows that changes in the form and meaning of words have been taking place at every stage of the language, and they are still going on today, in spite of the efforts of teachers and textbooks. Historical linguistics gives little encouragement to those who would guard the purity of English by fixing it in a permanent form. Changes are slow, however, and any one generation finds the language fairly stable. Dictionaries attempt to record the current state of the language, though they often include archaic or obsolete forms and meanings.

At any given stage, a language constitutes a system: certain ways of putting words together are acceptable whereas others are not. The system of a language at a given stage is its *grammar*, but the word *grammar* is used in other senses, too. W. Nelson Francis, in his often reprinted article, "Revolution in Grammar" (*Quarterly Journal of Speech*, October 1954), makes some useful distinctions. The meaning just described, which Francis calls Grammar 1, is the actual structure of a language—the way in which English words *must* go together if sentences are to be acceptable to other people who speak the language. Certain patterns of verbal sounds are used by all people who speak English; other patterns are never used. When a child learns to speak English—to use these acceptable patterns—he has at least made a start at learning the grammar of English in this first basic sense. A schoolboy may not know that he knows Grammar 1, but he would find a statement like "This my is book" unacceptable and "This is my book" a perfectly normal English sentence. Even though he cannot explain *why* the first sentence is wrong, he knows that it just isn't English.

Consider the following sentences:

1. Send me your new address.

2. Send your new address to me.

3. Send to me your new address.

4. Send your new address me.

No one would object to the first two sentences, though the pattern of the second sentence is probably a little less common. The third sentence, though intelligible, sounds stilted, slightly foreign. We would not be apt to use it ourselves, though we would understand it readily if a foreigner spoke it. The fourth sentence, however, is just not English, and everyone who recognizes this knows at least a part of Grammar 1.

The second meaning of *grammar* is suggested by a phrase like "a grammar of the English language," or by the word *grammarian*. If we want to know *why* "This my is book" is wrong, we need some systematic description of the acceptable forms and patterns of words in English sentences. Such generalized, explanatory descriptions may be called Grammar 2. The plural form "descriptions" is purposely used to indicate that there is no single correct way of describing and explaining English. Grammar 2 is any theoretical account of Grammar 1.

Language, like walking, is initially learned by trial and error. All normal children eventually learn to walk, though they may never learn exactly what happens to nerves and muscles when they are walking. Similarly, every normal child learns to speak the language of the adults around him, and he thus acquires the Grammar 1 of his particular dialect without conscious effort. If he wants to know, or is required to learn, the "theory" of the language he uses every day, he will have to study Grammar 2.

Is there any practical advantage to studying Grammar 2? There may be, though probably not so much as you think. Knowing something about the process of walking may improve our efficiency when we walk; it may help us distribute our weight properly and thus avoid weakened or flattened arches. Similarly, a knowledge of Grammar 2 may lead to greater efficiency in our use of the language; it may increase our knowledge of the possibilities of Grammar 1. It will not help much with simple sentences like "Send me your new address," but it may help us to communicate precisely more subtle or more complex meanings, or to redistribute the weight in a sentence so as to emphasize one part and play down another.

In the mind of the public, however, the chief reason for studying grammar at all is to enable us to speak and write "correct" English and to avoid "bad grammar." This is the third sense of the word in common use. Grammar 3 usually consists of prescriptive rules for "correct" English usage. Don't say "between you and I"; the preposition *between* requires a complement in the objective case. Don't say "Everyone brought their own lunch"; *everyone* is singular in number and must be followed by a singular pronoun. And so on.

Many people uncritically assume that studying Grammar 2, an analytic description of the language, is a necessary first step in correcting "errors" like those in the preceding paragraph, which are the main concern of Grammar 3. It may be that some grammatical analysis is useful in explaining why certain constructions are "wrong," but common sense suggests that a complete theoretical account of the structure of English is hardly necessary for correcting errors, in, say, agreement of subject and verb. Furthermore, an underlying assumption has not been proved: that if a student understands the theory of a language consciously, this knowledge will become usable on the subconscious level, where languages are really learned. Finally, linguists have raised serious doubts about the adequacy of the traditional Grammar 2 that has been taught since the Renaissance. Intelligent students are disturbed by the many exceptions to the grammatical principles they are taught, and linguists would add to the charge of inconsistency that of incompleteness.

Traditional Grammar 2 is concerned primarily with written, rather than spoken, English, and it thus simply ignores some very important ways of signaling meanings, like accent and pitch. A classic example from C. C. Fries is this headline:

PROFESSOR RAKES LEAVES AFTER CHAPEL

If we stress the word *rakes* and pronounce it with a relatively high pitch, we produce "Professor Rakes leaves after chapel." But if we stress the second syllable of *professor* and the word *leaves*, pronouncing both with a higher pitch than we give to *rakes*, we are saying "Professor rakes leaves after chapel." The point is that traditional Grammar 2 ignores completely the intonation of a sentence, an important element of spoken English.

Furthermore, traditional Grammar 2 attempts to fit written English into a theoretical framework derived from classical languages. The categories of our traditional grammar were borrowed from Latin and Greek. These are both highly inflected languages, in which the relationship between words is indicated by adding an ending to the root word. English has lost most of its inflectional endings; it depends on word order, rather than word endings, to indicate the difference between "Dog bites man" and "Man bites dog." The so-called parts of speech—eight categories into which all words are supposed to fit—had some meaning in Latin. One can tell from its form that *quies* is a noun, *quiesco* is a verb, and *quietus* is an adjective. But in English the word *quiet* may be, without change of form, a noun (*peace and quiet*), a verb (*to quiet down*), or an adjective (*a quiet hour*). To apply the Latin concept of parts of speech to English words is bound to produce some confusion. Since many English words fit into several categories, how can we say what part of speech a given word is?

One way out of the difficulty is to use terms like *noun, verb,* or *adjective* to refer to function in a sentence. That is, let function determine the part of speech, instead of vice versa. If *brick* is used to name an object, it is a noun. If it is used to describe an object (*a brick wall*), it is an adjective. This functional approach to grammatical analysis, using traditional Latin names to indicate function in a sentence, works fairly well for a rough analysis of sentence structure. But linguists have argued that new categories, derived from English as it is spoken rather than borrowed from Latin, might be more accurate and more useful.

In an effort to arrive at a Grammar 2 derived inductively from English, C. C. Fries studied fifty hours of transcribed telephone conversations among educated middle-class citizens of Michigan, analyzing their actual speech patterns. His book *The Structure of English* proposed new categories for English grammar, and they have since been modified and used by many structural linguists. Structural linguistics applies to English the objective approach used by anthropologists studying a native language in the field. Making no advance assumptions, the structural linguist tries to limit himself to statements about the forms of words and their structure in sentences, regardless of their meaning. Structural linguists pride themselves on being scientific: their statements are tentative (subject to change or qualification in the light of further data), verifiable by anyone who knows Grammar 1, and objective (they describe what is, instead of what should be). Although linguists do not yet agree on all details of structural analysis, nor on the terminology to be used in describing it, the method has uncovered some very important features of English that were obscured by traditional grammar.

More recently, however, a new school of linguists has been pointing out some shortcomings of structural linguistics. Perhaps the most serious, in the eyes of theorists, is that structural linguistics accounts for only part of a language: that is, it is limited to the "corpus" of words and sentences that it analyzes, and a manageable corpus must always be smaller than the entire language. If we were to analyze the structure of that part of the English language represented by fifty hours of telephone conversations among typical Americans (as Fries did), we could work out inductively some plausible principles for the formation of the past tense of verbs and the plural form of nouns. But suppose, as is not unlikely, that in the chosen fifty hours no one happened to use the words *weave* and *ox*. The grammar derived from this corpus would be imcomplete because it would fail to note that the past tense of *weave* is usually *wove*, rather than *weaved*, and that the plural of *ox* is *oxen*. Since any corpus is only a sample of a language, a grammar derived from the corpus is likely to be incomplete.

What some linguistic theorists wanted was an abstract method that could be used to "generate"—that is, account for—all the possible constructions in the language that native speakers would agree were acceptable, and none of the constructions that native speakers would reject. Such a system not only would be a significant addition to knowledge, but might provide a basis for ultimate computer translation from one language to another. Using concepts and symbols drawn from mathematics and symbolic logic, Noam Chomsky has devised the outlines of a system of this kind—a generative grammar that theoretically would account for all possible English sentences. Because of its use of "grammatical transformations" (rules for transforming one constituent structure into another), Chomsky's system is commonly called "Transformational Grammar," though the more general term "Generative Grammar" is sometimes employed.

Most linguists agree that transformational grammar gives the completest and most accurate description of the structure of English, and some have tried to make this particular Grammar 2 the basis of teaching English in the schools. Such an effort would be reasonable if it were generally agreed that the goal of English courses is a full understanding of the structure of English. But few schools or colleges aim so high. The student already knows (in the sense of being able to use) the basic Grammar 1 of his language, and English courses usually offer only the rough analysis considered necessary in the teaching of Grammar 3. For this, the terminology of the traditional Grammar 2 seems adequate, and it has the additional advantage of being at least in part familiar to most college students. This handbook attempts to utilize some of the insights of modern structural analysis without discarding entirely the older terminology.

Whatever system of grammatical analysis is used, we must meet squarely a basic question raised increasingly by modern linguists: Are the "errors" catalogued by Grammar 3 really errors? Is there a standard by which we can call certain usages correct and others wrong?

In some areas, like vocabulary, the answer is a qualified yes. All language is based on a social agreement to attach certain meanings to verbal symbols, and we all agree that in English *bread* is something we eat, not something we build walls with. There may be slight disagreement about the exact limits of a word's meaning: whether a certain bakery product is to be called *bread* or *cake*, for example. But it is our general agreement about the meanings of English words that makes communication possible, and we can say unequivocally that Mrs. Malaprop was wrong when she referred to "an allegory on the banks of the Nile."

Since the eighteenth century, a good many people have tried to give equally certain answers to questions about correct usage— about ending sentences with prepositions, or using contractions like *ain't*. Communication is not involved here: one construction conveys the meaning as well as the other. Is one usage right and another wrong? Among the rich varieties of expression possible in English, is there such a thing as *the* correct way of speaking or writing?

It is easy to ridicule this question as naive. To show its supposed triviality, Bergen Evans cites a hypothetical case: a student takes a mouse to a biologist with the question "Is this a correct mouse?" Such a question would seem nonsensical to a scientist. A biologist can tell about the species, age, sex, and physical condition of a mouse, but he has no standard for determining the "correctness" of mice. Evans is implying, of course, that linguistics, like other sciences, should be descriptive rather than evaluative, and he bolsters this point by citing another hypothetical example. Suppose that you want to make a grammar of the Eskimo language. The first thing you must do is to find some Eskimos. Then you must listen to what they say, record it, and by trial and error figure out how the language works. If while you are doing this, someone says, "Yes, but is this correct Eskimo?" all you can answer is, "Well, this is what they say in Baffinland." You might add that in Greenland they say it a little differently, but the implication is clear that the question is as nonsensical as the question about the correct mouse. What the Eskimos say is a fact, and all a linguist can do is record, analyze, and describe the facts. If English is what English-speaking people say and write, a linguist must base his analysis on what people are speaking and writing, without worrying about its "correctness."

Is one man's English, then, as good as that of the next? Are there no errors to be corrected by Grammar 3? It depends on the meaning one attaches to the term *error*. Certainly there are differences in the way different people speak English. When these differences are conspicuous, fairly regular, and confined to a particular area, we accept them as regional dialects, like Southern or Down East, or as racial, like the Black English dialect, widely spoken by Americans of African ancestry. But to a linguist, dialects are not necessarily limited to particular regions or races. People of different social classes in the same region may speak differently (on one side of the tracks "He don't" is common; on the other, nearly everyone says "He doesn't"), and any family is apt to have its own peculiarities of pronunciation, vocabulary, and syntax. It is probably true, in the last analysis, that no two people speak the language in precisely the same way—that is, each person has his own dialect (or idiolect, as the linguist would call it) of English. Why should any one dialect be called correct and others wrong?

The answer comes, in part, from history. In the past, the dialect of a metropolis has often gained prestige among the rural or provincial citizenry and has eventually been accepted as the standard. Modern English is a direct descendant of the dialect spoken in and around London in the fourteenth century. Furthermore, the written language of metropolitan areas has an advantage in its wider range of sentence patterns and its very much larger vocabulary, as compared with the dialects spoken in the provinces or backwoods.

But there is a sociological answer, too. In any given period there are apt to be differences between the language used by the educated classes and that used by uneducated people, rural or urban; and these differences almost always reflect different degrees of social prestige. In some countries, where society is more rigorously stratified than in the United States, one's speech determines one's social level, as Eliza Doolittle demonstrated in *My Fair Lady*. Language is not so important as a determinant of social prestige in the United States, but there is still a wide difference between the more prestigious "edited English" of the professional and executive classes and the dialects spoken, and sometimes written, by the less educated. It is unscientific for a linguist to ignore this difference, either by denouncing and banishing one level as "bad English," or by pretending that one level is "as good as" the other, since so many people speak it. Scientific objectivity calls for an accurate description of each dialect, and such a description should include some indication of the contexts in which either level gains or loses prestige for the speaker.

The kind of English prescribed by Grammar 3 might thus be redefined as a particular dialect of English that has special prestige because of the people who use it. A student ought to be able to write this dialect even though he usually speaks on a much more colloquial level. Why should we study the endless idiosyncracies of English spelling? *Beleive* is just as intelligible in written contexts as *believe*, but a person who misspells the word may lose caste in the eyes of others. Why should students be taught to write "I felt bad" instead of "I felt badly"? Because most people need to be concerned about the effect of their language on others. A person who confuses adjectives and adverbs may still communicate his meaning clearly enough, but he will reveal an ignorance of Grammar 3 that many people still regard as deplorable.

The motives behind studying Grammar 3 may thus be ultimately snobbish. The rules are often arbitrary conventions, without historical or rational justification, but they represent a level of usage found in practically all books, magazines, and newspapers; and this level of English cannot be ignored by teachers in a fluid society in which people are constantly trying to move upward in the social scale. Since this level of speech is not necessarily part of the Grammar 1 that children acquire unconsciously by imitating their elders, edited English, like table manners and polite behavior, must be studied and learned if one is to share whatever prestige attaches to speaking and writing "correctly."

Dictionaries and handbooks of composition usually try, as we have, in Chapters 8 and 9, to distinguish different levels of English usage. When descriptive labels such as *provincial, slang,* or *substandard* are used, they are meant as approximate guides to the social acceptability of different kinds of English. Almost everyone recognizes examples drawn from vocabulary. *Tired* is the normal English word, appropriate in both speech and writing, to indicate the feeling that follows overexertion. *Exhausted* is a little more literary; it is more apt to appear in writing than in speech. *Fatigued* is almost purely literary; though you know the word, you have probably never actually spoken it in conversation, and if you use it in informal writing, the chances are that your style is pompous. *Tuckered out* sounds provincial, as though the speaker came from the backwoods or were deliberately affecting folksy language. *Pooped* and *beat* are slang; you would not be likely to use either term when talking to the president of your college or in a letter applying for a job. A handbook is simply shirking part of its job if it does not point out that, things being what they are, the use of *like* as a conjunction may cast doubt on the social and educational background of the writer, even though one can find many examples of the usage on television and in the advertising columns of magazines.

In this handbook, the rules and the descriptive labels attached to examples of usage are not meant to be final judgments on what is, and what is not, correct by some mythical standard of "pure" English. Our purpose is more modest and more utilitarian; we are trying, among other things, to provide a guide for the perplexed. We are saying that, in our opinion, the level of usage implied by these rules and prescriptions is that of the people who determine the prestige values of the language: editors, writers, and educators. If you choose to violate the rules they follow, you should do so deliberately, not unwittingly.

Your choice of language, in writing or speaking, reflects a historical choice as well as a personal one. Whether you realize it or not, you are contributing to the history of your language, enriching it with your own exploration of words and sentences, or merely participating in a dialect. Your use of language is an unavoidable and sometimes thrilling responsibility, where the weight of the past, the variety of the present, and the possibility of the future meet.

11

REASONING

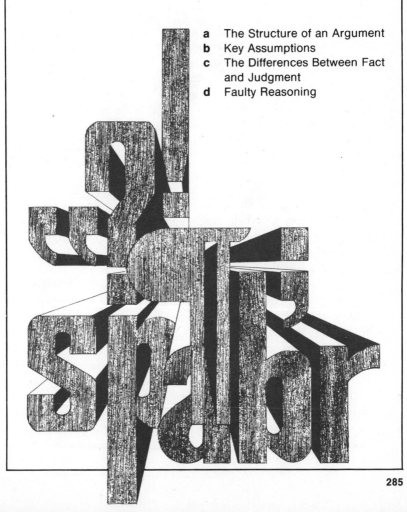

11
REASONING

Any expository writing that is more than just a bare summary of dates and events involves reasoning: making generalizations, drawing deductions, arriving at conclusions. You may be explaining your actions or beliefs; you may be discussing a book you find persuasive or unpersuasive; you may be arguing for or against some new policy. In each case, you are trying to convince your readers, and if you credit them with intelligence, you will want to convince them by reason.

As used in this chapter, the term "logic" applies in the broad sense of sound and adequate reasoning. The treatment is necessarily brief, ignoring many technicalities more suitably taken up in a full course in logic. It also omits discussion of certain specific expository techniques that help clear reasoning but are more properly taken up elsewhere: the definition and restriction of terms, the ways of achieving paragraph coherence, and the ways of achieving sentence unity (see the index).

This chapter cannot teach you "how to be logical." But it can supplement the comments of your teachers, who are often forced to confine themselves to such labels as "logic" or "coh" (coherence). Since these are only labels, the real challenge you face is the rethinking of your materials, and here the chapter may be helpful. It tries to indicate some of the most common errors in logic and some precautions you can take. Above all, the chapter argues that unsound reasoning is often the result of ignorance rather than intentional deception or incurable bigotry: the writer has not known enough, and perhaps not cared enough, about the subject and so has generalized hastily. Clear and persuasive arguments require clear and persuasive evidence.

11a

The Structure of an Argument

Definitions are usually the preliminaries of an argument. Having defined capital punishment as "execution, the death penalty for a crime," you can then argue for or against it. One "argument," or "reason," you might give for capital punishment is that it deters murder. A "reason" or "argument," against it might be that it does not deter murder. Note that the words "argument" and "reason" are interchangeable and that they imply an identical process of thinking.

In most discussions of logical analysis, the word *argument* signifies any two statements connected in such a way that one is drawn from the other. The argument has two parts: a *premise* (or evidence) and an *inference* (or immediate conclusion):

premise or evidence	inference or immediate conclusion
Capital punishment deters murder.	It should be continued.
Because it does not deter murder,	capital punishment should be abolished.

We use arguments constantly in writing and in speaking, and we recognize them by the actual or implied presence of connectives such as "because," "so," and "since," and by auxiliaries such as "ought," "should," and "must." The structure of an argument, then, is an observed fact or set of facts, or else a generalization presumably based on facts (the premise), leading to a conclusion (the inference). And usually we intend, though we may not always state explicitly, a final conclusion or *point* of the argument:

premise ————————→inference

I'm tired out **because** I've been studying too hard. ↓ final conclusion

So I'll take a break now.

final conclusion ←— inference ————————→premise

She wasn't angry. She didn't mean it **since** she was joking about it later.

Usually, a final conclusion has several arguments, not simply one, to support it. The inference of one argument may be the premise for the next, and so on in a chainlike pattern to the final conclusion, the clasp:

premise 1 and . . .	premise 2
Hayes has an A — average and an IQ of 130.	Brookes has a B— average and an IQ of 125.

(inference from premises 1 and 2 **becomes premise 3**)
Since Hayes is obviously brighter and more energetic,

(inference from premise 3 **becomes premise 4**)
he should do better work in a restricted creative writing course.

final conclusion
Consequently, he certainly should be given preference over Brookes.

Several distinct strands of argument may be knotted into the one final conclusion, itself often the beginning of a paper or conversation:

final conclusion
There is no clear reason for preferring Hayes over Brookes.

first argument introduced	**premise 1**

In the first place, both students are in the superior IQ range. The standard is irrelevant in this case (**inference** from premise 1).

second argument introduced	**premise 1**

In the second place, the fact that Hayes has a higher grade average is no proof that he has the special interest or talent this course requires (**negative inference** from premise 1).

third argument introduced	**premise 1 and so on to the end**

Moreover, I learned from talking with Brookes that. . . .

Just as a paragraph can develop several arguments to support one conclusion, so several paragraphs can each develop one or more arguments to support a thesis, itself a final conclusion. And just as an outline can help you sort out your arguments for the paragraph, it can also help you sort them out for the paper. But nothing has been said yet about the kind of argument used and its content. So far, we have considered an argument's structure, not its truthfulness. An argument's structure may be quite consistent, yet its premises and conclusions unsound. Two common causes for unsound arguments are the writer's failure to examine the key assumptions and the failure to distinguish between fact and judgment. Each of these causes requires a separate discussion.

11b

Key Assumptions

A key assumption is a connection between the premise and the inference, which is taken for granted *before* the argument is advanced; and it is a *presupposed* relationship between the argument and the final conclusion. Consider the argument we looked at earlier about the two students. Unless you *took for granted* that high grades and creativity are related, you couldn't very well argue that Hayes's superior average was proof that he would do better work in the writing course than Brookes and that *therefore* Hayes ought to be given priority. The key assumptions underlying the argument or arguments must be sound before they are built upon. If they are unsound, the whole thing collapses. If the assumptions are unjustified, the writer risks overlooking troublesome details that do not support them, and he may find unreal evidence that does. For example, if he were to assume that academic success and creativity are related, he would have to overlook the students with mediocre averages who are gifted painters, dancers, or dramatists and the intelligent honor students who seem to lack imagination, or at least seldom do more than safe, thorough work. The writer might, moreover, find an unreal significance in the difference between an IQ of 130 and one of 125 and from this trivial difference make a flimsy inference. And, finally, IQ tests are in themselves open to question in some areas.

To take another example, when students write about short stories narrated by a first person "I," they sometimes assume that there must be a one-to-one correspondence between the narrator and the author in real life—that what happens to the narrator of the story is exactly what happened to the author. By failing to distinguish between the "I" as a device for telling the story and the writer's personal identity, the analysis turns the story into autobiographical self-confession and distorts fact and fiction alike.

There are at least a couple of things you can do to help protect yourself against unsound assumptions and arguments built on them. First, you can get into the habit of detecting your own key assumptions by asking yourself what you have taken for granted in your argument. If the assumptions need defending, defend them; if they need explaining, explain them. Second, you can make it a practice to ask what other people are taking for granted in their arguments. If their key assumptions need challenging, challenge them.

Exercise 1

Consider each of the following arguments. Each (in one variation or another) is popular; each has one or more key assumptions. Analyze the argument to determine the key assumptions it makes and which of these assumptions, if any, would need to be explained or defended. For example, the argument that "A great many of the movies that Hollywood makes give an unfair picture of American life because they show mainly its violence and obsession with sex" makes several assumptions: that movies (or any other art) should give a "fair" picture of whatever they're picturing; that there is such a thing as a "fair picture"; that violence and obsession with sex are not "typical" of American life. Are these self-evident assumptions or do they need defending?

1. Enriched courses for gifted students are a valuable addition to the high school curriculum because such courses offer these students a chance to fulfill college requirements and to begin specializing earlier.
2. Civil rights laws are often useless because morality can't be legislated.
3. A politician who takes an unpopular position during an election is foolish because it simply increases his or her chances of losing.
4. A college education is becoming a worthless investment because it no longer guarantees admission to professional schools (such as law and medicine) and because the difference in average income between graduates and nongraduates is diminishing.
5. It's silly to argue with teachers because they'll only mark you down: just give them what they want and take a good grade.

11c

The Differences Between Fact and Judgment

As the preceding exercise may have suggested, what can be proved and what one approves of do not always coincide. The differences between fact and judgment, though not always easy to determine in a given case, are important. A *fact* may be defined as any statement, any declarative sentence, that can be proved true. The definition says nothing about who does the proving, what his or her qualifications are, or how he proves it. *It merely stipulates the possibility of verifying the statement,* the central idea intended here. It rules out commands, questions, and exclamations as provable assertions—no one will try to prove or disprove utterances like "Shut the door!" "How old is she?" or "Wow!"

The definition eliminates more than these obvious examples. "Water is wet"; "A yard has 3 feet"; "New York has more people than Chicago"; "Shakespeare was born in 1564"—most people would agree that such statements are all "facts." But saying "Water is wet" isn't the same as saying "The paint on the door is wet." The first sentence is either a *tautology,* a needless repetition of an idea to anyone familiar with the qualities of "waterness," or else instructions to a very young child on *how* to *identify* the feeling of liquid on his fingers. To say "A yard has 3 feet" is also to state a truth-by-definition—quite different from saying "The track was only 99 yards long." We can touch the paint and measure the track and thereby answer "Yes, it is" or "No, it isn't" to the assertion. But what point is there in responding "Yes, it is" or "No, it isn't" to statements like "Water is wet" or "A yard has 3 feet" except to agree with the definition?

Some statements are verifiable facts because they are stated in *quantifiable* terms, that is, in such a way that what is asserted can be weighed, measured, or counted: "Jean weighs 80 pounds," "The last discus throw was 147 feet long," "There are two bluebooks apiece for the thirty-five of you." Even in these cases of course, you assume that the scale or the tape measure is accurate, that neither has been jiggled, and that your index finger has not missed a cover or pointed at the same head twice. Other facts presuppose greater faith: If you believe that "New York has more people than Chicago" and "Shakespeare was born in 1564" are factual statements, you are not simply accepting the authority of an almanac and an encyclopedia. You are trusting the accuracy and conscientiousness of every census taker hired in these cities by the Bureau of the Census in 1980 and the reliability of scholars who have inspected the parish records of baptism in Stratford-on-Avon.

Admittedly, life is too short for anyone to verify personally more than a fraction of the "facts" he learns and many things have to be taken on authority. Still, you ought to cultivate the habit of skeptical analysis in reading and writing. It can help you detect those judgments that are unverifiable—that are often "proved" in writing by heavy underlining and double exclamation marks and in conversation by rising voices and tempers. How, for instance, can one prove (or disprove) such statements as "You can't change human nature" or "Materialism is the greatest threat to our way of life"?

A judgment is a conclusion expressing some form of approval or disapproval. The term should not be dismissed because it is taken to connote "mere opinion." There are, after all, reasonable grounds and confirming facts for "good judgment" as well as the arbitrary assumptions and disregarded facts in "poor judgment." Sometimes the judgment is a fairly simple, safe inference from the facts, as in the judgment "Helen Wills Moody was one of the finest tennis players in the game's history," which is based on her winning the Women's National Singles seven times, the Women's National Doubles three times, and the Women's Singles at Wimbledon eight times. The phrase "one of the finest" is a judgment of her record. Sometimes, a judgment is a complicated inference from many facts, none of which is immediately clear. Consider three propositions, in which the judgments are italicized:

1. In 1920, there were 6,448,343 farms in America with a total acreage of 955,844,000 acres; by 1975, *farms were larger and fewer,* totaling 2,808,000 in number and accounting for 1,086,000,000 acres.

2. Between 1920 and 1975, the American farm *has become more efficient through improved mechanization and specialization; it is now able to cultivate more land and feed a larger population with fewer people doing the farm work.*

3. *Profit-seeking specialization and mechanization are destroying the small, self-sufficient family farm in America and the deep attachment to the land and tradition that are so much a part of the family farm.*

The first statement contains the terms "larger" and "fewer," which possibly connote a judgment of greater efficiency but which certainly denote a factual inference—that fewer farms and a greater total acreage mean larger farms. The statement is clearly factual and the inference results from a simple computation. The second sentence, a judgment, not only presupposes the first statement's facts ("now able to cultivate more land . . .") but presupposes others. To prove "improved mechanization and specialization," the writer would need figures showing the increased use of electricity and various kinds of power machinery and the increased percentage of farms that raise only crops or livestock, or produce dairy goods. The evidence exists, of course, to defend the judgment that "the American farm has become more efficient."

In the third statement, the judgment is far more conspicuous than in the first two, and the facts are less immediately evident. To prove, for example, the existence of "the small, self-sufficient family farm" with its "deep attachment to the land and tradition" would require detailed information about income, expenses, size of family, acreage worked, period of ownership without tenancy, length of political and religious affiliations, and a study of attitudes toward marriage, education, and the like. Such information, whether in the form of statistics or the extensive observations of qualified reporters, would have to include the New York family raising sheep and a few cows, some acres of wheat, and garden tomatoes; the North Carolina family raising a hillside of tobacco and corn, supplemented by hogs and hunting; the Illinois family running a small dairy and orchard; and the Colorado family raising grain and beef near the foothills of the Rockies. Then the information about all of these families would have to be analyzed to see whether there is such a type as "the small, self-sufficient family farm" with distinct values or whether there are sharply different regional variations.

You can no more help making judgments about human actions and goals than the writer of the third statement could help feeling strongly about the changes taking place in the American farm. In fact, the writer might say that information about income and attitudes toward marriage had little to do with his judgment, that he was talking about qualities that could only be experienced personally. The grounds for this judgment might be his own life on a small Iowa farm or New Mexico ranch; novels like Willa Cather's *O Pioneers!*, Steinbeck's *The Red Pony*, or Harriet Arnow's *The Dollmaker*; short stories like those in Hamlin Garland's *Main-Travelled Roads*; movies like *Hud*; or the memories of a country doctor. The question would then be what other qualities are slighted. Do the films, fiction, and memoirs show only loyalty, belief, the close-knit family, and hard work? What of the fatigue and boredom, the bigotry and blighted vision, the drudgery and failure they reveal? Fiction, films, and memoirs are images of possibility, not mathematical probability: they can make us see, feel, and share the intensity and variety of human life in a particular time and place rather than convince us of statistical likelihood. If the writer argues that their details and experiences are "factually typical," he then *assumes as true* what only statistics or the extensive testimony of many qualified observers could confirm.

When you make judgments, then, express your facts clearly and accurately, and show clearly the way in which the facts warrant your judgment; when you don't know the facts, or have reason to suspect their authority, suspend judgment. And don't be reluctant to ask others to do the same. Try to distinguish between those judgments that involve personal preference and are not provable and those that may be supported by evidence and arguments. For your college writing, this advice implies your willingness to do research; to distinguish among facts, statements that may be factual, and judgments; and to tolerate uncertainty. The last is especially hard to do: often the experts in specialized fields are so much at odds that either you are tempted to give the matter up entirely or else arbitrarily decide "one side *must* be right, the other wrong, so I will choose." If, for example, you were to look up the statistics and analyses on capital punishment, you would find no clear-cut agreement among the criminologists, psychologists, and various law officials as to what the figures prove—and no agreement among the statisticians, either. But lives, the victim's, the accused murderer's, and their families', are too important to be forgotten about simply because you cannot prove conclusively that capital punishment is or is not a deterrent. There are other factual grounds that may help you form a judgment: How many innocent men have been executed, or how many saved at the last minute? Do the poor and the uneducated receive the death sentence more frequently than others convicted of murder? How often are murderers declared insane, later to be released to commit another murder?

As has been pointed out, we cannot verify personally more than a fraction of the "facts" we learn, and necessarily we have to take many things on authority. Still, when experts disagree about their facts and their judgments, there are a few helpful guides.

The *first guide* is to be sure that a supposed expert is an authority on the subject at hand. If a famous physicist and chemist differ about disarmament, you may have to suspend judgment as far as their argument about the technical difficulties is concerned, but you don't have to feel that either of them is an expert on Russia and Russian foreign policy. Other writers and scholars have made the study of Russian aims and behavior their life's work, and you should turn to them.

A *second guide* is to consider the experts' probable motives in relation to their testimony. An executive for a major car manufacturer who testifies that "all reasonable efforts have been taken to make economical, unpolluting cars" may well not be as reliable an authority as an independent trade magazine or engineering firm.

A *third guide* is to see whether others in the field agree about the strengths or weaknesses in an expert's research. Suppose that you are doing a project on the attitudes of high school students toward their teachers. If book reviewers generally praise a husband-and-wife team for their studies of suburban students but criticize their failure to study inner-city students as thoroughly, you would want to confine yourself to the couple's discussion of suburban students only, and look elsewhere for evidence about the feelings of inner-city students.

Exercise 2

For practice, consider the following statements. Determine which parts of each are facts and which parts are judgments. For each judgment, decide what kind(s) of facts or evidence, if any, could be cited to support the judgment.

1. Smoke Cigarmellos! They last longer, burn cooler, and are easier on you than cigarettes. They are cleaner and cheaper than pipes.
2. Julius Caesar, Rome's greatest general and ruler, was assassinated in 44 B.C. by Cassius, Brutus, and other personal enemies.
3. A meter equals 39.37 inches.
4. A kilometer contains 1,000 meters.
5. Kareem Abdul-Jabbar is one of the finest offensive players of all time in professional basketball.
6. If one compares the number of talented women now entering law schools with the number fifteen years ago, one sees how wasteful of abilities those sexist admissions policies were.
7. Since language changes, there can be no criteria of what is good or bad

usage except what the majority is willing to accept at any given moment.

8. Real mastery of a foreign language means the ability to think in the language, not simply to translate headlines and signs, word by word.

9. A recent classification of land use in Afghanistan estimates 76% wastelands, 5% meadows and pastures, 1.5% forests and woodland, 14% arable, and 3.5% cultivable but unused.

10. The early bird catches the worm—but who wants the worm?

11d
Faulty Reasoning

The failure to examine key assumptions and to distinguish between fact and judgment is not the only cause of faulty reasoning. Of the other causes, hasty generalizing is one of the most common.

1. Hasty Generalizations

To generalize is to *draw conclusions* about a *whole class* or *group*, after studying some members of the group. A hasty generalization is one drawn from too few individuals or from nontypical individuals. Suppose, for example, that after meeting three bright and articulate fraternity rush chairmen, you are convinced that most outstanding male students belong to fraternities. Do you have reason to question this generalization? Yes, because your sampling may be quite unrepresentative and in any case is quite small. The chairmen were probably chosen for their jobs because they are so impressive. But even so, suppose you still have a hunch that the outstanding students are fraternity members. How would you establish such a generalization?

Establishing an effective generalization usually requires several steps. First, you would have to identify the group "outstanding student" by defining it as, say, those on the college's honor roll. Otherwise, the generalization is no more than a vague judgment about a vague, unidentified group of people. You would then have to show that there was a higher percentage of fraternity men on the honor roll than of nonfraternity men. Otherwise, the outstanding student is no more likely to be a fraternity member than not.

To establish an effective generalization, you have to identify clearly the group or groups about which you are generalizing, and you must study enough individual members of the group to ensure that they represent the group as a whole. Failure to observe these principles usually results in hasty generalizations.

Not all generalizations can be as easily established as the one above. In cases where all the relevant facts about a limited group are available, one may indeed generalize by simply counting or checking accurately—a parking attendant inspects each car on the lot and generalizes that all headlights are off; a dean reviews all the high school transcripts and generalizes that every freshman has had at least a year of foreign language before entering the college. But much of the time it is not possible to do a complete check. Necessarily, one also generalizes by *induction,* that is, by observing a number of specific examples of the group and then concluding that other examples will *probably* be like those observed. Young children use induction when, after grabbing at two or three cats, they conclude that all cats scratch. Later, when they understand what grabbing is and when they have seen more cats, they learn to generalize that most cats will not scratch unless they are grabbed. Pollsters use induction when they question a representative *sample* of the voters to determine how all voters feel or will probably vote. If their cross section is not representative, as happened in 1948, they will be embarrassed. A consumers' research organization uses induction when it purchases all different brands of a mass-produced item, tests several samples of each brand carefully, and then generalizes about which brands are likely to be the best buys and in what ways.

The stereotype is one form of hasty generalizing—the trite, unchanging picture of an ethnic group, a profession, or a social role. "He was the typical Italian father, singing with gusto and crying 'Mamma mia!' " "She was the typical housewife, who could talk about nothing but her family and TV shows." Other stereotypes are mothers-in-law, the dumb athlete, and the crooked politician. Stereotypes are crude caricatures that deny the variety and diversity of actual life.

Oversimplification is another form of hasty generalizing. Usually, it entails making a question seem easier than it is. Statistics, especially, can lead to oversimplifying. For example, if two groups have a markedly different class average on a reading comprehension test, you could not generalize that every member of the first class was better than every member of the second. Since a few very high scores might have pulled up some mediocre ones in the averaging, you would have to compare all the individual scores to reach such a conclusion. Still less would you be entitled to simplify the results by generalizing that one group was "innately" better than the other. You would have to know a good deal about the income and education of the parents, the reading matter (if any) in the homes, each child's previous training, and other crucial factors before drawing any conclusions.

The unqualified generalization makes a third form of hasty generalizing, the exaggerated claim made from insufficient evidence. Several years ago, on the basis of a peace petition signed by a few thousand college students, a commentator generalized that all undergraduates were becoming pacifists. His sampling was highly inadequate. He ignored not only those who refused to sign but also those who were being drafted. The unqualified generalization is a rather frequent weakness in college writing—for example, "All the freshmen think 'Orientation Week' is a waste of time" or "Not one woman student in the whole college trusts the Dean." To the question "How do you know? Have you talked with *every* freshman or every woman?" the writer usually answers: "Of course not, but I know several [or some] people who feel . . . ." The least the writer can do is to rephrase the generalization more accurately and responsibly by identifying the approximate numbers involved and the source of the real evidence: "Several of us who are freshmen and attended 'Orientation Week' with high hopes have decided that . . ." or "After the women on our corridor had met with the Dean, we agreed that . . . ."

In order to generalize effectively, you need to know some criteria of generalizations. Since generalizations are made about classes or groups, *the first criterion of generalizations is that the evidence be typical of the class or group*. A theme using students in remedial English as the basis for generalizing about the writing abilities of all members of the freshman class would be as unconvincing as a theme that used the PLO to generalize about the political attitudes of all Arabs.

Often, though, the untypicality is less crude, more a question of interpretation than of outright error. Are Hemingway's heroes and heroines in *A Farewell to Arms* and *The Sun Also Rises* "typical" of the period in their disillusionment with World War I and its aftermath? Was the fear of "majority faction" by the authors of *The Federalist* "typical" of the Constitution's other proponents? If you read Hemingway's novels or *The Federalist* essays, you will agree on some conclusions: Hemingway's heroes and heroines do distrust "causes" and conventional moralities—they say so and ignore them; Hamilton and Madison often speak of "majority faction," especially in *Federalist 10*. Many of your most interesting writing assignments will be ones like these, or at least ones in which you use complex facts for complex judgments. *When you have to evaluate typicality, define what features you believe typical and show how these features are found in the evidence.* If you had read only the two Hemingway novels, but none by F. Scott Fitzgerald, John Dos Passos, or Ford Madox Ford about this period, you would want to confine your discussion of typicality to Hemingway's novels.

The second criterion of generalizations is that the evidence be adequate. Americans spending a few days in London or Madrid, Europeans touring in the United States for two weeks, or students visiting Washington, D.C., for a weekend have many superficial impressions, some of them probably accurate. But if they generalize "The English are reserved" or "Americans are friendly but ignorant," they reveal more about themselves than about the English or Americans. Other examples of inadequate evidence are the essay citing those convicted during the Watergate trials to show that all of the hundreds of peoples appointed by Nixon were unreliable, or a term paper citing Janis Joplin's death to show that all rock stars are deeply unhappy, tormented people. Like typicality, adequacy is sometimes difficult to judge—the anthropologist with only a jaw fragment and a few bones or the archeologist with only a faded temple painting may have to infer what he can and hope for more evidence. *But you can assist yourself and your reader by saying why you think your evidence is adequate and for what, if there is likely to be doubt.* If only one half of the 250 freshmen vote for class officers, you have adequate evidence that "something" is wrong with morale, but you would have to talk with many of the nonvoters to find out what it is.

The third criterion of generalizations is that the evidence be relevant. Figures showing that all sororities on campus have a "C" average or better would not be proof that sororities produce outstanding students. The figures would be more *pertinent* to the generalization that sororities care enough about their eligibility to satisfy academic requirements. In a different fashion, the fact that an artist or musician was once a communist or a fascist is irrelevant evidence to prove his work incompetent, if you define incompetence as a lack of artistic ability or skill. The only way he can be shown to be incompetent is by musical or artistic standards of performance. You might find it personally distasteful to attend his exhibit or recital, but if you condemn his present work because of his past associations, you adopt the propaganda view of art and the illogic used by the Nazis in persecuting "non-Aryan" writers and writing, and by the Soviets in their harassment of Pasternak, Solzhenitsyn, and others.

The fourth criterion of generalizations is that the evidence be accurate. This standard seems self-evident, yet if you were to read through the long, careful book reviews in such publications as *Scientific American*, the *American Historical Review*, or the *Journal of American Folklore*, you would find two common criticisms: that the writer has been careless about checking facts, and indiscriminate about sources. In cases of extreme carelessness, the reviewer legitimately questions the author's right to be trusted, regardless of how original the ideas are. In addition to the advice available in this volume (see Chapter 12), the most helpful guides you have are the ones for expert testimony: Does the information come from a recognized source? What are the person's announced motives or position in relation to the evidence? What agreement is there among others in the field about the strengths or weaknesses in the researcher's work? Like an editor or reviewer, your teacher has greater confidence and pleasure in conclusions based on accurate evidence.

2. Mistaken Causal Relationships

Mistaken causal relationships are errors in reasoning about cause and effect. Perhaps the two most frequent kinds are the *post hoc, ergo propter hoc fallacy* and the *reductive fallacy.*

The *post hoc, ergo propter hoc fallacy* is the error of arguing that because B follows A, A is the cause of B. Sequence is not proof of a causal relationship. The fact that B follows A is *not* proof that

B was caused by *A*. Primitive beliefs like a full moon "causing" pregnancy and their modern equivalent in the television commercial connecting marriage with a change in deodorant are easy enough to laugh at. But clear thinking on serious social problems can be obscured by this fallacy. For example, the assertion that heroin addiction is the result of smoking marijuana not only ignores the fact that most people who try or use pot never touch heroin but it may divert attention from the real need—the understanding of the psychological and physiological factors that do contribute to addiction. And what of the unqualified generalization that makes the loss of religious belief the cause of crime? Crimes are committed by people who profess religious belief; not every person who loses his faith commits a crime.

The reductive fallacy occurs when simple or single causes are given for complex effects, creating a generalization based on insufficient evidence. In history, when motives and events are enormously complicated and cannot be exactly duplicated, such generalizations as "Athens fell because of mob rule," "Luther caused the Reformation," or "The need to rebel caused the campus demonstrations of the 1960s" are *reductive*. That is, instead of specifying the mob or Luther as *one important condition*, these assertions make Luther or the mob the *single agent* of causation. Such generalizations tend to reduce history to caricature. Strictly speaking, historians rarely uncover the cause or causes of events. Rather, they try to decide which conditions were important and were more probably necessary for the event to take place. In scientific studies when a sequence cannot be directly observed and controlled and the investigator cannot know whether *Y* is the result of *X* only or *W* and *X* together, or whether *X* and *Y* are both the result of *W*, he speaks of a *correlation*. In 1964, when the Surgeon General announced a high correlation between cigarette smoking and lung cancer, he indicated that one was probably a *contributory cause* of the other. But since not all heavy smokers die of lung cancer and since there is evidence that industrial fumes and car exhaust are injurious in this regard, one cannot say that smoking is the *only* cause of lung cancer. Insofar as he cannot directly isolate, identify, and control each factor in a sequence, the scientist, like the historian, usually observes the test of sufficiency: *only if A alone is sufficient to produce B can it be called the cause.*

Except for laboratory reports in physics or chemistry and perhaps a research project in psychology or education, you will seldom have space or occasion in college writing to prove a strictly causal relationship. Usually, so far as causal relations are concerned, you will be judging or reporting on research done by others, or else trying to determine what the probable connections are between an effect you have observed or experienced and events preceding it.

To let your readers judge the *sufficiency* of your argument, define its conditions and limitations as clearly as you can. With complex relationships, it is often helpful to know that there is a significant difference between saying "It is due to" and "It has been helped by," just as there is between saying "Luther caused" and "Luther contributed to" or "The reason for the Revolution" and "One reason for the Revolution." The limited statement can be more exact because it is more tentative: it implies that other conditions, other contributing factors, may be as important as the one singled out for discussion. This kind of exact tentativeness requires careful, analytical thinking. When you analyze complex historical events and personalities, complex social issues, and complex motives, avoid the reductive fallacy.

3. Reasoning by Analogy

An analogy is a comparison between two different things or events showing the way or ways in which they are similar. To illustrate, for example, how the novelist works, one could draw the analogy between the writer and the potter: both begin with a rough idea or image, but discover the particular shape of the plot or vase as they work with their materials, often modifying the outlines several times before they are satisfied.

Analogies can vividly illustrate and clarify difficult ideas. They have been fruitful in science because they have suggested new lines of research and testing: Franklin saw a similarity between lightning and electric sparks; the similarity between X-rays and the rays emitted by uranium salts raised questions about the source and nature of this energy, and eventually led to Marie Curie's discovery of radium; mathematicians such as John von Neumann, instrumental during the early development of computers, saw an analogy between the way the human nervous system works and the way a relay of vacuum tubes can be made to work. In science, an analogy only sets up a hypothesis to be proved or disproved. Although it suggests a possibility, it is *not* proof by itself.

An analogy can be illustrative or suggestive, but it cannot be conclusive. You do well to suspect any conclusions that are supported only by an analogy. Sometimes, a false analogy offered as proof is relatively easy to detect. The student who argued that the new African countries should have federated into a United States of Africa to solve their political and economic problems ignored some obvious dissimilarities with the American colonies. The latter, unified by language and a common foe, had in most cases a long tradition of local self-government. African countries are separated from each other by deep linguistic and cultural differences and in several cases are inwardly divided by tribal rivalries. This analogy also ignores the difficulties we had—the failure of the Articles of Confederation and the opposition to the Constitution.

Often, however, false analogies may be even more deceiving. Two principles will help you cope with them:

1. The more concrete similarities there are, and the more instances that can be cited, the higher is the possibility that the conclusion is true.

2. The greater the magnitude of the differences and the more irrelevant the similarities that do exist, the less is the chance the conclusion is true.

False analogies obscure the real issues of and prevent clear thinking about serious and difficult questions. To detect analogies used as proof, examine the argument to see if any evidence is offered other than a comparison between two different things or events. In your own writing, if you think an analogy is essential to your argument, rethink your entire case: don't allow yourself to be taken in by shallow or deceiving similarities.

4. Avoiding the Question

When writers fail to give relevant evidence for their arguments or fail to draw relevant inferences, they are *avoiding the question*. *Begging the question* is one such common failure. A question is begged when writers use as a proven argument the very point they are trying to prove. For example, columnists who argue that the poor are lazy and cite families on welfare as "evidence" are assuming *without proof* that only lazy opportunists would take relief—the very point *to be demonstrated.*

The *ad hominem* argument is a second common form, the argument "to the man." Here, the tactic is to condemn the morals, the motives, the friends, or the family of one's opponent and to divert attention from the substance of the opponent's argument. The evaluation of expert testimony should not be confused with the *ad hominem* argument: in the former, you *ask* what a person's professional credentials are and the reasons for his position—that is, you attempt to distinguish between fact and judgment; in the latter, you *insinuate* by sarcasm or similar means that a person's word is untrue or his case unsound because there is something wrong with him.

The *straw man* is another device commonly used for avoiding the question. As the label implies, the technique is to stuff, set up, and knock down a position that is not being contested. If the question is whether or not Shylock deserves his punishment and the writer goes to great lengths to prove that bitterness can make a man lonely, he is erecting a straw man. The issue is whether Shylock is treated too severely, by either his own standards or Christian ones. No one argues the fact that bitterness can isolate people.

5. False Alternatives

The false either/or deduction is a common but easily avoided error. The error lies in assuming that there are only two alternatives and that if one of them is true, the other must be false. If parents tell a child, "You must be lazy because the only reasons for poor school work are laziness or stupidity, and I know you aren't dumb," the parents commit this error. They ignore other alternatives: the child may be bored with easy work, or he may lack adequate training, or he may be unhappy for a variety of reasons. Ideological slogans often make this kind of phony simplification—"Communism versus Capitalism," "The Free World versus Tyranny," "Education versus Indoctrination," and the like. The careful writer will rethink the false alternatives in order to discover what the more complex possibilities really are.

Exercise 3

To sharpen your eye for others' fallacies, take a newspaper and turn to the editorial and opinion section. Go through it carefully, isolating and analyzing the logical errors you find. Better still, if there's an issue you feel strongly about or a column you find particularly objectionable, write a letter pointing out how the reasoning is unsound.

Exercise 4

To sharpen your eye for fallacies in your own writing, go over some of your back papers as if they had been written by a stranger. What kinds of logical errors do you find? Now, try revising the material logically, as if you were doing a favor for a good friend.

Exercise 5

Analyze each of the following generalizations by the four criteria suggested. Be prepared to explain which generalizations are defective and in what ways.

1. From a recent faculty committee meeting: "Students are making a farce out of the government's low-interest loan program for college financing. The percentage of students who deliberately default is steadily rising, and there's no reason to think it will drop or that students will begin to feel responsible for paying the money they owe. The whole program is just a waste of the taxpayer's money."

2. From a recent "Letters to the Editor" column: "How can your editorial writer deny that Americans are the most wasteful, extravagant consumers of gas in the world! Drive along any expressway or freeway at rush hours and count all the cars with only one passenger and look at the miles of bumper-to-bumper traffic. If that isn't enough proof, just recall the long lines during the gas crunch, each owner greedily after his 10 gallons."

3. From a recent college newspaper: "This school has the worst meals of all the state colleges. Any athlete or debater can tell you the meals you get at other colleges make the ones we get look awful."

4. From the *Guinness Book of World Records:* "The only admissible evidence upon the true height of giants is that of recent date made

under impartial medical supervision. Biblical claims, such as that for Og, King of Bashan, at 9 Assyrian cubits (16 feet 2½ inches) are probably due to a confusion of units. Extreme mediaeval data from bone measurements refer invariably to mastodons or other non-human remains. Claims of exhibitionists, normally under contract not to be measured, are usually distorted for the financial considerations of promoters. There is an example of a recent 'World's Tallest Man' of 9 feet 6 inches being in fact an acromegalic of 7 feet 3½ inches."

Exercise 6

Analyze each of the following statements of causal relationship to determine which ones are guilty of the post hoc, ergo propter hoc fallacy *or the* reductive fallacy.

1. More than two thirds of the people in our state voted for the limitation on the state property tax and deliberately deprived local communities of all kinds of services. The only explanation is sheer selfishness; they were afraid of higher taxes.
2. All the children in the remedial reading class watch at least twenty hours of television a week. With all that passive sitting, no wonder they can't read.
3. No wonder the divorce rate is climbing: all those young couples splitting up now grew up during the chaos of the 1960s; they never had a chance at a stable environment.
4. Since 1940, the government has gotten bigger and bigger, and taxes have gone higher and higher. The conclusion is obvious.

Exercise 7

Analyze each of the following analogies to determine whether it is used as an illustration, a hypothesis suggesting further investigation, or proof.

1. From a student theme: "The sight of a monkey pushing through the jungle, leaping from tree to tree, seems 'natural' and, perhaps, graceful. However, when a monkey is placed in a small cage or zoo, his boundings from side to floor to side to ceiling seem antic and 'unnatural.' The satirist employs the same technique of limitation. He confines his subject, as it were, to a small cage, or at least one tree, for purposes of close observation. The setting in which he moves his object is limited and its barriers are precisely drawn. The satirist, in effect, traps the victim in his most ridiculous positions and does not allow him to wander off or in any way escape an intensely mocking portrayal."

2. From a composition handbook: "Many of the rules in this book, making no mention of exceptions or permissible alternatives, are dogmatic—purposely so. If a stranger is lost in a maze of city streets and asks for directions, one doesn't give him the several possible routes, with comments and cautions about each. He will simply become more confused and lost. One sends him arbitrarily on one route without mentioning equally good alternative ways. Likewise, the unskilled writer can best be set right by simple, concise, stringent rules."

3. From a student editorial: "The administration never gets tired of telling us that the state college is part of society as a whole. It harps on student responsibility for 'good taste' in plays and publications, student responsibility to obey state laws about drinking and driving, and student responsibility for property. By the same line of reasoning, then, how can the administration claim it has the final right to approve of campus organizations and their speakers? If the state university is part of 'society as a whole' it ought to recognize *our* rights as well as our obligations. We aren't asking for the privilege of being subversive; we are asking for the civil rights we have in 'society as a whole'—the rights to hear whom we wish and join the groups we wish."

4. From a student theme: "The college has the same obligation to satisfy the student that a store does to satisfy a customer. Students and their parents pay the bills and they ought to have a much freer say about what courses they take. No clerk would think of telling a customer he had to buy several things he didn't want before he could buy the item he came for. And no store would keep as clerks some of the men the college keeps as professors. They can't even sell their product."

5. From a medical journal: "If you place a number of mice together in fairly close quarters and then systematically introduce an increasing variety of distractions—small noises, objects, movements—you increase the probability of neurotic behavior. Cannot something like this process help explain the growth of neurotic behavior in our ever more crowded, complex society? The possibility is worth considering."

Exercise 8

Pick one of the following analogies and write a paragraph using the analogy as proof. Then, in a second paragraph, show precisely how the analogy is false or misleading, as you have developed it.

1. The family budget and the federal budget
2. The referee in boxing and the arbiter in labor disputes
3. The captain of a ship and the president of a democracy

4. Packaging the goods well and giving a lecture well
5. Determining the warnings on chemicals and determining the ratings of films

Exercise 9

The following statements contain unsound reasoning. Identify the different kinds of fallacies and specify what change, if any, would improve the argument.

1. Either you trust a person or you don't. And you don't do business with someone you don't trust. The same principle ought to be observed in foreign affairs: you don't do business with countries you can't trust.
2. Anyone with a grain of sense would have known that the county didn't need to buy land for a park. But those officials don't learn easily. It wasn't proof enough for them that a majority voted against the purchase in the election. They had to go to the state legislature and get voted down, too.
3. Freshman "Hell Week" is one of the oldest and dearest traditions of the college. Many of us alumni can remember having our heads shaved and getting up at midnight for roll calls and jogs around the track. Those of us on the Alumni Board oppose the abolition of the custom. We find the arguments for doing away with "Hell Week" childish and tiresome. We were good enough sports to go along with the sophomores in our time.
4. I don't see why I received such a low grade on this term paper. I put in hours of work on it and did several rough drafts. And I followed the format you asked for. It doesn't seem fair.
5. Any man who supports the Equal Rights Amendment has either been brainwashed by feminists or else has no guts.
6. To be an actor, you have to be on a real ego trip. That's why people become actors. All you have to do is look at any famous star and you'll see the living proof.
7. Laws against smoking on trains, in restaurants and theaters, and in other public places discriminate against my right of free choice. If I want to take the risks with my health because of the pleasure I get, that's my business. I'm not trying to tell others how to live their lives.
8. "Reflection on Ice-Breaking"
   Candy
   Is dandy
   But liquor
   Is quicker

   —OGDEN NASH

Exercise 10

The following is a satire, written by a student, of the arbitrary assumptions, unexamined generalizations, and misleading analogies, which all too often are found in print. In analyzing the argument, see how many of these logical errors you can find.

"Why Have Teachers?"

In the early days of America, before the establishment of compulsory schooling, moral standards were high. People were contented with the simpler virtues. Girls learned to sew, cook, and keep house; men, to farm or work at some trade. Marriages were stable and happy; there was no such thing as divorce. Today this happy scene has changed— the morals of modern America are corrupted. Every newspaper carries stories of murder, embezzlement, adultery, and divorce. What has caused this shocking situation? Is it possible to regain the happy state of early America?

The most influential institution during the formative years of each American is the school, governed and dominated by the teachers. From these teachers children learn the human faults of blind obedience, prejudice, and the betrayal of one's kind in the form of tattling. These early sown seeds bear the bitter fruit of low morality. Clearly, teachers do much to undermine the morality of American children, and through them, that of society.

The obvious solution is to eliminate the teacher as much as possible. The modern child is increasingly capable of educating himself. There are more college students today than ever before, a fact which proves that youth today possess superior intelligence. By educating themselves, they would not be subjugated to the influence of teachers. They would share their knowledge willingly, each gaining from the other, with no one person dominating the others.

As applied to colleges, this would mean that students would gather in pleasant informal surroundings and discuss intelligently matters with a common appeal, as was done in the medieval university. Not only would they enrich their knowledge, but they would also learn how to compromise and see each other's viewpoint. By obtaining many viewpoints instead of the one our system presents, the students would learn to know their own minds and think objectively instead of receiving opinions on a silver platter.

Cynics will sneer that this system is impractical, that students need guidance and even indoctrination in fundamentals before they can think on their own. Nothing could be further from the truth! One of the most clear-thinking, intelligent men in this nation's history, Abraham

Lincoln, was almost entirely self-educated. Think of the effect on our society of an entire generation with the training and characteristics of Lincoln. The present immorality would disappear; a high moral standard would be developed. The group that is undermining morality would be minimized in its influence, and the education of American youth placed where it belongs—in the hands of these same youth.

12

WRITING THE RESEARCH PAPER

12a

Why Do Research?

Research answers our deepest needs as thinking human beings. We hunger for facts. If you tell a friend, "My brother had the strangest experience last week," your friend is sure to ask, "What was it?" Millions of us read the daily newspaper to learn about events we have not seen, people we do not know, countries we will never visit.

We do not think when we read the newspaper that we are doing research, but we are. We are gathering information for tomorrow's argument about the mayor's latest conflict with the city council or about the stock market's response to the Federal Reserve Bank's new policy. We are doing research when we copy a recipe out of the food section, read a movie review, or glance through the want ads. Research is the texture of our lives—we want to know facts, so that we can live better.

We recognize, though, that we want more than information. Even when we have seen the game or the movie, we read the account or the review. We add to our own evaluation the judgments of the columnist: this play was the crisis of the game, that actor should have controlled his exuberance. We agree and disagree not only in the bar or the office or the classroom but in our silent conversation with the sports page or the entertainment section. Even in its most private moments, research is a social act.

Writing papers based on library research often enables us to join in a dialogue with thoughtful men and women, sharing their concerns, agreeing and disagreeing with them, reflecting and expanding upon their statements. If we look at a research paper as busywork, we will have much drudgery ahead; but if we consider the research assignment as an opportunity to enter an informed conversation, the result can be exciting and memorable.

Why should that be so? It is not merely that we are inquisitive. As E. M. Forster has pointed out, "Curiosity is one of the lowest of the human faculties." The spark of our curiosity is a desire for meaning, a desire to fit things into context. Behind every fact that engages us lies a question, or many questions: What is the consequence of this fact? How does it fit into the total picture? What would it mean if we were to discover the opposite?

Consider the research of Max Weber, the noted sociologist. He observed that the great period of industrial growth in Western Europe occurred after the Protestant Reformation. Curiosity might have led him to ask, "After the Middle Ages, after the Renaissance, after the Reformation, what next?" Instead, the search for significance led him to phrase the question in another way: Did the Reformation cause the Industrial Revolution, and if it did, what factors of the Reformation were most significant in that result? The answer to this question was one of the finest books of our century, *The Protestant Ethic and the Spirit of Capitalism.*

Your own research may not raise an entirely new set of issues for scholarly discussion, as Max Weber's did, but it should at least reveal the results of your own search for significance. That is a role in the dialogue among well-informed people that no one else can take.

12b
Writing the Long Paper

Perhaps the most disconcerting requirement of your research paper is that it must be so long. Most of your essays for your freshman composition course are short, from 500 to 700 words, filling two or three typed double-spaced pages. You can usually write a first draft in one sitting or two. Since you are almost always writing about something you know at firsthand, collecting information on the subject is no problem.

However, you will probably need to write at greater length in upper-division courses and later in life. A long paper may be required in a seminar or as a report on independent study; business men and women have to write reports, lawyers write legal briefs, journalists write feature articles. Such an assignment, often running to more than 1,000 words, presents special problems.

Of course, you have to gather the information for the paper. In most cases, you will have to do some research in the library if you are to know what you are talking about. You can't focus your topic, or adapt it to fit the space available, until you know what has been said about the subject. Part of this chapter, therefore, will be about locating material in the library.

A long paper cannot ordinarily be written at a single sitting, and you will need to plan your time accordingly. The venerable but foolish custom of neglecting an assignment until the day before and then sitting up all night to finish it simply will not work. After three or four hours, even professional writers feel fatigue and know that whatever they write thereafter will be poorer and poorer. The first rule, then, is to plan ahead and begin writing early enough so that you can finish in several sessions, a day apart, instead of in one desperate coffee-soaked night. The second is to set regular times for writing: you will have less difficulty sitting down to write if you have included writing sessions in your schedule.

Ernest Hemingway long ago laid down two additional rules for writers. First, always stop when you are going good. Don't write yourself out at any session, for if you say everything you have in mind, you may have trouble getting started next day when you return to the job. Make yourself stop when you still know exactly what is to come next, and you will find it easy to pick up the thread of your discourse next day. Second, to ensure continuity, begin each writing session by reading everything that has gone before, or at least the preceding five or ten pages. By the time you come to the place where you stopped writing, you should be back into the mood and spirit of the piece, and you may even have recovered your momentum. This is as important to the writer as to a football team.

Another temptation in the face of such a long assignment is to write a narrative, if not of your personal experience, then of the events your research uncovers. Retelling an old story is the easiest way of handling a large body of material, but this method rarely communicates your own thought about the research. A paper of exposition—descriptive or analytic or argumentative—better reflects your part in the dialogue of the well-informed.

You will also need to know the conventional methods of documentation, that is, indicating to the reader by footnotes or other references the sources of your material. Failure to indicate the source of a quotation or paraphrase will lead the reader to assume that it is your own writing and if it is not, you will be guilty of plagiarism. Passing off other people's words, sentences, or ideas as your own, whether it is deliberately or ignorantly done, is a serious offense. In college it can lead to dismissal; in the business world it can lead to a damage suit. Various safeguards against this misfortune will be discussed later in this chapter.

12c
Preliminary Strategies

1. Examine the Assignment

Teachers usually assign papers they think students can succeed in writing. Often, the assignment itself contains guiding questions that limit the focus of your research. When there is some freedom in the choice of a focus, review your class notes, and choose a subject that interests you—one about which you had an unanswered question, or a disagreement, or simply curiosity about the source of your teacher's remarks. Write down a set of questions, drawn from the assignment, or from your class notes (perhaps one question to a page). You can then write under each question a list of likely sources gathered from your research in the library.

2. Visit the Library

Sometimes examining the assignment doesn't help much. You have a vague sense of a subject, but you just don't know enough to focus your research. At this point, a preliminary visit to the library can clarify your aim—as long as you do not dive in too deeply. Check your library's encyclopedias and specialized reference works (some of which are listed in section 12d). Write down the statements that provoke your curiosity or your disagreement, and begin to compile your bibliography. Often, the reference work itself has a brief bibliography to help you get started.

12d

Using the Library

Any collection of written works might be considered a library. Thus the books that line the shelves of your room or sit on your desk constitute your own private library, and many are an immediate resource to which you can refer. You have probably discovered already the value of the dictionary and the thesaurus, and you may own other useful books—a desk encyclopedia, a world atlas, or an almanac.

In addition to books, magazines, and newspapers, libraries often collect other material that you can use in your research. A *review* is a periodical that aims at a college-educated audience and focuses on the arts and the humanities. You would not find much news in a review, but you would find articles about literature, film, theater, architecture, history, philosophy, and social or political thought. A *journal* is a periodical that aims at a professional audience and focuses on the problems of the profession. In the *Journal of the American Medical Association*, you might find an article about bone cancer but you will find nothing about literature or any nonmedical subject. *Government publications* include reports on commerce, census surveys, budgets, crime statistics, and thousands of other factual reports that can supply you with truckloads of information. Finally, many libraries collect the *correspondence* of the famous: the personal letters of Jane Fonda, John Kennedy, or F. Scott Fitzgerald can tell us much about the private lives of people whose public lives have meant a great deal to us or our parents. Usually, libraries do not allow everyone to use their collections of correspondence, but your librarian may give you a tour of the library's collection.

The vastness of the public and college library's holdings in comparison to the limitations of your personal library suggests both an opportunity and a difficulty. The opportunity, of course, is a chance to find much more information than your personal library can supply. The difficulty is locating that information. For this reason, every library organizes its material according to a system. Your guide to your personal library is your memory of what is in each resource and of where that resource is; your guide to the college and public library is what we might call a memory in print: the card catalog, the standard reference books, and the guides to periodical literature comprise a written record that makes research an organized exploration rather than a wishful, haphazard hunt. Learning the arrangement and the system of the library will help you make your research rewarding, not frustrating.

Within a week or two of coming to college, every student should take a tour of the college's library. Often, the library staff will offer such a tour, though many libraries do not have a staff large enough to provide this service. You can give yourself a tour of the library, identifying the three features of the library that will be most useful to you: the card catalog, the standard reference works, and guides to periodical literature.

1. The Card Catalog

The card catalog is the index of the library. All books and bound periodicals are listed on 3×5 cards, which are filed in alphabetical order in labeled drawers. (The entries in the card catalog include the standard reference works and the guides to periodical literature: these should be among the first books you look up when you begin a research project, whether you are looking for a few facts to support a brief argument, or beginning a long research paper.) A book is usually listed three or more times: by its author's name, by its title, and by the subject or subjects it covers. In large university libraries, the subject cards may be filed in a separate Subject Catalog, also in alphabetical order. Author and title cards usually make up the main catalog, in one single alphabetical listing.

Subject cards are intended to help you find books about a particular subject when you do not know any authors or titles. The chief value of subject cards is to guide you to the section of the stacks (the part of the library where the books are kept) that holds books about your subject. Some browsing around the area indicated by one call number will usually lead you to a number of relevant books. If your library has open stacks (that is, if you are allowed to go to the shelves where the books are kept), you should make it a point to browse. Serious studies of the subject will contain bibliographies (that is, lists of other printed sources for research about the subject), and soon you will have a long list of sources, from which you will be able to choose the most useful ones. Thus, the subject cards help you to get a start on a lengthy research project.

Catalog cards have many features, but the most valuable one for you is the *call number*, which indicates where the book is kept. Each call number corresponds to a subject heading according to a system of classification. The system of call numbers enables you to go from a subject card to a section of the library where you can find relevant books. There are two principal systems of classification, the Dewey Decimal System and the Library of Congress System. Your library will have a guide at the reference desk to tell you how the call numbers correspond to the subjects. Often, knowing the call number enables you to skip a step in your search, since you can go directly to the section of the stacks to which that number guides you.

Exercise 1

a. *By consulting the author cards, see if your library has the following books. If so, list the place of publication, the publisher, and the date of publication.*

1. *The Culture of Cities,* by Lewis Mumford
2. *Animals as Social Beings,* by Adolf Portmann
3. *The Subversive Science: Essays toward an Ecology of Man,* by Paul Shepard
4. *Literature and Film,* by Robert Richardson
5. *Structuralism,* by Jean Piaget
6. *Blues People,* by LeRoi Jones
7. *The Armies of the Night,* by Norman Mailer
8. *Language,* by Edward Sapir
9. *On the Contrary,* by Mary McCarthy
10. *Briefing for a Descent into Hell,* by Doris Lessing

Sample Catalog Cards

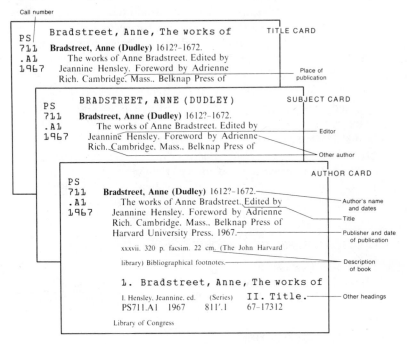

Call number

PS 711 .A1 1967   Bradstreet, Anne, The works of   TITLE CARD

Bradstreet, Anne (Dudley) 1612?-1672.
The works of Anne Bradstreet. Edited by
Jeannine Hensley. Foreword by Adrienne
Rich. Cambridge. Mass.. Belknap Press of

Place of publication

PS 711 .A1 1967   BRADSTREET, ANNE (DUDLEY)   SUBJECT CARD

Bradstreet, Anne (Dudley) 1612?-1672.
The works of Anne Bradstreet. Edited by
Jeannine Hensley. Foreword by Adrienne
Rich. Cambridge. Mass.. Belknap Press of

Editor

Other author

AUTHOR CARD

PS 711 .A1 1967

Bradstreet, Anne (Dudley) 1612?-1672.
The works of Anne Bradstreet. Edited by
Jeannine Hensley. Foreword by Adrienne
Rich. Cambridge. Mass.. Belknap Press of
Harvard University Press. 1967.

Author's name and dates

Title

Publisher and date of publication

xxxvii. 320 p. facsim. 22 cm. (The John Harvard

library) Bibliographical footnotes.

Description of book

1. Bradstreet, Anne, The works of

I. Hensley. Jeannine. ed.   (Series)   II. Title.
PS711.A1 1967   811'.1   67-17312

Other headings

Library of Congress

b. *Find a title card for a work of nonfiction and note any differences from the author card.*

c. *Select five of the books that are nonfiction and obtain the following information on each:*

1. What subject headings is each book cataloged under?
2. What are at least two other books—call number, author, and title— under one of the same general subject headings?

2. Standard Reference Works

It pays to become acquainted with standard reference books (encyclopedias, dictionaries, indexes, bibliographies) because they can shorten your time in the library immeasurably. Your personal library includes a few reference books, such as the dictionary or a desk encyclopedia, but your college library will own dozens of specialized reference works. These works fall into two categories: books that list facts, and bibliographies. The first category of reference works includes sources upon which you would rely if you are looking for a quick answer to a factual question; the second gives you a list of sources for a deeper understanding of a subject or for a major research project. We have not listed all the reference works you might find in your library, but we have listed some that will guide you to the appropriate section of the stacks for your research. Keep in mind that the first principle of research is to find exactly the book you need, and the second is to examine its neighbors. The best students accumulate a file, either in their memories or in a file box of 3 × 5 cards, of research aids, which are the keys to success in locating the information and sources they need. A plastic or metal file box filled with such cards is an excellent memory aid.

Here is a preliminary list of standard reference works.

GUIDES TO REFERENCE BOOKS

Gates, Jean Key. *Guide to the Use of Books and Libraries.* 3rd ed. 1973.
The Reader's Adviser. 3 vols. 12th ed. 1974–77.
Winchell, Constance M. *Guide to Reference Books.* 8th ed. 1967.

GENERAL INFORMATION

Chambers' Encyclopedia. 15 vols. 1973.
Collier's Encyclopedia. 24 vols. 1977.
Encyclopedia Americana. 30 vols. 1977.
Encyclopaedia Britannica. 30 vols. 1977. Many articles have brief bibliographies.
Encyclopedia International. 20 vols. 1977.
New Columbia Encyclopedia. 4th ed. 1 vol. 1975.

GAZETTEERS AND ATLASES

Barraclough, Geoffrey, ed. *Times Atlas of World History.* 1978.
National Geographic Society. *Atlas of the World.* 1963.
Palmer, R. R., ed. *Rand McNally Atlas of World History.* 1970.
Pergamon World Atlas. 1968.
Seltzer, L. E., ed. *Columbia-Lippincott Gazetteer of the World.* 1962.
Shepherd, William R. *Historical Atlas.* 9th ed. 1973.
Times (London) *Atlas of the World.* 5 vols. 1958–60.

REFERENCE BOOKS FOR SPECIAL SUBJECTS

Art and Architecture

Bryan, Michael. *Bryan's Dictionary of Painters and Engravers.* 5 vols. Rev. ed. by George C. Williamson. 1964.
Encyclopedia of World Art. 15 vols. 1959–68. Has brief bibliographies.
Haggar, Reginald C. *Dictionary of Art Terms.* 1962.
Hamlin, T. F. *Architecture Through the Ages.* Rev. ed. 1953. Has bibliographic entries.
Myers, Bernard S., ed. *Encyclopedia of Painting.* 3rd ed. 1970.
Zboinski, A., and L. Tyszynski. *Dictionary of Architecture and Building Trades.* 1963.

Biography

American Men and Women of Science. 13th ed. 1976. This set includes scholars in the physical, biological, and social sciences.
Current Biography. Monthly since 1940, with an annual cumulative index, and brief bibliographic entries.
Dictionary of American Biography. 22 vols. and index. 1928–58. Has bibliographic entries at the end of each article.
Dictionary of National Biography (British). 22 vols. and supplements. Each article is accompanied by a bibliography.
Directory of American Scholars. 4 vols. 7th ed. 1978. This set includes scholars in the humanities.
James, Edward T., and Janet W. James, eds. *Notable American Women 1607–1950.* 3 vols. 1971. Has bibliographic entries.
National Cyclopedia of American Biography. 1898–1906. Includes supplements.
Webster's Biographical Dictionary. 1976.
Who's Who (British), *Who's Who in America, International Who's Who.* Brief accounts of living men and women, frequently revised.
Who's Who of American Women. 1958–.

Classics

Avery, C. B., ed. *New Century Classical Handbook.* 1962.
Hammond, N. G. L., and H. H. Scullard, eds. *Oxford Classical Dictionary,* 2nd ed. 1970. Has bibliographic entries.
Harvey, Paul, ed. *Oxford Companion to Classical Literature.* 1937.

Current Events

Americana Annual. 1923–. An annual supplement to the *Encyclopedia Americana.*

Britannica Book of the Year. 1938–. An annual supplement to the *Encyclopaedia Brittanica.* Some entries have a brief bibliography.

Facts on File. 1941–.

New York Times Index. 1913–. This is, of course, a bibliography of articles in the *New York Times.*

Statesman's Year Book. 1864–. A statistical and historical annual giving current information (and brief bibliographies) about countries of the world.

World Almanac. 1968–.

Economics and Commerce

Coman, E. T. *Sources of Business Information.* 2nd ed. 1964. A bibliography.

Greenwald, Douglas, et al. *McGraw-Hill Dictionary of Modern Economics.* 2nd ed. 1973. Has bibliographic references.

Historical Statistics of the United States: Colonial Times to 1970. 1976. Includes indexes and bibliographies.

International Bibliography of Economics. 1952–.

Munn, Glenn G. *Encyclopedia of Banking and Finance.* 7th ed. 1973. Has bibliographic entries.

Statistical Abstract of the United States. 1897–.

Education

Burke, Arvid J., and Mary A. Burke. *Documentation in Education.* (The 5th ed., renamed, of Alexander's *How to Locate Educational Information and Data.*) 1967.

Deighton, Lee C., ed. *The Encyclopedia of Education.* 10 vols. 1971. Has bibliographic entries.

Ebel, Robert L., et al. *Encyclopedia of Educational Research.* 4th ed. 1969. Has bibliographic references.

World Survey of Education. 5 vols. 1972. Has bibliographic references.

History

Adams, James T., ed. *Dictionary of American History.* 3rd ed. 7 vols. 1976. A bibliography accompanies each article.

Cambridge Ancient History. 12 vols. 1923–39. 2 vols. 1970–75. Bibliographic footnotes.

Cambridge Medieval History. 8 vols. 1911–36. Bibliographic footnotes.

Langer, William L., ed. *Encyclopedia of World History.* 5th ed. 1972.

Morris, Richard B., and Graham W. Irwin, eds. *Harper Encyclopedia of the Modern World.* 1970.

New Cambridge Modern History. 14 vols. 1975. Bibliographical footnotes.

Sarton, George. *Horus: A Guide to the History of Science.* 1952. Primarily bibliographical.

Literature and Drama

A. American

Cunliffe, Marcus. *The Literature of the United States.* Rev. ed. 1967. Has bibliographic entries.

Hart, J. D. *Oxford Companion to American Literature.* 4th ed. 1965.

Kunitz, Stanley J., and H. Haycraft. *Twentieth Century Authors.* 1942. First supplement, 1955. A brief bibliography accompanies each entry.

Leary, Lewis. *Articles on American Literature 1900–1950.* 1954; *1950–1967.* 1970.

Parrington, V. L. *Main Currents in American Thought.* 3 vols. 1927–30. Brief bibliographic entries.

Spiller, Robert E., et al. *Literary History of the United States.* 4th ed. 2 vols. 1974. Entries include bibliographic essays.

B. British

Baugh, A. C., et al. *A Literary History of England.* 2nd ed. 1967. Has bibliographic entries.

Harvey, Paul, ed. *Oxford Companion to English Literature.* 4th ed. 1967.

Sampson, George. *Concise Cambridge History of English Literature.* 3rd rev. ed. by R. C. Churchill, 1970.

Watson, George, ed. *The New Cambridge Bibiliography of English Literature.* 4 vols. 1972.

Wilson, F. P., and Bonamy Dobree, eds. *Oxford History of English Literature.* Eleven of the fourteen projected volumes of this major series of reference works have been completed. Excellent bibliographic essays at the end of each.

C. Continental and General

Fleischmann, Wolfgang Bernard, ed. *Encyclopedia of World Literature in the Twentieth Century.* 4 vols. 1978. Brief bibliographies.

Grigson, Geoffrey. *The Concise Encyclopedia of Modern World Literature.* 1971. Brief bibliographic entries.

Leach, Maria, and Jerome Fried, eds. *Funk & Wagnall's Standard Dictionary of Folklore, Mythology, and Legend.* 1949–50.

MacCulloch, John A., et al. *Mythology of All Races.* 13 vols. 1964. Bibliography at end of each volume.

Preminger, Alex, F. J. Warnke, and O. B. Hardison, eds. *Encyclopedia of Poetry and Poetics.* 1965. A brief bibliography accompanies each article.

Steinberg, Sigfrid Henry. *Cassell's Encyclopedia of World Literature.* Rev. ed. by John Buchanan Brown. 3 vols. 1973. Brief bibliography at end of most articles.

D. Drama

Gassner, John, and Edward Quin, eds. *Reader's Enclyclopedia of World Drama.* 1969.

Hartnell, Phyllis, ed. *Oxford Companion to the Theater.* 3rd ed. 1967. A bibliography accompanies each article.

Music and Dance

Apel, Willi. *Harvard Dictionary of Music.* 2nd ed. 1969. Has brief bibliographies.

Beaumont, Cyril W. *A Bibliography of Dancing.* 1963.

De Mille, Agnes. *The Book of the Dance.* 1963.

Ewen, David. *The World of Twentieth Century Music.* 1968. Brief bibliographic entries.

Grove, George. *Dictionary of Music and Musicians.* 9 vols. 5th ed. 1954. Supplement, 1961. This work and the *Harvard Dictionary of Music* are the authorities in the field. Excellent bibliographies.

Sachs, Curt. *World History of the Dance.* 1937.

Scholes, P. A. *Oxford Companion to Music.* 10th ed. 1970. Includes bibliographies.

Thompson, Oscar. *International Cyclopedia of Music and Musicians.* 10th ed. 1975. Brief bibliographies.

Westrup, J. A., ed. *The New Oxford History of Music.* 10 vols. 1957–74. Includes bibliographies.

Philosophy

Copleston, Frederick. *A History of Western Philosophy.* 8 vols. Rev. ed. 1950. Bibliography at end of each volume.

Edwards, Paul, ed. *Encyclopedia of Philosophy.* 8 vols. 1967. Bibliographies.

Urmson. J. O. *The Concise Encyclopedia of Western Philosophy and Philosophers.* 1960. Brief bibliography at end of volume.

Political Science

Burchfield, Laverne. *Student's Guide to Materials in Poltical Science.* 1935. Useful bibliography for earlier periods.

Frankel, Joseph. *The Making of Foreign Policy: An Analysis of Decision-Making.* Rev. ed. 1967.

Huntington, Samuel P. *Political Order in Changing Societies.* 1968.

Morgenthau, Hans. *Politics among Nations.* 5th ed. 1974. Bibliography pp. 577–597.

Political Handbook of the World. 1927–.

Smith, Edward C., and A. J. Zurcher, eds. *Dictionary of American Politics.* 2nd ed. 1968.

White, Carl M., et al. *Sources of Information in the Social Sciences.* 2nd ed. 1973.

Psychology

Drever, James. *Dictionary of Psychology.* Rev. ed. by H. Wallerstein, 1964.

The Harvard List of Books in Psychology. 4th ed. 1971. Annotated.

Psychological Abstracts. 1927–.

Religion

Buttrick, G. A., et al. *Interpreter's Dictionary of the Bible: An Illustrated Encyclopedia.* 5 vols. 1976. Has bibliographic entries.

Cross, F. L., and Elizabeth A. Livingstone. *Oxford Dictionary of the Christian Church.* 1974. Has brief bibliographies.

Ferm, Vergilius. *Encyclopedia of Religion.* 1945. Brief bibliographic entries.

Hastings, James, ed. *Encyclopedia of Religion and Ethics.* 12 vols. and index. 1908–27. Footnotes, but no bibliography.

Jackson, S. M., et al. *New Schaff-Herzog Encyclopedia of Religious Knowledge.* 12 vols. and index. 1949–51.

McDonald, William J., et al., eds. *New Catholic Encyclopedia.* 15 vols. 1967. A bibliography follows each article.

Werblowski, R. J. Z., and Geoffrey Wigoder, eds. *The Encyclopedia of the Jewish Religion.* 1965.

Science

A. General

Deason, Hilary. *A Guide to Science Reading.* 1963.
McGraw-Hill Encyclopedia of Science and Technology. 15 vols. 4th ed. 1977. Has a bibliographical supplement.
Newman, James R., et al. *Harper Encyclopedia of Science.* 4 vols. Rev. ed. 1967. Brief bibliographic entries.
Van Nostrand's Scientific Encyclopedia. 5th ed. 1976.

B. Life Sciences

Benthall, Jonathan. *Ecology in Theory and Practice.* 1973. Includes bibliographical references.
De Bell, Garrett, ed. *The Environmental Handbook.* 1970. Bibliography at end of volume.
Gray, Peter, ed. *Encyclopedia of the Biological Sciences.* 2nd ed. 1970. Brief bibliographic entries.
Kerker, Ann E., and Esther M. Schlundt. *Literature Sources in the Biological Sciences.* 1961.
Smith, Roger C., and W. Malcolm Reid, eds. *Guide to the Literature of the Life Sciences.* 8th ed. 1972.

C. Physical Sciences

Kemp, D. A. *Astronomy and Astrophysics: A Bibliographical Guide.* 1970.
Larousse Encyclopedia of the Earth: Geology, Paleontology, and Prehistory. 1961.
Parke, Nathan G. *Guide to the Literature of Mathematics and Physics.* 2nd ed. 1958.
Universal Encyclopedia of Mathematics. 1964.
Van Nostrand's International Encyclopedia of Chemical Science. 1964.

Sociology and Anthropology

Hauser, Philip M., ed. *Handbook for Social Research in Urban Areas.* 1967. Includes bibliographies.
International Bibliography of Sociology. 1951–. Annual.
International Encyclopedia of the Social Sciences. 17 vols. 1968. Each article is followed by a bibliography.
Kroeber, A. L., ed. *Anthropology Today: An Encyclopedic Inventory.* 1953. Includes bibliographies.
Siegel, Bernard J. *Biennial Review of Anthropology.* 1959–. Contains a subject index.
Social Work Year Book. 1929–. Includes bibliographies.

Exercise 2

To familiarize yourself with Constance M. Winchell's Guide to Reference Books, *pick one of the following questions and run down the answer. Consult the* Guide *for likely sources; then check the sources themselves; finally, record on a 3 × 5 card the question, the answer(s), and the sources that were most helpful. Use complete bibliographic form for sources.*

1. If, in the eighteenth century, you had been convicted of "pradprigging," what would have been your crime and, in all probability, your punishment?
2. What Mexican hero-god carried a cross and what did it symbolize?
3. In what decade did the population of the United States shift from a predominantly rural to a predominantly urban one?
4. Why might a librarian view with alarm a type of book introduced in 1769 by James Granger?
5. Why are brushes made of camel hair and when did the practice begin?
6. What biographer of Johann Sebastian Bach has also written books on Jesus and St. Paul?

3. Finding Information in Periodicals and Newspapers

Often, the material you find in the reference books or in books you have located in the card catalog is neither specific nor current enough for your research. More current information usually appears in magazines and newspapers. To find this information, you will need to consult periodical indexes such as the following:

Reader's Guide to Periodical Literature. 1900–. Alphabetical list under author, title, and subject.

International Index to Periodicals. 1907–. Name changed to *Humanities and Social Sciences Index,* 1960. Separately published as *Humanities Index* and *Social Sciences Index,* 1965–.

Poole's Index to Periodical Literature. 1802–81; 1882–1906. Useful for earlier periodicals.

Book Review Digest. 1905–.

New York Times Index. 1913–.

These indexes list alphabetically, by author and by subject, important articles in magazines of general circulation. If you are investigating a more specialized subject, you may need to get information from reviews and journals such as those we list in the section below.

To find relevant articles in scientific and learned periodicals, use specialized indexes such as these:

Applied Science and Technology Index. 1957–.
Art Index. 1929–.
Biography Index. 1946–.
Biological Abstracts. 1926–. Includes ecological materials.
Business Periodicals Index. 1958–.
Current Anthropology. 1960–.
Economic Abstracts. 1953–.
Education Index. 1929–.
Engineering Index. 1884–.
Historical Abstracts. 1955–.
Music Index. 1949–.
Philosopher's Index.
PMLA, "Annual Bibliography." 1921–68. Since 1969 this index has been titled *MLA International Bibliography.* It is published separately from *PMLA* in four volumes: I, English and American Literature; II, foreign literature; III, linguistics; and IV, the teaching of foreign languages.
Psychological Abstracts. 1927–.
Public Affairs Information Service. 1915–. Political affairs, economics, and government.
Sociological Abstracts. 1955–.
Zoological Record. 1864–.

Here are two sample entries from the *Reader's Guide.* They refer to the same article, but the first is a subject entry, the second an author entry.

MASSACHUSETTS BAY colony
    Anne Hutchinson versus Massachusetts. W. Newcomb. il pors Am Heritage 25:12–15+ Je '74

NEWCOMB, Wellington
    Anne Hutchinson versus Massachusetts. il pors Am Heritage 25:12–15+ Je '74

Notice that these entries are not in the form you would use in the footnotes or bibliography of a research paper (see p. 339). The abbreviations are explained on the first pages of each volume of the guide, as the first pages of each index and reference book contain instructions for its use. The article referred to, "Anne Hutchinson versus Massachusetts," was written by Wellington Newcomb. It appeared in June, 1974, in Volume 25 of *American Heritage* on pp. 12–15 and later pages. The article is illustrated with portraits.

Exercise 3

Make a list of appropriate reference works to begin a preliminary bibliography for the following questions.

1. Why did Leibniz, Spinoza, and Newton discover the principles of differential calculus at the same time?
2. What is the relationship between Robert Frost's childhood and his poems about youth?
3. How are recent national movements (Israel, the Arab world) related to religious fundamentalism?
4. What would be the economic consequences of a national effort to develop solar energy?

12e

Organizing and Writing the Paper

1. Preliminary Bibliography

A list of books and articles related to a particular topic is called a bibliography, and you will need to make one of your own for a long paper. The bibliography you compile when you begin a paper is "preliminary" because you will alter it as you discover new references and discard references that turn out, as some will, to be useless. To make such changes easy, and to facilitate alphabetizing, you should put each reference on a separate card or slip of paper. A good size is 3 × 5 inches, easily distinguished from the larger slips on which you will put your actual notes.

Include on each bibliography slip all the information that will be needed for the final bibliography at the end of your paper. For a book you will need the name of the author or editor, the exact title of the book including any subtitle, the place and date of publication, and the name of the publisher. For an article in a periodical, you will need the author's name if the article is signed, the title of the article (in quotation marks), the name of the periodical (italicized), and an indication of the exact volume and pages. Ordinarily, volume number, date, and page numbers will serve, but in newspapers and in magazines such as *Newsweek*, which begin each issue with page 1, you will need to give the date of the particular issue in which the article appears. The standard form for bibliographic entries, which differs slightly from that of a footnote reference, is illustrated on page 345.

Use common sense in choosing the items for your preliminary bibliography. Don't waste time, for example, in collecting references to obscure publications not in your library. Interlibrary loans are possible but time-consuming, and you will find it much more rewarding to explore the resources of your own library. If your topic is new—a relatively recent event or discovery or notable person—look for information in newspapers and periodicals rather than in books. The writing and publishing of a serious book takes, usually, from two to five years; but magazines try to keep up with the times, and indexes to periodicals appear in monthly installments.

Remember, too, to check for original dates of publication whenever you are dealing with a paperback book or with a collection of essays. Some paperbacks will represent the original edition of a work, and some collections will be composed of material never printed before. But others will be reprints, or made up of reprints; and then you must be careful to get the original date of publication (which should be on the copyright page) or the source of the article (which should be either at the bottom of the first page of the article or in a list of sources at the beginning or end of the book). You need to do this for two reasons: first, because you will need this information for your footnotes and bibliography; and second, because you will feel like a fool if you refer to a 1975 paperback as "one of the latest works on this subject," only to discover too late that it's a reprint of something written in 1920.

Some teachers will ask you to submit an annotated bibliography. In addition to the standard bibliographic information about your source, you must write a brief comment evaluating the source's usefulness for your research: How well does it cover your subject? How much previous research does it use? Does it have a bibliography? Does it include an index?

2. Evaluating Material

When you look into the actual books and articles referred to in your bibliography, you will find some of them unsatisfactory—too skimpy, too prejudiced, or irrelevant. Pick out the useful ones and discard the rest, but be sure in discussing controversial issues that you are taking account of both sides. If your topic is, for example, "How Safe Is Nuclear Power?" you will run across pamphlets published by utility companies. These may not be actually biased, but they are almost certain to be extremely optimistic about the desirability of nuclear power plants. They should be checked with articles on the other side, which may in their turn be biased or exaggerated.

As authorities, scientists are generally preferable to public relations men, but scientists also disagree with each other. Read both sides—the scientists who signed Dr. Edward Teller's statement in favor of nuclear energy and those members of the Union of Concerned Scientists who have come out against expanding nuclear power plants. If you feel incompetent to judge between them, present both sides. Whether your paper is meant to prove a point or just to lay out the facts, you will need to report both sides of controversial questions.

3. Limiting the Topic

As you revise your own bibliography—discarding useless references and adding new and better ones—you should be looking ahead to the next two steps: collecting information and limiting the topic to a suitable size.

Suppose that you are looking into alternative sources of energy—that is, substitutes for our rapidly disappearing stocks of oil, coal, and natural gas. The more you read about solar energy—its direct application to heating water or houses and its various secondary forms, based on winds and waves and temperature gradients, not to mention planned biological transformation and concentration of sunlight—the more surprised you may be by the breadth of the subject. If you try to include all alternative sources of energy, you won't have time or space to do a thorough account of any one of them. The solution is obvious: limit your topic by choosing three or four alternative sources, or even just one, that can be treated in detail.

How do you choose? On what principle do you select parts of a topic and discard the rest? There are many answers. You might choose those that interest you most. Or, being severely down to earth, you might work only on those sources that have already been tested in the laboratory.

Or you could take up those that seem most practicable, technically or economically or even politically. You may find that you will need to limit your paper still further—perhaps to the technical and economic aspects of one alternative source, such as geothermal power.

Notice how these three processes—revising your bibliography, reading and evaluating material, and limiting your topic—go hand in hand. You have to find out something about the subject before you can know how to limit it, or how much limitation is needed. Limiting the subject will require changes in your bibliography, too. Not only will you discard references to articles no longer relevant, but you will be turning up new references in every book or article you read.

A useful guide in all three processes is a tentative plan. This can be a fairly detailed outline or a few notes to remind yourself what points you want to cover. The essential thing is to use the plan as a guide, but to keep it tentative and not be bound by it. The more you read, the more you may find it desirable to change this, or modify that, or emphasize some new points. No one can tell in advance what kind of material he will find, or what will interest him most. The tentative plan should develop as your reading extends and changes your original ideas on the subject.

4. Taking Notes

The most important advice here is to put each note on a separate card or sheet. Because your research paper presents your own point of view on the material, you will probably organize your research differently from the way you found it. To organize your material, you must break it into small units, and unless each unit is on a separate card, you will find it difficult to bring together from different sources all the notes on a single topic. Write your notes on cards (at least 4 × 6 inches) or on half-sheets of theme paper. If more than one card is needed for one point, use the back or clip on another card with the subject and source as a heading.

1. State the topic of the note in the upper left-hand corner. (Other corners may be used for the library call number and other information.) The exact source, including the author, the title, and the page, can go along the bottom edge of the card (see p. 334). It is not necessary to include the place of publication, the publisher, and the date on each card; your bibliography cards will contain this information.

2. Always put quotation marks around quoted material, and quote exactly, even to the punctuation marks and the spelling. Do not use quotation marks for paraphrases or summaries.

3. If parts of a quotation are omitted, ellipsis marks should be used to show where the omission occurs—three spaced periods (. . .) to indicate an omission within a sentence, four spaced periods (or three added to end punctuation) to indicate an omission at the end of, or beyond the end of, a sentence. Brackets should enclose words, not part of the quotation, that you have inserted for clarity. If, for example, there is an obvious error in the text, you may insert after it the word *sic* (Latin for "thus") in brackets, to show that the quotation is exact even though it contains an error: [*sic*].

A note is usually a direct quotation, a paraphrase in your own words, or a précis (see section 4d). The disadvantage of quoting directly is that it may waste space and time; a paraphrase or précis is usually shorter. However, the great advantage of direct quotation in your notes is that you can check the exact wording without going back to the book. When you actually write the paper you will use direct quotation rarely, usually when the exact words are worth commenting on; ordinarily, a paraphrase or a précis, sometimes including a brief excerpted phrase from the original, will show your mastery of the subject. In your notes, though, copy out as many direct quotations as time permits, indicating them, of course, by quotation marks.

DIRECT QUOTATION

> *Control of smoke*
> "Smoke is . . . more easy to handle than liquid effluents, because it proclaims itself to all the world. A stream of water running from a factory into a river or a sewer is not conspicuous, and the connivance of an official inspector may be arranged. But black smoke belching from a high stack stands out against the sky for every voter to see. The housewife in particular bristles up in wrath, and a politician recognizes a good vote-getting issue."
>
> George R. Stewart, <u>Not So Rich as You Think</u>, p. 125.

PARAPHRASE AND DIRECT QUOTATION

> *Control of smoke*
> Smoke is easier to control than liquid effluents. Since dirty water draining from a factory is usually invisible to the public, "the connivance of an official inspector" can be arranged more easily than when "black smoke [is] belching from a high stack . . . for every voter to see."
>
> George R. Stewart, <u>Not So Rich as You Think</u>, p. 125.

PRÉCIS

> *Control of smoke*
> Smoke can be more easily controlled than liquid effluents because it is more conspicuous. Liquid factory wastes are usually invisible to the public, but smoke from a high stack attracts the attention of voter and politician alike.
>
> George R. Stewart, <u>Not So Rich as You Think</u>, p. 125.

5. Writing the Paper

When you have collected as much information as you need or have time for, you will have arrived at the same stage in your writing as you did after organizing your jottings or outline for a short theme. What remains is to report the influence your research has had on your own thinking, to weave the material you have discovered into the fabric of your thought. In some cases, you may disagree with the authors you have read. In others, you may show how their views or information support your own conclusions or have led you to change your mind.

At this point, many researchers write a "comment card" to correspond to each note card, reminding them of their reasons for taking the note and serving as a jotting to develop into a few sentences in the essay. This practice guarantees that the paper will not be a mere splicing together of quotations but a contribution of the writer to the dialogue.

The next step is to convert your tentative plan into a final outline. Expand, cut, and reorganize so that the outline represents what you finally want to say. The new outline should be as detailed as possible, because you will actually write your paper from it.

Next, sort out your notes, putting together those that relate to the various subpoints in your outline. This will bring together the notes that explain or justify or give evidence for the points you want to make. If you find you have no notes at all for a subpoint in the outline, ask yourself some questions. Is the point really important? Should you look for more material, should you try to write it up out of your own head, or should you simply omit the point altogether? You're in charge here. Use your judgment.

From this point on, beyond reminding you of the principles of order, coherence, emphatic statement, and careful choice of words—matters already discussed in this handbook—a teacher can only give you advice based on experience. We find, for example, Hemingway's advice very useful: write the first draft by hand, not on the typewriter. A soft pencil or a smooth-flowing ballpoint pen helps your writing to flow naturally, instead of jerking along in a staccato mechanical rhythm. It also helps to keep the first draft fluid and easy to revise. There is something final-looking about typewritten copy that discourages the impulse to make changes. Moreover, deleting a typed sentence is awkward and time-consuming, but with one satisfying swoop of the pen you can wipe out a whole sentence, or even a paragraph, and start over again. Allow plenty of space so that words or phrases can be inserted between the lines, in place of those you cross out. If the order of sentences in a paragraph needs to be changed, you can indicate this quickly and clearly with freehand lines as visual guides.

In writing the first draft, try free-writing so that you don't lose your train of thought. If you can't think of the right word, leave a generous blank and go on. The main idea at this stage is to get your ideas down on paper while they are hot. The time to agonize in cold blood over the exact word or the most concisely emphatic sentence pattern is in revision. Hemingway's other bit of advice is also worth remembering: Don't write yourself out. Stop while you're going good and know just what's coming next, so that you can get started readily at your next writing session.

Don't neglect transitional words, phrases, and sentences. Give the reader lots of signposts so he will know at all times where he is. *However* signals a concession to the opposite point of view; *in the second place* locates a stage in a progressive pattern. A sentence like "Two types of evidence support this theory" alerts the reader to the structure of the paragraphs that follow. If in doubt, use more transitional phrases rather than fewer. They can always be crossed out in revision, but if they seem appropriate to you, they will probably be helpful to a reader and should be retained.

If you have time, put the first draft of the whole paper in a drawer for a day or two (at least overnight) before beginning to revise it. Revision is the hardest part of a writer's task, and it is helpful to come at it refreshed and with a clear mind. This is the time for simple mechanical repairs: looking up the spelling of difficult or troublesome words, checking rules of punctuation and mechanics, looking for your likely faults in sentence structure. Decide how much direct quotation you will use, how much summary. If you see too many long quotes on a page, look again to see whether they can be shortened. Check your paraphrases to make sure they're not uncomfortably close to plagiarism. Put footnotes into their full form now, while there's still time for a last mad dash to the library; check spellings of names and titles, correctness of page numbers. Most important, this is the time to test each sentence to see if it really says what you intend. Set a high standard here. Don't be satisfied with the mere hope that a reader will be able to understand your meaning. Try to write so that your reader cannot misunderstand.

The final version of your paper—the one you will hand in—should be typed, double-spaced, or written neatly in ink. Follow the suggestions in section 17a for manuscript style. If your instructor requires it, prepare and submit a detailed outline, which will serve as a table of contents. Double-check footnotes for correct form, and prepare a final bibliography. When you submit the paper, put it in a folder or secure it by paper clips, but do not staple the pages together. Most instructors will want to separate the pages to facilitate checking and making corrections.

6. Plagiarism

Because the research paper represents the ideas you have developed in response to the research of others, you will find it necessary to distinguish your own thoughts from the rest of the material. Unless you name your sources, your reader will assume that he is reading your own observations, opinions, and ideas and the results of your own surveys and interviews. It is plagiarism to pass off the work or ideas or language of someone else as your own, whether you do so intentionally or accidentally. Intentional or not, plagiarism can have serious consequences.

Keep in mind two devices that help mark off others' ideas from your own. The first is the *establishing phrase*, such as "According to . . . " or "Benedict has stated that . . . ." Your reader will assume that any statement that precedes an establishing phrase is your own thought, unless it has a footnote. The second device is the footnote number itself. Your reader will assume (except in the case of factual material) that any material after the establishing phrase and before the footnote is from your source.

Avoiding plagiarism is not always as clear-cut and simple as it may sound. In practice, it is often impossible to give the sources for everything one writes. Where, for example, did we get the definition of plagiarism just given? We really don't know. For years we have heard plagiarism talked about, have read about it, and have even studied examples of it in student papers. In short, our knowledge of what the term means is common knowledge, part of our understanding. Generally known facts, such as the discovery of America by Columbus, are also considered common knowledge. One is not required to indicate the sources of the fact that a mile is 5,280 feet or that a red traffic light, in this country at least, means Stop.

If, however, you write that "a study of 125 randomly selected freshmen showed that only 29 percent considered snitching more reprehensible than cheating," your failure to indicate who did the study implies that you did it yourself. If you didn't, you could be accused of plagiarising the work of someone else. If you write "a study by A. G. White[1] showed that 29 percent . . .," and if you indicate in a footnote* that the source is an article entitled "Moral Judgments in the Classroom," which appeared in 1972 on page 223 of Volume 6 of the *Review of Education,* you are using White's material properly.

Even if you indicate the source of your information, you may be plagiarizing if your paraphrase or précis is too close to the language of the original.

Suppose that a paragraph in White's article reads

The students used in the study were chosen from a middlewestern university thought to be generally representative of middle-class views on ethical questions. Standard statistical techniques were employed to ensure an adequate sample of the freshman class.

If in your paper this turns up as "The students were selected from a midwestern university in which middle-class views on ethical matters prevail. To ensure a representative sampling of freshmen, standard statistical techniques were used," you are guilty of plagiarizing.

It is true that in a paraphrase or a précis, you will need to use some of the words that occur in the original; it is both difficult and unnecessary to find accurate synonyms for "middlewestern," "university," "freshman," and the like. But it is not enough merely to invert the order of the clauses in the second sentence of the original and to change "chosen" to "selected," and "adequate sample" to "representative sampling." To use material legitimately, you must say it in your own language, fit it into your own context, and con-

---

* For the proper form of a footnote, see the next section.

nect it with what goes before and after in your paper. A patchwork of paraphrases and quotations, loosely connected, is not a paper you can call your own—nor, in all probability, would you want to. If it is to be your paper, you must use the source material to support, or test, or illustrate your own thoughts, and in most instances, you will paraphrase rather than quote directly. When you do quote you must do so exactly.

7. Footnotes

The number of footnotes in a long paper cannot be prescribed in hard-and-fast rules. All quotations, paraphrases, and précis should be documented, of course, and all titles of books. Beyond this, use your judgment. Give references to the most important sources of your information, especially on controversial issues. If you have only four footnotes in a 1,000-word paper, you probably aren't doing justice to your sources. If you have five footnotes on every page, you probably are documenting needlessly.

When a paper is to be submitted for publication, most editors prefer to have the footnotes on separate sheets at the end of the paper. Some instructors also prefer this method for term papers. Ask about it. If footnotes are placed at the bottom of each page, the first footnote should be separated from the last line of the text by triple spacing. Footnotes and bibliography entries are double-spaced for college papers. Use arabic numerals rather than asterisks or other symbols to indicate the reference of the footnote in the text. Number the footnotes consecutively throughout the paper. In the text the reference numerals should be placed slightly above the line and immediately after the name, quotation, sentence, or paragraph to which the footnote refers. In the footnote itself, the reference number should also be placed slightly above the line. Information given in the text of the paper need not be repeated in the footnote. For example, if you say "Angus Wilson maintains that . . .," the footnote would begin with the title of the book, instead of the author's name.

A footnote can be thought of as an abbreviated sentence. Its first line is indented five spaces from the left-hand margin, and the first word is capitalized. The footnote ends with a period. Only the first footnote reference to a book or periodical article needs to be written out in full. For later references, use the brief form illustrated below and in the sample paper.

The footnote form prescribed and used in this section follows that of *The MLA Style Sheet*, Second Edition. A footnote should contain the following items in the sequence here given:

1. The author's name, first name first. Since footnotes are not in alphabetical order, there is no need to put the last name first.

2. The title of the book, underlined to indicate italic type. If the reference is to an article in a periodical or in a book, the author's name is followed by the title of the article, in quotation marks, and this is followed by the name of the periodical (or book) underlined. Use commas to separate these elements.

3. Information regarding the place and date of publication. For books, this consists of the city in which the book was published, a colon, an abbreviated name of the publisher, and the date, all enclosed in parentheses. Months of more than five letters are abbreviated. For articles in reviews and journals, the title of the periodical is underlined, followed by the volume number in arabic numerals, the date in parentheses, and the page number. For articles in newspapers and magazines, the volume number is omitted and the date is enclosed in commas. In referring to the newspaper articles, include the section of the newspaper if it is separately numbered, and the column number, counting from the left.

4. Page number. The abbreviation of *page* is *p.*; the plural is *pp.* If a book is printed in more than one volume, use Roman numerals to indicate numbers between one and ten. In such a case, the abbreviation *p.* is not used: for example, II, 46.

The following six footnotes illustrate first and second footnote references.

[1] Perry Miller and T. H. Johnson, *The Puritans* (New York: Harper, 1963), p. 18.

[2] Rosemary M. Laughlin, "Anne Bradstreet: Poet in Search of Form," *American Literature*, 42 (1970), 16.

[3] Miller and Johnson, p. 65.

[4] Ann Stanford, "Anne Bradstreet," in *Major Writers of Early American Literature*, ed. Everett Emerson (Madison: Univ. of Wisconsin Press, 1972), p. 37.

[5] Ibid.

[6] Laughlin, p. 19.

The following additional words and abbreviations are sometimes used in footnotes, bibliographies, and references:

anon.	anonymous
b.	born
c. or **ca.** (circa)	about (used with dates)
cf. (confer)	compare or consult
d.	died
diss.	dissertation
ed.	edition, editor, or edited by
et al.	and others (used of people only)
f., plural **ff.**	and following page(s)
ibid.	the same
id. or **idem**	the same; usually the same author
l., plural **ll.**	line(s)
loc. cit. (loco citato)	in the place already cited
ms, plural **mss**	manuscript(s)
n., plural **nn.**	note(s)
N.B. (nota bene)	take notice, mark well
n.d.	no date (of publication) given
n.p.	no place (of publication) given
n. pag.	no pagination used in book

The three preceding abbreviations tell your reader that the publisher of your reference work has omitted information you would normally include in your footnote.

op. cit. (*opere citato*)	in the work cited

This abbreviation must be used with the author's name, to identify the work being cited. If two works by the same author have been referred to, this abbreviation cannot be used. The general tendency today is to avoid such abbreviations altogether, and to use the author's name, plus a short title if one is needed.

passim	here and there, throughout
rev.	revised, revision; review, reviewed by (Write out word if necessary to prevent ambiguity.)

rpt.	reprint of an earlier edition
sc.	scene
sic	so, thus
st., plural sts.	stanza(s)
trans.	translator, translation, translated by
v., plural vv.	verse(s)
vol., plural **vols.**	volume(s)

The following is a list of the chief footnote forms used in the first reference.

BOOK BY ONE AUTHOR

[1] Elizabeth Wade White, *Anne Bradstreet: "The Tenth Muse"* (New York: Oxford Univ. Press, 1971), p. 52.

BOOK BY ONE AUTHOR, REVISED OR LATER EDITION

[2] Roy Harvey Pearce, ed., *Colonial American Writing,* 2nd ed. (New York: Holt, 1969), p. 34.

BOOK BY ONE AUTHOR, REPRINT OF AN OLDER EDITION

[3] Sumner Chilton Powell, *Puritan Village* (1963; rpt. New York: Anchor, 1965), p. 61.

BOOK BY ONE AUTHOR, TRANSLATED

[4] Ursula Brumm, *American Thought and Religious Typology,* trans. John Hoaglund (New Brunswick, N.J.: Rutgers Univ. Press, 1970), pp. 49–50.

BOOK BY ONE AUTHOR, PART OF A SERIES

[5] George M. Waller, ed., *Puritanism in Early America,* 2nd ed., Problems in American Civilization (Lexington, Mass.: Heath, 1973), p. 67.

[6] Josephine K. Piercy, *Anne Bradstreet,* Twayne's United States Authors Series, No. 72 (1965; rpt., New Haven, Conn.: College and University Press, 1965), p. 14.

BOOK BY TWO AUTHORS

⁷ Perry Miller and T. H. Johnson, *The Puritans* (New York: Harper, 1963), II, 47.

A work with three authors would use this same style, with the authors being listed as A, B, and C. If a work has more than three authors, the custom is to cite only the name of the first author mentioned on the title page and to complete it with "et al." or with the English equivalent, "and others."

AN EDITED TEXT

⁸ Robert Hutchinson, ed., *Poems of Anne Bradstreet* (New York: Dover, 1969), p. 48.

⁹ William Bradford, *Of Plymouth Plantation: 1620–1647*, ed. Samuel Eliot Morison (New York: Knopf, 1952), pp. 101–102.

SIGNED ESSAY IN A BOOK BY SEVERAL CONTRIBUTORS

¹⁰ Ann Stanford, "Anne Bradstreet," in *Major Writers of Early American Literature*, ed. Everett Emerson (Madison: Univ. of Wisconsin Press, 1972), p. 38.

¹¹ Robert D. Richardson, Jr., "The Puritan Poetry of Anne Bradstreet," *Texas Studies in Lit. and Lang.*, 9 (1967), rpt. in Sacvan Bercovitch, ed., *The American Puritan Imagination: Essays in Revaluation* (London and New York: Cambridge Univ. Press, 1974), pp. 112–113.

ARTICLE IN A JOURNAL

¹² Rosemary M. Laughlin, "Anne Bradstreet: Poet in Search of Form," *American Literature*, 42 (March 1970), 5.

Notice that when there is a volume number, you do not write "p."

ARTICLE IN A WEEKLY OR MONTHLY MAGAZINE

¹³ D. Davis, "American Hurrah: European Vision of America," *Newsweek*, 5 Jan. 1976, p. 36.

Do not include the volume number of a magazine or newspaper, or put the date in parentheses.

ANONYMOUS ARTICLE IN A PERIODICAL

[14] "ALA Pictorial Scrapbook," *American Libraries,* 7 (Jan. 1976), 42–43.

ANONYMOUS ENCYLOPEDIA ARTICLE

[15] Bradstreet, Anne Dudley," *Encylopaedia Britannica,* 1974, Micro-paedia.

Do not give page numbers of alphabetically arranged reference works.

ANONYMOUS NEWSPAPER ARTICLE

[16] "Women's Roles to Be Featured," *Boston Sunday Globe,* 4 April 1976, p. 93, col. 5.

A BOOK REVIEW

[17] John Harris, "A Free Press Underground," rev. of *The Books of the Pilgrims,* by Lawrence D. Geller and Peter J. Gomes, *Boston Sunday Globe,* 11 April 1976, p. A15, col. 1.

The article is in section A of the newspaper.

8. The Final Bibliography

At the end of the paper (after the footnotes, if they are on separate sheets), add your final, alphabetized, bibliography. This may be a list of all those works mentioned in either your text or your footnotes (often called a "List of Works Cited"), or it may include all books and articles you have consulted at length, whether they were actually used in writing the paper or not. This would be a "List of Works Consulted." If your instructor does not specify one form of bibliography or the other, the choice is up to you.

The form of a bibliographic entry differs slightly from that of a footnote reference. Authors are listed with surname first, to make alphabetizing easy. The items within each reference are generally separated by periods instead of commas, but colons and semicolons remain as they were. Bibliographic entries are never numbered, and the second and following lines of an entry are indented five spaces.

SAMPLE BIBLIOGRAPHY

"ALA Pictorial Scrapbook." *American Libraries*, 7 (Jan. 1976), 42–43.

"Bradstreet, Anne Dudley." *Encylopaedia Britannica*. 1974. Micropaedia.

Brumm, Ursula. *American Thought and Religious Typology*. Trans. John Hoaglund. New Brunswick, N.J.: Rutgers Univ. Press, 1970.

Laughlin, Rosemary. "Anne Bradstreet: Poet in Search of Form." *American Literature*, 12 (1970), 1–17.

Miller, Perry, and others, eds. *Major Writers of America*. 2 vols. New York: Harcourt, 1962.

————, and T. H. Johnson. *The Puritans*. New York: Harper, 1963. Vol. 2.

The long dash indicates that Miller is the first-named author for this as well as for the preceding book. Books by the same author, or having the same senior author, are listed in alphabetical order.

Powell, Sumner Chilton. *Puritan Village*. 1963; rpt. New York: Anchor, 1965.

Richardson, Robert D., Jr. "The Puritan Poetry of Anne Bradstreet." *Texas Studies in Lit. and Lang.*, 9 (1967); rpt. in *The American Puritan Imagination: Essays in Revaluation*. Ed. Sacvan Bercovitch. London and New York: Cambridge Univ. Press, 1974, pp. 105–122.

Stanford, Ann. "Anne Bradstreet." *Major Writers of Early American Literature*. Ed. Everett Emerson. Madison: Univ. of Wisconsin Press, 1972, pp. 33–58.

Waller, George M., ed. *Puritanism in Early America*, 2nd ed. Problems in American Civilization. Lexington, Mass.: Heath, 1973.

SAMPLE PAPER

Autism: A Certain Uncertainty

Jeanne M. Petrillo

Rhetoric 102

April 13, 1980

Comment

Jeanne made this topic outline to guide her writing of the paper.

Outline for "Autism: A Certain Uncertainty"

I.   Introduction

Thesis: There is much disagreement about the cause and cure of autism.

II.   Features of autism

A. Withdrawal from the environment

B. Passivity in some autists

C. Hyperactivity in others

D. Self-destructiveness of autists

E. Robotlike behavior

F. Muteness

G. High intelligence of autistic children

III. Cause of autism disputed

A. Functional theories not always convincing

1. Genetic defect disproved by studies of twins

2. Some evidence for abnormalities associated with birth

3. Some evidence for organic defects in the left hemisphere of the brain

B. Theory of prenatal emotional influences not convincing

C. Theory of postnatal emotional attitudes
    also questioned
    1. Coldness of parents often observed
    2. Stress or inexperience of parents
        suggested by frequency among first-
        born.
    3. Objection to theory: parents should
        not feel guilty about autistic
        children
IV. Treatment of autism also controversial
    A. Freudian psychotherapy as a cure
        1. Basis of Freud's theory of hidden
            conflict
        2. Method of treatment: insight,
            support, patience
        3. Wing's critique: regression for
            autistic children is inappropriate
    B. Behavior modification as a cure
        1. Basis in systematic reward and
            punishment
        2. Method of the procedure: to
            punish bad and reward good
            behavior

3. Objections to behavior modification

    a. Cruel

    b. Ineffective: produces imitation, not understanding

    c. Still, shock or behavior modification often effective

C. Sign language as a cure

    1. Basis: sign language related to right side of the brain

    2. Uses of sign language

        a. Positive reinforcement to teach autistic child to pay attention

        b. Rewards effort to communicate

        c. Teaches practical vocabulary

        d. Social rewards and group approval

    3. Creedon, who invented technique, critical of behavior modification

    4. Yet uses method of behavior modification

V. Conclusion: We need more research and experimentation if we are to find the cause and cure of autism.

Comments

Jeanne begins by discussing the principal issue of her paper, which she believes is interesting enough to attract the attention of her readers.

Jeanne indents and single-spaces this long quotation. Notice that there are no quotation marks.

She uses a paraphrase here: the material is Dr. Wing's, but the words are Jeanne's.

Autism: A Certain Uncertainty

How can we begin to discuss autism when we
hardly know what it is? Autistic children have
only recently attracted popular attention in the
United States. Lorna Wing, M.D., states:

> It seems likely that there have always
> been autistic children, although it is
> only in the last twenty-five years that
> they have been named as a group and thought
> of separately from other severely mentally
> handicapped children. Perhaps they were the
> reason for the legends of the fairy changeling
> children, in which the fairies were believed
> to steal away a human baby and leave a fairy
> child in its place.[1]

The word autism stems from the Greek word autos,
meaning "self"; psychiatrists use the term to describe self-absorbed and withdrawn behavior.[2] The
cause of autism is unknown and diagnosis is difficult because the symptoms of autism are as different as the personalities of its victims. Because
the origin of autism remains a mystery, we cannot
agree upon a fairly certain cure for this frightening disorder.

Autism usually appears in children within the
first two and a half years of life. It occurs in
four or five children in every ten thousand. The
autistic child is usually the first born into a

Comment

Jeanne constructs her own sentence to fit grammatically with the phrase she has quoted.

family, and the occurrence of autism in males outnumbers that in females by almost three to one. The autistic child is withdrawn from his environment. He fails to establish normal parent-child relationships. In some cases, the autistic child is apathetic. Some have been described as being "as nearly dead as it is possible to be and still go on functioning."[3] In other cases, the child is hyperactive and may throw frequent temper tantrums for seemingly senseless reasons. Autistic children are reported as having excellent memories. Leo Kanner, an American child psychologist who first identified autism in 1943, described one hyperactive victim of autism with an exquisite memory "who screamed in implacable fury when one block was experimentally turned in a jumble of blocks and toys left on the floor during the child's absence. Each block had to be returned to its exact place before the child was satisfied."[4]

One terrifying habit exhibited by autistic children is their self-destructiveness. Some mutilate their hands and shoulders by biting them to the bone. Others will bang their hands against the wall until bloody. They also behave in other

Comment

Jeanne makes the transition into the second part of her paper with no overt device. Instead, she expects the reader to recognize the change of focus in her use of the word "cause" at the beginning of the paragraph, which appears for the first time since its mention in her thesis.

peculiar ways. Some engage in repetitive motions that would make a robot look human. They wave their hands in front of their faces or walk back and forth in a straight line for hours. Another strange symptom of autism, according to Dr. Bernard Rimland, author of several works on the subject, is the child's failure to speak or the loss of already acquired speech and the use of a "non-communicative, parrot-like monotone."[5]

Surprisingly, some autistic children show advanced spatial ability and coordination, while others, according to Anne Alvarez, are "limp, like a puppet whose strings have been dropped."[6] It must be remembered, though, that these children are not stupid or retarded by any means. As Dr. Rimland states: "It has been noted by a number of writers that autistic children can sometimes assemble jig-saw puzzles as readily when the picture is facing down as when it is visible."[7]

The cause of autism has eluded scientists and psychologists since its identification in 1943. Many experts believe that it is the result of a genetic defect, but this has been disproven by the discovery, reported by Nikolass Tingergen

Comment

The mention of Dr. Ferreira's name and the title of his article is a signal of the précis that follows.

that in two known sets of twins, only one in each set became autistic.[8] Others, he states, believe it is caused by "irreparable abnormalities" that occur at birth.[9] Dr. Rimland believes that autistic children may suffer from some organic defect in the left hemisphere of the brain. These children are deficient in skills associated with that side of the brain, such as speech, but not in spatial and musical tasks, which the right side of the brain appears to perform.[10]

Some specialists contend that autism is caused, or greatly influenced by, the emotional attitudes of the parents. Antonio Ferreira, M.D., in his article, "The Pregnant Woman's Emotional Attitude and Its Reflection on the Unborn," set up tests to determine whether a prenatal emotional environment exists and whether the mother's attitude could cause deviant behavior similar to the behavior displayed by autistic children. He questioned the mothers in two areas of interest, "Fear of Harming the Baby" and "Rejection of Pregnancy." The results of his tests showed a high correlation between those mothers who were indeed fearful of harming their babies or who rejected their preg-

Comments

Until now, Jeanne has principally recorded the results of her research. Since the footnote indicates the end of her précis of Ferreira's article, this comment shows her own judgment of the inadequacy of his research.

Jeanne decides to quote Rimland because his list of adjectives is rhetorically powerful.

nancy and those babies who exhibited behavior deviant from that of normal babies. Thus, he concluded that the prenatal emotional attitude of the mother can affect the behavior of her child.[11] He did not bother to ask whether the mothers continued to fear harming their children or felt guilt about their rejection of their pregnancies after the children were born.

The postnatal emotional attitudes of both parents of autistic children have, however, been considered causes of the disorder. The parents have been described by Dr. Rimland as being highly intelligent, "cold, bookish, formal, introverted, disdainful of frivolity, humorless, detached, and highly, even extensively, rational and objective," and as giving "mechanical attention" to their children.[12] Nikolass Tinbergen believes that these people are under stress themselves or are simply inexperienced as parents, possibly the reason autism is prevalent in the firstborn.[13] Dr. Rimland has said that autistic children are "the offspring of highly organized, professional parents, cold and rational, who just happened to defrost long enough to produce a child."[14] Still, some

Comments

Jeanne begins to indicate a transition to the next major section of her paper with this summary of the previous section.

Her mention of "treatment" as a synonym for "cure" completes the transition.

experts believe that the behavior and attitudes of
a victim's parents have little to do with the
child's autism, and that parents should not be
made to feel guilty for their child's disorder.
Such uncertainty is quite characteristic of the
controversy surrounding the cause of autism.

Treatments for autism have been proposed by
numerous specialists, most of whom assert that
theirs is the most effective procedure. Bruno
Bettelheim is a major proponent of Freudian psy-
chotherapy as a means to rehabilitate autistic
children. The principle behind Freudian psychology is the existence of an underlying conflict,
some tragic experience that has disrupted a critical stage of development, a problem that must be
discovered and rooted out in order to change the
behavior. The treatment of autistic children,
he contends, is the "combination of Freudian insight, a warm environment that makes no demands,
and infinite patience by the therapist."[15] Psy-
choanalysis, however, involves long hours and
tedious work and has largely been ineffectual.
Dr. Wing criticizes the Freudian approach: "The
use of psychotherapeutic techniques, which en-

Comment

Here is a copy of Jeanne's note card corresponding to footnote 17. Observe that she adds her own comment on the card below the quotation.

Behavior modification
"Behavior modification is a scientific procedure for systematically changing behavior through the use of rewards, punishments, or both. It works by increasing or decreasing the likelihood of a specified behavioral response through systematic reward and punishment."

positive reinforcement = reward
negative reinforcement = punishment

Wing, Rimland report success with this method. See Wing, p. 53.

Andrews and Karlins, Psychology, p. 6.

Jeanne uses her comment, slightly revised, in the paper after the quotation.

courage 'regression' (for example, bottle feeding
a child of seven to encourage him to go back to
the baby stage and 'start again'), seems particularly inappropriate for autistic children."[16]

Dr. Wing, with many others, is a proponent of
the behavioral psychologist's method of treating
the autistic child: behavior modification. It is,
according to Lewis M. Andrews and Marvin Karlins,
"a scientific procedure for systematically changing
behavior through the use of rewards, punishments,
or both. It works by increasing or decreasing the
likelihood of a specified behavioral response through
systematic reward and punishment."[17] This method
involves the use of "positive" and "negative" reinforcement to correct wrong and encourage proper
behavior. Numerous instances of how this procedure
has succeeded in changing the behavior of autistic
children lead one to wonder why it was ignored for
so long. Dr. Wing explains a situation in which
autistic children in an institution were given
attention only when they started to harm themselves;
otherwise, they were ignored: "it is easy to see how
this will make this self-injury occur more often than
ever." Some of the staff then started to punish

Comment

By setting up a contrast between the proponents and the critics of behavior modification, Jeanne sharpens the issues involved, particularly the ethical ones. To make this contrast effective, she has balanced two well-developed paragraphs, one favorable to behavior modification, the other unfavorable; she has signalled the contrast by the connective "Nonetheless," a forceful word placed at the beginning of the second paragraph.

self-destructive behavior and reward the children
when they behaved properly. These children soon
stopped their harmful behavior. [18]

Nonetheless, many critics have objected to
this therapy; they believe that it is cruel to
punish children who do not realize that they are
doing anything wrong. Bruno Bettelheim is one of
them. He states that when this method is used
for the purpose of conditioning a child to speak,
it does nothing but produce "verbal imitation" and
no comprehension. He believes that it adds one
more trauma to the many the child has already
faced. He briefly describes a session he observed of a behaviorist and an autistic child:

> During the training session, the child and
> adult sat facing each other, their heads
> about 30 cm. apart. The adult physically
> prevented the child from leaving the train-
> ing situation by holding the child's legs be-
> tween his own legs. Rewards, in the form
> of a single spoonful of the child's meal,
> were delivered after correct responses.
> Punishment (spanking, shouting by the adult)
> was delivered for inattentive, self-destruc-
> tive, and tantrumous behavior which inter-
> fered with the training, and most of these
> behaviors were suppressed within one week. [19]

Bettelheim thinks that behavior modification is
"brutal experimentation" and insists that although
the child is behaving correctly, he is doing so

Comments

Though fair in her treatment, Jeanne takes a clear position on the side of behavior modification.

Here Jeanne uses an overt device ("an alternative method") to show her transition to the third part of this section of her paper.

either to avoid punishment or to receive food.
Although the behavioral psychologists have found
a therapy that does help control the autistic
child, it might be compared with the training of
a dog. Therefore, many therapists believe that behavior modification is not the answer. However,
the first step in treating a victim of this disorder is to make him recognize that he is not in
his own world. If this realization requires
changing his environment in a sometimes painful
way, perhaps a shock is worthwhile to bring him
out of his fantasy and into reality.

An alternative method in the rehabilitation of
autistic children is beginning to look promising to
a few specialists. Carole Wade Offeir explains
"visual speech" or sign language as a treatment.
Sign language was used to treat autists earliest
by Margaret Creedon in the late 1960s and early
1970s. It is important to recognize that sign
language is primarily controlled by the right side
of the brain, possibly the stronger side in these
children. Using visual speech, autistic children
"let their fingers do the talking," a form of
communication used only by the deaf until then.

Comment

This ellipsis of four spaced periods shows that Jeanne has come to the end of a sentence and is skipping to a sentence that appears later in the article.

The therapist first teaches the child to pay attention to her, using positive reinforcement, along with sign language: "The therapist orders the child to 'look at me' at the same time she makes the corresponding sign slowly and deliberately....If the child meets the therapist's eyes, he gets praised, verbally and in sign language. He may also get a tickle or a tender pat."[20]

The therapists do not look for perfection at first, only an effort to communicate. "Communication, not speech, is the goal. It is wrongheaded to concentrate on mindless imitation of sounds, syllables, and words as many therapies do." The therapists teach children signs that enable them to request personal needs, food, toys, help. Soon the autists can handle a small vocabulary to attain all their physical needs easily. Creedon emphasizes group encounters and approval in her treatment of these children. She encourages them to touch each other, play group games, wrestle, and make signs with each other. Creedon is also skeptical of behavior-modification techniques, claiming that a "one-to-one relationship" between the therapist and the patient does not encourage the

Comments

Since there is no other footnote in this paragraph, we can assume that both summary and quotation are from p. 76 of the article.

Although Jeanne approves of Margaret Creedon's methods, she believes that Ms. Creedon does not entirely understand why they succeed.

Jeanne paraphrases and quotes from the article of Ann Alvarez to show another reason for Creedon's success in treating autistic children.

child to relate to other people and the outside world. As for rewards and punishments, she states: "We don't want these kids talking for M&M's all their lives."[21] She may not realize that praise is the reward she gives, or that praise is a form of reinforcement.

The physical aspect of Creedon's treatment also seems appropriate. Although the prognosis for autistic children who speak is much better than for those who do not speak, increasing the awareness among speaking autistic children of their bodies could help them as much as it does autistic mutes. They could learn to communicate with others, also. Autistic children who do speak, Anne Alvarez reports, always refer to themselves as "you" or "we," never as "I". It is "as if one thought of oneself in the third person rather than the first." Encouraged to touch and play with similar children, the autistic child who speaks could come into the world more readily.[22]

There are many theories about the causes of autism, from chills at birth to fear of castration. No one psychologist or scientist seems to be able to find an unambiguous answer. Autistic children's symptoms differ with their personalities; therefore,

Comment

In her final paragraph, Jeanne summarizes her main points and suggests solutions. Her last three sentences (beginning with "However, it seems . . . .") round out the paper and explain the aptness of her title—"Autism: A Certain Uncertainty."

treatments for each victim might also differ to accommodate each one's individuality. Perhaps the experts should consider a mixture of methods; for instance, sign language and behavior modification, which Ms. Creedon seems to have stumbled upon quite innocently. However, it seems that all one ever hears or reads about autism is the uncertainty surrounding it. If some of these children have made a full recovery from autism and others can function normally in society, then we can hope for a discovery of the cause and cure of autism. For such a discovery, we certainly need more research and experimentation.

Comments

The author's name need not be included in footnote 6 because it is mentioned in the text of the paper.

Because *Psychology Today* is not a journal but a magazine, the volume number and parentheses around the date are omitted in footnote 10.

Notes

[1]Lorna Wing, <u>Autism: A Guide for Parents and Professionals</u> (New York: Brunner/Mazel, 1972), p. 6.

[2]Wing, p. 4.

[3]Peter Gay, "The Empty Fortress," <u>The New Yorker</u>, 18 May 1968, p. 160.

[4]Quoted in Bernard Rimland, <u>Infantile Autism</u> (New York: Meredith Publishing Co., 1964), p. 11.

[5]Rimland, p. 11.

[6]"Children in the Shadows," <u>Parent's Magazine</u>, March 1972, p. 72.

[7]Rimland, p. 11.

[8]"Ethology and Stress Diseases," <u>Science</u>, 5 July 1974, p. 20.

[9]Tinbergen, p. 20.

[10]Reported by Carole Wade Offeir, "Visual Speech: Their Fingers Do the Talking," <u>Psychology Today</u>, June 1976, p. 78.

[11]In <u>American Journal of Ortho-Psychiatry</u>, 30 (1969), 553-561.

[12]Rimland, p. 25.

[13]Tinbergen, p. 22.

[14]Rimland, p. 25.

[15]Quoted in Richard Steele, "World Without I," Newsweek, 27 March 1976, p. 70.

[16]Wing, p. 53.

[17]Lewis M. Andrews and Marvin Karlins, Psychology: What's in It for Us? (New York: Random House, 1975), p. 6.

[18]Wing, p. 83.

[19]Gay, p. 170.

[20]Offeir, pp. 72-78. The quotation is from p. 76.

[21]Quoted in Offeir, p. 76.

[22]Alvarez, p. 72.

Bibliography

Alvarez, Anne. "Children in the Shadows." Parent's
     Magazine, March 1972, pp. 54-55, 72.

Andrews, Lewis M., and Marvin Karlins. Psychology:
     What's in It for Us? New York: Random House,
     1975.

Bettelheim, Bruno. The Empty Fortress. London:
     Collier-Macmillan, 1967.

Ferreira, A. J. "The Pregnant Woman's Emotional
     Attitude and Its Reflection on the Newborn."
     American Journal of Ortho-Psychiatry, 30
     (1960), 553-561.

Gay, Peter. "The Empty Fortress." The New Yorker
     18 May 1968, pp. 160-170.

Offeir, Carole Wade. "Visual Speech: Their Fingers
     Do the Talking." Psychology Today, June 1976,
     pp. 72-78.

Rimland, Bernard. Infantile Autism. New York:
     Meredith Publishing Co., 1964.

Steele, Richard. "World Without I." Newsweek,
     27 March 1967, pp. 70-71.

Tinbergen, Nikolass.   "Ethology and Stress Diseases."

 Science, 5 July 1974, pp. 20-27.

Wing, Lorna.   Autistic Children: A Guide for Parents

 and Professionals. New York: Brunner/Mazel,

 1972.

13

SENTENCE FRAGMENTS AND COMMA SPLICES

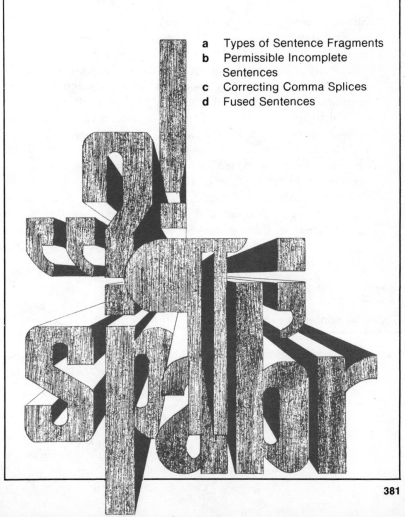

Shards of sentences on the page, broken phrases, or two sentences jammed together carelessly with a comma—such piecemeal, lumpy writing is as exasperating to read as it is easy for the writer to remedy. It is silly to alienate your audience, in particular the instructor who must evaluate your work, with fragments and fused sentences, especially when they are not difficult to identify. An eye trained to spot subjects and finite verbs and an ear tuned to the intonations of speech are sufficient to catch fragmented and run-together sentences. To develop a sense of the sight and the sound of complete sentences, read your writing aloud, listening to the accents, pitch, and rhythms of the words on the page. Notice the different breath pauses for different marks of punctuation, the rising and falling pitch at different points in the sentence. Read aloud the sentences of other writers for cadence and intonation. Once again, remember that grammar and the human voice often coincide in remarkable ways.

13a

Types of Sentence Fragments

A series of words that does not contain an independent clause, that is, a clause with a subject and a finite verb, is a *sentence fragment.*

Fragment   The purpose of reciting five minutes in French was to encourage imitation of the recording. Thus putting emphasis on intonation, rhythm, and pronunciation.

Correct   The purpose of reciting five minutes in French was to encourage imitation of the recording, thus putting emphasis on intonation, rhythm, and pronunciation.

This statement, which expresses one idea, should be contained in one sentence. The second series of words in the faulty version, however, is a fragment, a participial phrase without a subject or a verb. The phrase should be joined, as it is in the corrected example, to the previous sentence.

Listed below are common types of sentence fragments. Learn to recognize and to correct them.

1. Appositive Phrase

Fragment   The crowd that attended the local track meet was the usual one. Parents, friends of the athletes, and people looking for a good tan.

Correct   The crowd that attended the local track meet was the usual one—parents, friends of the athletes, and people looking for a good tan.

The three nouns "parents," "friends," and "people" are in apposition to "one," and the appositive phrase should be attached to the rest of the sentence with a dash or a colon.

2. Prepositional Phrase

Fragment   The council meeting was to have been conducted in an orderly and democratic fashion, but it was impossible. With demonstrators seizing the microphone and the chair banging her gavel for order.

Correct   The council meeting was to have been conducted in an orderly and democratic fashion, but it was impossible with demonstrators seizing the microphone and the chair banging her gavel for order.

The prepositional phrase beginning with "with" modifies "impossible," and it should be attached to it. Or the phrase might be made into an independent clause and written as a separate sentence.

Correct   The council meeting was to have been conducted in an orderly and democratic fashion, but it was impossible. The demonstrators seized the microphone, and the chair banged her gavel for order.

3. Participial Phrase

Fragment   I was surprised at the commotion in the magazine's office. Reporters, copywriters, and secretaries were rushing all over the place. Running up and down the aisles, conferring with the editors, and talking in little groups.

Correct   I was surprised at the commotion in the magazine's office. Reporters, copywriters, and secretaries were rushing all over the place, running up and down the aisles, conferring with the editors, and talking in little groups.

"Running," "conferring," and "talking" are participles parallel in structure with "rushing"; that is, they are part of the first sentence and should be attached to it.

Fragment   She had good reason for coming to college and choosing the one she did, unlike some of her classmates. Having planned for several years to become a doctor.

Correct   Unlike some of her classmates, she had good reason for coming to college and choosing the one she did, having planned for several years to become a doctor.

The participial phrase modifies "she," and it is best placed close to it. To avoid confusion, the phrase "unlike some of her classmates" should begin the sentence.

4. Infinitive Phrase

Fragment   After a good deal of arguing, I finally received permission from my parents. To work for Project Head Start that summer and perhaps even during the fall semester.

Correct   After a good deal of arguing, I finally received permission from my parents to work for Project Head Start that summer and perhaps even during the fall semester.

"To work . . ." is an infinitive phrase modifying "permission" and should not be separated from the main clause.

5. Dependent Clause

Usually, the best way to correct a sentence fragment is to join it to the sentence of which it is logically a part.

Fragment   Often I stay up late in my room, studying, writing, or thinking about the future. While all the other people in the dorm are asleep.

Correct   Often I stay up late in my room, studying, writing, or thinking about the future while all the other people in the dorm are asleep.

Note that the fragment could have been corrected by omitting the conjunction "while" and making two complete sentences.

Fragment   After so many weeks of worrying, I was grateful to learn of the college's loan funds. Because I didn't know where I could turn for help or see how I could take a part-time job.

Correct   After so many weeks of worrying, I was grateful to learn of the college's loan funds because I didn't know where I could turn for help or see how I could take a part-time job.

Sometimes, however, it is better to change the fragment into a full sentence, by adding a verb, a subject, or whatever else is lacking.

Fragment   After completing the sonnet sequence, the reader is hardly optimistic about marriage. The wife returning to an impossible relationship, hiding from the neighbors, nursing her sick husband, sitting by his deathbed, and finally seeing no purpose to it all.

Correct   After completing the sonnet sequence, the reader is hardly optimistic about marriage. The wife returns to an impossible relationship, hides from the neighbors, nurses her sick husband, sits by his deathbed, and finally sees no purpose to it all.

13b

Permissible Incomplete Sentences

Certain elliptical expressions are equivalent to sentences because the missing words are clearly understood. Such permissible incomplete sentences include the following:

1. Questions and Answers in Conversation

Why not? Because it's late.

How much? Two dollars.

2. Exclamations and Requests

At last!

This way, please.

3. Transitions

So much for the first point.

Now to consider the next question.

In addition, fragments are sometimes deliberately used for particular effects, especially in narrative or descriptive writing. In most expository writing, however, there is seldom occasion or excuse for writing fragmentary sentences.

Exercise 1

For each of the following sentences, identify the cause of the fragment and correct it in whatever way seems most effective.

1. When you really get down to it, homework is more likely to be assigned in the academic subjects. Whether they are English, math, science, or some language.

2. One thing that I dislike very much is a person with a mean streak. A person who will go out of his way to do harm to others.

3. During the day the eel lies buried in the mud or concealed under rocks or in seaweed. But at night begins its prowling for food.

4. As this summary indicates, the first part of the story is deceiving. So far, just another tale about a college boy—maybe the all-American ideal— who gets his girl and job and is living on easy street.

5. For some people, life is only boring or painful. Especially if the person has no purpose, no goal in life.

6. The number of the very rich and the very poor having been reduced, leaving most Americans in one large middle class.

7. I now think that my high school was too progressive in some ways. Meaning that it didn't teach how to read and write correctly.

8. The head librarian threatened to close the stacks to all students. Because the cost of replacing stolen books was mounting each year.

9. Tyrone Guthrie's movie production of *Oedipus Rex* was very impressive. Although it took me a while to get used to the masked actors.

10. The City Council's decision to limit speed on a road in the campus but not on a street near an elementary school seemed ridiculous. Since small children are less able to cross streets responsibly.

11. Long hours of practice after classes, the weekends usually taken up with games, and most evenings spent in study. Athletes have little time for working their way through college.

12. Historians are interested only in the more civilized societies that have existed in the past. The ones that have produced great works of art, science, or technology.

13. Every month, the entire research staff spends a full day together in informal conference. To discuss at length current problems and propose and criticize new ideas.

14. A description of being lost in the Grand Canyon when Schuyler's life was saved by a discarded semirotten orange.

15. The distance between the stars is immense. So immense that it is difficult to find a unit of measurement that will help one grasp it imaginatively.

13c

Correcting Comma Splices

A comma splice—sometimes called a "comma fault"—is two or more independent clauses separated only by a comma.

> **Comma Splice** I wonder if he is thinking, he probably won't tell.

The comma splice, as in this sentence, can lead to misreading. Is he thinking that he won't tell? Or won't he tell whether or not he is thinking? The comma splice can fail to show clear sequence and relationship, as in

> **Comma Splice** There was an extremely heavy rain on Monday night, after the storm was over, the streams were overflowing.

You can catch many comma splices in revision by reading your paper aloud; if you drop your voice or pause conspicuously at a comma, check the sentence to see if it is two separate statements.

There are several alternatives for correcting comma splices.

1. Subordination of One Main Clause

Correct the comma splice by subordinating one of the main clauses. The commonest subordinating conjunctions include *because, which, since.*

Comma Splice	The banks were closed, John couldn't get the necessary money.
Correct	Since the banks were closed, John couldn't get the necessary money.
Comma Splice	There are many good reasons for working in the summer, only a few of them can be discussed.
Correct	There are many good reasons for working in the summer, only a few of which can be discussed.
Correct	Of the many good reasons for working in the summer, only a few can be discussed.

2. Coordination of Clauses by Conjunction

Correct the comma splice by using a coordinating conjunction to join the two main clauses if you want to give them equal emphasis.

Comma Splice	We will add another room to the house this summer, painting will have to wait until next year.
Correct ·	We will add another room to the house this summer, but painting will have to wait until next year.
Comma Splice	Reading is partly a matter of personal taste, every reviewer ought to keep this fact in mind.
Correct	Reading is partly a matter of personal taste, and every reviewer ought to keep this fact in mind.

The most usual pattern is the coordinating conjunction (*and, but, for, nor, or*) preceded by a comma. When long, complex clauses punctuated internally by commas are joined, a semicolon along with a coordinating conjunction may be needed to show the main division of the sentence.

Comma Splice	As the development of the atomic bomb, the computer systems, and guided missiles shows, technology, indeed basic scientific research itself, is often determined by

political and military considerations, many people do not recognize this interdependence and instead regard changes in technology as changes that simply "happen."

Correct   As the development of the atomic bomb, of computer systems, and of guided missiles shows, technology, indeed basic scientific research itself, is often determined by political and military considerations; *but* many people do not recognize this interdependence and instead regard changes in technology as changes that simply "happen."

3. Coordination of Clauses by Semicolon

Correct the comma splice by using a semicolon to join the two main clauses. This method is appropriate when the relationship between the two statements is to be implied rather than stated explicitly.

Comma Splice   Gambling is like a drug, after a while the gambler finds it impossible to stop.

Correct   Gambling is like a drug; after a while the gambler finds it impossible to stop.

4. Separation of Clauses into Sentences

Correct the comma splice by making each main clause into a sentence. Use this method if you want to emphasize the separation between the two statements.

Comma Splice   There was an extremely heavy rain on Monday night, after the storm had passed, the streams were overflowing.

Correct   There was an extremely heavy rain on Monday night. After the storm had passed, the streams were overflowing.

5. Commas with Short Independent Clauses

Commas without conjunctions may be used between short independent clauses for special effects or emphasis. Short, closely related independent clauses in a series are occasionally joined only by commas. Such punctuation is used often in narratives but more sparingly in expository writing.

Correct	The wind blew, the shutters banged, the children trembled.

6. Semicolon with Conjunctive Adverbs

Two main clauses linked by a conjunctive adverb require a semicolon or a period between them. One of the most common forms of the comma splice is the use of the comma between two main clauses linked by a conjunctive adverb. Such conjunctive adverbs as *also, besides, hence, however, instead, moreover, then,* and *therefore* should be preceded by a semicolon or period when they introduce a second independent clause.

Comma Splice	I hadn't read the test very carefully, therefore I was surprised that I had done so well on it.
Correct	I hadn't read the test very carefully; therefore, I was surprised that I had done so well on it.
Comma Splice	To a majority of the economists a gloomy forecast seemed inevitable, however three of the experts were unfashionably cheerful.
Correct	To a majority of the economists a gloomy forecast seemed inevitable; however, three of the experts were unfashionably cheerful.

One way to tell a conjunctive adverb from a pure conjunction is to try to change its position in the sentence. A conjunctive adverb need not stand first in its clause:

We had been told to stay at home; **moreover,** we knew that we were not allowed to play outside after dark.

We had been told to stay at home; we knew, **moreover,** that we were not allowed to play outside after dark.

A pure conjunction will fit into the sentence only at the beginning of its clause:

We had been told to stay at home, **and** we knew that we were not allowed to play outside after dark.

We knew we were not allowed to play outside after dark **because** we had been told to stay home.

13d

Fused Sentences

A fused sentence is one in which two main clauses are joined with no punctuation between them.

Fused   He took the job he was offered otherwise he would have had to borrow more money.

The fused sentence is a more blatant error than the comma splice because it often results in serious misreadings. To correct a fused sentence, use any of the means for correcting the comma splice.

Correct To avoid borrowing money, he took the job he was offered.

Correct He took the job he was offered; otherwise, he would have had to borrow more money.

Fused   Congress passed the bill only after long hours of debate there was strong feeling on both sides.

Correct Congress passed the bill only after long hours of debate. There was strong feeling on both sides.

Correct Because there was strong feeling on both sides, Congress passed the bill only after long hours of debate.

Exercise 2

In the following sentences, revise the comma splices or fused sentences by whatever means seems most effective. Be prepared to explain the reasons for the means you choose.

1. On most report cards there is a special place for marking effort this is put there so that the teacher can show how hard a student has tried.
2. I obeyed my elders, but I always weighed the facts and formed my own judgments, apparently this independence of mine made some adults angry.
3. But why shouldn't carols be played in shops and stores it's all in the spirit of Christmas.
4. But Huck doesn't pray, instead he thinks of all the times that Jim has been good to him.

5. Once in her room she did a few dance steps, looked at her unmade bed, and shrugged unconcernedly, then she glanced out the window in hopes of catching sight of her little brother.

6. But with the first of September the warm days were over, cold winds began to blow, stirring up freshly turned dirt in the graveyard and causing old Charles to cast apprehensive glances at the sky.

7. Ironically, the population migration has been especially great to places like Arizona, New Mexico, and southern California, these are places with a limited water supply.

8. In the first sonnet of the sequence she returns to her husband, this is because he is mortally ill.

9. We found the sea too choppy for sailing or swimming, we stayed on shore.

10. Permission was not granted for the interview, however the reporters never gave up hope.

11. The new dictionary was more than a revision of the old one, the compilers had redefined each entry and included many more examples of usage.

12. The critic wrote that as the commercials became longer and more offensive, the shows became shorter and more innocuous, also she felt advertisers ought to be forced to watch the commercials.

13. In speech class he announced he would give a demonstration-lecture on how not to pack a suitcase, after he was finished, the other students clapped reluctantly.

14. The counselor gathered the paddles, came down to the pier, and untied the canoe then he waited while the campers climbed in.

15. The medical insurance was cheap and comprehensive, according to its advertisers, the people who bought it soon claimed otherwise.

14

GRAMMATICAL USAGE

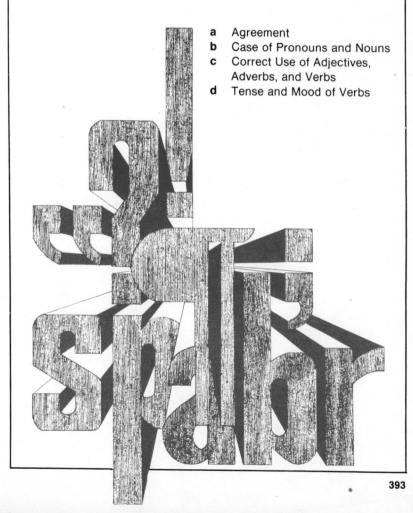

a Agreement
b Case of Pronouns and Nouns
c Correct Use of Adjectives, Adverbs, and Verbs
d Tense and Mood of Verbs

14a

Agreement

In standard English a verb agrees with its subject in person and number. That is, if the subject is first person (*I*), the verb is first person (*am*); if the subject is plural, (*they*), the verb is plural (*are*). The rule is simple enough in theory, but in practice we occasionally make agreement errors for a number of reasons.

In the first place, the third person singular of many verbs is formed by the addition of *s* (he/she/it walks), while *s* added to a noun forms the plural (nouns). We have to live with this inconsistency in the language, but we should be aware that it can be a source of confusion. Another difficulty is that some writers speak a dialect that does not observe the agreement convention. Furthermore, all of us from time to time violate the principle in conversation, either in haste or carelessness or in sheer forgetfulness of how we began the sentence. It is easy to understand why agreement is a troublesome rule for some writers. Perhaps the pronoun is so far away from its antecedent (the word it refers to) that the writer forgets what the antecedent is. Or a writer may be uncertain whether a compound subject such as "Either Angela or Carol," should be considered singular or plural. Such questions will be discussed in following sections.

Another problem, sociological rather than grammatical, arises from the lack in English of a singular pronoun that refers to either sex. For centuries it has been a convention to use the masculine third-person singular pronoun to refer to a noun of which the gender is either unknown or irrelevant.

A **child** should be taught to take care of **his** teeth.

This convention, however, has led to some bizarre constructions:

At her strongest and most characteristic, she [Edith Wharton] is a brilliant example of the writer who relieves an emotional strain by denouncing his generation.

—EDMUND WILSON

To avoid such a logical inconsistency, don't hesitate to use the feminine pronoun where its antecedent is clearly female, as in the example above. You can avoid the problem entirely by casting general statements about human beings in the plural: "*Children* should be taught to take care of *their* teeth."

Avoid the "everyone . . . his" construction when possible, in consideration of those women in your audience who might feel uncomfortable with a pronoun that sometimes refers to them, sometimes not. Some writers in published books use first "he," then "she" to refer to the sexually neutral *person, artist, student*; others frown on this practice as confusing and inconsistent. A number of new pronouns have been suggested to replace "his or her": *tes, shis, vis*. Experimenting with these forms will teach you, if nothing else, how difficult it is to break ourselves of old language patterns and introduce new words into our grammar.

1. Agreement of Subject and Verb

In English the subject and verb of a sentence must agree in person and number. If the subject is in the first-person singular ("I"), the verb must be in the first-person singular ("am"). If the subject is in the third-person singular ("she"), the verb must be in the third-person singular ("is"). Most verbs are not as highly inflected as the "to be" verb ("am," "is," "are"). In fact, the only inflection in most verbs is the third-person singular, which adds an "s": "he walks," "she runs," "it rains." It is with the third-person singular that most students have problems. Remembering, perhaps, that nouns add an "s" to the plural, some writers add an "s" to the third-person plural and write "they walks." And being unwilling to add an "s" to what they know to be a singular person, such writers drop the "s" from the third-person singular and write "he walk." If such a pattern is habitual and if the writer speaks a dialect that does not sound the "s" in the third-person singular, then memory, drill, and vigilance must be practiced to change the habit.

Uncertainty about which word is the subject of the sentence can result in an agreement error. Modifying phrases may seem to change the number of the subject, but if the subject is singular, so is the verb.

Incorrect   A program of two Bergman films were shown last night.

Correct   A program of two Bergman films was shown last night.

Because "films," which is the object of the preposition "of," is closer to the verb than is "program," it seems as if the verb should agree with the plural noun "films." But "program," although modified by the prepositional phrase, is singular, and it is the subject of the sentence. The verb, then, must agree with that singular subject.

Phrases such as "accompanied by," "as well as," and "together with" suggest a plural idea, but they do not change the number of the subject.

Incorrect   The prisoner, accompanied by guards and her lawyer, were in the courtroom.

Correct   The prisoner, accompanied by guards and her lawyer, was in the courtroom.

Incorrect   The property, as well as the guest house and the extra garage, are up for rent.

Correct   The property, as well as the guest house and the extra garage, is up for rent.

When two nouns are connected by some form of the verb *to be*, the first noun is the grammatical subject, and the verb agrees with it.

Correct   The first **thing** we noticed **was** the **tuna boats**.

Correct   The **tuna boats were** the first **thing** we noticed.

Simply remember to make the verb agree with the number of the first noun in the sentence.

Remember, too, that the verb always agrees with the subject even if the subject follows it.

Incorrect   Beyond the old mud fort was the endless sands of the desert.

Correct　Beyond the old mud fort were the endless sands of the desert.

What was beyond the fort? The "sands," and they are plural and demand the plural verb "were."

In sentences beginning with *there is* or *there are*, the subject always follows the verb and always agrees with it.

There **are** a million **laughs** in this bouncy little comedy.

There **is** only one correct **solution** to the problem.

There **is** a long **list** of jobs to be done before we leave.

There **are** many **jobs** to be done before we leave.

Confusion about the number of the subject, whether it is singular or plural, can also cause agreement problems. When compound subjects are joined by *and*, they are usually considered to be plural.

Mathematics and **science are** my best subjects.

The **evaluating, hiring,** and **training** of the applicant **are** left to the Personnel Department.

There are, however, some exceptions to this principle. If the two nouns of a compound subject refer to the same person, the verb should be singular.

This young bachelor and man-about-town **was** finally discovered to be an imposter.

Sometimes two compound nouns are needed to indicate one thing.

Bacon and eggs **is** the typical American breakfast.

In informal English, a singular verb is occasionally used when a compound subject follows the verb.

In the office there **are** a **desk**, a **chair**, and a filing **cabinet**.

In the office there **is** a desk, a chair, and a filing cabinet.

When *each* or *every* is used to modify the compound subject, a singular form of the verb is used.

Each soldier and sailor **was** given a complete examination.

Every camera and light meter **has** been reduced in price.

Two or more subjects joined by *or* or *nor* usually take a singular verb form.

Local information or a good road map **is** needed to get you to the camp.

Neither the producer nor the consumer **was** treated fairly.

When one subject is singular and one is plural, the verb agrees with the subject nearer it.

Neither my brother nor my sisters **have** ever been there.

In informal English, a plural verb is occasionally used when a *neither . . . nor . . .* construction expresses a plural idea.

Neither the union nor the company **seem** to like the plan.

COLLECTIVE NOUNS

Collective nouns, such as *class, committee, team, family, number,* are considered singular when they refer to the group as a unit. If you want to emphasize the individual members of the group, you may use the plural form of the verb.

The **committee was** unanimous in its recommendations.

The **class were** unable to agree on a day for the party.

Many writers would feel this sentence to be awkward, even though correct, and would rephrase it: "The members of the class were unable. . . ."

A large **number** of votes **is** required.

A large **number** of notes in her journal **are** inaccurate.

The **number** of correct answers **was** small.

INDEFINITE PRONOUNS

Indefinite pronouns, such as *each, every, either, neither, any, some,* and their compounds with *-one* or *-body,* are singular in number and should be followed by singular verb forms.

Each of the boys **was** tested.

Either of them **is** qualified for the job.

Neither of the speakers **was** willing to answer questions.

In speech and in informal writing, especially in questions, a plural verb is common.

None, some, more, most, and *all* may be either singular or plural, depending on the context and the intended meaning.

> **None** of the money **was** wasted.
>
> **None** of the dresses **are** paid for.
>
> **Most** of the pie **has been** eaten.
>
> **Most** of the students **have read** that play.

RELATIVE PRONOUNS

The relative pronouns *who, which,* and *that* take a singular verb form when the antecedent is singular, a plural verb form when the antecedent is plural.

> Betsy is the kind of **woman who prefers** to earn her living.
>
> *The antecedent of "who" is* woman.
>
> This is one of those **motors that were** imported from Japan.
>
> *The antecedent of "that" is "motors." The sentence is about one of a group of motors—those that were imported from Japan.*

NOUNS ENDING IN *s*

Some abstract nouns that are plural in form are grammatically singular—for example, *aesthetics, economics, linguistics, mathematics, news, physics, semantics.*

> Physics **was** the hardest course I had in high school.

Note that certain nouns ending in *s* have no singular form and are always plural: *trousers, scissors, measles, forceps.* Some nouns ending in *ics (athletics, politics, statistics)* may be either singular or plural, often with a distinction in meaning.

> Athletics [the collective activity] **builds** the physique.
>
> Athletics [particular sports and teams] **are** his favorite pastime.
>
> Statistics **is** my most difficult course.
>
> Statistics **show** that . . . .

LATIN PLURALS

Words like *data* and *strata* are Latin plurals, but there is a strong tendency in current English to treat them as collective nouns, which may be either singular or plural.

We must classify all the data that **have** been collected.

This data **was** collected in a survey.

These **strata go** back to the Miocene period.

Exercise 1

Give reasons for using the singular or the plural verb form in the following sentences.

1. Every one of the nine men on the team (is, are) important.
2. The close relationship with professors and fellow students (makes, make) the small college the choice of many entering freshmen.
3. Doug sprawled in the chair and knocked over one of the lamps which (was, were) on display.
4. There (has, have) never been hard feelings between the families on this street.
5. The symptoms of lead poisoning (varies, vary) with each individual case.
6. Next in the waiting line (was, were) an elderly lady and her grandson.
7. He believes that athletics (improves, improve) school morale.
8. Up goes the starter's gun, and each of the runners (becomes, become) tense.
9. The doctor said that there is always a possibility that the infection will return but that so far there (has, have) been no signs of its recurrence.
10. The family (takes, take) its annual vacation during August.
11. Each of the hospital's patients (has, have) some kind of medical insurance.
12. Either the *Times* or the *Tribune* (is, are) a reliable source of news.
13. The catcher, as well as the pitcher and the coach, (was, were) arguing furiously with the umpire.
14. Her chief interest in life (was, were) politics.
15. Slater is one of those legislators who (has, have) always opposed spending.

Exercise 2

In the following sentences, determine the cause of the faulty agreement and supply the correct form of the verb.

1. In addition, there is the students who cheat because they have never been taught differently.
2. The author's portrayal of the guests and the games add up to an extremely vivid picture of that particular society, with its petty concerns and rituals.
3. Another of the unpopular activities that take place during freshman week are the roll calls.
4. The theme of suffering, its causes and its consequences, are treated by Shakespeare, Tolstoy, and Conrad.
5. The first thing that catches your eye are the headlines.
6. The fact that the children are so beautiful and so intelligent add to their goodness and make the ghosts appear even more evil.
7. Everyone else in the story have readjusted to their roles, and Pam is the only one who is injured by the experience.
8. However, their way of expressing themselves are totally different.
9. These products of automation may have made life more pleasant but has reduced the population from hardworking pioneers to button-pushing time-servers.
10. She is one of the women who has made this country what it is.

2. Agreement of Pronoun and Antecedent

Pronouns should agree in number with the words they refer to—their antecedents.

> Many **people** pay a genealogist to look up **their** ancestry.

"People," the antecedent, is plural, so the correct pronoun is "their."

> My **uncle** paid a genealogist to look up **his** ancestry.

"His" agrees with "uncle."

Such indefinite antecedents as *each, either, neither, everyone, everybody, someone, somebody, anyone, anybody* are followed in Edited English by a singular pronoun.

> **Everyone** at times finds **himself** facing failure.

> **Anybody** can eat **his** meals at the Club.

The terms *everyone* and *anybody*, however, include my sister, and she never finds "himself facing failure" nor eating "his meals at the Club." Many women object to this illogical construction, but to fill it out—"eats his or her meals"—is awkward and wordy. Such a sentence, however, can often be improved by rewriting.

Everyone at times faces failure.

Anybody can eat meals at the Club.

Compound antecedents are usually considered plural when joined by *and*, singular when joined by *or* or *nor*.

My father encouraged **Henry** and **me** not to postpone **our** trip.

Neither the senator nor his press secretary would admit that **he** was responsible.

If a singular pronoun, even though correct, produces an awkward or clumsy sentence, the plural pronoun is often acceptable in informal writing.

Almost everybody eats some fruit as a part of **their** basic diet.

When the antecedent is a collective noun, the singular pronoun is used to emphasize the cohesiveness of the group, the plural to emphasize the separate individuals.

The **audience** showed **its** approval by applause.

The **audience** were cheering, booing, whistling, and stamping **their** feet.

Note in the sentence above that the verb "were" also is in the plural form. Be consistent. If the verb form shows the antecedent to be singular, the pronoun should be singular. If the verb is plural, the pronoun should be plural.

Incorrect   The **jury is** about to return and give **their** verdict.

Correct   The **jury is** about to return and give **its** verdict.

Demonstrative pronouns (*this, these; that, those*) are sometimes used as adjectives and should then agree in number with the words they modify.

Incorrect   **These kind** of vegetables are grown in the Valley.

Correct   **This kind** of vegetable is grown in the Valley.

Correct   **These kinds** of vegetables are grown in the Valley.

Exercise 3

Give reasons for using the singular or plural form of the pronoun in the following sentences. Be prepared to say which pronoun forms would be acceptable in speech and informal writing but would be discouraged in college writing.

1. Maybe some day each person will have (his, their) own helicopter for commuting to the city.
2. Nobody needs servants because nobody has more housework than (he, they) can manage.
3. The school was preparing to put on (its, their) annual May Day Dance.
4. Any parent hopes to get the best education for (his, their) children.
5. The congregations were divided in (its, their) feelings about the new minister.
6. Neither Faulkner nor T. S. Eliot won the Nobel Prize in Literature until well after (he, they) had written (his, their) most important works.
7. Each man and woman must make (his, their) own decision.
8. The United States has to look out for the rights of (its, their) citizens.
9. Neither Macbeth nor the Emperor Jones cared how (he, they) got what (he, they) wanted.
10. I believe that a person should never ask someone else for advice on (his, their) problems.

Exercise 4

In the following sentences, determine the cause of the faulty agreement and supply the correct form of the pronoun.

1. Either the members or the secretary may submit their objections.
2. The family was quite frank in stating their opinions.
3. These kind of scrimmages can be very bruising.
4. Each camper was supposed to bring their own bedding.
5. Now that everything was perfect, he was going to make sure they stayed that way.
6. Dorm meetings are always a spectacle because someone always loses their temper.
7. The prisoner's attitude toward society is largely determined by the treatment they receive in prison.
8. Every new proposal was vetoed by the chairman because he thought they weren't practical.

14b

Case of Pronouns and Nouns

Case means the changes in the form of a noun or pronoun that show how it is used in a sentence: *student, student's, he, his, her, them,* and so on. English nouns used to have many case forms, but over the centuries the forms have been reduced to those that indicate possession. Most pronouns, however, have three case forms: NOMINATIVE (or subjective) when the pronoun is the subject of a verb, the POSSESSIVE (or genitive) case to show possession, and the OBJECTIVE case when the pronoun functions as a complement—the object of a verb or preposition.

Nominative	I	we	he	she	it	they	who
Possessive	my	our	his	her	its	their	whose
Objective	me	us	him	her	it	them	whom

As with agreement, people usually get case right without consciously thinking about it. But a few constructions can cause writers trouble.

1. Compound Constructions

A noun and a pronoun used in a compound construction should be in the same case; the same principle applies to constructions like *we boys* and to appositives.

My father and I often hunt together.·

"I" is a subject of the verb "hunt."

The professor invited my father and me to his house.

Because a construction such as "my father and I" is so familiar, it is easy to slip into using it even when, as here, the objective case is needed. He invited my father and he invited "me," not "I."

Between you and me, Porter doesn't have a chance to win.

The compound construction "you and me" is the object of the preposition "between."

Our parents always rewarded us children for getting good grades.

We children always tried to please our parents by getting good grades.

*In the first sentence, "us children" is the object of the verb "rewarded."
In the second, "we children" is the subject of "tried."*

Most of the float was designed by two members of the class, Howard
and **me**.

*Since "two members" is the object of the preposition "by," the apposi-
tive should also be in the objective case. However, in speech, "Howard
and I" would be fairly common, though incorrect.*

2. *Who* in Dependent Clauses

When in doubt about the case of the relative pronoun *who*, try a
personal pronoun in its place. If *he* or *they* sounds right, use *who*; if
him or *them* fits the grammatical context, use *whom*.

Here is a woman **who** can explain eclipses.

*Ask of the relative clause following "woman," "who can explain
eclipses?" Obviously, "she" can. We would not say, "her can explain
eclipses."*

Manabe is the man **whom** I told you about.

*In this sentence the pronoun is not the subject of the clause but the
object of the preposition "about" and, therefore, is in the objective
case. The clause means: "I told you about him."*

Note that a parenthetical expression such as *I think* or *he says* does
not change the case of the pronoun.

The man **who** I thought would accept the nomination changed his
mind.

*The sense of the clause is "I thought that 'he' would accept the nomi-
nation," so the relative pronoun should be the nominative "who."*

Here are extra bluebooks for **whoever** needs them.

*The relative pronoun is the subject of "needs": they need them.
"Whomever" would be correct in a sentence like "Give the tickets to
whomever you choose," where the sense of the sentence is "You choose
to give the tickets to them." Most speakers and many writers would find
that the construction sounds too much like a fussy grammarian talking
and would change the phrasing: "Give the tickets to anyone you
choose."*

In formal writing the interrogative pronouns *who* and *whom* are used exactly like the relative pronouns.

> **Who** is coming to the party? (**They** are.)
>
> **Whom** are you expecting at the party? (I am expecting **them**.)

In speech and in much informal writing, there is a tendency to use **who** as the interrogative form whenever it begins a sentence, no matter what its construction in the sentence.

> **Who** are you expecting for dessert?
>
> **Who** are you driving with?

In Edited English it is safer to be formal.

> **Whom** are you expecting for the party?
>
> With **whom** are you driving?

3. Complement of *to be*

In formal writing, the complement of the linking verb *to be* is in the nominative case.

> The members of the delegation are **you**, your **sister**, and **I**.
>
> We hoped the speaker would be President Markson, but it was not **he**.
>
> A voice on the telephone asked for President Poynter, and I said, "This is **she**."

In speech and informal writing, the form "It is me" and analogous forms like "I thought it was her" and "It wasn't us" are commonly used. In college writing, such forms usually occur in dialogue, where informality is appropriate.

When the infinitive form of *to be* is used, its complement is always in the objective case.

> I wouldn't want to be **him**.

4. Pronoun after *than, as,* or *but*

After *than* or *as*, the case of a pronoun is determined by its use in the shortened clause of which it is a part.

My cousin is taller than **I** [am].

They take more photographs than **we** [do].

I can type as well as **he** [can].

He chooses you more often than [he chooses] **me**.

I thought her [to be] as guilty as [I thought] **him** [to be guilty].

But is sometimes used as a preposition meaning *except*. In such constructions, the object of *but* should be in the objective case.

By morning everyone had left but **them**.

At Judy's party all the children had a good time but Judy and **me**.

5. Possessives with Gerund

A noun or pronoun modifying a gerund should be in the possessive case.

Julie's acting amazed those of us in the audience.

Alan's father and mother approved of **his** climbing the mountain.

The subject of a gerund, however, should be in the objective case.

We could hear **John** snoring.

We saw **them** washing the dishes.

Exercise 5

In each sentence, choose the proper case form and be prepared to explain your choice.

1. My sister is a better skier than (I, me).
2. If Harvey hadn't finished college, my parents would never have permitted Betty and (he, him) to get married.
3. There was no comment from the two members (who, whom) I thought were sure to protest.
4. All the students (who, whom) I talked to seemed to like the new coach.
5. My father used to nag us—my sister and (I, me)—about using his pipe cleaners to make bracelets.
6. All the family went to the funeral but (I, me).
7. The new dictator won't be sure of (who, whom) he can trust.

8. His father objects to (him, his) watching sports every spare minute he can.
9. The reward was divided between my older brother and (I, me).
10. The Holes have not lived here as long as (we, us).
11. That year we finally had a teacher (who, whom) won the respect of all of (we, us) students (who, whom) she had in class.
12. Only two members of the family are double-jointed in the thumb, my mother and (I, me).
13. Another good reason for (him, his) joining the Coast Guard is the chance for special training.
14. The ten remaining tickets will be given to (whoever, whomever) applies first.
15. I would hate to be (he, him).

14c

Correct Use of Adjectives, Adverbs, and Verbs

Most adverbs are formed by adding -ly to the adjective: *clear, clearly; immediate, immediately.* But note that some adjectives also end in -ly: a *friendly* gesture, a *manly* appearance, *monthly* payments. A few adverbs have the same form as the adjective: the *far* corner, *much* pleased, I *little* thought, do it *right*, run *fast*, go *slow.* The dictionary will tell you whether a word functions as an adjective or an adverb, or both.

The car stopped **suddenly.**

The adverb modifies the verb "stopped."

The car came to a **sudden** stop.

The adjective modifies the noun "stop."

1. Adjectives with Linking Verbs

Verbs such as *be, become, seem, appear,* as well as verbs indicating the use of the five senses (*look, feel, taste, sound, smell*), are often used to link an adjective to the subject of a sentence. Do not use the adverbial form as the complement of a linking verb.

The swimmer $\begin{cases} \text{looked} \\ \text{seemed} \\ \text{felt} \\ \text{sounded} \\ \text{became} \\ \text{was} \end{cases}$ **cold.**

I felt **terrible** about my mistake.

I knew I had played **terribly.**

The melon tasted **sweet,** and my aunt smiled **happily.**

Although the surgeon looked **tired,** he felt my ankle **carefully.**

I smelled the fish **cautiously,** but it smelled **fresh.**

Watching him, Betty felt **uneasy.** *(tells something about Betty)*

Betty watched him **uneasily.** *(tells how she watched him)*

I felt **bad** about her illness. *(adjective complement of "felt")*

I felt **badly** bruised. *(adverb modifying "bruised")*

In speech, the following adjectives are often used to modify a verb or an adjective. Such expressions are considered colloquial.

He looks **real** good in blue.

I slept **good** last night.

I feel **some** better today.

We were **sure** glad to see them again.

In edited writing, however, the corresponding adverbs are expected.

He looks **really** good in blue.

I slept **well** last night.

I feel **somewhat** better today.

We were **surely** (or **certainly**) glad to see them again.

2. Comparatives and Superlatives

Formal writing distinguishes between the comparative and superlative in making comparisons. The comparative is used in speaking of two persons: "He was the *taller* of the two." The superlative is used when three or more are being compared: "She was the *tallest* person on the team." In speech and informal writing this distinction is not always observed, and the superlative is often used in comparing two persons or things.

> Of the two styles offered, the first was the **most** popular.

Formal writing, however, requires that the distinction be made.

> She was the **more** influential of the two vice-presidents and the **most** powerful of all the stockholders.

According to logic, adjectives like *perfect* or *unique* should not have comparative or superlative forms; a thing is either perfect or not perfect, and since *unique* means *the only one of its kind*, no object can be more unique than another. Consequently, formal writing tends to avoid expressions like *most perfect* or *more unique*, even though it regularly uses modifiers indicating an approach to the absolute, such as *nearly perfect* playing or an *almost unique* diamond. Informal writing often uses the superlative form, *most perfect*, but *rather unique* and *the most unique* were considered unacceptable by 94 percent of the Usage Panel of *The American Heritage Dictionary.*

Formal	Holmes is the **most nearly perfect** actor we have seen this season.
Informal	Holmes is the **most perfect** actor we have . . . .
Acceptable	We, the people of the United States, in order to form a **more perfect** union . . . .

Exercise 6

Correct the use of adjectives and adverbs as may be necessary to bring the following sentences up to the level of standard written English.

1. If you listen close, you should be able to hear it quite distinct.
2. The colors in the living room contrasted harshly and looked shockingly.
3. People today live more secure because of new drugs and antibiotics.
4. I am sure I didn't do too good on the objective part of the final.
5. The sky was clear and the air smelled freshly.
6. In the laboratory we were shown a seemingly impossibility.
7. An exciting documentary affects me quite different from a dramatized story about the same thing.

8. We were real pleased that so many people were willing to help.
9. That disastrous Thursday started out quite normal.
10. The sunset was beautiful that evening, but the sky looked threateningly the next morning.
11. During the whole time that Jane Blaisdel was chairman, business went along very smooth.
12. The trick worked as perfect as we had hoped.
13. By looking real close at the ballot, I could see that somebody had changed it.
14. A small minority of students have given this university a real bad image.
15. At the end of the play, he finds that defeat tastes bitterly.

14d

Tense and Mood of Verbs

Tense means variations in the form of a verb to indicate time differences. There are six principal tenses in English.

Present

I **believe** this is the right thing to do.

Past

I **mowed** the lawn, and my sister **pruned** the bushes.

Future

I **will fly** to Denver next month.

Present Perfect

I **have tried** to encourage him, but he **has** never **dared** to dive.

Past Perfect

She **had finished** the assignment by the time I arrived.

Future Perfect

He **will have arrived** before we get to the station.

1. Sequence of Tenses

English observes the following tense patterns:

When I **press** this button, the motor **begins** to run.

The instant he **pressed** the button, the motor **began** to run.

If you **press** (or **will press**) the button, the motor **will start**.

Now that he **has pressed** the button, he **expects** the motor to start.

Since he **had pressed** the button, he **expected** the motor to start.

If these patterns are not followed, a sentence like the following can result:

When he died, his fellow citizens realized how much he contributed to the community, and since then they collected funds for a memorial.

The tense relationships are more complicated than the sentence indicates. Here is the proper sequence of tenses:

When he **died** [a particular time in the past], his fellow citizens **realized** [from that time on] how much he **had contributed** [up to the time of his death] to the community, and since then they **have been collecting** [from that time to the present] funds for a memorial.

An infinitive should be in the present tense unless it represents an action earlier than that of the main verb.

July 14, 1789, must have been a great day **to be alive** [not **to have been alive**].

I realized later that it was a mistake **to have chosen** [not **to choose**] the life of an artist two years earlier.

Statements that are permanently true should be put in the present tense (sometimes called the "timeless present") even though the main verb is in the past.

Copernicus **found** that the Sun **is** the center of our planetary system. [Not **was**; it still **is**.]

I **insisted** that the Amazon River **is** longer than the Nile.

The present tense is often used in book reviews and criticism for describing a novel, play, or movie. But statements about the facts of a dead author's life are normally in the past tense.

Oliver La Farge's novel **is** the story of a young Navajo whose wife **seeks** revenge for her mistreatment by a white man.

The setting of Hawthorne's short stories is the New England village that Hawthorne **knew** so well. [The setting of the stories is still the same; Hawthorne knew them in the past.]

2. Principal Parts of Irregular Verbs

Irregular verbs are a small group which, instead of forming their past tenses by adding -ed *(start, started)*, take varied ways to indicate the past tense and the past participle *(begin, began, begun)*. The principal parts are (1) the present infinitive *(begin)*, (2) the past tense *(began)*, and (3) the past participle *(begun)*. All tense forms can be derived from the three principal parts. The first principal part is the basis for all present and future tenses, including the present participle; the second principal part is used for the simple past tense—"I began the job yesterday." The third principal part is used in all the compound tenses: "I have begun," "he had begun," "the job was begun."

In the speech of children, errors in the use of principal parts of the irregular verbs are common: "I throwed the ball," "We brung it home," "He has went home." The following list gives the principal parts of some irregular verbs that are apt to be confused.

infinitive	past tense	past participle
arise	arose	arisen
be	was, were	been
begin	began	begun
bid (offer)	bid	bid
bid (command)	bade	bidden
bite	bit	bitten
blow	blew	blown
break	broke	broken
bring	brought	brought
burst	burst	burst
buy	bought	bought
choose	chose	chosen
come	came	come
deal	dealt	dealt
dive	dived, dove	dived
do	did	done
drag	dragged	dragged

draw	drew	drawn
drink	drank	drunk
drive	drove	driven
eat	ate	eaten
fall	fell	fallen
fly	flew	flown
forget	forgot	forgotten, forgot
freeze	froze	frozen
get	got	got, gotten
give	gave	given
go	went	gone
grow	grew	grown
know	knew	known
lay (put)	laid	laid
lead	led	led
lie (recline)	lay	lain
ride	rode	ridden
ring	rang	rung
rise	rose	risen
run	ran	run
see	saw	seen
shrink	shrank, shrunk	shrunk
sing	sang	sung
speak	spoke	spoken
spring	sprang, sprung	sprung
steal	stole	stolen
swim	swam	swum
swing	swung	swung
take	took	taken
teach	taught	taught
tear	tore	torn
throw	threw	thrown
wear	wore	worn
write	wrote	written

3. *Shall* and *Will*

To express the simple future (the tense that indicates an event yet
to occur), Formal English demands *shall* in the first person and *will*
in the second and third persons. To express determination, promise,
or prophecy, *will* is used in the first person and *shall* is used in the
second and third person.

Simple Future

If you don't mind, I **shall join** you and we **shall go** together.

If you don't hurry, you **will be** late.

When he arrives, he **will** probably **be** tired.

Determination, Promise, Prophecy

Despite the inconvenience, we **will pay** the bill.

He **shall do** as I tell him.

You **shall** not **escape** the consequences of your crime.

In most speech and writing these distinctions are ignored. To express the simple future, *will* is used for all three persons. *Shall* is rarely used at all in informal speech and writing, except in questions, as a polite substitute for *let's*, or to find out what the person addressed wants.

Shall we go now? (Meaning "Let's go.")

Shall I leave the window open? (Meaning "What would you like?")

4. Subjunctive Mood

Subjunctive forms of the verb are used much less than formerly. In speech, the subjunctive is retained only in formulas like "If I were you . . . ." Informal writing, however, often uses the subjunctive, and formal writing demands it on a few occasions:

Condition Contrary to Fact

I wish I **were** younger.

If this **were** Saturday, we would be at the lake.

Although the dog has just had his supper, he acts as if he **were** still hungry.

Indirect Imperative

The terms of the will require that the funds **be spent** on education.

Her lawyer insists that she **open** a savings account.

Motions and Resolutions

I move that the minutes **be approved.**

Resolved, that this question **be submitted** to arbitration.

Exercise 7

Correct any errors in the use of verbs in the following sentences.

1. She wore a faded blue dress, and her dusty gray shoes were once white.
2. The astronomer said that the moon was approximately 239,000 miles from the earth.
3. For a reader who had never run across advertising of this kind, a further explanation may be necessary.
4. Zephyr, our cat, would lay on the floor for hours and played with a ball of string.
5. He would have liked to have told her what he thought of her.
6. If I had chose physics as my major, I wouldn't have to write all these papers.
7. It was a serious mistake to have been so candid.
8. The book had laid right where I had put it.
9. The water level began to raise, and by noon it had rose 10 feet.
10. She recognized the boy who had spoke to her in her calculus class.

Exercise 8

For each of the following sentences choose the proper verb form and be prepared to justify your choice.

1. I wouldn't tolerate such noise if I *(were, was)* you.
2. He moved that the motion *(is, be)* approved.
3. His mother insists that he *(come, comes)* in right now.
4. If Alaska *(was, were)* a warmer state, its population would be larger.
5. He acts as if he *(was, were)* drunk, and he probably is.
6. *(Shall, Will)* the play begin promptly at eight?
7. I am determined that he *(shall, will)* not escape punishment.
8. That bell sounds as though it *(was, were)* cracked.

Exercise 9

Correct all grammatical errors in the following sentences.

1. Most ski accidents are the results of someone being careless or thinking they are more skillful than they really are.
2. Still, along with increased speed comes many new problems in jet design.
3. Their bird was setting right on the perch, right where they left him three hours earlier.
4. The adolescent feels that if they do not conform, they will be unpopular.

5. Intercollegiate sports, even though the whole student body does not participate in it, provides amusement for most of the students.
6. Certain basic traits in humans, such as love of power, is a real obstacle to a peaceful world.
7. I know several people in my class whom I'm convinced scarcely opened a book in four years.
8. Criminals receive very fair trials in our country in that he is considered innocent until proved guilty.
9. Her favorite reading matter are novels, preferably science fiction.
10. According to the report, the company will give a bonus to whomever discovers the source of leakage.
11. Extra work was assigned to we students who came in late.
12. Every time any of us open a newspaper, we read of new trouble abroad.
13. The foreman of the lumber gang told Stan and I to report early the next morning.
14. Anyone with a little practice can learn to drive, can't they?
15. Within the broad limits of the assignment there are a great variety of topics for students to choose from.
16. He says he always feels bad after he had worked hard.

15

PUNCTUATION

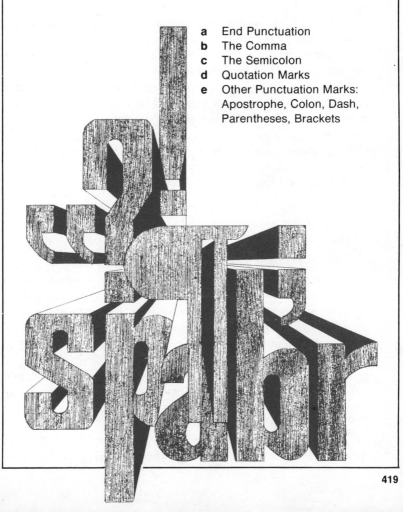

Punctuation is to writing what notation is to music: it allows the eye to re-create from the page the sounds the author of the composition had in mind. Both are necessary and exacting systems. Just as musicians know the crucial difference between a quarter-note and a half-note, so writers know the crucial difference between a comma and a semicolon, between brackets and parentheses. The brief and moderate and extended pauses noted by punctuation give cadence and rhythm to prose, but, more important, they signal meaning. Only a person who understands punctuation knows how the drop in the voice signaled by the commas makes one of these sentences mean something quite different from the other.

> The students who have worked diligently and completed all the assignments on time will not have to take the final.

> The students, who have worked diligently and completed all the assignments on time, will not have to take the final.

Contrary to popular mythology, there is nothing mysterious or arbitrary about punctuation. There are choices and options and the freedom, within certain unexceptional rules, to write with frequent or infrequent marks, in a liberally or conservatively punctuated fashion, depending upon the writer's taste and style. Good writers use these wide margins to punctuate with originality and flair, to give their voices further distinction on the page. Only an indifferent writer will sprinkle commas and dashes randomly during a last-minute reading, much as our ancestors sprinkled sand over the paper to dry the ink.

The rules in the following sections specify where punctuation marks are needed and, occasionally, where they are acceptable. Beyond this, you must use your judgment. If you are in doubt and no positive rule covers the point, the habit of less rather than more applies: omit the punctuation mark.

15a
End Punctuation

1. The Period

Use a period to mark the end of a declarative or imperative sentence.

> This is an example of a declarative sentence.
>
> Use a period at the end of a sentence like this.

A period is also used after abbreviations, like *Dr.*, *Mr.*, *Ph.D.*, *etc.*, A.D., *Calif.*, *Inc.* For the proper use of abbreviations, see Chapter 17.

Three spaced periods (. . .), called ellipsis marks, are used to indicate the omission of a word or words from a quoted passage. If the omitted words come at the end of a sentence, a fourth period is needed.

> We hold these truths to be self-evident: that all men . . . are endowed by their Creator with certain unalienable rights. . . .

Similarly, three (or four) periods are sometimes used in dialogue and interrupted narrative to indicate hesitation and pauses. Beginning writers should use these with caution.

> He inspired uneasiness. That was it! Uneasiness. Not a definite mistrust—just uneasiness—nothing more. You can have no idea how effective such a . . . a . . . faculty can be.
>
> —JOSEPH CONRAD

2. The Question Mark

Use a question mark after a direct question.

> Where did you find such information?

How much of the White Sands is gypsum?

Looking at me, the officer said, "Where do you live?"

An indirect question should be followed by a period, not a question mark.

He asked what had caused the delay.

I wonder how many Americans walk to work these days.

A request that is phrased as a question for politeness' sake is followed by a period.

Will you please send me your latest catalog.

3. The Exclamation Mark

Exclamation marks are appropriate only after statements that would be given unusual emphasis if spoken.

Four hours of taking lecture notes without a break! Will my fingers ever unbend?

Seldom is it suitable to expository writing. Nor is it advisable to use the exclamation mark to underscore flat statements or ironic remarks.

Ineffective The professor suggested that we take out our notebooks since he was going to give us a little (!) test.

15b

The Comma

The comma is perhaps the most used and, consequently, the most abused punctuation mark. It separates coordinate elements within a sentence and sets off certain subordinate constructions from the rest of the sentence. Since it represents the shortest breath pause and the least emphatic break, it cannot separate two complete sentences.

A primary function of the comma is to make a sentence clear. Always use commas to prevent misreading: to separate words that might be erroneously grouped together by the reader.

1. To Separate Independent Clauses

Two independent clauses joined by a coordinating conjunction (*and, or, nor, but, for*) should be separated by a comma. Note that the comma is always placed before the conjunction.

> I failed German in my senior year of high school, **and** it took me a long time to regain any interest in foreign languages.
>
> She went through the motions of studying, **but** her mind was elsewhere.

Very short independent clauses need not be separated by a comma if they are closely connected in meaning.

> The bell rang and everyone left.

Coordinating conjunctions are often used to join the parts of a compound predicate: that is, two or more verbs with the same subject. In such a sentence a comma is not required to separate the predicates. However, if the two parts are long or imply a strong contrast, a comma may be used to separate them.

> We **measured** the potassium and **weighed** it on the scale.
>
> Mr. Fossum **demonstrated** the differences between preserving wood with oil and with shellac, **and advised** the use of oil for durable tabletops.
>
> To our dismay, the suede could not be **washed** at home or **dry cleaned** at an ordinary place, **but had to be sent** to a specialist.

When the clauses of a compound sentence are long and are also subdivided by commas, a stronger mark of punctuation than a comma may be needed to separate the clauses from each other. For this purpose a semicolon is regularly used.

> For purposes of discussion, we shall recognize two main varieties of English, Standard and Nonstandard; and we shall divide the first type into Formal, Informal, and Colloquial English.

2. To Separate Elements in a Series

Separate words, phrases, or clauses in a series by commas. The typical form of a series is *a, b,* and *c.* A series may contain more than three parallel elements, and any of the coordinating conjunctions may be used to connect the last two. If *all* the elements of a series are joined by coordinating conjunctions (*a and b and c*), no commas are necessary to separate them.

Series of Adjectives

The shy devilfish blushes in **blue, red, green, or brown.**

Series of Phrases

Water flooded over the riverbed, over the culverts, and over the asphalt road.

Series of Predicates

The bear jumped away from the garbage can, snarled at the camper, and raced up the tree.

Series of Nouns

Resistors, transistors, capacitors, and connectors are small electronic parts.

Series of Independent Clauses

Stone was hauled twelve miles, a casing was built as the hole deepened, and a well 109 feet deep was completed in Greensburg, Kansas.

The comma before the last item in a series is omitted by some writers, but its use is generally preferred because it can prevent misreading.

Misleading   The three congressional priorities are nuclear disarmament, the curtailment of agricultural trade and aid to underdeveloped countries.

Without the comma before "and," "agricultural trade" and "aid to underdeveloped countries" can be read as compound objects of "curtailment of," and the reader reaches the end of the sentence still waiting for the third priority. No such misreading occurs if the comma is included.

3. Uses with Coordinate Elements

Adjectives modifying the same noun should be separated by commas if they are coordinate in meaning. Coordinate adjectives are those that could be joined by *and* without distorting the meaning of a sentence.

Bus lines provide inexpensive, efficient transportation.

The adjectives are coordinate: transportation that is "inexpensive" and "efficient."

Sometimes, however, an adjective is so closely linked with the noun that it is thought of as part of the noun. Such an adjective is not coordinate with a preceding adjective.

The Paynes bought a spacious summer cabin.

This does not mean "a cabin that is spacious and summer." "Summer" indicates the kind of cabin; "spacious" describes the summer cabin.

Note that numbers are not coordinate with other adjectives and are not separated by commas.

They screened in two large, airy outdoor porches.

"Two" and "large" should not be separated by a comma. But since the two outdoor porches were "large" and "airy," a comma is used to separate these two coordinate adjectives.

Coordinate words or phrases that are sharply contrasted are separated by commas.

He is ignorant, not stupid.

Our aim is to encourage question and debate, not criticism and argument.

An idiomatic way of asking a question is to make a direct statement and add to it a coordinate elliptical question. Such a construction should be separated by a comma from the direct statement.

You will come with us, won't you?

He won't test us on last semester's units, will he?

Another idiomatic construction that requires a comma is the coordinate use of adjectives, as in *the more . . ., the more . . . .*

The faster the bird, the higher the metabolism.

The more a candidate meets voters, the more he may learn about their concerns.

Exercise 1

Insert the proper punctuation marks where they are required in the following sentences, and give a reason for your choice.

1. Seven legislators from the southern part of the state changed their votes and with their aid the bill was passed.
2. During many periods of history men's clothing has been no less extravagant in cut color and richness of fabric than women's and there have been times when men's clothes have been the gaudier.
3. By the end of the twenty-mile hike we were all fairly tired and some of · us were suffering from sore feet as well.
4. Three of the editors argued that the article was biased and malicious and voted to reject it in spite of the distinguished name of the author.
5. The teller at the bank looked dubiously at the check I offered her and even though I knew the check was good I could feel a guilty look freezing on my face as her doubts increased.
6. Painted surfaces should be washed with a detergent sanded lightly and covered with a thin coat of plastic varnish.
7. I painted the house a warm deep pearl gray.
8. Her latest novel was marred by pretentious writing the absence of solid characterization and a hackneyed plot.
9. I believe that a state lottery can be useful because it can provide revenue for education increase employment and relieve the tax burden.
10. I judge people of any race by what they say and how they act not by the color of their skin.

4. To Set Off Nonrestrictive Modifiers

A dependent clause, participial phrase, or appositive is nonrestrictive when it can be omitted without changing the main idea of the sentence. A nonrestrictive modifier gives additional information about the noun to which it refers. A restrictive modifier, on the other hand, restricts the meaning of the word to which it refers to one particular group or thing. If it is omitted, the main idea of the sentence is changed. One check is to read the sentence aloud: if the voice pauses and drops slightly before and after the modifier, the modifier is probably nonrestrictive; if the voice is sustained and unhesitant before and after the modifier, the modifier is probably restrictive and is *not* set off by commas.

NONRESTRICTIVE CLAUSES AND PHRASES

Note that *two commas* are required to set off a nonrestrictive modifier in the middle of a sentence; one comma is sufficient if the modifier is at the beginning or end of the sentence.

Nonrestrictive Clause

My faculty advisor, **who had to sign the program card,** was hard to find.

If the clause were omitted, some information would be lost, but the sentence would make the same point: that my advisor was hard to find.

Restrictive Clause

A faculty advisor **who is never in his office** makes registration difficult.

Omitting the clause here changes the sense completely. The purpose of the clause is to limit the statement to a certain kind of faculty advisor—those who are never in their offices.

nonrestrictive clause

I found the letter under the door, **where the postman had put it.**

restrictive clause

The letter was still **where the postman had put it.**

nonrestrictive clause

Uncle Jasper's letter, **lying unclaimed in the dead letter office,** contained the missing document.

restrictive phrase

We have had many complaints about letters **undelivered because of careless addressing.**

Notice how the meaning of a sentence may be altered by the addition or the omission of commas:

The board sent questionnaires to all members, who are on Social Security.

Nonrestrictive clause. The sentence implies that all members are on Social Security.

The board sent questionnaires to all members who are on Social Security.

Restrictive clause. The questionnaire is sent only to some members, those on Social Security.

NONRESTRICTIVE APPOSITIVES

Appositives are usually nonrestrictive and hence are set off by commas. If, however, an appositive puts a necessary limitation upon its noun, it is restrictive and no punctuation is necessary.

Appositive

...rking with cryogenics have produced temperatures within a ...of a degree of absolute zero, **approximately 459.7 below zero Fahrenheit.**

Restrictive Appositive

The noun cryogenics comes from a Greek word meaning "icy cold."

Note that an appositive used to define a word is often introduced by the conjunction *or.* Such appositives are always set off by commas to distinguish them from the common construction in which *or* joins two coordinate nouns.

The class found a fine specimen of pyrite, **or fool's gold.**

We couldn't decide whether to plant phlox or coral bells.

Note that an abbreviated title or degree (K.C.B., USMC, M.D., Ph.D.) is treated as an appositive when it follows a proper name.

He was introduced as Robert Harrison, **L.L.D.,** and he added that he also held a Ph.D. from Cornell.

Exercise 2

Insert commas in the following sentences to set off nonrestrictive clauses and participial phrases. In doubtful cases, explain the difference in meaning produced by the insertion of commas.

1. King Leopold of Belgium who was Queen Victoria's uncle also gave her a great deal of advice.
2. Many people who have never been to the United States think of it as a country of wealth and luxury where everyone lives on the fat of the land.
3. Some years ago I lived in a section of town where almost everyone was a Republican.
4. With the advent of the jet engine which is more efficient at high than at low altitudes aircraft could attain greater heights.
5. The astronauts who had been trained for any circumstance were calm when launching was called off at the last minute.
6. The student hoping to get a "C" without too much work should stay out of Economics 152.
7. We shall have to hire a caretaker if you can't find time to keep the place neat and orderly.

8. The packing plant where I worked all summer is on the Aleutian Islands.
9. She has made a special study of the native women who are monogamous.
10. The average American tired of last year's models and seeking something new is an easy prey for the designers who capitalize on herd psychology and the craving for novelty.

5. To Set Off Parenthetic Elements

Parenthetic is a general term describing explanatory words or phrases that are felt to be intrusive and subordinate. That is, they interrupt the normal sentence pattern to supply additional, supplementary information, and they are accordingly set off by commas or other punctuation marks. In the widest sense of the term, nonrestrictive modifiers are a kind of parenthetic element. Many other sentence elements may become parenthetic if they are removed from their regular place and inserted so that they interrupt the normal order of a sentence.

For example, adjectives normally are placed before the words they modify: *Two tired, hungry boys came into camp.* If the adjectives are inserted elsewhere in the sentence, they become parenthetic and should be set off: *Two boys, tired and hungry, came into camp.* Similarly, it is possible to rewrite a sentence like *I am certain that space science will bring some unexpected discoveries* so that one clause becomes parenthetic: *Space science, I am certain, will bring some unexpected discoveries.*

The minutes, I regret to say, need several additions.

The discovery that mammals can learn to breathe under water may, in the opinion of some experts, lead to a technique that will prevent drowning.

TRANSITIONAL WORDS

Transitional words and phrases, such as *however, moreover, indeed, consequently, of course, for example, on the other hand,* are usually set off by commas, especially when they serve to mark a contrast or the introduction of a new point. In short sentences where stress on l word is not needed or desired, the commas are

ng violinist needs patience. For example, six lines of music can have 214 bowing variations.

The best beef should be bright red and be marbled with pure white fat. However, a customer may be fooled by tinted lighting, which, in fact, cheats the buyer.

The court ruled, consequently, that no damages could be collected.

Notice that *however* is sometimes used as a regular adverb, to modify a particular word rather than as a sentence modifier, and that when so used it is not set off by a comma.

However much he diets, he does not lose enough weight.

Since "however" modifies "much," it is not set off.

DATES AND ADDRESSES

Multiple elements of dates, addresses, and references are set off by commas. If only one element (day of month, year, city) appears, no punctuation is needed.

April 4 is her birthday.

New York is her native state.

Act IV moves toward the climax.

But if other elements are added, they are set off by commas.

April 4, 1953, is the date of her birth.

The return address was 15 South Main Street, Oxford, Ohio.

The quotation is from *King Lear*, II, ii, 2.

DIRECT ADDRESS, INTERJECTIONS, *YES* AND *NO*

Nouns used as terms of direct address, interjections, and the words *yes* and *no* should be set off by commas.

Miss Kuhn, would you like to be a teaching assistant?

This preposterous charge, ladies and gentlemen, reveals my opponent's ignorance.

Oh, yes, we have a more expensive rental.

QUOTATION EXPRESSIONS

Quotation expressions such as *he said* are set off by commas when used with a direct quotation.

"When I was young," he said, "seeing a monoplane was exciting."

Do not use a comma to set off an indirect quotation.

The jeweler said that he could reset the sapphire.

They told us that they had sent a wire.

When the quotation contains two independent clauses and the quotation expression comes between them, a semicolon may be required to prevent a comma fault (see section 13c).

"Please try," he said; "you could win."

"Please try," he said. "You could win."

"I'd like you to try," he said; "I won't insist, though."

For other rules regarding the punctuation of direct quotations, see section 15d.

ABSOLUTE PHRASES

An absolute phrase should be set off by commas. An absolute phrase consists of a participle with a subject (and sometimes a complement) not part of the basic structure of the sentence but serving as a kind of sentence modifier. It usually tells when, why, or how something happened.

The gale having quieted, highway workers began to clear fallen trees and signs from the roads.

The marks on her transcript didn't annoy her, grades representing only part of her education.

Exercise 3

Insert commas where they are required to set off parenthetic elements or to follow conventional usage.

1. Money is not to be sure the only problem that people worry about.

2. Yes I have lived in Minnesota most of my life but I was born in Seattle Washington.
3. My uncle formerly one of the richest men in Woodstock promised to put me through college.
4. In the first place there is no evidence Mr. Jones that my client was driving a car on July 14 1965.
5. Teaching of course has certain disadvantages class size being what it is.
6. "From here" said Mr. Newman "you can see the car double-parked in the alley."
7. The study of Latin or of any other foreign language for that matter helps to clarify English grammar.
8. My cousins tired and wet returned from their fishing trip at sunset.
9. Stricter laws it is argued would be of no use without more machinery for their enforcement.
10. Portland Maine was not as I remember an unpleasant place for a boy to grow up in.

6. To Set Off Introductory Elements

A dependent clause coming first in the sentence is usually set off by a comma. If a dependent clause follows the main clause, however, a comma is used only when the dependent clause is nonrestrictive.

If you see him, tell him to write me soon.

Introductory adverbial clause, set off by a comma.

Tell him to write me as soon as he can.

Restrictive adverbial clause following main clause.

Take a trip abroad now, even if you have to borrow some money.

Nonrestrictive adverbial clause following main clause.

An introductory verbal phrase (participial, gerund, or infinitive) is usually followed by a comma. A prepositional phrase of considerable length at the beginning of a sentence may be followed by a comma.

participial phrase

Suffering from disease, overcrowding, and poverty, the people of Manchester were prime victims of the early Industrial Revolution in England.

gerund phrase

After seeing the poverty and unfair treatment of the working-class people, Mrs. Gaskell wrote several protest novels.

infinitive phrase

To understand Hemingway's uneasy friendship with F. Scott Fitzgerald, one must know something of Hemingway's attitude toward Fitzgerald's wife, Zelda.

long prepositional phrase

Soon after his first acquaintance with Fitzgerald, Hemingway took an intense dislike to Zelda.

7. To Prevent Misreading

Use a comma to separate any sentence elements that might be incorrectly joined in reading and thus misunderstood. *This rule supersedes all others.*

Incorrect   Ever since he has devoted himself to athletics.

Correct   Ever since, he has devoted himself to athletics.

Incorrect   Inside the house was brightly lighted.

Correct   Inside, the house was brightly lighted.

Incorrect   Soon after the minister entered the chapel.

Correct   Soon after, the minister entered the chapel.

Incorrect   To elaborate the art of flower arranging begins with simplicity.

Correct   To elaborate, the art of flower arranging begins with simplicity.

8. Misuse of the Comma

Modern practice is to use less, rather than more, punctuation in narrative and expository prose. A good working rule for the beginner is to use no commas except those required by the preceding conventions. Here are some examples of serious errors caused by excessive punctuation. In all the following sentences, the commas should be omitted.

Incorrect His ability to solve the most complicated problems on the spur of the moment, never failed to impress the class.

The comma erroneously separates subject and predicate.

Incorrect The men who lived in the old wing of the dormitory, unanimously voted to approve the new rules.

If the clause is restrictive, no commas should be used; if the clause is nonrestrictive, two commas are required.

Incorrect During chapel the minister announced, that the choir would sing Handel's *Messiah* for Easter.

The comma erroneously separates an indirect quotation from the rest of the sentence.

Incorrect Gigi is so tall, that she may break the record for rebounds.

The comma erroneously splits an idiomatic construction, "so tall that."

Do not put a comma before the first member or after the last member of a series, unless the comma is required by some other rule.

Incorrect For lunch I usually have, a sandwich, some fruit, and milk.

The comma after "have" separates the whole series from the rest of the sentence. It should be omitted.

Incorrect Rhode Island, New Jersey, and Massachusetts, were the most densely populated states in 1960.

The comma after "Massachusetts" erroneously separates the whole series from the rest of the sentence.

Correct Rhode Island, New Jersey, and Massachusetts, in that order, were the most densely populated states in 1960.

The comma after "Massachusetts" is required to set off the parenthetic phrase "in that order."

Exercise 4

Some of the following sentences omit necessary commas, while others contain unnecessary and misleading ones. Punctuate the sentences correctly and be prepared to justify each comma you use and the eliminations you make.

1. The person who used to speak precisely and clearly, may now mumble and run words together the way a favorite television star does.

2. Some parents feel there should be a limit to the amount of homework that students are assigned but I feel most teachers are quite reasonable about the amount given.
3. When people cheat, they cheat no one, but themselves.
4. This purity of spirit combined with the courage to stand up for what he believes, makes Huck the great character that he is.
5. Finally when Ike is fully initiated the chase begins.
6. A certain coffee commercial is amusing because it uses puppets, and is different from other advertisements.
7. The skeptical writer proposes questions hoping for answers.
8. I could readily understand for instance, that primitive human beings who were ignorant and easily terrified, might develop a caste of medicine men.
9. The band, bunting and fireworks were planned but these were not enough to assure the parade's success.
10. It is soon evident, in the story, *Lucky Jim*, by Kingsley Amis, that Margaret is unstable, and that Dixon feels insecure and inferior.
11. He is apparently disgusted with his job, and the rest of his environment.
12. Their faces, like the faces of the rest of the villagers are grotesque and primitive.

15c

The Semicolon

The semicolon indicates a greater break in the sentence than the comma does, but it does not have the finality of a period. Its most important use is to separate two independent clauses not joined by a conjunction. As a device for creating compound sentences from shorter sentences, the semicolon may easily be overworked. If a conjunction expresses the relationship between the two parts of a sentence, use the conjunction. The semicolon should be reserved for use when the relationship between two statements is so clear that it is unnecessary to state it explicitly.

1. To Separate Principal Clauses

When the independent clauses of a compound sentence are not joined by a conjunction, a semicolon is required.

I do not say that these stories are untrue; I only say that I do not believe them.

In India fourteen main languages are written; several hundred dialectical variations are spoken.

The conjunctive adverbs (*so, therefore, however, hence,. nevertheless, moreover, accordingly, besides, also, thus, still, otherwise,* and so on) are inadequate to join two independent clauses. A semicolon is required to separate two independent clauses not connected by a pure conjunction. Using a comma instead produces a comma splice (see section 13c).

Our plan was to sail from Naples to New York; however, an emergency at home forced us to fly instead.

From the high board, the water looked amazingly far away; besides, I was getting cold and tired of swimming.

The loan account book must be sent with each monthly payment; otherwise, there may be disputes as to the amount still owing.

If the clauses are short and closely parallel in form, commas are frequently used between them even if conjunctions are omitted.

The picture dimmed, the sound faded, the TV failed.

The curtains fluttered, the windows rattled, the doors slammed.

2. To Separate Clauses When Commas Are Inadequate

Even when two independent clauses are joined by a coordinating conjunction, a semicolon may be used to separate the clauses if the clauses are long or are subdivided by commas.

The Northwest Ordinance of 1787, drafted by Jefferson, is generally noted because it established government of territory north of Ohio and west of New York; yet one of its most important statutes was the allocation of land and support for public schools.

In recognition of her services, the principal was given a farewell dinner, a record, and a scroll; **and** a new elementary school was named after her.

Use a semicolon to separate elements in a series when the elements contain internal commas. That is, when a comma is not a strong enough mark of separation to indicate the elements of a series unmistakably, a semicolon is preferable.

Incorrect One day of orientation was led by Mr. Joseph, the chaplain, Mrs. Smith, a French teacher, and the Dean.

Correct One day of orientation was led by Mr. Joseph, the chaplain; Mrs. Smith, a French teacher; and the Dean.

The punctuation of the corrected sentence indicates clearly how many people led the orientation.

Correct Bibliography may include Randall Jarrell, *Poetry and the Age*; Northrup Frye, *Anatomy of Criticism*; and Edmund Wilson, *The Shock of Recognition.*

Be sure that semicolons separate coordinate elements. Using a semicolon to separate an independent clause and a subordinate clause is an error similar to writing a sentence fragment, and just as serious.

Incorrect Young people tend to reject parental authority; although they are searching for other adults as models.

Correct Young people tend to reject parental authority, although they are searching for other adults as models.

Exercise 5

Some of the following sentences contain semicolons that are unnecessary or incorrect, while other sentences lack needed semicolons. Correct the punctuation and be able to justify each semicolon you use or omit.

1. Joseph is reluctantly picked up by a passing stagecoach; and then only after one of the passengers notes that they could be held legally responsible if a naked stranger should die for lack of aid.
2. More understandable than any of her other criticisms are her remarks about the educational system, however, even these are not very specific.
3. Our technology has developed the telephone for the talebearer; the car for the speedster; and the elevator for children.
4. A novel dealing with the affectations of a past society may become dated, and one must consider this possibility when judging it, otherwise, the book will suffer undue criticism.
5. He was not admitted to the honor society; although he was a good athlete and a top student.
6. The second edition of the book, published in 1922, is relatively scarce and hard to find; but the third edition, published four years later, can be seen in almost any store selling old books.

7. Sometimes I get so interested in a book that I stay up until I finish it; regardless of whether I have classes the next morning or not.
8. Since air is dissolved by water at the surface only, the shape of an aquarium is important, too small an opening may cause an oxygen deficiency.
9. I might ask here; "What is the most important thing in life?"
10. The sculptor can work for more than a week on the same clay model; because clay can be kept soft and pliable for a long time.

Exercise 6

Explain the punctuation in the following sentences. To do so, you will need to distinguish among principal clauses, subordinate clauses, and phrases.

1. There are no set rules that actors must follow to become proficient in their art; however, there are certain principles regarding the use of mind, voice, and body that may help them.
2. The book covered the life of Lotta Crabtree from birth to death; it painted her as one of the most colorful figures of early California.
3. Her forehead was wrinkled, her mouth was firm and tense, but her eyes had a dreamy, reminiscent look.
4. The unconscious sailor would then be taken to an outbound ship to be sold to the captain at a price ranging from $100 to $300, depending on how pressed the captain was for men; and he would regain consciousness somewhere in the Pacific Ocean, without the slightest idea of where he was or where he was going.
5. Among the colorful figures in the book are Johnny Highpockets, a simple-minded settler; Charley Tufts, formerly a professor at Yale; and the author of the book himself.
6. A grove of cypress trees, wind-blown and shaggy with Spanish moss, still grows on the headland, as it did when Stevenson first explored the area.
7. Somervell, the only son of a hard-working country doctor and a mother who had been trained as a schoolteacher, was born in a quiet, secluded farming town in Arkansas on August 21, 1892.
8. In most respects the hotel is admirably located; it is near the corner of Fifth Avenue and 52nd Street, within walking distance of convention headquarters.
9. On the postcard was a reproduction of a watercolor by John Piper; it showed the interior of Ingelsham Church.
10. My interview, which lasted over an hour, was successful; I got the job.

15d

Quotation Marks

1. To Enclose Direct Quotation

Use quotation marks to enclose a direct quotation, but not an indirect quotation. A direct quotation gives the exact words of a speaker. An indirect quotation is the writer's paraphrase of what someone said.

Indirect Quotation   He said that he would call.

Direct Quotation   He said, "I will call."

The expression *he said* is never included within the quotation marks. If the actual quotation is interrupted by such an expression, both halves must be enclosed by quotation marks.

"I am interested," he said, "so let's talk it over."

"It all began accidentally," Jackson said. "My remark was misunderstood."

2. To Quote Several Sentences

If a quotation consists of several sentences, uninterrupted by a *he* or *she said* expression, use one set of marks to enclose the entire quotation. Do not enclose each separate sentence. If a quotation consists of several paragraphs, put quotation marks at the beginning of each paragraph and at the end of the last paragraph.

Barbara replied, "Right now? But I haven't finished my paper for economics. Call me in a couple of hours."

Poor Richard has a number of things to say about diet: "They that study much ought not to eat so much as those that work hard, their digestion being not so good.

"If thou art dull and heavy after meat, it's a sign thou hast exceeded the due measure; for meat and drink ought to refresh the body and make it chearful, and not to dull and oppress it.

"A sober diet makes a man die without pain; it maintains the senses in vigour; it mitigates the violence of the passions and affections."

3. Quotations Within Quotations

A quotation within a quotation is enclosed with single quotation marks. Be sure to conclude the original quotation with double marks.

> The lecture began, "As Proust said, 'Any mental activity is easy if it need not take reality into account.'"

In the rare instance when a third set of marks must be included within a quoted passage, they become double:

> In her edition of Flanneny O'Connor's letters, Sally Fitzgerald writes: "Anything but dour, she never ceased to be amused, even in extremis. In a letter after her return from the hospital and surgery, in 1964, she wrote: 'One of my nurses was a dead ringer for Mrs. Turpin. . . . Her favorite grammatical construction was "it were." . . . I reckon she increased my pain about 100%.'"

4. To Indicate Implied Speech

Quotation marks are frequently used for implied speech:

> He tried to cry, "She is there, she is there," but he couldn't utter the words, only the sounds.
>
> —JAN DE HARTOG

They are not customarily used for unspoken thoughts:

> It was a momentary liberation from the pent-up anxious state I usually endured to be able to think: At least I'm not them! At least I'm not those heavy, serious, righteous people upstairs.
>
> —ROBERT LOWRY

5. Misuse in Paraphrase

Use quotation marks around material directly quoted from another writer, but not around a paraphrase of an author's ideas.

> John Selden pinpoints our attitude toward virtues when he defines humility: "Humility is a virtue all preach, none practice, and yet everybody is content to hear. The master thinks it good doctrine for his servant, the laity for the clergy, and the clergy for the laity."

John Selden describes humility as a virtue we all praise, but few practice. We expect to observe it in those who deal with us, while overlooking our own chances to be humble.

If you quote only a few words from a well-known writer and work them into your own sentence, quotation marks may be omitted.

During childhood it was easy to see that others should share toys, but during adulthood it is not easy to do unto others as you would have them do unto you.

6. Longer Quotations

When a borrowed quotation runs to several lines of print, it should be set off by indenting and single-spacing. Quotation marks should not be used to set off such material, though they may be required within the quotation.

T. S. Eliot begins the essay "Tradition and the Individual Talent":

In English writing we seldom speak of tradition, though we occasionally apply its name in deploring its absence. We cannot refer to "the tradition" or to "a tradition"; at most, we employ the adjective in saying that the poetry of So-and-so is "traditional" or even "too traditional." Seldom, perhaps, does the word appear except in a phrase of censure. If otherwise, it is vaguely approbative, with the implication, as to the work approved, of some pleasing archaeological reconstruction.

7. Verse Quotations

A quotation of more than one line of poetry should be set off by indenting and single-spacing, without quotation marks. Be sure to keep the line lengths exactly as they are in the original.

Boileau has captured a quality inseparable from fine satire:

But satire, ever moral, ever new,
Delights the reader and instructs him too.
She, if good sense refine her sterling page,
Oft shakes some rooted folly of the age.

A quotation of one line of verse, or part of a line, should be enclosed in quotation marks and run in as part of your text.

> Lytton disliked the false heroics of Henley's "My head is bloody but unbowed."

If parts of two lines of verse are run in to the text, indicate the line break by a slash (/):

> Stark Young and Rex Stout both found book titles in Fitzgerald's "never grows so red / The rose as where some buried Caesar bled."

8. Punctuation with Quotation Marks

At the end of a quotation, a period or comma is placed inside the quotation mark; a semicolon or colon is placed outside the quotation mark.

> "Quick," said my cousin, "hand me the flashlight."
>
> The bride and groom said, "I do"; the audience wept.
>
> I have only one comment when you say, "All people are equal": I wish it were true.

A question mark or exclamation mark goes inside the quotation mark if it applies to the quotation only, and outside the quotation mark if it applies to the whole sentence.

> My mother asked, "Did you arrive on time?"
>
> Did the invitation say "R.S.V.P."?
>
> He called irritably, "Move over!"
>
> Above all, don't let anyone hear you say, "I give up"!

9. To Indicate Titles

Titles of books, poems, plays, musical compositions, and so on, may be enclosed in quotation marks, but the preferred practice is to italicize titles of books, journals, plays, and major poetic or musical works, and to use quotation marks for the titles of chapters, articles, short poems, and songs. Italics on the typewriter and in handwriting are represented by underlining. Titles of paintings and other objects of art are regularly enclosed in quotation marks.

The fourth section of Isak Dinesen's **Out of Africa** is entitled "From an Immigrant's Notebook."

Carl Orff's cantata **Carmina Burana** opens and closes with "Fortune, Empress of the World."

10. Misuse for Humorous Emphasis or with Slang

If occasionally you want to indicate that a word or phrase should be heavily stressed or deserves special attention, use italics, not quotation marks. Humor or irony should be indicated by the context. Using quotation marks to call attention to an ironic or humorous passage is like poking your listener in the ribs when you have reached the point of a joke. If you use slang at all, take full responsibility for it. Do not apologize for a phrase by putting it in quotation marks.

Exercise 7

Insert punctuation marks where they are needed in the following sentences.

1. The Dean replied that he knew very well that freshmen had trouble getting adjusted. But, he added, it doesn't usually take them eight months to find themselves.
2. I hope said Professor Painter that someone can identify a quotation for me. It's from the end of a sonnet, and all I can remember is like a lean knife between the ribs of Time.
3. President Turini, according to the *Alumni Magazine*, believed that the chief values of a liberal education were nonmaterial; but on another page she was quoted, in the course of a speech delivered in Seattle, as saying that a college education is essential for any person who does not plan to marry money.
4. I asked whether Professor Lawrence still began his first lecture by saying My name is Lawrence and I wish I were not here, as he always did when I was in college.
5. The program said that the musical *Hello, Dolly* is based on Thornton Wilder's play *The Matchmaker.*
6. Take a chair, said my tutor. He picked up my paper. Tell me honestly, he said. Is this the best you can do?
7. Madame Lenoir said, As my first number I will sing the song Der Leiermann, from Schubert's *Winterreise.*
8. When asked To what do you attribute your success? Henderson always answered Sleeping late in the morning.

15e

Other Punctuation Marks: Apostrophe, Colon, Dash, Parentheses, Brackets

1. The Apostrophe

The chief uses of the apostrophe are to indicate the possessive case of nouns and indefinite pronouns, to mark the omission of letters in a contracted word or date, and to indicate the plural of letters or numerals.

POSSESSIVE CASE

Nouns and indefinite pronouns that do not already end in *s* form the possessive by adding an apostrophe and an *s*.

a child's toy	children's toys
one's dignity	Cole Porter's songs

Plural nouns that end in *s* *(boys, girls)* form the possessive by adding an apostrophe only.

girls' hockey	the Ellises' orchard
boys' jackets	the Neilsons' garage

Singular nouns that end in *s* *(Thomas, kiss)* form the possessive by adding an apostrophe and an *s* if the *s* is to be pronounced as an extra syllable.

Thomas's poems   King James's reign   the kiss's effect

But if an extra syllable would be awkward to pronounce, the possessive is formed by adding the apostrophe only, omitting the second *s*.

Socrates' questions   Moses' life   Euripides' plays

The personal pronouns *never require an apostrophe*, even though the possessive case ends in *s*: *his, hers, its, ours, yours, theirs*. In joint possession the last noun takes the possessive form.

Marshall and Ward's St. Paul branch

In individual possession each name should take the possessive form.

John's, George's, and Harold's separate claims

＊Note also these preferred forms: *someone else's book; my sister-in-law's visit; nobody else's opinion.*

CONTRACTIONS

Use an apostrophe to indicate omissions in contracted words and dates.

haven't	doesn't	isn't	it's	o'clock
have not	does not	is not	it is	of the clock

the class of '38
the class of 1938

PLURAL OF LETTERS AND NUMERALS

The plural of letters and of numerals is formed by adding an apostrophe and an *s*. The plural of a word considered as a word may be formed in the same way.

Her **w**'s were like **m**'s, and her **6**'s like **G**'s.

His conversation is too full of **you know**'s punctuated by **well**'s.

2. The Colon

The colon is a formal mark of punctuation, used primarily to introduce a formal enumeration or list, a long quotation, or an explanatory statement.

Consider these three viewpoints: political, economic, and social.

Tocqueville expresses one view: "In the United States we easily perceive how the legal profession is qualified by its attributes . . . to neutralize the vices inherent in popular government. . . ."

I remember which way to move the clock when changing from Daylight Saving Time to Standard Time by applying a simple rule: spring ahead, fall backward.

Note that a list introduced by a colon should be in apposition to a preceding word; that is, the sentence preceding the colon should be grammatically complete without the list.

Incorrect   We provide: fishing permit, rod, hooks, bait, lunch, boat, and oars.

Correct   We provide the following items: fishing permit, rod, hooks, bait, lunch, boat, and oars.

Correct   We provide the following: fishing permit, rod, hooks, bait, lunch, boat, and oars.

Correct   The following items are provided: fishing permit, rod, hooks, bait, lunch, boat, and oars.

The colon may be used between two principal clauses when the second clause explains or develops the first.

Intercollegiate athletics continues to be big business, but Robert Hutchins long ago pointed out a simple remedy: colleges should stop charging admission to football games.

A colon is used after a formal salutation in a business letter.

Dear Sir: Dear Mr. Harris: Gentlemen:

A colon is used to separate hour and minutes in numerals indicating time.

The train leaves at 9:27 A.M., and arrives at Joplin at 8:15 P.M.

In bibliographical references, a colon is used between the place of publication and the name of the publisher.

New York: Oxford University Press

Between the parts of a Biblical reference a colon may be used.

Proverbs 28:20

3. The Dash

The dash, as its name suggests, is a dramatic mark. Like the comma and the parentheses, it separates elements within the sentence, but what the parentheses says quietly the dash exclaims. The dash is indicated on the typewriter by two hyphens. To signal a summary statement, the dash is more informal than the dignified colon—and more emphatic. Use the dash cautiously. Its flashy interruption can create suspense and energy in a sentence, but its frequent use often indicates a writer who has not learned how to punctuate with discrimination.

A dash is used, as a separator, to indicate that a sentence is broken off or to indicate a sharp turn of thought.

> The application requested a transcript and had space to enter extracurricular activities, interests, hobbies—need I say more?

> From noon until three o'clock, we had an excellent view of all that can be seen of a battle—i.e., nothing at all.
>
> —STENDHAL

Dashes may be used to set off appositives or parenthetic elements when commas are insufficient.

> Three pictures—a watercolor, an oil, and a silk screen—hung on the west wall.

> *If the commas were used to set off "a watercolor, an oil, and a silk screen" the sentence might be misunderstood to refer to six pictures. The dashes make it clear that only three pictures are meant.*

> By the time the speech was over—it lasted almost two hours—I was dozing in my chair.

> *Since the parenthetic element is an independent clause, commas would be insufficient to set it off clearly.*

When a sentence begins with a list of substantives, a dash is commonly used to separate the list from the summarizing statement which follows.

> Relaxation, repose, growth within—these are necessities of life, not privileges.

> The chance to sit on a committee with no big issues to debate, the prospect of introducing bills which will never be reported, the opportunity to write speeches that will rarely be delivered—these are not horizons toward which an able man will strain.
>
> —HAROLD LASKI

4. Parentheses

Parentheses, like dashes and commas, are used to enclose or set off parenthetic, explanatory, or supplementary material. Arbitrary rules indicating which marks to use cannot be laid down. Commas are most frequently used, and are usually sufficient, when the parenthetic material is very closely related in thought or structure to the rest of the sentence. If the parenthetic material is long or if it contains commas, dashes would customarily be used to set it off. Parentheses are most often used for explanatory or supplementary material of the sort which might be put in a footnote—useful information that is not essential. Parentheses are also used to enclose numbers that mark an enumeration within a sentence.

> It was, perhaps, this very sensibility to the surrounding atmosphere of feeling and speculation which made Rousseau more directly influential on contemporary thought (or perhaps we should say sentiment) than any writer of his time.
>
> —James Russell Lowell

> His last story ("Success à la Steinberg") lacked imagination and any relevance to the cartoonist named in the title.

> In general, the war powers of the President cannot be precisely defined, but must remain somewhat vague and uncertain. (See Wilson's *Constitutional Government in the United States*.)

> The types of noncreative thinking listed by Robinson are (1) reverie, or daydreaming, (2) making minor decisions, (3) rationalizing, or justifying our prejudices.

5. Brackets

Brackets are used to enclose a word or words inserted in a quotation by the person quoting.

> "For the First Amendment does not speak equivocally. It prohibits any law 'abridging the freedom of speech, or of the press.' *It must be taken as a command of the broadest scope that explicit language, read in the context of a liberty-loving society, will allow.*" [Italics added.]

> "It is clear [the message read] that the Muscle Shoals development is but a small part of the potential public usefulness of the entire Tennessee River."

"We know more about its state [the state of the language] in the later Middle Ages; and from the time of Shakespeare on, our information is quite complete."

The word *sic* (meaning *thus*) enclosed in brackets is sometimes inserted in a quotation after a misspelling or other error to indicate that the error occurs in the original.

He sent this written confession: "She followed us into the kitchen, snatched a craving [*sic*] knife from the table, and came toward me with it."

If one parenthetical expression falls inside another, then brackets replace the inner parentheses. (Avoid this situation whenever possible; usually [as here] it is distracting.)

Exercise 8

Insert colons, dashes, parentheses, and brackets as they are needed in the following sentences.

1. Each of its large rooms there were no separate cells in this prison housed some twenty prisoners.
2. I took part in a number of activities in high school the rally committee, dramatics, *Ayer* staff the *Ayer* is our annual, and glee club.
3. He joined the Quakers and became an occasional speaker the Quakers have no ordained ministers at their meetings in Philadelphia.
4. According to an inscription on the flyleaf, the book had been owned by Alburt *sic* Taylor.
5. The sect permits dancing but forbids some other seemingly innocent recreations card playing, for example, is banned as being the next thing to gambling.
6. According to the *Mason Report* Stearns testified as follows "I made his John Brown's acquaintance early in January 1857, in Boston."
7. The midnight programs at the Varsity Theater feature horror films, science-fiction thrillers, movies of strange monsters from the sea you know the kind of thing.

Exercise 9

Some of the following student sentences contain incorrect or misleading punctuation, while others lack needed punctuation. Correct each sentence and be prepared to justify your changes.

1. The author mentions spontaneous and joyous effort, but what is a spontaneous and joyous effort.

2. Lincoln born in 1809 in Kentucky, was brought up in a poor family in the woods.

3. What would imply greater silence and quiet meditation than the numerous s's in the sentence.

4. You have a carwash for your car; a combination washer and dryer for your laundry; and a portable dishwasher for your dishes.

5. His goal had been to set up camp at this particular place along the river—No other place would do even though other places would have been faster to get to, and now he had done it.

6. It is the setting that is significant, without the setting there would be no story.

7. Now we reach the inevitable question, how do our liberally educated people make use of their knowledge when they enter the business world?

8. However, Bernard Shaw's main purpose is not to show the tragedy of St. Joan (that is already quite evident)—but to explain the character of St. Joan.

9. In our new house, the kitchen the bathroom and the utility rooms, will have plain wood floors

10. Under the system just established a student from a family that cannot afford to send a child away to college, will have a chance for a scholarship, especially if he or she is interested in science or engineering.

Exercise 10

Punctuate the following paragraphs and be ready to give a reason for each mark used.

I could tell without turning who was coming. There wasnt a big flat-footed clop-clop like horses make on hard-pack but a kind of edgy clip-clip-clip. There was only one man around here would ride a mule at least on this kind of business. That was Bill Winder who drove the stage between Reno and Bridgers Wells. A mule is tough all right a good mule can work two horses into the ground and not know it. But theres something about a mule a man cant get fond of. Maybe its just the way a mule is just as you feel its the end with a man whos that way. But you cant make a mule part of the way you live like your horse is its like he had no insides no soul. Instead of a partner youve just got something else to work on along with the steers. Winder didnt like mules either but thats why he rode them. It was against his religion to get on a horse horses were for driving

Its Winder Gil said and looked at Davies and grinned. The news gets around dont it

I looked at Davies too in the glass but he wasnt showing anything just staring at his drink and minding his own thoughts.

—WALTER VAN TILBURG CLARK

16

SPELLING

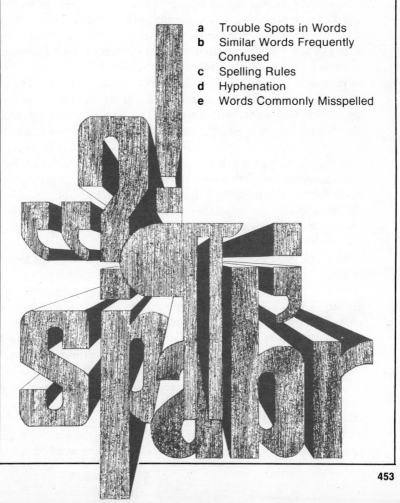

Orthography, or the art of correct spelling, is derived from two Greeks roots: *ortho* (right) and *graphy* (write). Spelling right, then, is writing straight. Since the time of Aristotle, correct spelling has distinguished the scholar from the dolt. Indeed, Lord Chesterton could write in the eighteenth century that one false spelling would fix ridicule on a gentleman for the rest of his life: "I know many of quality," he claims, "who never recovered from the ridicule of having spelled *wholesome* without the *w*." In the next century, such American rebels as Walt Whitman and Mark Twain could ridicule the English aristocratic passion for correctness. "Morbidity for nice spelling," Whitman scolded, "means . . . impotence in literature," and Twain pouted, "I don't see any use in spelling a word right, and never did. . . . We might as well make all our clothes alike and cook all dishes alike." No impotence in literature for Twain, who then wrote one of the greatest works in the language in which many of the words are misspelled.

In *Huck Finn* Twain catches by means of misspellings the sound of Huck speaking a dialect that is not Standard English. Our language, which scholars began to standardize in the late seventeenth century, grows out of hundreds of dialects such as the one Huck spoke, and that variety of origins accounts for many of the peculiarities of English spelling. English is not an easy language to spell, and it is in the American spirit to chafe at the propriety of good spelling. Still, many people, especially college teachers, feel, like Aristotle, that good spelling is the result of study and memory, and that its presence on a piece of paper is a mark of intelligence and effort.

The first step in mastering orthography is to make a list of words you often misspell. Ask a friend to test you on the words listed in section 16e. Write down the words you miss. Add to this list all words that are misspelled on your themes, and study the list. Look carefully at the letters of each word, pronounce the word a syllable at a time, write the word repeatedly to fix the pattern in your mind. Invent mnemonic devices—pictures, jingles, associations—to help you remember particular spellings. If you have written the word "sentance" and it is circled on your paper, remember that a se*nce* is a f*ence* built around an idea. If you have written "mispell," remember that in a spelling bee we miss a word when we "misspell" it. Learn the common prefixes and suffixes, and analyze words to see how they are formed. For example:

disappoint = dis + appoint
dissatisfied = dis + satisfied
misspelling = mis + spell + ing
really = real + ly
unnecessary = un + necessary
undoubtedly = un + doubt + ed + ly
government = govern + ment
carefully = care + ful + ly
incidentally = incident + al + ly

See how many words in the list of Words Commonly Misspelled (page 463) can be analyzed into a root word with prefixes or suffixes. If you find exceptions, look for an explanation in the Spelling Rules (page 458).

When you have finished the final draft of a paper, proofread it carefully before you hand it in. Proofread for spelling errors separately if you have trouble with spelling. It is no excuse to say that you knew the correct spelling of a word but that your pen slipped. Misspellings because of typographical errors or general carelessness are still misspellings.

16a

Trouble Spots in Words

Learn to look for the trouble spots in words and concentrate on them. Common words are almost always misspelled in the same way. That is, a particular letter or combination of letters is the trouble spot, and if you can remember the correct spelling of the trouble spot, the rest of the word will take care of itself. *Receive*, like *deceive, perceive,* and *conceive,* is troublesome only because of the *ei* combination; if you can remember that it is *ei* after *c,* you will have mastered these words. To spell *beginning* correctly, all you need to remember is the double *n.*

Careful pronunciation may help you to avoid errors at trouble spots. In the following words, the letters in boldface italic are often omitted. Pronounce the words aloud, exaggerating the sound of the boldface letters:

accident*all*y	February	li*a*ble
cand*i*date	gener*all*y	library
everybody	laboratory	liter*a*ture
occasion*all*y	recognize	su*r*prise
proba*b*ly	sophomore	temper*a*ment
quan*t*ity	stric*t*ly	us*u*ally

Many people add letters incorrectly to the following words. Pronounce the words, making sure that no extra syllable creeps in at spots indicated by boldface italic type.

a*th*letics	en*t*rance	mischie*v*ous
disas*t*rous	heigh*t*	remem*br*ance
drown*ed*	hin*d*rance	simil*ar*
e*lm*	light*n*ing	um*br*ella

Trouble spots in the following words are caused by a tendency to transpose the boldface italic letters. Careful pronunciation may help you to rember the proper order.

child*r*en	per*f*orm	pre*j*udice
hund*r*ed	per*s*piration	pre*s*cription
irrele*v*ant	pre*f*er	trage*d*y

16b

Similar Words Frequently Confused

Learn the meaning and spelling of similar words. Many errors are caused by confusion of such words as *effect* and *affect.* It is useless to spell *principal* correctly if the word that belongs in your sentence is *principle.* The following list distinguishes briefly between words that are frequently confused.

accept	receive	capital	city
except	aside from	capitol	building
access	admittance	choose	present
excess	greater amount	chose	past
advice	noun	clothes	garments
advise	verb	cloths	kinds of cloth
affect	to influence (verb)	coarse	not fine
effect	result (noun)	course	path, series
effect	to bring about (verb)	complement	to complete
		compliment	to praise
aisle	in church	conscience	sense of right and wrong
isle	island	conscious	aware
all ready	prepared		
already	previously	corps	group
		corpse	dead body
allusion	reference		
illusion	misconception	costume	dress
		custom	manner
altar	shrine		
alter	change	council	governmental group
alumna	a woman	counsel	advice
alumnae	women		
alumnus	a man	decent	proper
alumni	men	descent	slope
angel	celestial being	desert	wasteland
angle	corner	dessert	food
ascent	climbing	device	noun
assent	agreement	devise	verb
berth	bed	dairy	milk supply
birth	being born	diary	daily record
boarder	one who boards	dual	twofold
		duel	fight
border	edge	formally	in a formal manner
breath	noun		
breathe	verb	formerly	previously

forth	forward	respectfully	with respect
fourth	4th	respectively	in the order named
ingenious	clever		
ingenuous	frank	shone	from shine
		shown	from show
its	of it		
it's	it is	stationary	adjective
		stationery	noun
later	subsequently		
latter	second of two	their	possessive
		there	in that place
lead	metal	they're	they are
led	past tense of verb lead		
		than	comparison
		then	at that time
loose	adjective		
lose	verb	to	go to bed
		too	too bad, me too
peace	not war	two	2
piece	a portion		
		weather	rain or shine
personal	adjective	whether	which of two
personnel	noun		
		who's	who is
principal	most important	whose	possessive
principle	basic doctrine		
		you're	you are
quiet	still	your	possessive
quite	entirely		

16c

Spelling Rules

Learn the available spelling rules. Spelling rules apply to a relatively small number of words, and unfortunately almost all rules have exceptions. Nevertheless, some of the rules may help you to spell common words that cause you trouble, especially those words formed with suffixes.

It is as important to learn when a rule may be used as it is to understand the rule itself. Applied in the wrong places, rules will make your spelling worse, instead of better.

1. Final Silent *e*

Drop a final silent *e* before suffixes beginning with a vowel (*-ing, -age, -able*). Keep a final silent *e* before suffixes beginning with a consonant (*-ful, -ly, -ness*).

hope + ing = hoping	hope + ful = hopeful
love + able = lovable	nine + teen = nineteen
stone + y = stony	arrange + ment = arrangement
guide + ance = guidance	late + ly = lately
plume + age = plumage	pale + ness = paleness
white + ish = whitish	white + wash = whitewash
write + ing = writing	sincere + ly = sincerely
dote + age = dotage	bale + ful = baleful

Learn the following exceptions:

dyeing	hoeing	judgment	awful
ninth	truly	duly	wholly

The *e* is retained in such words as the following in order to keep the soft sound of *c* and *g*:

noticeable	courageous
peaceable	outrageous

Exercise 1

Following the rule just given, write the correct spelling of each word indicated below.

use + ing	pale + ing
use + ful	manage + ment
argue + ment	write + ing
guide + ance	advantage + ous
nine + ty	refuse + al
pale + ness	waste + ful
immediate + ly	hope + less
please + ure	absolute + ly
manage + able	sure + ly

2. Doubling Final Consonant

When adding a suffix beginning with a vowel to words ending in one consonant preceded by one vowel (*red, redder*), notice where the word is accented. If it is accented on the last syllable or if it is a monosyllable, *double* the final consonant.

pre**fér** + ed = preferred	**bén**efit + ed = benefited
o**mít** + ing = omitting	**pró**fit + ing = profiting
oc**cúr** + ence = occurrence	**dí**ffer + ence = difference
réd + er = redder	**trá**vel + er = traveler

Note that in some words the accent shifts when the suffix is added.

re**férr**ed	**réf**erence
pre**férr**ing	**préf**erence

There are a few exceptions to this rule, such as *transferable* and *excellent;* and a good many words that should follow the rule have alternative spellings: either *worshiped* or *worshipped; traveling, traveler,* or *travelling, traveller.*

Exercise 2

Make as many combinations as you can of the following words and suffixes. Give your reason for doubling or not doubling the final consonant. Suffixes: -able, -ible, -ary, -ery, -er, -est, -ance, -ence, -ess, -ed, -ish, -ing, -ly, -ful, -ment, -ness, -hood.

occur	scrap	ravel	man	libel	glad
happen	red	kidnap	defer	will	profit
begin	equip	hazard	sum	skill	avoid
god	commit	read	stop	expel	level
shrub	equal	rid	clan	rival	jewel

3. Words Ending in *y*

If the *y* is preceded by a consonant, change the *y* to *i* before any suffix except *-ing.*

lady + es = ladies	lonely + ness = loneliness
try + ed = tried	accompany + es = accompanies
study + ing = studying	

The *y* is usually retained if it is preceded by a vowel:

valleys   monkeys   displayed

Some Exceptions   laid, paid, said, ladylike

Exercise 3

Add suffixes to the following words. State your reason for spelling the word as you do.

mercy	relay	hardy	bounty	medley
duty	study	wordy	jockey	galley
pulley	essay	fancy	modify	body

4. *ie* or *ei*

When *ie* or *ei* is used to spell the sound *ee*,
Put i before *e*
Except after c.

achieve	grieve	retrieve	ceiling
belief	niece	shield	conceit
believe	piece	shriek	conceive
brief	pierce	siege	deceit
chief	relief	thief	deceive
field	relieve	wield	perceive
grief	reprieve	yield	receive

Some Exceptions either, leisure, neither, seize, weird.

16d

Hyphenation

A hyphen is used, under certain circumstances, to join the parts of compound words. Compounds are written as two separate words (*city hall*), as two words joined by a hyphen (*city-state*), or solid as one word (*townspeople*). In general, the hyphen is used in recently made compounds and compounds still in the process of becoming one word. Because usage varies considerably, no arbitrary rules can be laid down. When in doubt consult the latest edition of an unabridged dictionary. The following "rules" represent the usual current practice.

1. Compound Adjectives

Words used as a single adjective *before* a noun are usually hyphenated.

fine-grained wood	three-quarter binding
strong-minded woman	matter-of-fact statement
far-sighted proposal	so-called savings
well-informed leader	old-fashioned attitude

When these compound adjectives *follow* the noun, they usually do not require the hyphen.

The snow-covered mountains lay ahead.

The mountains are snow covered.

When the adverb ending in *-ly* is used with an adjective or a participle, the compound is not usually hyphenated.

highly praised organization, widely advertised campaign.

2. Prefixes

When a prefix still retains its original strength in the compound, use a hyphen. In most instances, however, the prefix has been absorbed into the word and should not be separated by a hyphen. Contrast the following pairs of words:

ex-president, excommunicate	pre-Christian, preconception
vice-president, viceroy	pro-British, procreation

Note that in some words a difference of meaning is indicated by the hyphen:

She recovered her strength.

She re-covered her sofa.

3. Compound Numbers

A hyphen is used in compound numbers from twenty-one to ninety-nine.

Correct twenty-six, sixty-three, **but** one hundred thirty.

4. Hyphen to Prevent Misreading

Use a hyphen if necessary to avoid ambiguity.

Ambiguous   A detail of six foot soldiers was on duty.

Clear   A detail of six foot-soldiers was on duty.

        OR

Clear   A detail of six-foot soldiers was on duty.

Exercise 4

Should the compounds in the following sentences be written solid, with a hyphen, or as two words? Consult a recent edition of a good dictionary, if necessary.

1. We need an eight foot rod.
2. All the creeks are bone dry.
3. She gave away one fourth of her income.
4. The United States is a world power.
5. Who was your go between?
6. He is extremely good looking.
7. The younger son was a ne'er do well.
8. Let us sing the chorus all together.
9. They are building on a T shaped wing.
10. She is getting a badly needed rest.
11. Are you all ready?
12. The leak was in the sub basement.
13. He was anti British.
14. She does her work in a half hearted manner.
15. I don't like your chip on the shoulder attitude.
16. They always were old fashioned.
17. A high school course is required for admission.
18. I do not trust second hand information.
19. He is as pig headed a man as I ever knew.
20. She will not accept anything second rate.

16e

Words Commonly Misspelled

The following list is composed of some ordinary words that are often misspelled. If you learn to spell correctly those which you usually misspell, and if you will look up in a dictionary words that are obviously difficult or unfamiliar, your spelling will improve remarkably.

Have a friend test you on these words—fifty at a time. Then concentrate on the ones you miss. To help you remember correct spellings, trouble spots are indicated by boldface italic type in most of the words.

absence
absorption
absurd
abundant
academic
accidentally
accommodate
accumulate
accurate
achievement
acquainted
acquire
across
additionally
address
adequately
aggravate
airplane
allotment
allotted
all right
already
altogether
always
amateur
among
analysis
annually
apology
apparatus
apparent
appearance
appetite
appreciate
appropriate
arctic

argument
arithmetic
arrangement
article
ascend
association
athletic
attacked
attendance
audience
available
awkward
bargain
basically
becoming
beginning
believe
benefited
boundary
brilliant
Britain
business
calendar
candidate
career
category
cemetery
certain
challenge
changeable
changing
Christian
column
coming
commission
committee

comparatively
competent
competition
conceit
concentrate
condemn
confidence
conqueror
conscientious
conscious
consider
consistent
contemporary
continuous
controlled
convenience
coolly
copies
courteous
criticism
dealt
deceive
decision
definitely
descendant
describe
description
desirable
despair
desperate
dictionary
different
difficult
dining room
disappear
disappoint

disastrous
discipline
disease
dissatisfied
dissipate
divide
doctor
dying
effect
eighth
eliminate
embarrass
emphasize
entirely
entrance
environment
equipped
especially
etc. (et cetera)
exaggerate
exceed
excellent
exceptionally
exercise
existence
expense
exorbitant
expense
experience
explanation
familiar
fascinate
feasible
February
fictitious
finally
foreign
forty
friend
gauge
government
grammar

guard
harass
hardening
height
hindrance
humorous
hurriedly
hypocrisy
illiterate
imagination
imitation
immediately
incidentally
incredibly
independent
indispensable
infinite
initiative
intelligence
interest
involve
irrelevant
irresistible
itself
jealousy
knowledge
laboratory
laid
led
leisure
library
license
literature
loneliness
lose
luxury
magazine
maintenance
manufacturer
marriage
mathematics
mattress

meant
medieval
merely
miniature
municipal
murmur
mysterious
necessary
neither
nineteen
noticeable
nowadays
nucleus
obstacle
occasionally
occurred
occurrence
omission
omitted
opinion
opportunity
optimism
origin
paid
pamphlet
parallel
paralyzed
parliament
particularly
partner
pastime
perform
perhaps
permanent
permissible
persistent
personnel
persuade
physical
pleasant
politician
possess

possible
practically
preceding
predominant
prejudice
preparation
prevalent
primitive
privilege
probably
procedure
proceed
profession
professor
prominent
pronunciation
prove
psychology
pursue
quizzes
really
receive
recognize
recommend
reference
referred
religious

reminisce
repetition
representative
rhythm
ridiculous
sacrifice
safety
scene
schedule
secretary
seize
sense
separate
sergeant
severely
shining
siege
similar
sincerely
soliloquy
sophomore
specimen
speech
stopping
strenuous
stretch
studying

succeed
suppress
surprise
susceptible
syllable
sympathize
temperament
tendency
thorough
together
tragedy
transferred
truly
typical
tyranny
undoubtedly
unnecessary
until
using
usually
vengeance
village
villain
weird
writing

Exercise 5

Write the infinitive, the present participle, and the past participle of each of the following verbs (e.g., **to stop, stopping, stopped**):

prefer	slam	hop	acquit	drag	recur
profit	begin	differ	commit	equip	confer

Exercise 6

Write the following words together with the adjectives ending in -able derived from them (e.g., **love, lovable**):

dispose	compare	imagine
move	console	cure
prove	blame	measure

Exercise 7

Write the following words together with their derivatives ending in -able (e.g., notice, noticeable):

trace	marriage	damage
service	charge	peace
change	place	manage

Exercise 8

Write the singular and the plural of the following nouns (e.g., lady, ladies):

baby	remedy	treaty	turkey
hobby	enemy	delay	decoy
democracy	poppy	alley	alloy
policy	diary	attorney	corduroy
tragedy	laundry	journey	convoy

Exercise 9

Write the first and third persons present indicative, and the first person past, of the following verbs (e.g., I cry, he cries, I cried):

fancy	spy	vary	worry
qualify	reply	dry	pity
accompany	occupy	ferry	envy

Exercise 10

Study the following words, observing that in all of them the prefix is not diss- but dis-:

dis + advantage	dis + obedient
dis + agree	dis + orderly
dis + approve	dis + organize
dis + interested	dis + own

Exercise 11

Study the following words, observing that in all of them the prefix is not u- but un-:

un + natural	un + numbered
un + necessary	un + named
un + noticed	un + neighborly

Exercise 12

Study the following words, distinguishing between the prefixes **per-** and **pre-**. Keep in mind that **per-** means **through, throughout, by, for;** and that **pre-** means **before.**

perform	perhaps	precept
perception	perspective	precipitate
peremptory	perspiration	precise
perforce	precarious	precocious
perfunctory	precaution	prescription

Exercise 13

Study the following adjectives, observing that in all of them the suffix is not **-full,** but **-ful:**

peaceful	forceful	healthful
dreadful	shameful	pitiful
handful	grateful	thankful
graceful	faithful	plentiful

Exercise 14

Study the following words, observing that in all of them the ending is not **-us,** but **-ous:**

advantageous	specious	fastidious
gorgeous	precious	studious
courteous	vicious	religious
dubious	conscious	perilous

Exercise 15

Study the following words, observing that in all of them the suffix **-al** precedes **-ly:**

accidentally	terrifically	exceptionally
apologetically	specifically	elementally
pathetically	emphatically	professionally
typically	finally	critically

Exercise 16

Study the following words, observing that the suffix is not **-ess,** but **-ness:**

clean + ness   plain + ness   stern + ness

| drunken + ness | stubborn + ness | keen + ness |
| mean + ness | sudden + ness | green + ness |

Exercise 17

Study the following words, observing that the suffix is not -able, but -ible:

accessible	discernible	imperceptible
admissible	eligible	impossible
audible	feasible	incompatible
compatible	flexible	incredible
contemptible	forcible	indefensible
convertible	horrible	indelible
intelligible	perceptible	responsible
invincible	permissible	sensible
invisible	plausible	susceptible
irresistible	possible	tangible
legible	reprehensible	terrible

Exercise 18

Study the following groups of words:

-ain	-ain	-ian	-ian
Britain	curtain	barbarian	guardian
captain	fountain	Christian	musician
certain	mountain	civilian	physician
chieftain	villain	collegian	politician

Exercise 19

Study the following groups of words:

-ede	-ede	-eed
accede	precede	exceed
antecede	recede	proceed
concede	secede	succeed

Exercise 20

Fill the blanks with **principal** *or* **principle.** **Principle** *is always a noun;* **principal** *is usually an adjective.* **Principal** *is also occasionally a noun: the* **principal** *of the school, both* **principal** *and* **interest.**

1. The _____ will be due on the tenth of the month.

2. Her refusal was based on _____.
3. This is my _____ for going.
4. The _____ has asked that we hold our meeting tomorrow.
5. He did not even know the first _____ of the game.
6. Can you give the _____ parts of the verb?

Exercise 21

Fill the blanks with **affect** *or* **effect:**

1. I do not like his _____ ed manner.
2. An entrance was _____ ed by force.
3. The _____ upon her is noticeable.
4. The law will take _____ in July.
5. It will be an _____ ive remedy.
6. The hot weather will _____ the crops.
7. There was no serious after _____.
8. She _____ ed ignorance of the whole matter.

Exercise 22

Fill the blanks with **passed** *or* **past. Passed** *is the past tense or past participle of the verb* **pass;** **past** *can be an adjective, noun, adverb, or preposition.*

1. We _____ your house.
2. She went _____ me.
3. They whistled as they _____ by.
4. He is a man with a _____.
5. My cousin is a _____ master at the art of lying.
6. That vocalist is _____ her prime.
7. Many years _____ before he returned.
8. It is long _____ bedtime.

Exercise 23

Fill the blanks with:

a. **Its** *(pronoun in the possessive case) or* **it's** *(contraction of* **it is**).
    1. _____ raining.
    2. The cat has had _____ supper.
    3. The clock is in _____ old place again.
    4. _____ now six years since the accident.
    5. I think that _____ too late to go.

b. **Your** (*pronoun in the possessive case*) or **you're** (*contraction of* **you are**).

1. _____ mistaken; it is _____ fault
2. _____ position is assured.
3. _____ to go tomorrow.
4. I hope that _____ taking _____ vacation in July.

c. **There** (*adverb or interjection*), or **their** (*pronoun in the possessive case*), or **they're** (*contraction of* **they are**).

1. It is _____ turn.
2. _____ ready to go.
3. _____, that is over with.
4. _____ car was stolen.
5. _____ back from _____ trip.

d. **Whose** (*pronoun in the possessive case*) or **who's** (*contraction of* **who is**).

1. _____ turn is it?
2. There is the woman _____ running for mayor.
3. _____ responsible for this?
4. _____ book is this?
5. He is one _____ word can be trusted.
6. Bring me a copy of _____ *Who*.
7. _____ ready to go?

Exercise 24

Circle the boldface word that is spelled correctly in each of the following sentences. Consult section 16b if necessary.

1. Everyone is going **accept, except** me.
2. People came to her every day for **advice, advise,** and she was always ready to **advice, advise** them.
3. At so high an altitude it was hard to **breath, breathe.**
4. His **breath, breathe** came in short gasps.
5. One of the sights of Washington, D.C., is the **Capital, Capitol.**
6. Albany is the **capital, capitol** of New York.
7. Before dinner I had time to change my **clothes, cloths.**
8. The tickets were sent with the **complements, compliments** of the manager.
9. The country was as dry and dreary as a **desert, dessert.**
10. The shack in which we **formally, formerly** lived is still standing.
11. It's **later, latter** than you think.
12. The winners were **lead, led** up onto the stage.
13. Button the money in your pocket so you won't **lose, loose** it.

17

MECHANICS

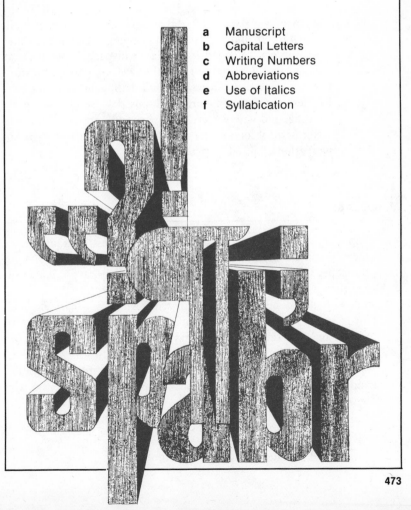

The appearance of a paper, like the appearance of a person, indicates regard for self and for the world at large. Confidence and pride in writing call for good typing, a clean page, observance of editing conventions. Crossed out pencil scrawls on paper torn from an old notebook witness a rather gray and shabby outlook on everything. Readers are always favorably disposed to scrubbed, neatly dressed writing, and wise writers use any means—from varying sentence patterns to observing the principles of syllabication—to ensure a sympathetic and attentive audience.

17a

Manuscript

Paper should be 8½ × 11 inches in size, unless your instructor specifies some other kind. If you type your themes, and you should, the paper should be unruled. If you used ruled paper for handwritten themes, the lines should be widely spaced to prevent crowding. Themes should be either typed or written in ink—black or blue-black; pencil is difficult to read and often smears. Write legibly. An instructor or an editor grows cranky with a manuscript that has to be puzzled out, one word at a time. Give your words and the responses of your reader a fair break. Lines jammed into one another and out to the edge of the margins are as boorish as a person who never stops talking.

Here are some sensible guidelines for arranging material on the page:

1. Write on one side of the sheet only.

2. Leave a generous margin—at least an inch and a half—at the left side of each page and at the top. Leave about an inch of margin at the right side and at the bottom.

3. In typewritten manuscript, double-space the lines throughout, including footnotes or endnotes. In handwritten manuscript, leave an equivalent space between lines. Use alternate lines on narrow-lined paper.

4. Number all pages except the first in the upper right-hand corner. Use arabic numerals, not roman.

5. Indent uniformly for paragraphs. The usual indentation for typewritten manuscript is five spaces. Indent about an inch in handwritten manuscript.

6. Center the title at least two inches from the top of the page, or on the first line if you use ruled paper. Leave extra space between the title and the first line of the composition.

Do not underline your title or put quotation marks around it (unless it is a quotation or the title of a book). Capitalize all words in the title except articles, short conjunctions, and short prepositions.

1. Arrangement of Quotations

Observe the following conventions in reproducing quotations:

1. A quotation of only a few words may be incorporated into the text.

> In *Childhood and Society,* Erik Erikson says that the young adult, "emerging from the search for and insistence on identity," is now "ready for intimacy."

2. A quotation of more than two lines of verse or more than 100 words of prose should be set off from the main text, without quotation marks. It should be introduced by a colon if the preceding sentence has referred to the quotation, and it should begin on a new line. It should be indented from the left-hand margin. (Poetry should be centered on the page.) It should be single-spaced.

> Ruth Benedict's strong belief that individual rituals reflect a larger cultural whole is apparent in her description of the dance of the Zuñi Indians in New Mexico:

The dance, like their ritual poetry, is a monotonous compulsion of natural forces by reiteration. The tireless pounding of their feet draws together the mist in the sky and heaps it into the piled rain clouds. It forces out the rain upon the earth. They are bent not at all upon an ecstatic experience, but upon so thorough-going an identification with nature that the forces of nature will swing to their purposes. This intent dictates the form and spirit of Pueblo dances. There is nothing wild about them. It is the cumulative force of the rhythm, the perfection of forty men moving as one, that makes them effective.

As an anthropologist, Benedict is particularly drawn to rituals because. . . .

3. A quotation of poetry should be divided into lines exactly as the original is divided. If an entire line of verse cannot be written on one line of the page, the part left over should be indented.

Allons! the inducements shall be greater,
We will sail pathless and wild seas,
We will go where winds blow, waves dash, and the Yankee
    clipper speeds by under full sail.

—WALT WHITMAN

4. When quoting a conversation from a story, novel, or play, be sure the quotation is exactly as it appears in the original, including the paragraphing and punctuation. (British writers commonly use a single quotation mark where we would use two.)

"Are you better, Minet-Chéri?"
"Yes. I can't think what came over me."
The grey eyes, gradually reassured, dwelt on mine.
"I think I know what it was. A smart little rap on the knuckles from Above."
I remained pale and troubled and my mother misunderstood:
"There, there now. There's nothing so terrible as all that in the birth of a child, nothing terrible at all. It's much more beautiful in real life. The suffering is so quickly forgotten, you'll see! The proof that all women forget is that it is only men—and what business was it of Zola's, anyway?—who write stories about it."

—COLETTE

2. Correcting the Manuscript

If a reading of your final draft shows the need of further alterations or revisions, make them unmistakably clear. It is not necessary to recopy an entire page for the sake of one or two insertions or corrections. Copying is necessary only when there are so many corrections as to make the page difficult to read or messy in appearance.

Words to be inserted should be written above the line, and their proper position should be indicated by a caret ($\wedge$) placed below the line. Words so inserted should not be enclosed in parentheses or brackets unless these marks would be required if the words were written on the line. Cancel words by drawing a neat line through them. Parentheses or brackets should never be used for this purpose.

17b

Capital Letters

The general principle is that proper nouns are capitalized; common nouns are not capitalized. A proper noun is the name of a particular person, place, or thing: *Richard Wright, Virginia Woolf, Alaska, New Orleans, the Capitol, the United States Senate, Colorado River.* A common noun is a more general term that can be used as a name for a number of persons, places, or things: *engineer, doctor, county, town, court house, legislative body, harbor.*

Note that the same word may be used as both a proper and a common noun.

Of all the peaks in the Rocky Mountains, Pike's Peak is the mountain I would most like to climb.

Our beginning history class studied legislative procedure and the part our representatives play in it. When I took History 27 our class visited the Legislative Committee hearing in which the Representative from Ohio expressed his views on the Alliance for Progress.

Abbreviations are capitalized when the words they stand for would be capitalized: USN, ROTC, NBC.

1. Proper Nouns

Capitalize proper nouns and adjectives derived from them. Proper nouns include the following:

1. Days of the week, and months

2. Organizations such as political parties, governmental bodies and departments, societies, institutions, clubs, churches, and corporations: the Socialist Party, the Senate, the Department of the Interior, the American Cancer Society, the Optimists' Club, the J. E. Caldwell Company

3. Members of such organizations: Republicans, Lions, Presbyterians, Catholics

4. Historical events and periods: the Battle of Hastings, the Medieval Age, the Baroque Era

5. Geographic areas: the East, the Midwest, the Northwest

6. Race and language names: Japanese, English, Indian, Caucasian

7. Many words of religious significance: the Lord, the Son of God, the Trinity

8. Names of members of the family when used in place of proper names: a call from Mother telling about my father's trip

9. In biological nomenclature, the names of genera but not of species: *Homo sapiens, Salmo irideus, Equus caballus*

10. Stars, constellations, and planets, but not the earth, sun, or moon unless used as astronomical names

2. Titles

1. Capitalize titles of persons when they precede proper names. When used without proper names, titles of officers of high rank should be capitalized; other titles should not.

Senator Marsh, Professor Stein, Admiral Byrd, Aunt Elsa. Both the Governor and the Attorney General endorsed the candidacy of our representative. The postmaster of our town appealed to the Postmaster General.

2. Capitalize the first word and the important words of the titles of books, plays, articles, musical compositions, pictures, and other literary or artistic works. The unimportant words are the articles *a*, *an*, and *the*; short conjunctions; and short prepositions.

I, Claudius; Summer in Williamsburg; Friar Felix at Large; Childhood and Society; Measure for Measure; Beethoven's *Third Symphony;* Brancusi's "Bird in Space"; Joni Mitchell's *For the Roses.*

3. Capitalize the first word and any titles of the person addressed in the salutation of a letter.

Dear Sir, Dear President Stark, My dear Sir.

In the complimentary close, capitalize the first word only.

Very truly yours, Yours sincerely, Yours very truly.

3. Sentences and Quotations

1. Capitalize the first word of every sentence and of every direct quotation. Note that a capital is not used for the part of a quotation that follows an interpolated expression like "he said" unless that part is a new sentence.

"Mow the lawn diagonally," said Mrs. Grant, "and go over it twice."

"Mow the lawn twice diagonally," said Mrs. Grant. "It will be even smoother if the second mowing crosses over the first one."

Mrs. Grant said, "Mow the lawn twice."

Following a colon, the first word of a series of short questions or sentences may be capitalized.

The first-aid questions were dull but important: What are the first signs of shock in an accident victim? should he be kept warm? should he eat? should he drink?

2. Capitalize the first word of every line of poetry except when the poem itself does not use a capital.

I'll walk where my own nature would be leading:
　　It vexes me to choose another guide:
Where the grey flocks in ferny glens are feeding;
　　Where the wild wind blows on the mountain-side.

　　　　　　　　　　　　　—EMILY BRONTË

> last night i heard
> a pseudobird;
> or possibly
> the usual bird
> heard pseudome.
> —EBENEZER PEABODY

Exercise 1

What words in the following sentences should be capitalized? Why?

1. A canary-colored buick convertible was driving north on fountain avenue.
2. Although many of the natives can speak spanish, they prefer their own indian dialect.
3. A novel experiment in american education was announced on monday by the yale school of law and the harvard school of business administration.
4. "I'm going out to the country club," said chris; "want to come along?"
5. Although technically a veteran, he had served in the coast guard for only two weeks toward the end of the second world war.
6. the douglas fir, often sold under the name oregon pine, is neither a fir nor a pine.
7. He makes these regional divisions: the east, the old south, the middle west, and the far west.
8. When I left high school I intended to major in economics, but in college I became interested in science and graduated as a biology major.
9. Buddhists, christians, jews, and moslems attended the conference, which was held at ankara, the capital of turkey.
10. Both the rotarians and the lions meet in the private dining room of the piedmont inn.

17c

Writing Numbers

Usage varies somewhat, but the following practices are widely accepted. One general principle is that all related figures in a particular context should be treated similarly: for consistency, do not use figures for some and words for others.

1. Numbers from one to ten and round numbers that can be expressed in one or two words are usually written out: *three people in line,* **seven hundred** *reserved seats,* **five thousand** *tickets.* All numbers that begin a sentence are spelled out, even though they would ordinarily be represented by figures: **Four hundred sixty** *dollars was too high a price.*

2. For ordinary usage, figures are appropriate for the day of the month *(June 23),* the year *(1929),* and street numbers *(400 University Circle).*

3. Figures are used for long numbers *(a capacity of 1,275 gallons),* page and chapter numbers *(Chapter 14, page 372),* time expressed by A.M. and P.M. *(from 11 A.M. to 2 P.M.),* and exact percentages, decimals, and technical numbers *(7.31 inches, 8.5 percent interest, 38th parallel).*

4. After a dollar sign ($) figures are always used: *My share of the job paid $177.90, but I had $27.50 in expenses.* If a number is short and followed by *dollars* or *cents,* it may be spelled out: *I paid* **twelve dollars** *for the reservation.*

17d

Abbreviations

Minimize the use of abbreviations in ordinary expository prose. Spell out Christian names, the words in addresses *(Street, Avenue, New Jersey),* the days and months of the year, units of measurement *(ounces, pounds, feet, hour, gallon).* Volume, chapter, and page should be spelled out in references in the text, but abbreviated in footnotes, parenthetical citations, and bibliographies.

Eliott Brodie of 372 West 27th **Avenue,** Kenosha, moved on **December** 16, 1970.

The quotation is on **page** 267 of the **third edition.**

For further information on proper terms for addressing dignitaries, consult the appropriate section in the latest Webster unabridged dictionary ("Forms of Address," **pp.** 51a–54a).

The following conventions are generally observed:

1. A few standard abbreviations are in general use in all kinds of writing: *i.e.* (that is), *e.g.* (for example), *etc.* (and so forth), *vs.* (versus), A.D., B.C., A.M., P.M., (or *a.m.*, *p.m.*), Washington, D.C. Names of some organizations and of many government agencies are commonly represented by their initials: *CIA, GOP, NATO, CAA, NAACP.* Dictionaries vary in their preferences for using periods with these abbreviations.

   Some abbreviations require periods (*Ph.D., N.Y., Col., oz.*), but others are regularly written without periods (*FBI, Na, ERA*). The correct form of standard abbreviations can be found in your dictionary, usually in regular alphabetical order, sometimes in a separate appendix.

2. Civil, religious, and military titles are spelled out except the following ones:

   a. Preceding names: *Mr., Messrs., Ms., Mrs., Dr., St.* (for *Saint*). *(The) Rev.* and *(The) Hon.* are used only when the surname is preceded by a Christian name: *Rev. Henry Mitchell,* (or *Mr. Mitchell* or *Father Mitchell*), not *Rev. Mitchell.*

   b. Following names: *Esq., M.D., Sr., Jr., Ph.D., M.A., LL.D.* Do not duplicate a title before and after a name.

   Incorrect **Dr.** Rinard Z. Hart, **M.D.**

   Correct **Dr.** Rinard Z. Hart, or Rinard Z. Hart, **M.D.**

   For the correct forms of titles used in addressing officials of church and state, consult an unabridged dictionary.

3. In technical writing, directions, recipes, and the like, terms of measurement are often abbreviated when used with figures.

   Correct 32°**F**; 1,500 **rpm**; 25 **mph**; ½ **tsp.** salt and 2 **tb.** sugar; 12 **ft.** 9 **in.**; 5 **cc**; 2 **lb.** 4 **oz.**

   Abbreviations such as *Co., Inc., Bros.,* should be used only when business organizations use them in their official titles. The ampersand (&) is used only when the company uses the symbol in its letterhead and signature.

Incorrect   D. C. Heath & Co., D. C. Heath and Co.

Correct   D. C. Heath and Company

Exercise 2

Correct any errors in abbreviations in the following sentences.

1. Dr. Geo. C. Fryer lives on Sandy Blvd. near Walnut St.
2. I have worked for the Shell Oil Co. since Oct., '57.
3. We expected to go to N. Y. for Xmas.
4. The Acme Corp. ships mail-order goods C.O.D.
5. I was in Wash., D.C., on Aug. 10, 1975.
6. Mt. Whitney, which is 14,495 ft. high, is located in SE California.
7. The drive to Lexington, Ky., took us 3 hrs., 17 min.
8. A temperature of 32°F. is equivalent to zero on the cent. scale.
9. He bought three fl. oz. of aromatic spirits of amm.
10. Turn back to the 1st page of Ch. 3 and read pp. 18–22.

17e

Use of Italics

Italics are used for certain titles, unnaturalized foreign words, scientific names, names of ships and aircraft, and words considered *as* words. To italicize a word in a manuscript, draw one straight line below it, or use the special underlining key on the typewriter, thus: King Lear.

1. In the titles of books, monographs, musical works, and such separate publications, italicize all words. (Do not italicize the author's name.) In the titles of newspapers, magazines, and periodicals, only the distinctive words are italicized. The article *The* in newspaper titles is usually not italicized, but printed in regular (roman) type. (Note that *The* is italicized in the preceding sentence since it refers to the word itself, used as the subject of *is*.)

> *The Blithedale Romance,* Edmund Wilson's *The Shock of Recognition. Of Stars and Men. Dictionary of Foreign Terms.* The *Atlantic Monthly. Christian Science Monitor.* The *Southern Review.* The *New York Times.*

Titles of parts of published works and articles in magazines are enclosed in quotation marks.

The assignment is "Despondency" from William Wordsworth's long narrative poem, *The Excursion.*

I always read filler material in the **New Yorker** entitled "Letters We Never Finished Reading."

She hoped to publish her story entitled "Nobody Lives Here" in a magazine like **Harper's.**

2. Italicize foreign words that have not yet become accepted in the English language. If you are not certain whether a foreign word has become naturalized, consult a dictionary. Be sure to consult the Explanatory Notes to see how foreign words are indicated. Scientific names for plants and animals are italicized.

The dancer unties a knot with her feet in the Mexican **reboza.**

The technical name of Steller's jay is **Cyanocitta stelleri.**

3. Italicize the names of ships and aircrafts, but *not* the names of the companies that own them.

The liner **S. S. Constitution** sails for Africa tomorrow.

He went to Hawaii on a Matson liner and returned on one of United's **Royal Hawaiian** flights.

4. When words, letters, or figures are spoken of as such, they are usually italicized.

The misuse of **cool** and **real** is a common fault.

The letter *e* and the figure *2* on my typewriter are worn.

17f

Syllabication

Dividing a word at the end of a line is mainly a printer's problem. In manuscripts it is not necessary to keep the right-hand margin absolutely even, so it is seldom necessary to divide a word at the end of a line. If such a division is essential, observe the following principles, and mark the division with a hyphen (-) at the end of the line.

1. Divide words only *between* syllables—that is, *between* the normal sound divisions of a word. When in doubt as to where the division between syllables comes, consult a dictionary. One-syllable words, such as *through* or *strength,* cannot be divided. Syllables of one letter should not be divided from the rest of the word. A division should never be made between two letters that indicate a single sound. For example, never divide *th* as in *brother, sh* as in *fashion, ck* as in *Kentucky, oa* as in *reproaching, ai* as in *maintain.* Such combinations of letters may be divided if they indicate two distinct sounds: *post-haste, dis-hon-or, co-au-thor.*

Incorrect   li-mit, sinec-ure, burg-lar-ize, ver-y, a-dult, co-ord-in-a-tion

Correct   lim-it, sine-cure, bur-glar-ize, very, adult, co-or-di-na-tion

2. The division comes at the point where a prefix or suffix joins the root word, if pronunciation permits.

be-half, sub-way, anti-dote, con-vene, de-tract

lik-able (or like-able), like-ly, place-ment, Flem-ish, en-force-ment, tall-er, tall-est, fall-en

Exceptions Because of Pronunciation

prel-ate, pred-e-cessor, res-ti-tu-tion, bus-tling, prej-u-dice, twink-ling, jog-gled

3. When two consonants come between vowels (me*mb*er), the division is between the consonants if pronunciation permits (*mem-ber*). If the consonant is doubled before a suffix, the second consonant goes with the suffix (*plan-ning*).

remem-ber, pas-sage, fas-ten, disman-tle, symmet-rical (**but** symme-try), prompt-er (**but** promp-ti-tude), impor-tant, clas-sic, rum-mage, as-sur-ance, oc-cident, at-tend, nar-ration, of-fi-cial-ly, com-pen-di-um, fit-ting

BUT NOTE: knowl-edge

4. The division comes after a vowel if pronunciation permits.

modi-fier, oscilla-tor, ora-torical, devi-ate

Exercise 3

Correct in the following sentences any errors in abbreviations, numbers, capitals, and italics.

1. He made a survey of Athletics in the Universities and Colleges in the U.S.
2. When grandmother was a girl, she lived in Lincoln, Nebr.
3. She always adds a P.S. to her letters.
4. He was traveling in the East last Winter.
5. I spent fifty cents for a pattern, $6.80 for my material, and a dollar and ten cents for trimming; so you see that my dress will cost only $8.40.
6. 1975 brought us good fortune.
7. "You will surely decide to go," he said, "For you will never have such a chance as this again."
8. After each war we resolve "That these dead shall not have died in vain."
9. Our country entered the second world war in nineteen hundred and forty-one.
10. The use of the word like as a conjunction is a very common error.
11. My Chemistry and Math. grades were high, and my grade point average was 3.2.
12. Roosevelt was elected president for a 2nd term by an Overwhelming Majority.
13. They discussed the eighteenth amendment and the methods of repealing an amendment to the constitution.
14. The president of the United States rose to greet the president of our university.
15. Queen Elizabeth 1 tried to preserve the status quo.

18

DEFINITIONS OF GRAMMATICAL TERMS

absolute construction, absolute phrase   An absolute phrase consists of a participle with a subject (and sometimes a complement) grammatically unconnected with the rest of the sentence but usually telling when, why, or how something happened.

> **The floodwater having receded,** people began returning to their homes.
> I hated to leave home, **circumstances being as they were.**

abstract language   Words expressing general ideas, states, or conditions: *generosity, love, goals.* (See **concrete language.**)

active voice   See **voice.**

adjective   A part of speech used to describe or limit the meaning of a substantive. There are the following kinds:

Descriptive	a **true** friend, a **poor** man.
Limiting	**an** apple, **the** woman, **two** boys.

Notice that many kinds of pronouns regularly perform the function of an adjective.

Possessive	**my** book, **his** sister, **your** house.
Demonstrative	**this** chair, **these** papers.
Interrogative	**whose** hat? **which** one?
Indefinite	**any** card, **each** boy, **some** candy.

adjective clause   See **clause.**

adverb   A part of speech used to modify a verb, an adjective, or another adverb. An adverb answers the questions: *Where? When? How? Why?* or *To what extent?*

He bowed **politely.**

"Politely" modifies the verb "bowed."

A **very** old woman came in.

"Very" modifies the adjective "old."

He was **too** much absorbed to listen.

"Too" modifies the adverb "much."

Substantives may be used adverbially:

He walked **two miles.**

"Two miles" modifies the verb "walked."

He walked **two miles** farther.

"Two miles" modifies the adverb "farther."

adverb clause   See **clause.**

agreement   The correspondence in number and person between the subject and verb in a sentence and the correspondence in number, person, gender, and case between a pronoun and its antecedent (see section 14a).

antecedent   A word, phrase, or clause to which a pronoun refers.

I saw the **house** long before I reached **it.**

"House" is the antecedent of "it."

This is a **problem which** cannot be solved without calculus.

"Problem" is the antecedent of "which."

appositive   A substantive attached to another substantive and denoting the same person or thing. A substantive is said to be **in apposition** with the substantive to which it is attached.

Alice, my **cousin,** was enjoying her favorite sport—**sailing.**

"Cousin" is in apposition with "Alice"; "sailing" is in apposition with "sport."

article   The word *the* is called the **definite article;** the word *a* or *an* is called the **indefinite article.** In function, articles can be classed with adjectives.

auxiliary   When the verbs *be, have, do, shall, will, may, can, must,* and *ought* assist in forming the voices, modes, and tenses of other verbs, they are **auxiliaries.**

A message **was** given to me.

He **should have** known better.

He **has been** gone a week.

cardinal number   Any of the numbers *one, two, three, four,* etc., denoting quantity, in distinction from *first, second, third,* etc., which are **ordinal numbers** and show sequence. Cardinal and ordinal numbers can function as adjectives or as nouns.

case   The inflection of a noun *(girls', friend's)* or pronoun *(she, her, hers)* to show its relationship to other words. In English, pronouns are classified into three cases (see section 14b).

Nominative (or Subjective)

I spoke; **they** listened; **she** dozed.

The inflected pronouns function as subject.

Objective

John tossed **me** the ball. I collided with two other players and knocked **them** down.

The inflected pronouns function as indirect object, and object of the verb.

Possessive (or Genitive)

His score and **mine** were identical. **Our** scores were higher than **theirs.** They wondered **whose** grade was the highest.

The inflected pronouns show possession or a similar relationship.

In modern times, English nouns are inflected only to indicate the genitive case: "*Jerry's money* and *Sarah's* money was invested at their *parents'* advice; this allayed the *relatives'* fears about the *boy's* future and the *girl's* education."

clause   A group of words containing a subject and predicate (see Chapter 5). Clauses that can stand alone as complete sentences are **independent** (**principal** or **main**) clauses. Clauses that are not by themselves complete in meaning are **dependent (subordinate)** clauses. Subordinate clauses are used as nouns, adjectives, or adverbs. They are usually introduced by subordinating conjunctions or relative pronouns.

We heard him **when he came in.**

"We heard him" is the main clause; "when he came in" is the subordinate clause.

That she will be late is certain.

Subordinate clause used as a noun.

The woman **who spoke to us** is our sheriff.

Subordinate clause used as an adjective.

He will come in **when he is ready.**

Subordinate clause used as an adverb.

Clauses that play the same part in a sentence, whether they are main or subordinate, are called **coordinate clauses.**

The bell rang and **everyone stood up.**

Coordinate main clauses.

He left **because he did not like the work** and **because the pay was low.**

Coordinate subordinate clauses.

collective noun A noun that is singular in form (**class, crowd, orchestra**) but that denotes a group of members.

colloquial language Language appropriate to speech but not to formal writing, unless a relaxed and casual tone is intended.

comparison Inflection of an adjective or adverb to indicate an increasing degree of quality, quantity, or manner.

Positive Degree   Our house is **cold.**

Comparative Degree Their house is **colder.**

Superlative Degree Their house is the **coldest** in town.

When adjectives have one or two syllables, the comparative degree is usually formed by adding *-er* to the positive; and the superlative degree is usually formed by adding *-est* to the positive. To form the comparative degree of adverbs and of adjectives with more than two syllables, place *more* before the positive form; the superlative degree is usually formed by placing *most* before the positive. Some adjectives have irregular comparison: e.g., *good, better, best; bad, worse, worst* (see section 14c).

complement Traditionally, a word or phrase added to a verb to complete the sense of the statement. It may be the direct object of a transitive verb, an indirect object, or a predicate noun or adjective (see sections 5a, 14b, and 14c).

Direct Object	A big wave swamped our **boat.**
Indirect Object	I paid **him** the money.
Predicate Noun	Our destination was **Corsica.**
	The referee called Sanchez the **winner.**
Predicate Adjective	The waves were **enormous.**
	A limber branch made the tree-house **shaky.**

"Corsica" and "enormous" are called subjective complements (see section 5a). "Shaky" and "winner" are sometimes called objective complements (see **objective complement***).*

complex sentence See **sentence** and section 5b.

compound sentence See **sentence** and section 5b.

concrete language Words describing specific things, perceptible by the senses: *smooth, bitter, yellow, creaky, shrill.* (See **abstract language.**)

conjugation The inflected forms of a verb which show person, number, tense, voice, and mood. The following is a simplified conjugation of the indicative mood of the verb *see:*

		Active Voice	Passive Voice
		PRESENT TENSE	
sing.	1.	I see	I am seen
	2.	you see	you are seen
	3.	he (she, it) sees	he is seen
pl.	1.	we see	we are seen
	2.	you see	you are seen
	3.	they see	they are seen

PAST TENSE

sing.	1.	I saw	I was seen
	2.	you saw	you were seen
	3.	he saw	he was seen
pl.	1.	we saw	we were seen
	2.	you saw	you were seen
	3.	they saw	they were seen

FUTURE TENSE

sing.	1.	I will see	I will be seen
	2.	you will see	you will be seen
	3.	he will see	he will be seen
pl.	1.	we will see	we will be seen
	2.	you will see	you will be seen
	3.	they will see	they will be seen

PERFECT TENSE

sing.	1.	I have seen	I have been seen, etc.
	2.	you have seen	
	3.	he has seen	
pl.	1.	we have seen	
	2.	you have seen	
	3.	they have seen	

PAST PERFECT TENSE

sing.	1.	I had seen	I had been seen, etc.
	2.	you had seen	
	3.	he had seen	
pl.	1.	we had seen	
	2.	you had seen	
	3.	they had seen	

FUTURE PERFECT TENSE

1.	I will have seen, etc.	I will have been seen, etc.

See section 14d on *Shall-Will*. See also **principal parts**.

conjunction   A part of speech used to connect words, phrases, and clauses. There are the following kinds:

Coordinating

Pure, or simple, conjunctions: **and, or, nor, but, for, yet.**

Coordinating

Correlatives: either . . . or, neither . . . nor, both . . . and, not only . . . but [also].

Subordinating

Conjunctions introducing noun clauses, adjective clauses, or adverb clauses: **that, when, where, while, whence, because, so that, although, since, as, after, if, until,** etc.

Coordinating conjunctions (see section 13c) connect sentence elements that are logically and grammatically equal; i.e., they may connect two subjects or two verbs or two clauses, etc. Subordinating conjunctions (see section 13c) connect subordinate (or dependent) clauses with their principal (or independent) clauses.

conjunctive adverb An introductory adverb, or sentence modifier, that indicates the relationship between principal clauses: *however, moreover, therefore, nevertheless, also, hence, consequently, then, furthermore,* etc. Between independent clauses a conjunctive adverb must be reinforced by a semicolon or by a coordinating conjunction (see section 13c).

connotation The associations, suggestions, feelings that a word brings to mind as opposed to its literal, dictionary meaning. For example, both *baby* and *infant* denote, or mean literally, a small child, but *baby* connotes coddling, affection, tender protection, and sexuality. (See **denotation.**)

coordinate Sentence elements that are parallel in grammatical construction are coordinate. In the sentence *He and she talked lengthily and earnestly, and at last agreed, he* and *she* are coordinate; *talked* and *agreed* are coordinate; *lengthily* and *earnestly* are coordinate.

copula, or linking verb A verb, like *to be, to seem, to appear, to become, to feel, to look,* which acts mainly as a connecting link between the subject and the predicate noun or predicate adjective. (See **denotation.**)

correlative conjunctions Coordinating conjunctions used in pairs:

both my father **and** my mother

neither my father **nor** my mother

not only deceived us **but also** accused us of deception.

declension   See **inflection.**

demonstrative   See **adjective** and **pronoun.**

denotation   The literal or dictionary definition of a word. (See **connotation.**)

diction   Choice of words, especially as those words affect the tone of the writer's voice, depending on their formality or informality, the range of which is suggested below:

highly formal	———————→		highly informal
residence	home	pad	crib
affluent	wealthy	rich	loaded
obtuse	ignorant	stupid	dumb

direct address   A grammatical construction in which the speaker or writer addresses a second person directly.

Mary, wait for me.

Friends, Romans, countrymen, lend me your ears.

direct object   See **object** and section 5a.

elliptical expression   An expression that is grammatically incomplete, but the meaning of which is clear because the omitted words are implied.

Elliptical   **If possible,** bring your drawings along.

Complete   **If it is possible,** bring your drawings along.

euphemism   The substitution of an "inoffensive," often trite and sentimental expression for one considered to be unpleasant or indelicate: *in an interesting condition* or *in the family way* are euphemisms for *pregnant.* (See section 9e.)

finite verb   A verb that makes an assertion and can serve as a predicate, as distinguished from infinitives, participles, and gerunds.

Finite Verb   The alarm **rang** and I **got** up.

Verbal   The **ringing** alarm awoke me and I hurried **to get** up.

gender In grammar, the division of nouns *(actor, actress)* and pronouns *(he, she, it)* into sexual categories: masculine, feminine, and neuter.

genitive See **case** and section 14b.

gerund A verb form ending in *-ing* and used as a noun. It should be distinguished from the present participle, which also ends in *-ing* but is used as an adjective. (See **participle**.)

Subject of Verb	**Fishing** is tiresome.
Object of Verb	I hate **fishing**.
Object of Preposition	I have a dislike of **fishing**.
Predicate Noun	The sport I like least is **fishing**.

Like a noun, the gerund may be modified by an adjective. In the sentence *They were tired of his long-winded preaching, his* and *long-winded* modify the gerund *preaching*. A noun or pronoun preceding a gerund is normally in the possessive case—e.g., *his preaching*. Since a gerund is a verb form, it may take an object and be modified by an adverb.

He disapproved of our **taking luggage** with us.
"Luggage" is the object of the gerund "taking."

Our success depends upon his **acting promptly**.
"Promptly" is an adverb modifying the gerund "acting."

idioms An expression whose meaning cannot be determined from the literal meaning of the individual words, but which as a whole is understood and used by speakers of a particular language or region.

She **was taken in** by the practical jokes.

Every now and then, I **have a mind to tell her off.**

He is, **after all,** my brother, and I have to **stick up for him.**

He was **out of his head** for a while, but he finally **pulled himself together.**

imperative See **mood**.

indicative See **mood**.

indirect object   See **object** and section 5a.

infinitive   That form of the verb usually preceded by *to. To* is called the **sign of the infinitive.** Since it is a verb form, the infinitive can have a subject, can take an object or a predicate complement, and can be modified by an adverb.

> They wanted **me** to go.
>
> *"Me" is the subject of "to go."*
>
> They asked to meet **him.**
>
> *"Him" is the object of "to meet."*
>
> We hope to hear **soon.**
>
> *"Soon" is the adverbial modifier of "to hear."*

The infinitive may be used as a noun (*To meet her* is a pleasure. He wanted *to buy my car*), or as an adjective or adverb (He gave me a book *to read.* He waited *to see you.* We are happy *to help*).

inflection   A change in the form of a word to show a change in meaning or use. Nouns may be inflected to show number (*man, men*) and the genitive case (*dog, dog's*). Pronouns may be inflected to show case (*he, him*), person (*I, you*), number (*I, we*), and gender (*his, hers*). Verbs are inflected to show person (I *go*, he *goes*), number (she *is*, they *are*), tense (he *is*, he *was*), voice (I *received* your letter, your letter *was received*), and mood (if this *be* treason). Adjectives and adverbs are inflected to show relative degree (*strong, stronger, strongest*). The inflection of substantives is called **declension;** that of verbs, **conjugation;** that of adjectives and adverbs, **comparison.**

intensive pronoun   When the pronouns *myself, himself, yourself,* etc., are used in apposition, they are called intensives because they serve to emphasize the substantives that they are used with; e.g., *I myself will do it. I saw the bishop himself.* When one of these words is used as the object of a verb and designates the same person or thing as the subject of that verb, it is called a **reflexive pronoun;** e.g., *I hurt myself. They benefit themselves.*

interjection   An exclamation that has no grammatical relation with the rest of the sentence; e.g., *oh, alas, please.*

intransitive   See **verb.**

irregular verb   A verb which does not form its past tenses by adding *-ed* or *-t*: *sing, sang, sung; drink, drank, drunk.* Such a verb is sometimes called a **strong verb.** See section 14d for a table of irregular verbs.

jargon   The specialized, technical language of a profession, class, group, or discipline, that is usually obscure to the general public.

linking verb   See **copula.**

modifier   A word or group of words that functions as an adjective or an adverb to limit, define, or qualify another word or group of words. In the sentence "I dislike these sour oranges" *sour* describes *oranges* and *these* limits them to a nearby group. They are adjectival modifiers. In the sentence "She sang for half an hour," the phrase, *for half an hour,* which tells how long she sang, is an adverbial modifier.

mood   Inflection of a verb to indicate whether it is intended to make a statement or command or to express a condition contrary to fact.

The **indicative mood** is used to state a fact or to ask a question.

The wind is blowing.

Is it raining?

The **imperative mood** is used to express a command or a request.

Do it immediately.

Please answer the telephone.

The **subjunctive mood** is used to express a wish, a doubt, a concession, a condition contrary to fact (see section 14d). In speech and in all but "edited" writing, the subjunctive mood has largely been replaced by the indicative.

Wish

I wish that I **were** able to help you.

Condition Contrary to Fact

If she **were** older, she would understand.

nominative See **case** and section 14b.

nonrestrictive modifier A dependent clause or phrase that adds information without limiting the meaning of the word it modifies. See section 15b.

noun A part of speech: a noun names a person, place, thing, or abstraction. There are the following kinds:

A **common noun** refers to any member of a group or class of things, or to abstract qualities; e.g., *man, village, book, courage.* Common nouns are not usually capitalized.

A **proper noun** or **proper name** is the name of a particular person, place, or thing, or event; e.g., *Jane Austen, Chicago, Domesday Book, Revolutionary War.* Proper nouns are capitalized.

A **collective noun** is the name of a group or class considered as a unit; e.g., *flock, class, group, crowd, gang, team.*

Nouns may also function as modifiers; e.g., *town hall.*

noun clause See **clause.**

number Inflection of verbs, nouns, and pronouns to indicate singular or plural.

object The **direct object** (see section 5a) of a verb names the person or thing that completes the assertion made by a transitive verb. It answers the question *what* or *whom.*

Father dried the **dishes** and broke a **plate.**

I trusted **him** and followed his **advice.**

The **indirect object** (see section 5a) of a verb is the person or thing to which something is given or for which something is done. The indirect object can usually be made the object of the preposition *for* or *to.*

I built my **wife** a shelf. = I built a shelf **for my wife.**

I wrote **him** a letter. = I wrote a letter **to him.**

objective (accusative) See **case** and Chapter 14.

objective complement Either a noun or an adjective that completes the predicate by telling something about the direct object.

noun
They called him a **fool**.

adj.
I like my coffee **hot**.

ordinal number   See **cardinal number.**

parallelism   The putting of equal ideas into equivalent structures in a sentence, such as this one—She wants *fame, prestige,* and *power*—where the italicized words are equally weighted as objects of the verb, *wants. That she must work hard, that many obstacles stand in her way, that few encourage her endeavors—* these facts do not affect her pluck one bit. In this sentence, clause is balanced against clause to create parallel structure.

participle   A verb form used as an adjective. The present participle ends in -ing; e.g., *eating, running.* The past participle ends in -ed, -d, -t, -en, -n or is formed by vowel change; e.g., *stopped, told, slept, fallen, known, sung.*

   Since a participle is a verbal adjective, it has the characteristics of both a verb and an adjective. Like an adjective, it modifies a substantive:

The **inquiring** reporter stopped him.

Encouraged by his help, she continued her work.

Having just **returned** from my vacation, I had not heard the news.

Like a verb the participle may take a direct or an indirect object and may be modified by an adverb:

Wishing us success, he drove away.

"Us" is an indirect object, "success" a direct object, of the participle "wishing."

Stumbling awkwardly, he came into the room.

"Awkwardly" is an adverb modifying the participle "stumbling."

parts of speech   The classification of words according to the special function that they perform in a sentence: nouns, pronouns, verbs, adjectives, adverbs, prepositions, and conjunctions.

passive voice   See **voice** and section 5c.

person Inflection of verbs and personal pronouns to indicate the speaker (**first person**), the person spoken to (**second person**), and the person spoken of (**third person**).

First Person   I am, we are; I go, we go.

Second Person   you are; you go.

Third Person   she is, they are; he goes, they go.

phrase A phrase is a group of words without a subject and predicate, and used as a single part of speech—as a substantive, verb, adjective, or adverb. See Chapter 5.

predicate A group of words that makes a statement about, or asks a question about, the subject of the sentence (see section 5a). Thus in the sentence *Jim drove the car, drove the car* is the predicate, because it tells what the subject *Jim* did. The predicate always contains a finite verb; e.g., *drove, had driven.*

The **simple predicate** is the verb alone. The **complete predicate** is the verb and its modifiers and complements.

Jim drove the car into the garage.

"Drove" is the simple predicate. "Drove the car into the garage" is the complete predicate.

predicate adjective, predicate noun See complement.

prefix Letters added before a word's base to form a new word: *pre-, re-, com-.* (See **suffix**.)

preposition A part of speech that shows the relationship between a substantive and another word in the sentence; e.g., *in, on, into, to, toward, from, for, against, of, between, with, without, before, behind, under, over, above, among, at, by, around, about, through.* The word that completes the meaning of the preposition is called the object of the preposition. In English many words may be used as either prepositions or adverbs, their classification depending on their function in the sentence. If they are followed by a substantive which, with them, forms a phrase, they are prepositions (see section 5a); if by themselves they modify a verb, they are adverbs.

He stood **behind** the chair. *(Preposition)*

The money is **in** the bank. *(Preposition)*

He came **in** while we were there. *(Adverb)*

principal clause See **clause** and Chapter 5.

principal parts In English, the three forms of a verb from which all other forms are derived. They are (1) the present infinitive, (2) the past tense, and (3) the past participle: *send, sent, sent; choose, chose, chosen; swim, swam, swum.* All present and future tense forms, including the present participle, are derived from the first principal part: I *send,* he *sends,* we *will send.* The second principal part is used for the simple past tense: he *sent,* I *chose,* you *swam.* Compound past tenses and the forms of the passive voice employ the third principal part: he *has chosen,* they *had swum,* the package *was sent,* or *may be sent, is being sent, will be sent,* etc.

In learning a foreign language or in correcting unconventional English, one must know the principal parts of the irregular verbs (see section 14d). The verb *to be* is too irregular to be reduced to three principal parts.

pronoun A part of speech, a word used to refer to a noun already used (or implied). Pronouns may be classified as follows:

Personal	*I, you, he, she, it,* and their inflectional forms I listened to **her.**
Demonstrative	*this, that, these, those* (see section 7a) **This** is my favorite book.
Interrogative	*who, which, what* **Who** can answer this question?
Relative	*who, which, that,* and compounds like *whoever* (see section 4a) This is the house **that** Jack built.
Indefinite	*any, anyone, some, someone, no one, nobody, each, everybody, either,* etc. (see section 14a)
Reflexive	*myself, yourself,* etc. I hurt **myself.**
Intensive	*myself, yourself,* etc. He **himself** is to blame.

Reciprocal   *each other, one another*
John and Mary looked at **each other.**

regular verb   A verb that forms its past tenses by adding *-ed* or *-t: start, started; dream, dreamed* or *dreamt.* Also called a **weak verb.**

relative pronoun   A pronoun (*who, which,* or *that*) used with a double function: to take the place of a noun and to connect clauses as does a subordinating conjunction (see section 5a).

restrictive modifier   A dependent clause or phrase intended to define or limit the word it modifies (see section 15b).

restrictive

The students **who come regularly to class** do better work and earn

restrictive

higher marks than the students **who attend only periodically.**

sentence   An independent utterance, usually including a subject and predicate, that can stand by itself and is set off by capitalization of its beginning and a period or other terminal punctuation at the end. A sentence may range in length from one word (Why?) or short phrases (What an absurd idea!) to a main clause (I saw him sitting on the fence). See Chapter 5.

From the point of view of structure, sentences are classified as **simple, compound, complex,** or **compound-complex.** See section 5b.

From the point of view of meaning or function, sentences may be classified as follows:

1. A **declarative sentence** asserts something about a subject.

    The man felt ill and called the doctor.

2. An **interrogative sentence** asks a question.

    When is she coming?

3. An **imperative sentence** expresses a command.

    Call him again.

4. An **exclamatory sentence** expresses strong feeling.

    What a fool he was!

For further discussion, see Chapters 6 and 7; see also Chapter 13, especially for the discussion of so-called "incomplete" forms.

subject   The part of the sentence or clause naming the person or thing about which something is said. The subject of a sentence is usually a noun or pronoun, but it may be a verbal, a phrase, or a noun clause. See sections 5a and 14a.

Noun   Beyond the ridge lay a high **plateau**.

Verbal   Nowadays **flying** is both safe and cheap.

Phrase   "**To fear the worst** oft cures the worse."

Clause   **That she will be promoted** is certain.

The **simple subject** is a substantive, usually a noun or pronoun. The **complete subject** is the simple subject and its modifiers.

The young trees that we planted last year have grown tall.

"Trees" is the simple subject. "The young trees that we planted last year" is the complete subject.

subjective complement   See **complement** and section 4a.

subjunctive   See **mood** and section 14d.

subordination   Making one element of a sentence grammatically dependent on another in order to show the relationship of ideas.

When the party was over, I left.

The subordinate clause beginning with "when" limits the time of the action. (See section 5a).

substantive   Any word or group of words used as a noun. It may be a noun, a pronoun, a clause, an infinitive, or a gerund.

suffix   Letters added at the end of a word's base to form a new word: *-tion, -ship, -ing.* (See **prefix**.)

syntax   The way in which words are put together to make phrases, clauses, and sentences.

tense   Different forms of a verb that indicate distinctions in time. In English there are six tenses: the present tense, the past tense, the future tense, the perfect (present perfect) tense, the past perfect tense, and the future perfect tense. See **conjugation** for example. See Chapter 14 for discussion.

verb   A part of speech whose function is to assert that the subject exists, acts, or has certain characteristics. (The man who *is* on my left *wrote* the book; he *is* very difficult to talk to.) The verb may be a word or a group of words, but in either case its form changes to indicate time, person, mood. (He *was saying* that I *am* too young but *should have* a chance next year).

A **transitive verb** is a verb that requires a direct object (noun or other substantive) to complete its meaning.

He **shut** the **door**.

"Door" completes the statement by telling what was shut.

They **greeted** her.

An **intransitive verb** is a verb which does not require a direct object.

After a heated argument, he **left**.

The child **sat** near the fire.

A **copula**, or **linking verb**, acts mainly as a connecting link between the subject and the predicate noun or predicate adjective.

That **is** correct.

He **seems** sleepy.

She **felt** warm.

verbals   Forms of a verb *(stealing, stolen, to steal)* used as nouns, adjectives, or adverbs. See **gerund, participle, infinitive,** and section 5a.

voice   Inflection of a verb to indicate the relation of the subject to the action expressed by the verb. A verb is in the **active voice** when its subject is the doer of the action. A verb is in the **passive voice** when its subject is acted upon.

Active Voice I rang the bell.

The subject "I" did the act of "ringing."

Passive Voice The bell was rung by me.

The subject "bell" was acted upon by "me."

weak verb See **regular verb.**

FURTHER READING ABOUT WRITING AND LANGUAGE

Aristotle. *Rhetoric and Poetics.* Westminster, Md.: Modern Library, 1974.

Barzun, Jacques, and Henry Graff. *The Modern Researcher.* 3d ed. New York: Harcourt Brace Jovanovich, 1977.

Burke, Kenneth. *A Grammar of Motives.* Berkeley: University of California Press, 1969.

Christensen, Francis. *Notes Toward a New Rhetoric.* New York: Harper and Row, 1967.

Daiker, Donald A., et al., eds. *Sentence Combining and the Teaching of Writing.* Akron, Ohio: Land S. Brooks, 1979

Emig, Janet. "Writing as a Mode of Learning." *College Composition and Communication* 28 (May 1977), 122–28.

Follett, Wilson. *Modern American Usage: A Guide.* Ed. Jacques Barzun. New York: Hill and Wang, 1963.

Galbraith, John Kenneth. "Writing, Typing, and Economics." *Atlantic,* March 1978, 102–6.

Kinneavy, James L. "Freshman English: An American Rite of Passage." *Freshman English News* 6 (Spring 1977), 1–3.

———. *A Theory of Discourse.* Englewood Cliffs, N.J.: Prentice-Hall, 1971.

Murray, Donald M. *A Writer Teaches Writing.* Boston: Houghton Mifflin, 1968.

Ohmann, Richard. *English in America.* New York: Oxford University Press, 1976.

Pei, Mario A. *The Story of Language.* Philadelphia: Lippincott Co., 1949.

Toulmin, Stephen. *The Uses of Argument.* London: Cambridge University Press, 1964.

Weaver, Richard M. *The Ethics of Rhetoric.* Chicago: Henry Regnery and Co., 1953.

INDEX

1   2   3   4   5   6   7   8   9   0